RESEARCH IN LABOR ECONOMICS

WITHDRAWN

RESEARCH IN LABOR ECONOMICS

Series Editor: Solomon W. Polachek

IZA Co-Editor: Konstantinos Tatsiramos

RESEARCH IN LABOR ECONOMICS

EDITED BY

SOLOMON W. POLACHEK

*Department of Economics, State University of
New York at Binghamton and IZA*

KONSTANTINOS TATSIRAMOS

University of Leicester and IZA

United Kingdom – North America – Japan
India – Malaysia – China

Emerald Group Publishing Limited
Howard House, Wagon Lane, Bingley BD16 1WA, UK

First edition 2012

Copyright © 2012 Emerald Group Publishing Limited

Reprints and permission service
Contact: permissions@emeraldinsight.com

British Library Cataloguing in Publication Data
A catalogue record for this book is available from the British Library

ISBN: 978-1-78190-357-5
ISSN: 0147-9121 (Series)

ISOQAR certified Management Systems, awarded to Emerald for adherence to Quality and Environmental standards ISO 9001:2008 and 14001:2004, respectively

ISOQAR
REGISTERED

UKAS
MANAGEMENT
SYSTEMS

0026

Certificate Number 1985
ISO 9001
ISO 14001

INVESTOR IN PEOPLE

CONTENTS

LIST OF CONTRIBUTORS

Adam Clemens	CNA Corporation, Alexandria, VA, USA
Lorenzo Corsini	Department of Economics, University of Pisa, Italy
Ronald G. Ehrenberg	Department of Economics and CHERI, Cornell University, Ithaca, NY, USA
Robert W. Fairlie	Department of Economics, University of California, Santa Cruz, CA, USA
Kevin F. Hallock	Department of Economics and HR Studies, Cornell University, Ithaca, NY, USA
Antti Kauhanen	The Research Institute of the Finnish Economy, Helsinki, Finland
Penka Kovacheva	Economics Department, Princeton University, Princeton, NJ, USA
Harry Krashinsky	Department of Management and Centre for Industrial Relations and Human Resources, University of Toronto, Canada
Krishna B. Kumar	Economics & Statistics Department, Pardee RAND Graduate School, RAND Corporation, Santa Monica, CA, USA
Audrey Light	Department of Economics, Ohio State University, Columbus, OH, USA
Sami Napari	Economics Department, Ministry of Finance, Government of Finland, Helsinki, Finland
Xiaotong Niu	Economics Department, Princeton University, Princeton, NJ, USA
Yoshiaki Omori	Department of Economics, Yokohama National University, Japan

Konstantinos   University of Aberdeen Business School,
Pouliakas   Scotland

Ronald L. Seeber   School of Industrial and Labor Relations,
                        ILR School, Cornell University, Ithaca, NY,
                        USA

Nikolaos   Department of Economics, University of
Theodoropoulos   Cyprus, Cyprus

Kenneth T. Whelan   Deceased

Julie Zissimopoulos   Department of Clinical and Pharmaceutical
                        Economics and Policy and Schaeffer Center
                        for Health Policy and Economics, University
                        of Southern California, Los Angeles, CA,
                        USA

EDITORIAL ADVISORY BOARD

PREFACE

Pay varies across individuals. Some variation is endemic to a country's institutions including a country's level of development and its technological infrastructure. Some variation is based on differences in individual attributes, particularly an individual's ability to acquire human capital. Finally, some variation is based on incentives instigated by the government, by one's employer, or by one's family. These incentives often operate indirectly by influencing educational choices, labor force participation, and even cohabitation and marital arrangements. This volume contains eight articles on aspects of the distribution of income. One deals with technology change and the distribution of earnings, two deal with internal labor markets, four deal with incentives that motivate work related behavior, and finally one deals with immigrant labor market success.

Underlying the first article are well known paradoxical findings. Worker skills have risen, boosting the relative supply of skilled workers. Yet, wage differences between skilled and unskilled workers have not fallen as a result of skilled workers becoming relatively more plentiful. As many have argued, one reason the skilled wage premium could have remained high is that technological change likely increases the productivity of skilled workers relatively more than the productivity of less trained workers. Lorenzo Corsini confirms that technological change measured by R&D expenditures is a driving force. However, he shows there must be other reasons, as well, because variations in technological change do not fully explain changes in the skill premium across European countries. As a result, Corsini shows that variations in these inter-country differences must also depend on institutions such as minimum wage and unemployment insurance, as well as opportunities for country-wide bargaining, the latter of which in part depends on outside options of skilled employees.

Wages also vary within firms in a given country. In the next article, Antti Kauhanen and Sami Napari utilize a 26-year panel of employer–employee data for Finland. They assess theories of internal labor markets previously tested by Baker, Gibbs, and Holmstrom (1994) and reach some similar, but a number of different conclusions. Most important, they find that human capital explains most of the variance in earnings, but job type and job level play important roles, as well. As such, aspects of the internal labor market are important with respect to advancement. For example, they find that one's promotion probability decreases with the time spent in the current and previous job level. Being at a higher wage level in one's current job makes one more likely to be promoted. Further, the share of internal hires increases as one moves up the job ladder. But not all promotions are internal. Outside hiring is also important at all job levels. However, whereas incumbents are promoted more quickly than external hires during the first year, incumbents are also demoted more often. In short, the internal labor market is important in understanding how well workers do.

The next article by Adam Clemens also examines the internal labor market. Clemens finds persistent differences in the speed at which jobs lead to promotion. Some jobs are "fast track" characterized by human capital accumulation that is more valuable in higher-level positions than the human capital acquired in "slow jobs." Incumbents in these higher-level jobs tend to be younger and better educated than their peers suggesting that firms choose promising employees to prepare for promotion. To explain these patterns Clemens modifies the Gibbons and Waldman (2006) model to allow for two type entry level jobs: one in which the experience gained is of high value at the next level, and a second in which experience gained is not as valuable. A number of predictions emerge both about the type of workers picked for each job and the resulting rates of promotion to the higher level. These predictions are tested using data from the financial sector.

Absenteeism is also affected by workplace incentives. In the next article, Konstantinos Pouliakas and Nikolaos Theodoropoulos examine the effects of a variety of performance-related pay schemes on absence rates in a matched employer–employee representative sample of private sector British firms. They find establishments that link pay to individual performance have lower absentee rates. These lower absentee rates are especially true for nonmanagerial workers, and the effect is greater for jobs linking a greater proportion of pay to performance. Also, the effect is bigger in firms facing higher absentee rates. Finally, Pouliakas and Theodoropoulos find that firms with high absentee rates are the ones most likely to adopt incentive plans to reduce absenteeism. Taking account of endogeneity indicates a feedback mechanism in which a firm's high past absenteeism leads to more reliance on performance-related-pay schemes, which, in turn, causes lower absentee rates.

A firm's pay-incentive schemes can also affect retirement decisions. In the next article, Kenneth T. Whelan, Ronald G. Ehrenberg, Kevin F. Hallock, and Ronald L. Seeber use data from a major university affected by the recent economic downturn. In 2008, it implemented a voluntary retirement program, rather than cut costs. The incentive was full pay for a year along with a 30% base-pay contribution to the employees' fixed-contribution pension fund. Whereas, the approach induced a number of employees to retire, the take-up rate was asymmetric. Weaker less productive workers in units of the university hardest hit by budget cuts were most likely to accept the offer. Concurrently, the most productive employees were not significantly more likely to take the incentive. In short, the incentive program had its intended effect.

Not always is one's expected income during retirement actualized. Obviously, when this happens, well-being diminishes; but in what ways? In the next article, Penka Kovacheva and Xiaotong Niu answer this question. They exploit a one-time shock in the Russian economy that occurred in 1966. In that year, a decline in economic output and hence tax revenues brought about a temporary decline in pension payments, only to be restored the very next year in 1997. The short-term impact of the crisis was sufficiently severe to double poverty rates among the affected pensioners. Large non-pecuniary effects of this exogenous shock were estimated using a difference-in-difference approach. Whereas life satisfaction declined significantly, self-assessed health did not. However, the shock's negative effects extended to non-pensioner members of pensioner households. Also, the data indicate pensioners bore the financial brunt themselves, as they neither received more nor sent less money to their extended family. To the extent Russian pensioners are not unique, crises in the United States and other country pension benefits could have the same non-pecuniary effects.

Incentives based on public policy could also affect non-pecuniary behavior. In the next article, Audrey Light and Yoshiaki Omori examine how government policies affect cohabitation and marriage. They concentrate on expected income tax burdens, AFDC or TANF benefits, Medicaid expenditures, and parameters of state divorce laws. They develop a sequential model detailing long-term marital transitions from being single, to cohabitating, to becoming married, to getting divorced, and finally to remarriage. They follow single 18-year-old women contained in the NLSY79 data over a 30-year period and emphasize the probability of staying in a marital or cohabitating union, rather than merely concentrating only on transitioning out. They find policy variables to have little impact. Apparently love (or at least familial unions) transcends these economic incentives.

Workplace and public policy incentives motivate behaviors that affect labor market success, but so do upbringing, education, and background even before migrants enter a country, let alone the labor market. As it turns out, Indian businessmen in the United States consistently do better than other immigrant entrepreneurs. Surprisingly, they do better than home-grown American entrepreneurs, as well. Indian businesses yield higher profits, hire more employees, and fail at lower rates. Similar patterns occur in Canada and the United Kingdom. But why? What is it about Indian immigrants that bring such success? In the final article, Robert W. Fairlie, Harry Krashinsky, Julie Zissimopoulos, and Krishna B. Kumar find the main reason to be human capital. Sixty-eight percent of Indian entrepreneurs are college educated which is twice the rate for white Americans. Of course, the educational advantage is related to the type of business. Over 15% of the businesses are medical practices.

As with past volumes, we aim to focus on important issues and to maintain the highest levels of scholarship. We encourage readers who have prepared manuscripts that meet these stringent standards to submit them to *Research in Labor Economics* (RLE) via the IZA website (http://rle.iza.org) for possible inclusion in future volumes. For insightful editorial advice, we thank Dan Anderberg, Dirk Antonczyk, Daniel Baumgarten, Keith A. Bender, John Bennett, Raquel Bernal, Petri Böckerman, Michael Bognano, Donghun Cho, Alexander Danzer, Leif Danziger, Tirthatanmoy Das, Polona Domadenik, Tor Erikkson, Alfonso Flores-Lagunes, Markus Frolich, Delia Furtado, Vladimir Gimpelson, Daniel Henderson, Luojia Hu, Martin Kahanec, Melanie Khamis, Johannes Koettl, Fidan Ana Kurtulus, Marco Leonardi, Magnus Lofstrom, Alexander Muravyev, Andreas Peichl, Matteo Picchio, Tiziano Razzolini, Indhira Santos, Judith Scott-Clayton, Zahra Siddique, Steven Stillman, Nikos Theodoropoulos, Raymundo M. Campos Vazquez, and Anne Winkler.

Solomon W. Polachek
Konstantinos Tatsiramos
Editors

REFERENCES

Baker, G., Gibbs, M., & Holmstrom, B. (1994). The internal economics of the firm: Evidence from personnel data. *Quarterly Journal of Economics*, *109*(4), 881–919.

Gibbons, R., & Waldman, M. (2006). Enriching a theory of wage and promotion dynamics inside firms. *Journal of Labor Economics*, *24*(1), 59–107.

INSTITUTIONS, TECHNOLOGICAL CHANGE AND WAGE DIFFERENTIALS BETWEEN SKILLED AND UNSKILLED WORKERS: THEORY AND EVIDENCE FROM EUROPE

Lorenzo Corsini

ABSTRACT

This article studies the evolution of the wage differentials between graduate (skilled) and non-graduate (unskilled) workers in several European countries from the beginning of the 1990s to the beginning of this century. The starting point is that all European countries show a common increase in the relative supply of skilled workers but different evolution of wage differentials. Economics theory usually relates the evolution of wage differentials not only to relative supply but also to skill-biased technological progress. I complement this explanation providing a theoretical model of wage bargaining where wage differentials are determined also by labour market institutions. My empirical findings show that both technological progress and labour market institutions are important in the determination

Research in Labor Economics, Volume 36, 1–33
ISSN: 0147-9121/doi:10.1108/S0147-9121(2012)0000036005

1

of wage differentials. As for the former, I find that differentials depend on the pace and intensity at which technological progress takes place. As for labour market institutions, their effect, though important, is not always straightforward. In fact, some aspects of institutions, like minimum wage and the duration of unemployment benefits, favour unskilled workers while other aspects, like bargaining power and replacement rates from unemployment benefits, may magnify the differences in outside options and actually increase wage differentials.

Keywords: Wage differentials; skills; technological progress; wage bargaining; labour market institutions

JEL classifications: J24; J31; J51; J52; O33

INTRODUCTION

A large number of studies have reported how in the last decades the relative supply of skilled workers in industrial countries has been constantly rising but it was not mirrored by a decrease in the wage differentials between skilled and unskilled workers. In other words, while the relative supply of a factor was increasing, a fall in its relative price was not observed. One of the first and most influential analysis that documents this pattern is Katz and Murphy (1992), where wage differentials between graduated workers (considered the skilled) and non-graduated workers (the unskilled) are analysed for the United States and the non-negative relationship between relative supply and relative wages is found. This pattern is also confirmed by more recent empirical analyses on wage inequalities: Machin and Van Reenen (2008) covering US and UK, Dustmann, Ludsteck, and Schönberg (2009) and Antonczyk, DeLeire, and Fitzenberger (2010a) for Germany.

Given the lack of reduction in wage differentials in the presence of increasing relative supply of skilled labour, there must be something that, at the same time, is also increasing the relative demand for skilled workers. Several explanations are possible for this shift in the demand and the first that has been brought forth is related to technological progress. According to this view, the introduction of new technologies increases the demand for workers that have the skills to use them so that skilled workers become relatively more demanded than the rest. In particular, a number of studies provided evidence that skilled workers benefit relatively more than unskilled ones from technological progress: this phenomenon has been called skill-biased technological change (SBTC). This is the conclusion that Katz and Murphy (1992) reach in their analysis for US, and several other papers have confirmed the presence of SBTC: Acemoglu (1998) is particularly relevant, trying to endogenize SBTC, while Beaudry and Green (2005) update the analysis of Katz and Murphy (1992) with more recent data. A smaller number of papers have appeared covering cross countries evidence: studies by Berman, Bound, and Machin (1998) and Machin and Van Reenen (1998) tackle the consequences of technological change examining wage inequalities in a larger group of countries but do not use exact measures of wage differentials between skilled and unskilled workers.

More complex relationships between technology adoption and labour demand have also been proposed. In particular, Autor, Levy, and Murnane (2003) suggest that jobs that require routine tasks, mostly found in middle wages clerical occupations, are being substituted by new technological devices, so that there is a downward pressure on wages for this kind of jobs. On similar lines, Manning (2004) argues that since wages at the bottom of the distribution are related to manual but non-routine jobs, they might not experience a decrease due to technological progress. The above literature suggest that employment might become polarized, with new technologies producing relatively high demand for high and low wage occupations and relatively low demand for medium wage occupations. Indeed, Spitz-Oener (2006) shows that non-routine tasks within the German occupations have become ever more important and it points to the fact that task changes within occupations are probably the best dimension to assess the presence of a skill-biased technology: according to this view, the skill-bias is present but is somehow nuanced, appearing with different shades depending on the actual tasks of different jobs. This is confirmed also by Dustmann et al. (2009) who observe a polarization of German employment, with medium wage occupations that require routine tasks being less demanded than non-routine occupations at both ends of the wage distribution.

Apart from the effect of technological progress, there are at least two other possible explanations for the evolution of wage differentials: the rise in the international commerce, which increased the competition with less developed countries possibly decreasing low skilled wages, and changes in the labour market conditions. The former has been widely studied and the general conclusion of the empirical analyses on this subject is that the effect of international trade on college premium is, at most, feeble. This is the conclusion reached, for example, by Berman et al. (1998) and by Machin and Van Reenen (1998). A detailed description of several empirical analyses on this aspect is contained in Machin and Van Reenen (2008) where they argue that, all things considered, there is little support for trade-based explanations of demand shifts.

The last possible explanation, the changes in labour markets conditions, has received some attention but has still to be fully assessed. Previous literature on this aspect has provided empirical evidence on the importance of institutions in determining wage inequality. In particular, DiNardo, Fortin, and Lemieux (1996) and DiNardo and Lemieux (1997) point to the importance of union density and minimum wages in producing wage compression; however, Card (1998) argues that the effect of union density on wage compression may be smaller than expected. In addition, there are some empirical studies (Card, Lemieux, & Riddell, 2003 for Canada, US and UK and Antonczyk, Fitzenberger, & Sommerfeld, 2010b for Germany) which suggest that it is the diffusion of bargaining agreements (i.e. the coverage rate) to be particularly important for wage compression, further strengthening the idea that unions are relevant in determining income inequalities. However, the above studies, with the partial exception of Antonczyk et al. (2010b), are not measuring explicitly differentials between skilled and unskilled wage so that an assessment of the relationship between labour market institutions and this specific form of inequality has still to be carried out. Even fewer studies have formalized these aspects in a theoretical framework: an exception is Koeniger, Leonardi, and Nunziata (2007) where a very interesting model that relates income differentials to labour market institutions is built. In that article, however, the analysis focuses on the differences between the earnings of workers from different quantiles of income distribution (the 90th to the 10th percentile mostly) with no exact measure of wage differentials between graduate and non-graduate individuals.

In this article, I focus on the wage gap between workers holding a graduate degree (that I consider skilled) and those without such a degree (unskilled). This measure is similar to the one used by Katz and Murphy (1992) and Beaudry and Green (2005) but has rarely been analysed outside US or in a cross-country perspective. I have data covering 11 European countries: Austria, Belgium, Denmark, Finland, France, Germany, Greece, Ireland, Italy, Spain and UK, in a time span that ranges from the beginning of the 1990s to the beginning of the new century. There are no official data that measure the ratio of wages of graduates and non-graduates and I derive such values using surveys on individual workers: the British Household of Panel Studies for UK (BHPS), the German Socio Economic Panel for Germany (GSOEP) and the European Community Household Panel (ECHP) for the rest of the countries. The differentials have a quite different evolution among those countries: in some cases they rise, in other cases decrease and in a few they stay constant. Overall, the average ratio of the wages of the two groups of workers is quite comparable across the countries, ranging from 1.424 in Denmark to 1.756 in Spain (and Spain has a remarkably higher ratio than the rest of the countries). On the contrary, the share of skilled workers over total workers is increasing in all countries (with the partial exception of Ireland) but it greatly differs in its average level: from 0.11 in Austria to 0.46 in UK. Obviously, this great variety is due to the differences in participation rates to tertiary education but also to the differences that the concept of 'graduate degree' assumes in different countries.

The variety in the evolution patterns of wage differentials poses an interesting puzzle when compared to the common growth of relative supply. When considering the role of technological progress, there are a couple of possible explanations for this behaviour: (1) technological change does not happen at the same rate in different (though quite similar and near) countries, (2) technological change happens at a similar rate, but its effect is different in different countries or (3) a combination of the two.

Clearly, as mentioned earlier, the different evolutions of actual data may also be explained by other factors. One of them is international trade, which I take into account in the analysis but do not explore further given that the conclusion from the previous literature discussed above was that such effect is at most feeble. On the contrary, I do focus on the role of institutions in the labour market and I provide theoretical arguments and empirical evidence on the importance of this aspect. In particular, I present first a model with perfectively competitive labour market and then I build a model where wages are determined through union bargaining so that wage differentials are influenced by the labour market institutions and by the outside options of workers. Then, in the empirical analysis, I introduce several aspects of labour market institutions (unions, minimum wages, employment protection and unemployment insurance) and assess their role in determining wage differentials between skilled and unskilled workers.

The aim of this article is then threefold: (i) to examine the evolution of wage differentials between skilled and unskilled workers using a direct measure of them (i.e. wage differentials between workers with and without an university degree), (ii) to assess the role of technological progress investigating if it is biased and how it is possible to measure its effect and (iii) to analyse how institutions in the labour market and elements like benefits generosity, employment protection and union density may, favouring some groups of workers over the others, help in explaining the evolution of the differentials. In my own view, considering the role of institutions is particularly important. While previous literature usually concluded that institutions regulating the labour market promote wage compression, I argue instead how different institutions affect differently the differentials and some of them may actually magnify the differentials.

The article is organized as follows: the second section explains how I derived my data and briefly describe them; the third section introduces some theoretical models that explain the determination of wage differentials, both with and without union bargaining; the fourth section presents the econometrical analysis, first focusing on the role of technological change and then addressing the role of institutions; finally, the fifth section draws the conclusion.

DATA DESCRIPTION

The main variable I am interested in is the wage ratio between graduate and non-graduate workers. There are no official data describing this variable so I have to build it starting from national surveys on workers. Basically I need a measure for the average wage of graduated workers (the skilled) and for the average wage of the rest of them. The surveys which I use in the analysis are the BHPS (from 1991 to 2003), the GSOEP (from 1992 to 2003) and the ECHP (from 1994 to 2001), which contain data on income, education attainment and other demographic and economic information for individual workers. I use data for all male and female employees in working age (16–65), both full-time and part-time (clearly the latter display lower weekly working hours). I do not consider data on self-employed to obtain a more comparable and trustworthy measure of wages. All surveys contain sampling weights and I use them to guarantee that the true representativeness of the population is respected. For each worker I obtain a measure of his/her wage using the 'current gross wage' variable and weighting it by the weekly working hours. As for the data on education attainment, I rely on the International Standard Classification of Education (ISCED) and I consider him/her a graduate (and skilled) worker if he/she has an ISCED level of at least 5 (that is defined as first stage of tertiary education).

In principle, I could simply calculate the average wage of skilled and unskilled in a given year in a given country. However, I would like to remove from this measure some possible compositional effects which may influence the average wage but that are not particularly relevant for the analysis. In particular, it is possible that the composition in terms of gender and working experience inside each group changes over time, influencing the wage differential. Since I am not interested in variations due to compositional change I want to remove them. This issue has already been noticed in the previous literature and I proceed then to build a series of skill premium cleaned-up from these compositional effects: to do that I adopt the procedure presented in Katz and Murphy (1992), which I describe here below.

What I do is to group and weight data to obtain a homogeneous composition of workers so that influences on wages from variation in the composition in terms of experience and gender is removed. To obtain this, I divide the sample into the two educational groups. For each group (skilled and unskilled) I pick out 6 classes of experience (0–2 years, 3–10, 11–20, 21–30, 31–40 and 41 and more) in turn divided by gender. By means of this I obtain two matrices of 12 cells for every year: each cell identifies workers of a given gender and of a given experience level. For each cell, and for each year studied, I compute the average wage of skilled and unskilled workers using the current gross wage (using sample weights contained in the surveys) divided by the number of weekly working hours.[1] The average wages per cell are assembled in two yearly values: one for skilled and one for unskilled workers. Then I obtain the aggregate average wages as the weighted average of all the cells in a matrix. The weights are the same for all years (allowing to take away the compositional effects) and are computed as the average through time (for each single country) of the occupational rate (the share of workers belonging to that cell over the total workers) in each cell. After having obtained the average wages for both types of workers, I compute their ratio.

The other important variable that I need for the analysis is the ratio of labour supply between skilled and unskilled workers. A simple way to measure this would be to compute the ratio of total weekly working hours between the skilled and the unskilled workers. However, I would like to aggregate quantities of work that are homogeneous in terms of efficiency units. Then, following the previous literature on this subject (in particular this method is followed both in Katz & Murphy, 1992 and Beaudry & Green, 2005), I suppose that real wage is a measure of the efficiency of each unit. Then again I pick each country separately and I divide the workers into two matrices of 12 cells per year, as already discussed. For each cell, and for each year studied, I calculate the sum of weekly hours worked by all the workers and the average wage. The supply of the skilled (or of the unskilled) workers is then obtained through a weighted aggregation of total weekly hours in each cell of a given year. These weights are given by the ratio between the average through time of the wage of each cell over the average through time of the wage of a particular cell chosen as reference. Finally, I generate the time series of relative supply as the ratio between the total supply of skilled over the total supply of unskilled workers.[2]

I obtain data for the following countries[3]: Austria (1995–2001), Belgium (1994–2001), Denmark (1997–2001), Finland (1996–2001), Germany (1992–2005), Greece (1994–2001), Ireland (1994–2001), Italy (1994–2001), Spain (1994–2001) and UK (1991–2003).

An Overview of the Data

I start by showing the average share of skilled employed workers on total employed workers in each country in the related years (Fig. 1(a)).[4]

The shares are quite different across nations and range from about 10% in Italy and Austria to nearly 50% in Belgium and UK with an average across countries of 29.4%. Obviously, such variability is due both to the different participation of the population to tertiary education and to the differences in the exact definition of 'graduate degree' (and on how difficult it is to obtain this qualification). This wide variability is not met by a comparable phenomenon in the ratio between wages of graduated and non-graduated workers (see Fig. 1(b)). This variable seems to be rather

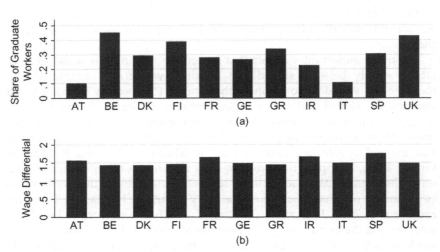

Fig. 1. (a) Share of Workers Holding a Graduate Degree. (b) Skilled-Unskilled Wage Ratio.

stable across the countries: from around 1.43 in Denmark and Belgium to 1.756 in Spain, with an average of 1.53. The general impression from a comparison across countries is that those countries with a smaller (greater) share of graduate workers do not display higher (lower) wage differential: countries with a low relative supply, like Italy and Austria, have below average wage differentials, while those with high relative supply, like UK and France, have average differentials and quite high differentials, respectively. Only in Belgium a very high share of skilled workers correspond to one of the lowest wage differential. Overall, the negative relationship between differentials and relative supply does not arise from a comparison among countries' averages. In any case, I am more interested in these variables' evolution through time within each country.

The time patterns of the share of graduate is shown, for each country, in Fig. 2. The patterns are clearly similar for most countries with an upward trend in relative supply of graduates. The only exception is Ireland where this variable has been pretty much constant.

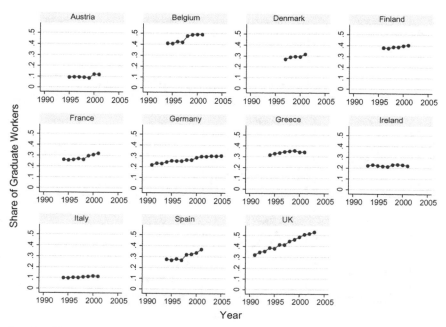

Fig. 2.   The Evolution of Relative Supply of Skilled Labour in European Countries.

The same pattern homogeneity is not found in the evolution of wage differentials (Fig. 3). While almost all countries experienced an increased in the share of skilled work, wage differential shows a variety of patterns. In Austria, Belgium, Denmark and Finland it is increasing, in France, Ireland, Spain and UK, it is decreasing, while in Germany and Italy it does not have a clear trend.[5]

Considering the basic model, which explains the magnitude of wage gap on the basis of the scarcity of skilled workers, there is still much left unexplained. Not only in several cases the basic inverse relationship between relative wages and relative supply is not confirmed but, moreover, the same phenomenon produces different outcomes. Even in the presence of a demand shift due to technological change that drives the evolution of wage differentials, it is quite clear that such demand shift should be either different across countries (so that changes cannot be seen as a common trend) or the technological change was the same but it produced different effects. The aim of the next sections is to solve this puzzle.

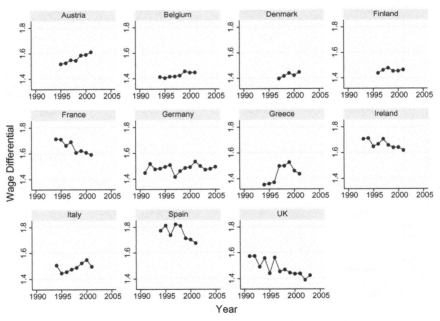

Fig. 3. The Evolution of Wage Differentials in European Countries.

THEORETICAL MODELS

The aim of this section is to give a theoretical foundation to the relationship between wage differentials, relative supply and technological change. To do that I start by describing a model of perfect competition and then I move to build a simple model where wages are determined through union bargaining.

Perfect Competition

I assume that production function is given by[6]

$$Y = \alpha(aS)^\gamma + (1 - \alpha)(bU)^\gamma \qquad (1)$$

where S is the quantity of skilled labour, U the quantity of unskilled labour, a and b are two productivity parameters and α measures how the two factors are aggregated: since a is the productivity of skilled workers it is likely that $a > b$, though this is not a necessary condition in what follows. The parameter γ determines the returns to scale, which are the same for both factors: I assume diminishing returns so that $\gamma < 1$. I imagine that S and U are exogenous variables.

Firms are operating in perfect competition so that real wages (w_s for skilled workers and w_u for unskilled ones) are set equal to marginal productivity (e.g. $w_s = dY/dS = \alpha\gamma a(aS)^{\gamma-1}$) implying that relative wage w_s/w_u is

$$\frac{w_s}{w_u} = \frac{\alpha a^\gamma S^{\gamma-1}}{(1 - \alpha)b^\gamma U^{\gamma-1}} \qquad (2)$$

or, defining w^R as the logarithm of the above ratio

$$w^R \equiv \log\frac{w_s}{w_u} = \log\frac{\alpha}{1 - \alpha} + \gamma\log\frac{a}{b} + (\gamma - 1)\log\frac{S}{U} \qquad (3)$$

Eq. (3) describes what I will refer to as wage differentials: from the equation above I can state that as long as the parameters are constant, relative wage is solely determined by relative supply. If, following an increase in the relative supply S/U, I do not observe a decrease in wage ratio, then the rest of parameters must have changed, that is, a shift in the demand for labour has occurred. It is quite obvious that both the productivity parameter a and b should increase through time as an effect of the technological change;

nevertheless, this is not enough to modify relative wages. As long as the ratio a/b is constant, the change in productivity has no effect on the differentials. Instead, if one of the parameters grows at a higher rate than the other, this affects wage differentials and a biased technological change is observed.

It is possibly to imagine that technological level (and its change) may be measured, in a given period t, by a certain variable T_t. Therefore I can write Eq. (3) as

$$w_t^R = C + \rho T_t + \sigma R_t \tag{4}$$

where C is a constant, R_t is the exogenous relative supply at time t and ρ and σ are parameters that determine the effect of T and R. If $\rho > 0$, then technological change is biased in favour of skilled workers, while if it is zero, there is no effect of technology. An obvious problem in this specification is the exact measurement of T_t: this is usually approximated by a time trend. Under this interpretation, technology level displays a constant increase through time and if $\rho > 0$, at each increase of technology the level of productivity of skilled workers grows more than those of the unskilled ones. This is usually explained asserting that skilled workers are better in exploiting more complex technologies, so that the demand and the reward for their skills grow according to the technological level. The adoption of a time trend to approximate the technological level is probably a too simple approach. In section "Empirical Analysis" I will propose different ways of measuring T_t and investigate how they perform empirically.

Imperfect Competition and Wage Bargaining

I now examine how wage bargaining and labour market institutions might affect wage differentials. An interesting model that introduces bargaining in a context with two categories of workers is contained in Koeniger et al. (2007). Here, for simplicity, I build just a very basic model that includes bargaining. Though simple, it allows to relate institutions to differentials and to grasp their role.[7]

Consider an economy with two kinds of firms i and j. They produce the same good but each one uses only skilled and unskilled labour respectively: each firm employs only a single worker and the resulting production is a for firm i and b for firm j (prices are exogenously set at a given level which for simplicity I set equal to 1). In other words, a and b are the productivity of a skilled and unskilled worker respectively. The resulting real profits π are

$$\pi_i = a - w_s \tag{5}$$

$$\pi_j = b - w_u \tag{5a}$$

Workers bargain with firms to determine real wages and I assume that bargaining is carried out at the central level by identical unions, so that each worker has the same bargaining power. Union utility is given by the surplus of wages over outside option (z_s for the skilled workers and z_u for the unskilled ones): this is a common assumption and the outside option is usually given by the state paid unemployment benefits, by the competitive wage or by a combination of the two. This form of utility can be obtained assuming that unions have utilitarian preferences: for a detailed discussion of different union utility functions see Oswald (1985).

To maximize their utility, unions would like to obtain a wage that is equal to their productivity (since in the absence of fixed costs, firms would never offer a wage higher than labour productivity) and would never accept a wage lower than the outside option. On the other hand, firms try to increase their profits by settling on a lower wage. The final bargained real wage is a weighted average between outside option and productivity, with the weight being the actual bargaining power of unions (which I call β and that ranges from 0 to 1).[8] The resulting bargained wage is then $w_s = \beta a + (1 - \beta)z_s$ and $w_u = \beta b + (1 - \beta)z_u$ so that the wage differentials (in logarithmic terms) are

$$w^R = \log \frac{w_s}{w_u} = \log \frac{\beta a + (1 - \beta)z_s}{\beta b + (1 - \beta)z_u} \tag{6}$$

Alternatively, I could have assumed that bargained wage is given by a geometric weighted average between productivity and outside options (with bargaining power β being still the weight). In this case, I have $w_s = a^\beta z_s^{1-\beta}$ and $w_u = b^\beta z_u^{1-\beta}$, and wage differentials (in logarithmic terms) are given by

$$w^R = \log \frac{w_s}{w_u} = \beta \log \frac{a}{b} + (1 - \beta)\log \frac{z_s}{z_u} \tag{7}$$

Finally, I allow for the possibility that unions' objectives include wage compression and that they actively push for it. If λ is the union strength in pushing towards wage compression, I obtain

$$w^R = \log \frac{\beta a + (1 - \beta)z_s}{\beta b + (1 - \beta)z_u} - \lambda \tag{6a}$$

or

$$w^R = \beta \log \frac{a}{b} + (1 - \beta)\log \frac{z_\text{s}}{z_\text{u}} - \lambda \tag{7a}$$

with Eq. (6a) obtained starting from Eq. (6), and Eq. (7a) obtained starting from Eq. (7).

In all these cases (and also in the detailed model introduced in Appendix A) relative wages have a component similar to the case of perfect competition, since they still depend on a ratio of the productivity parameters. However they also depend on the outside options and on the union preferences in terms of wage compression. The ratio of the productivity parameters should still be related to technology and we can imagine that the ratio between reservation wages depends on the probability for each group to find another job and on the generosity of unemployment benefits. The preferences of the unions may be related to union density if it is true that larger unions promote wage compression. An important point here is that the bargaining power of unions does not have, a priori, a determined effect on the wage ratio: depending on the actual level of productivity and reservation wages, they might magnify or reduce the gap (note that in the case depicted in Eq. (7) the gap is magnified). According to this model, it is quite possible that bargaining acts as a magnifying device of the differences in productivity growth and of the initial differences in the outside options. Another relevant aspect is that relative supply does not enter the equation for wage differentials: this result is robust to changes in the mechanism of wage bargaining. In fact, if I allow for actual bargaining, supply becomes endogenous and does not enter directly in the equation for wages.[9]

In addition, I should mention that I did not introduce minimum wages in the bargaining problem. Were minimum wages in place, and supposing they are relevant only for unskilled workers, a new constraint for the lowest unskilled wage that can be bargained should be inserted. As long as this constraint is binding, I would obtain a new solution where unskilled wage would be higher and wage differentials would be lower than in the previous case. Finally, it is important to stress the role of institutions in a non-competitive labour market that emerges from this model. In particular, the effect of institutions does not run in just one direction: some institutions favour workers with lower wages and produce wage compression while others may act as a magnifying device of the differences in productivity and initial conditions, producing an increase in differentials.

EMPIRICAL ANALYSIS

In this part I turn to the empirical evidence on wage differentials and I look for a confirmation of the above models. I start from the first one, focusing on the role of technological change and then I move to the second one, introducing labour market institutions. In both cases, before estimating the models, I discuss which are the reasonable proxies for some of the variables I am interested in and, in the light of the models I presented above, what should be their role in the determination of wage differentials.

All the analyses are carried out through fixed effects panel regressions using a feasible general least square estimator. This estimator operates minimizing the sum of weighted square residuals, where weights are determined by the elements of the estimated variance–covariance matrix G of the disturbance vector. In particular, in all regressions, I allow for the matrix G to have groupwise heteroskedasticity and panel-specific (country-specific in this case) autocorrelation. In the last part of the analysis, I also relax the assumption on groupwise heteroskedasticity and allow for cross-country errors correlation.[10] The use of Fixed Effects and thus of country-specific constants is fundamental for the analysis. In principle, the adoption of the same formal definition of 'skilled' for all countries could imply different levels of actual skill. This possibility is captured by the country-specific constant so that each country has a different baseline wage differential (i.e. a different constant term in the regression). The evolution of wage differentials within each country is captured by the evolution (variation) of the skilled supply and of the other variables so that I can assess the determinants of such evolution.

From an estimation point of view, the technological level and the supply of skilled might be related in that the former may promote the latter. However, given the length of time necessary to obtain a university degree, it is unlikely that the technological level in a given year affects the supply of graduated workers in the economy.[11] In any case, even if such relationship existed, I would simply observe multicollinearity between two independent variables: this could produce scarce statistical significance of the related coefficients but it would not bias the estimation results. In addition, I do find these coefficients to be significant, which indicate that the results seem not to be affected by their reverse causality.

Technological Change

According to the model I presented in section "Perfect Competition", relative wages depend on relative supply of skilled workers and on a variable which captures the relative productivity of skilled with respect to unskilled workers: this variable should be related to technological progress. If I add a country-specific constant I can estimate the following model

$$w_{i,t}^R = C + c_i + \rho T_{i,t} + \sigma R_{i,t} + \varepsilon_{i,t} \tag{8}$$

where $w_{i,t}^R$ is the log ratio between skilled and unskilled wage in country i, $R_{i,t}$ the relative supply of skilled workers (measured in log) and $T_{i,t}$ the technological variable; C and c_i are the constant terms with the latter being country specific.

Several proxies can be used to measure T and, depending on which one I choose, I imply a different mechanism that links technology to relative productivity: in any case, should ρ be significantly different from zero, I would detect the presence of biased technological progress (skill-biased for $\rho > 0$).

The first way to approximate technological progress is through a linear trend. This implies that technological progress happens at a steady pace that is the same in all countries and has the same effect across them. I test the model of Eq. (8) following the above mentioned estimation technique: the results are given in column (i) of Table 1.

The estimation clearly shows that a common time trend is not present. This is not surprising given the pattern in Figs. 2 and 3. While relative supply of skilled workers was increasing almost everywhere, wage differentials were having different evolutions in different countries. This implies that they could hardly be experiencing a common trend. I also find that the coefficient of relative supply is negative, which is in line with what the theoretical model predicts.

If we still believe that technological progress is relevant in explaining the evolution of wage differentials, then we need a variable that could measure the differences in technology in each country. To do so I consider a measure of technological level obtained as the cumulated sum through the years of R&D expenditures over GDP.[12] In practice, I normalize to zero the technological level in a base year (1990 in my case) and I assume that $T_{i,t} \equiv \sum_{y=1990}^{t} R\&D_{i,y}$ where $R\&D_{i,y}$ indicates the expenditures over GDP in year y in country i (measured in logs). Obviously it is possible that the initial technological level is different in different nations but such (likely) case would be captured by the country-specific constant and would not be a problem. This measure should capture the cumulated dimension or stock of

Table 1.   Regressions for Wage Differentials in the Perfectly
Competitive Case.

	Wage Differentials		
	(i) Technological Time Trend	(ii) Technological Level	(iii) Intensity of Technological Change
Relative supply	−0.054**	−0.086***	−0.084***
	(0.025)	(0.019)	(0.009)
Time trend	−0.001		
	(0.0014)		
Cumulated R&D		0.0001	
		(0.005)	
R&D			0.209***
			(0.021)
Observations	93	85	85
Number of countries	11	10	10

Standard errors in parentheses.
*Significant at 10%; **significant at 5%; ***significant at 1%.

knowledge and innovation that a given country has reached. To the best of my knowledge the cumulated R&D expenditure over GDP has not been considered in previous literature. However, it is related to some other measures that have been proposed by Beaudry and Green (2005) where they adopt the stock of physical capital and total factor productivity. All these measures share the idea that it is the level of technology (i.e. the stock of technology) that might cause the skill-bias. In this they follow the spirit of Katz and Murphy (1992) though proposing different measurement methods.

The results are presented in column (ii) of Table 1.[13] Once again, the technological variable is not statistically significant, suggesting that technological level on itself does not imply a bias towards a certain category of workers.

Finally, I turn to a different approach and I assume that the relevant factor is the intensity of technological change. Then I can measure the technological variable directly through the R&D expenditures over GDP, setting $T_{i,t} \equiv R\&D_{i,t}$. The results of the estimation (column (iii), Table 1) are much better than in the previous case as the intensity of the change seems to strongly affect relative wages. There is a clear interpretation of these results: it appears that technological bias comes from the pace of the progress, not from the progress itself. Under this view, skilled workers seem to be quicker to adapt, taking advantage from rapid changes in technology. This interpretation is partly new but it is also compatible with the nuanced version of SBTC highlighted in Autor et al. (2003) and Spitz-Oener (2006). In fact, the capacity of adapting to fast changes or rapid innovations is probably more relevant in non-routine occupations rather than in routine ones. In any case, my findings appear to be relevant and allow to identify one of the driving forces in the evolution of wage differentials in the intensity of technological change. The relationship between the intensity of progress and differentials can be also seen plotting the change in the wage differentials against the change in R&D expenditures measured as the log ratio of the final and initial values in each country (Fig. 4).

Obviously, this is only an intuitive representation of this relationship as it neglects the exact evolution of the variables and focuses only on the first and last values of each country. Nonetheless, the relationship is striking clear and positive, with countries with growing R&D expenditures having an increase in wage differentials and vice versa. The figure also explains the division into groups of countries that I made in the previous section: Austria, Belgium, Denmark and Finland have increasing differentials and are in the top right of the figure, with R&D expenditures increasing as well. Germany and Italy are in the centre, with stable differentials and R&D. Finally, in the bottom left there are France, Ireland and UK, with

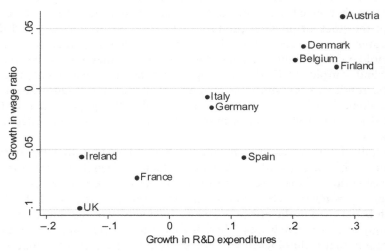

Fig. 4.   Growth of Wage Ratio Against Growth of R&D Expenditures.

decreasing differentials and R&D; only Spain remains partly out of this description, with a slight increase in R&D but falling differentials. Note also that according to the above figure, a constant R&D would be associated to decreasing differentials. This is not a real issue because the graph is neglecting that relative skilled supply was increasing throughout the period in almost all countries, thus contributing to the fall of the differentials.

To better explore this relationship, to analyse differences across countries and to check how robust my specification is, I now consider a specification in which the technological effect due to the R&D intensity differs across countries.[14] This allows to determine whether the magnitude (and the sign) of the skill bias is the same in different countries and to further address the issue that my definition of skilled might actually imply different skills in different countries. I proceed in estimating

$$w_{i,t} = C + c_i + \alpha R_{i,t} + \beta_i T_{i,t} + \varepsilon_{i,t} \tag{9}$$

where the coefficient β_i is specific to country i. The results are presented in Table 2 in which I present the coefficient associated to their R&D expenditures separately for each country.

It is easy to see that once I have taken into account standard errors most of the countries have coefficients that are reasonably close to each other. The exceptions are France, which has a higher coefficient, Finland which is a bit lower than average and Spain which has a negative (but not significant) coefficient. The result for Spain is the only one that creates some concerns, in fact, unless I consider an unskilled biased technology, the negative effect has no theoretical explanation. A possible explanation for this may come from the fact that the Spanish labour market was undergoing several changes in the period of analysis, with a strong increase in flexibility. Given the reforms Spain undertook, it is likely that new entrant workers ended up having fixed term contracts in contrast to incumbents workers, which mostly had permanent contracts. This, in combination with a higher share of skilled in new entrants than incumbent (due to the increase in tertiary education attainment) and with the usual lower wage associated with fixed term jobs, may explain the decline in wage differentials. From a statistical point of view, I can test the equality of the coefficients. The results (reported in Table 2), indicate that equality of the coefficient for all countries is rejected but it cannot be rejected for a large subset of countries (Austria, Belgium, Denmark, Germany, Ireland, Italy and UK).

There is a final aspect concerning technological progress that needs to be mentioned. Technological progress might somehow be contagious between countries so that by measuring it within single countries this aspect might

Table 2.   Regression with Country Specific Coefficient Technological
Change.

	Wage Differentials
Relative supply	-0.081^{***}
	(0.014)
Austria	0.289^{***}
	(0.052)
Belgium	0.303^{***}
	(0.061)
Denmark	0.203^{***}
	(0.035)
Finland	0.047^{*}
	(0.029)
France	0.621^{***}
	(0.083)
Germany	0.245^{***}
	(0.094)
Ireland	0.252^{***}
	(0.082)
Italy	0.494^{**}
	(0.224)
Spain	-0.175
	(0.126)
UK	0.212^{**}
	(0.089)
Observations	85
Number of countries	10
Test for equality of all the R&D coefficients	$\chi^2(9)=74.45$
	$\text{Prob}>\chi^2=0.000$
Test for equality for a subset of R&D coefficients	$\chi^2(9)=4.67$
	$\text{Prob}>\chi^2=0.587$

Standard errors in parentheses.
*Significant at 10%; **significant at 5%; ***significant at 1%.

be overlooked. Actually, previous analyses on this subject have usually
adopted measures confined to single countries and indeed I follow this
approach. However, in the next subsection, once I have developed a richer
specification for my model, I will also adopt an estimation technique that
partly amends for this issue.

So far the analysis has neglected the effect of international commerce on
wage differentials. While I did not introduce a formalized model for it,
I discussed earlier how international trade may affect the differentials as

competition from other countries might affect some sectors more than others and, in particular, competition from less developed countries may induce a reduction of the unskilled wages. To control for this, I introduce a measure of international trade in the regression. The simplest way to do this is to consider what is called the openness to imports of a country, that is, the share of imports of goods and services over the GDP. Obviously, the share of imports of goods and services is a crude approximation and, in particular, it is possible that the wages of unskilled workers are particularly sensitive to competition from less developed countries. In the attempt of tackling this aspect, I proceed to build a more accurate measure, which I call 'adjusted imports'. This variable is given by the total imports from non-developed countries[15] net of the imports of mineral fuels (oil, carbon and gas) from those countries and it should be able to capture the competition that unskilled intensive goods suffer because of imports from less developed countries. It is possible to build this variable only for the years after 1994, therefore the sample slightly shrinks. I use both these measures in regression (i) of Table 3 (where I allow for different coefficients for R&D as before) but

Table 3. Regression with Controls for International Commerce.

	Wage Differentials		
	(i) Openness & Adjusted Imports	(ii) Openness Only	(iii) Adjusted Imports Only
Relative supply	−0.042**	−0.063***	−0.038**
	(0.020)	(0.011)	(0.019)
R&D	0.232***	0.274***	0.236***
	(0.030)	(0.026)	(0.031)
R&D for Finland	0.040	0.048*	0.043
	(0.031)	(0.029)	(0.031)
R&D for France	0.624***	0.586***	0.634***
	(0.144)	(0.091)	(0.140)
R&D for Spain	−0.272*	−0.174	−0.281**
	(0.145)	(0.127)	(0.142)
Openness	−0.031	−0.028	
	(0.032)	(0.018)	
Adjusted imports	0.006		−0.016
	(0.026)		(0.017)
Observations	72	84	73
Number of countries	10	10	10

Standard errors are in parentheses.
*Significant at 10%; **significant at 5%; ***significant at 1%.

I fail to find a significant effect. Even if I use only one of these measures (regressions (ii) and (iii)), I still fail to find any significant effect. Over all, even, when I use what I believe to be a proper measure for imports, international commerce and competition from less developed countries do not seem to be relevant.

The Role of Institutions

Now I turn to evaluate how institutions can affect the wage differentials. In the theoretical discussion, I have introduced the mechanism of wage bargaining and I have concluded that, in such a context relative supply is not directly relevant and wage differentials should depend not only on the relative productivity of workers (which might be related to technological progress) but also on their reservation wage (which depends on the employment possibilities and on unemployment benefits) and on the preferences of unions. In general, these factors should be relevant only if they differ across the two groups while it is very likely that some institutions, or at least labour legislation, are the same for both groups. In all, I am going to use the following variables: employment rates (ER) of skilled and unskilled workers (which measure the probabilities of finding a job), replacement ratio (RR) and benefits duration (BD) (which determines the generosity of unemployment benefits), overall union density (UD),[16] employment protection level (EP) (both these variables can be thought to be proxies of overall bargaining power and possibly of unions preference) and the minimum statutory wage (MW).[17]

Even when the institutions and the variables measuring them are the same for both groups, I have reasons to believe that they may have different effects on the reservation wages and bargaining power of the two groups. In what follows I describe the variables and I explain what effects should be expected.

The employment rate should measure the employment opportunities of a worker and it is the only variable which can be effectively measured distinguishing between the skilled and unskilled workers. It is given by the ratio between the number of workers that are employed and the sum of them plus those workers that declare being unemployed and searching for a job. The effect of this variable should be quite clear: when the employment rate of a certain group is high it means that it is easy to obtain a job for people belonging to that group so that their outside option should be better. I measure differences in employment opportunities by means of the ratio of the employment rate of the skilled workers and those of the unskilled ones and I expect that this variable has a positive effect on wage differentials.

The replacement ratio measures the share of the past wage that an unemployed worker receives when out of work and entitled to unemployment benefits. It follows that this variable should be more relevant in the determination of reservation wage for the group whose past wages are on average higher. This should be the case for the skilled workers so the relationship between RR and the wage differentials should be positive.

The duration of unemployment benefits measures the maximum duration of unemployed benefits. The same reasoning as for the replacement ratio should be true for the benefits duration. However, it must be underlined that the group which shows higher employment probability could take less advantage from long duration. Since the skilled workers exhibit higher employment probability, the final effect might be ambiguous.

Union density is the percentage of workers that are members of unions. This variable is usually associated with the bargaining power of unions, which in my model should have no clear effect on the wage ratio.[18] However, there is evidence that unions are able to compress wages, so that the effect could be negative, even if there is no clear evidence that this compression happens also in the differentials between skilled and unskilled. On the other hand, there are at least two reasons why its effect could be positive. First of all, bargained wages depend on outside options and it may be possible that bargaining power amplifies the differences in the starting positions, so that the group of workers with better outside options gains more from higher bargaining power (my theoretical model indeed shows that this case is possible). Second, there may be a relationship between the union density and the composition of the members. It is likely that when only few workers belong to unions, those members belong to the unskilled group (that probably forms the core of the unions) while the relative number of skilled members increases with the increase of union density. Then, a shift in the preferences of the union could be observed (from the unskilled to the skilled) as its density increases. The overall effect is then uncertain.

The level of employment protection is an index that measures the rigidity of the labour market. It should not directly affect the wage but it is possible that high protection increases the bargaining power of workers making them less likely to be fired when too high bargained wages generate an excess in the number of employed. As discussed above, a stronger bargaining power may promote wage compression but it might also amplify the differences in the outside options of the groups. This mechanism is in any case dubious so its effect on the differentials is uncertain.

The minimum statutory wage is the minimum hourly wage a worker is entitled to receive if he or she holds a contract. It is measured as a percentage of median wages. In this perspective, the minimum wage poses a constraint to the unskilled bargaining wage, while skilled workers should be unaffected by it as their wage is usually above that level. Then, when the constraint is binding, the minimum wage increases the wages of the unskilled workers only and decreases the wage differentials.

After having described the variables I use, I perform the estimation of the following equation adopting the same estimator as before

$$
\begin{aligned}
w_{i,t} = C + c_i + \alpha ER_{i,t} + \beta T_{i,t} + \gamma_1 RR_{i,t} + \gamma_2 BD_{i,t} + \gamma_3 UD_{i,t} \\
+ \gamma_4 EP_{i,t} + \gamma_5 MW_{i,t} + \varepsilon_{i,t}
\end{aligned} \tag{10}
$$

The results are shown in column (i) of Table 4.[19]

The estimations are quite in line with what the theoretical model predicts. They confirm that the ratio of employment rate and the replacement ratio have a positive effect on the differentials. On the contrary, the duration of benefits has a negative effect, implying that skilled workers tend to take less advantage of benefits that last long; similarly the minimum wage has a negative effect on differentials, as it is probably binding for unskilled workers only. The result on union density seems to negate that unions induce wage compression, at least between the skilled and unskilled workers. On the contrary, the employment protection level is positive but not significant. As discussed before, there are two possible explanations for the former effect: first, the composition and unions' preferences may shift to favour the skilled workers when union density increases; second, union power might have an amplifying effect of the outside options. We must bear in mind that the lack of wage compression is strictly confined to the differentials between graduate and non-graduate workers. In fact, it is possible that unions produce wage compression and reduce inequality within these two groups or even between other groups (e.g. groups identified by the percentiles in the income distribution, as in the case of Koeniger et al., 2007). Anyway, the results confirm the relevance of institutions in the determination of wage differentials and they give evidence to the fact that their effect is complex with some specific institutions compressing the differentials and others magnifying them.

I showed above that some countries have different coefficients for R&D from the rest so, in regression (ii), I allow for these differences. The results do not change much with the only exception of EP, which is still positive but now significant.

Table 4. Regression for Wage Differentials in the Imperfectly Competitive Case.

	Wage Differentials		
	(i) Common R&D coefficient	(ii) Different R&D Coefficients	(iii) Cross-Sectional Correlation
Employment rate ratio	0.260***	0.107 *	0.166***
	(0.083)	(0.062)	(0.025)
R&D	0.200***	0.229***	0.189***
	(0.024)	(0.014)	(0.014)
R&D for Finland		0.067*	
		(0.040)	
R&D for France		0.838***	0.927***
		(0.126)	(0.086)
R&D for Spain		−0.215	−0.189***
		(0.137)	(0.067)
Replacement ratio	0.179***	0.189***	0.186***
	(0.024)	(0.021)	(0.008)
Benefits duration	−0.073***	−0.087***	−0.082***
	(0.020)	(0.017)	(0.008)
Union density	0.060**	0.050**	0.027**
	(0.026)	(0.022)	(0.014)
Employment protection level	0.025	0.031**	0.030***
	(0.018)	(0.015)	(0.010)
Minimum wage	−0.033**	−0.028**	−0.026***
	(0.016)	(0.015)	(0.005)
Observations	83	83	56
Number of countries	10	10	10

Standard errors in parentheses.
*Significant at 10%; **significant at 5%; ***significant at 1%.

Finally, to further check the robustness of the results I allow for a different assumption on the errors structure. So far I have assumed that there was no correlation in the errors across countries, while now I allow for this. Technically, this means that in the estimation of the variance–covariance matrix G I allow for its off-diagonal elements to be different from zero. The correlation between cross-country error terms implies that unobservable factors might have similar effects on the different countries. This partly captures also some possible contagious effects of technological progress in that, shocks due to such technological spillover may happen at the same time and with similar magnitude in different countries. The introduction of this technique has the drawback that in order to estimate the matrix G I need a balanced panel. Therefore, I am forced to use only a subset of the data, confining the analysis only to Austria, Belgium, France, Germany, Ireland, Italy, Spain and UK. Using only a subset of the countries might reduce the efficiency of the estimation, but it also allows to further test the robustness of the analysis, checking whether the results hold true even for just a subsample.

The results are presented in column (iii) of Table 4 and are extremely satisfactory. Even when I allow for cross correlation and use only a sub-sample, the estimates are still accurate and all the results hold (and even the absolute values of the coefficients are very similar). As before, R&D is still significant, once again confirming that skill bias originates from the intensity of technological change. Moreover, all the institutions seems to behave as in the above case: note that once again EP seems to have a positive effect so that the amplifying effect might indeed be present. Actually, the coefficient for R&D is now slightly lower than before, implying that R&D from a single country is now slightly less important in the determination of the differentials. This could be a signal that technological progress is contagious (as, in the presence of correlated errors, differentials respond less to country-specific R&D) but the magnitude of the reduction is so small that the degree of contagiousness would be feeble at most and not capable of significantly altering my conclusions. This is an aspect that might be worth investigating in future research.

CONCLUSIONS

In this article I have examined the evolution of wage differentials between skilled (graduate) and unskilled (non-graduate) workers in several European countries in a period that goes from the beginning of the 1990s to the beginning of this century. The main stylized fact for this period is that, while all European countries have seen a rise in the relative supply of skilled workers, the evolution of the wage differentials has been widely different across these countries. These patterns suggest not only that a simple supply and demand model is not sufficient in explaining the evolution of the differentials, but also that the adoption of a common technological trend is not enough to identify the effect of technological progress. In the first part of this study I analysed the relationship between technological progress and the wage differentials and I found that the intensity of technological change, measured with R&D expenditures, seems to be the (technological) driving force of wage differentials. The interpretation of this result is that skilled workers are more able to adapt themselves to changes in technology and so they take advantage of periods of rapid progress. The different degree of R&D across Europe helps to explain the differences in the evolution of the differentials. I have also tried to take into account the effect of international competition of less developed countries, building what I believe to be an appropriate measure for it: the results seem to neglect any effect of this factor.

In the second part I consider the labour market institutions by presenting a simple theoretical model of non-competitive labour market which I test empirically. The introduction of institutions shifts the attention towards the analysis of the differences between the outside options of workers and how institutions may reduce or amplify these differences. In particular, skilled workers are likely to have better outside options and thus, according to my model, the institutions that amplify the differences in the outside options also increase the wage differentials between skilled and unskilled workers. This should be the case for union density (which is a proxy for union power) and for the generosity of unemployment benefits (in terms of replacement rates). The empirical analysis shows that these two aspects indeed increase wage differentials. On the contrary, some institutions directly favour the unskilled more than the skilled workers and should thus decrease differentials. In particular, the maximum duration of unemployment benefits (which unskilled workers are more likely to fully exploit) and the minimum wage (that should not be binding for skilled workers) fall in this category and, once again, the empirical analysis confirm these results. The overall conclusion is then that institutions have a relevant role in the determinations of wage differentials, but their effect is not clean cut and, depending on the particular institution, it may run in both ways. The magnifying aspects of some institutions is particularly interesting and should be further tackled in future research.

NOTES

1. Actually, to obtain an exact measure of the hourly wage I should multiply this by 4.33. Since in the end I am interested in the ratio between two average wages, this can be omitted.

2. In any case the patterns of relative supply obtained by means of this method are not so different from those obtained using directly total weekly hours. I also tried to use this latter variable in the empirical analysis contained in section "Empirical Analysis", but the results were qualitatively similar.

3. While ECHP survey covers also Luxembourg, Netherland and Sweden, the quality of those data is not good enough to obtain a measure of wage differentials. In particular: data on Luxembourg do not cover gross income; educational data on Netherland are clearly incorrect (according to them only around 5% of workers has achieved more than primary education) and data on Sweden cover too few years. Things are different for Portuguish data which are complete enough to calculate wage differentials. However, the result for Portugal is completely out of scale, with an average value of the wage ratio above 3, whereas the average of the other countries is around 1.52. I do not know whether this is due to the quality of data or if they reflect the real Portuguish situation, but in order not to compromise this analysis I prefer not to use them.

4. The measure is given by the total weighted work hours of skilled workers over total work hours of all the employed workers. The weights allow me to measure efficient units of labour, as explained above.

5. Other empirical studies report a general rising trend in wage inequality in Germany (Antonczyk et al., 2010a) and UK (Machin & Van Reenen, 2008), but they are not totally incompatible with this analysis since I focus only on the differential between graduate and not graduate workers. In addition, Dustmann et al. (2009) examine the evolution of inequality between groups of differently skilled workers in Germany, focusing on three groups, high skilled (with college degree), medium skilled (with post-secondary degree) and low skilled (the rest) and report an increase in inequality between the medium and low skilled and no clear pattern for the high skilled compared to the medium; again this is not incompatible with the substantial stability of the graduate/non-graduate German differentials that I report.

6. I choose this particular functional form for its simplicity. However, I would have reached exactly the same results using a CES production function.

7. In Appendix A, I provide a more detailed model in which bargaining is formalized by means of a Nash Bargaining solution: the main conclusions remain the same.

8. This simplification is not particularly strange, first because it has already been done in some other relevant papers (see, e.g. Pissarides, 1985) and second because if I instead solve the bargaining through a Nash Maximandum, I would obtain, in this context, exactly the same result (see Appendix A).

9. This is what I obtain in the more detailed model presented in Appendix A. See Layard, Nickel, and Jackman (1991) for a text-book case of wages determined through bargaining.

10. See Greene (2002, pp. 322–329) for a detailed description of these methods.

11. In addition, I tried to run fixed effect panel regressions of the relevant technological variable on the supply of skilled worker: the resulting coefficient was not statistically significant indicating that this problem should not be present.

12. Data are obtained from EUROSTAT statistics database, available at http://epp.eurostat.ec.europa.eu/portal/page/portal/statistics/themes.

13. Data on R&D expenditures for Greece are not available. This explains the reduction in sample size.

14. To evaluate the robustness of the estimation I also tried to remove one country at time. The results obtained in all cases are the same as above, ruling out the possibility that a single nation is driving our estimations results.

15. This is obtained subtracting from total imports the imports from Euro-15 countries, Australia, Japan, New Zealand, Norway, Switzerland and US. While some minor developed countries are still present, their impact should be negligible.

16. In principle there could exist an exact measure of union density for each group, but I do not have such data nor do I know possible sources that would cover all countries.

17. The source of data for RR, UD, EPL MW is OECD; for BD is Nickell (2006). For ER I am using my own computations from the survey data used in the rest of the analysis.

18. There is another important variable that can be associated to bargaining power and to the relevance of unions: the coverage rate. When I include in the regressions both the coverage rate and the union density they are not statistically significant: this is probably due to collinearity as the two variables display high in-group correlation. When used separately, they appear significant, with the same sign and quite close magnitude, indicating that indeed they are probably capturing the same effect. In the end, I chose to use union density only because I have more data for it and so I can use a larger sample. However, results for regressions with coverage rate are reported in Appendix B.

19. Once again, even if I do not report the results, I also tried to remove a country at a time and the results were unchanged.

ACKNOWLEDGEMENTS

The present research was (co-)funded by the European Commission under the 6th Framework Programme's Research Infrastructures Action (Transnational Access contract RITA 026040) hosted by IRISS-C/I at CEPS/INSTEAD, Differdange (Luxembourg). I am grateful to IRISS-CEPS/INSTEAD for hosting me and for the help received from all its staff. I thank Konstantinos Tatsiramos and two anonymous referees for their useful suggestions. Finally, I am deeply in debt with Silvia Demi for her help in re-editing the revised version of this article.

REFERENCES

Acemoglu, D. (1998). Why do new technologies complement skills? Directed technical change and wage inequality. *Quarterly Journal of Economics, 113*(4), 1055–1089.

Antonczyk, D., DeLeire, T., & Fitzenberger, B. (2010a). *Polarization and rising wage inequality: Comparing the U.S. and Germany.* IZA Discussion Paper No. 4842, IZA, Bonn.

Antonczyk, D., Fitzenberger, B., & Sommerfeld, K. (2010b). Rising wage inequality, the decline of collective bargaining, and the gender wage gap. *Labour Economics, 17*(5), 835–847.

Autor, D., Levy, F., & Murnane, R. (2003). The skill content of recent technological change: An empirical exploration. *The Quarterly Journal of Economics, 118*(4), 1279–1333.

Beaudry, P., & Green, D. (2005). Changes in U.S. wages, 1976–2000: Ongoing skill bias or major technological change? *Journal of Labor Economics, 23*(3), 609–648.

Berman, E., Bound, J., & Machin, S. (1998). Implications of skill-biased technological change: International evidence. *Quarterly Journal of Economics, 113*(4), 1245–1279.

Card, D. (1998). *Falling union membership and rising wage inequality: What's the connection?* NBER Working Papers No. 6520, NBER, Cambridge, MA.

Card, D., Lemieux, T., & Riddell, W. C. (2003). *Unionization and wage inequality: A comparative study of the U.S., the U.K., and Canada.* NBER Working Papers No. 9473, NBER, Cambridge, MA.

DiNardo, J., Fortin, N. M., & Lemieux, T. (1996). Labor market institutions and the distribution of wages, 1973–1992: A semiparametric approach. *Econometrica, 64*(5), 1001–1044.

DiNardo, J., & Lemieux, T. (1997). Diverging male wage inequality in the United States and Canada, 1981–1988: Do institutions explain the difference? *Industrial and Labor Relations Review, 50*(4), 629–651.

Dustmann, C., Ludsteck, J., & Schönberg, U. (2009). Revisiting the German wage structure. *The Quarterly Journal of Economics, 124*(2), 843–881.

Greene, W. H. (2002). *Econometric analysis* (5th ed.). Prentice Hall, 2007.

Katz, L. F., & Murphy, K. M. (1992). Changes in relative wages, 1963–1987: Supply and demand factors. *Quarterly Journal of Economics, 107*(1), 35–78.

Koeniger, W., Leonardi, M., & Nunziata, L. (2007). Labor market institutions and wage inequality. *Industrial and Labor Relations Review, 60*(3), 340–356.

Layard, R., Nickel, S., & Jackman, R. (1991). *Unemployment: Macroeconomic performance and the labour market.* Oxford: Oxford University Press.

Machin, S., & Van Reenen, J. (1998). Technology and changes in skill structure: Evidence from seven OECD countries. *The Quarterly Journal of Economics, 113*(4), 1215–1244.

Machin, S., & Van Reenen, J. (2008). Changes in wage inequality. In S. N. Durlauf, & L. E. Blume (Eds.), *The new Palgrave dictionary of economics* (2nd ed.). New York, NY: Palgrave Macmillan.

Manning, A. (2004). We can work it out: The impact of technological change on the demand for low-skill workers. *Scottish Journal of Political Economy, 51*(5), 581–608.

Nickell, W. (2006). *The CEP-OECD Institutions Data Set (1960–2004).* CEP Discussion Paper No. 759, London School of Economics and Political Science, London.

Oswald, A. J. (1985). The economic theory of trade unions: An introductory survey. *The Scandinavian Journal of Economics, 87*(2), 160–193.

Pissarides, C. (1985). Short-run equilibrium dynamics of unemployment vacancies, and real wages. *American Economic Review, 75*(4), 676–690.

Spitz-Oener, A. (2006). Technical change, job tasks, and rising educational demands: Looking outside the wage structure. *Journal of Labor Economics, 24*(2), 235–270.

APPENDIX A: A MORE DETAILED MODEL OF BARGAINING

Here I present a better specified model of bargaining than the one presented in section "Theoretical Models". The key difference is that now bargaining is fully formalized by means of the solution of a Nash Bargaining. However, as it is shown at the end of this appendix, the final results will be similar.

Suppose again that there are two kinds of firms i and j: they produce the same goods but they only use skilled and unskilled labour respectively. They sell it at an exogenously set price (which I set equal to 1) and their production function is given by

$$Y_i = (aS)^\gamma + aS \tag{A.1}$$

$$Y_j = (bU)^\gamma + bU \tag{A.2}$$

For simplicity, I assume that firms share the same returns to scale, though I could opt for different ones without altering my conclusions. Workers are organized in decentralized unions which bargain with firms for real wages through a Right to Manage mechanism. Unions utility is given by the expected wage per member and their fallback values are z_s for skilled workers and z_u for unskilled workers. The utility for firms is given by their real profits and their fallback value is zero. The solution of the bargaining is obtained from the maximization of a Nash Maximandum and, for skilled workers, it is given by

$$\left\{ \arg \max \ _{w_s}[(w_s - z_s)S]^\beta \ [Y_i - w_sS]^{1-\beta} \quad \text{s.t.} \quad \frac{dY_i}{dS} = 0. \tag{A.3}$$

where the constraint represents the firms' right to manage. The solution of the above gives

$$w_s = \left(2\beta + \frac{\gamma}{\gamma - 1}\right)^{-1}\left[\beta a + \left(\frac{\gamma}{\gamma - 1} + \beta\right)z_s\right] \tag{A.4}$$

Through an equivalent procedure I can obtain bargained wages of unskilled workers

$$w_u = \left(2\beta + \frac{\gamma}{\gamma - 1}\right)^{-1}\left[\beta b + \left(\frac{\gamma}{\gamma - 1} + \beta\right)z_u\right] \tag{A.5}$$

so the relative wages are

$$\frac{w_s}{w_u} = \frac{a\beta + \left(\frac{\gamma}{\gamma-1} + \beta\right) z_s}{b\beta + \left(\frac{\gamma}{\gamma-1} + \beta\right) z_u} \tag{A.6}$$

Even if it does not exactly share the same functional form as Eq. (6) or (7), the above result displays the same effect for all the relevant parameters and, moreover, it does not directly include relative supply, exactly as in the case presented in the main text.

APPENDIX B: ESTIMATION RESULTS INCLUDING COVERAGE RATE

I report in Table B1 the results for the estimation of Eq. (10) when Coverage Rate is used as an independent variable.

Table B1. Regressions Including Coverage Rate.

	Wage Differentials	
	(i) Union Density & Coverage Rate	(ii) Coverage Rate Only
Employment rate ratio	.028***	0.29***
	(.006)	(0.09)
R&D	0.200***	0.1754***
	(0.028)	(0.018)
Replacement ratio	0.138***	0.146***
	(0.038)	(0.0367)
Benefits duration	−0.037	−0.043
	(0.034)	(0.029)
Union density	0.066	
	(0.048)	
Coverage rate	0.021	0.073***
	(0.046)	(0.026)
Employment protection level	0.027	0.032*
	(0.018)	(0.026)
Minimum wage	−0.045	−0.029
	(0.054)	(0.05)
Observations	62	62
Number of countries	10	10

Standard errors in parentheses.
*Significant at 10%; **significant at 5%; ***significant at 1%.

CAREER AND WAGE DYNAMICS: EVIDENCE FROM LINKED EMPLOYER-EMPLOYEE DATA

Antti Kauhanen and Sami Napari

ABSTRACT

We study career and wage dynamics within and between firms using a large linked employer-employee panel dataset spanning 26 years. We construct six-level hierarchies for more than 5,000 firms. We replicate most of the analyses from Baker, Gibbs, and Holmström (1994) and make some extensions. Many of our results corroborate their findings. Careers within firms are important, but the strong version of the theory of internal labor markets does not fit the data. Recent theories of career and wage dynamics explain our findings well.

Keywords: Internal labor markets; employer changes; promotions; wage growth; human capital

JEL classification: M51; M12; J62; L22

Research in Labor Economics, Volume 36, 35–76
ISSN: 0147-9121/doi:10.1108/S0147-9121(2012)0000036006

INTRODUCTION

During the last three decades, the fields of personnel economics and organizational economics have started to develop and test models of internal workings of firms. In this respect, they have moved beyond the traditional treatment of firms as "black boxes." A particular area that has received a lot of attention is internal labor markets, which refer to a set of practices through which firms restrict entry to certain positions and thereafter careers progress on a more or less specified path. The theory of internal labor markets also implies that wages are strongly tied to jobs and not to the characteristics of the jobholder.

Economic studies of careers in organizations were spurred by the seminal contribution of Baker, Gibbs, and Holmström (1994). They studied the personnel records of a single US firm for a period of 20 years, focusing on the hierarchical structure of the firm, career, and wage dynamics, and the role of hierarchical levels as determinants of pay. They found that the allocation of labor in the firm resembles an internal labor market in some respects, and that human capital, both general and firm-specific, and learning about employee ability are important for career dynamics.

These findings led to more elaborate theories of promotion and wage dynamics (e.g., Gibbons & Waldman, 1999, 2006). One reason for the significant impact of the single-firm study by Baker et al. (1994) on theoretical work was its broad approach to careers in organizations. Indeed, Waldman (2007) argues that studies that consider many related phenomena of careers are especially helpful for theory development, given that a theory of careers in organizations should ideally describe many, if not all, empirical findings. Baker and Holmström (1995), on the other hand, have cautioned against using results from a single case study as a guide to theoretical research.

Yet, many of the empirical findings by Baker et al. (1994) have received support from other case studies, including Seltzer and Merrett (2000), Treble, van Gameren, Bridges, and Barmby (2001) and Dohmen, Kriechel, and Pfann (2004), which use data from different institutional environments, time periods, and industries. Nevertheless, there are also some important differences in the results between these studies, leaving open the question of which of the results hold true across various settings and which are particular to the specific case studies. Lazear and Oyer (2004) contribute to the literature by going beyond case study research and studying entry into and exit from firms using a large Swedish dataset. Their results suggest that outside competition, or external labor market, plays an important role both in the hiring process and wage setting at all levels of firms' hierarchies in Sweden.

An additional aspect of career dynamics in firms that have recently received attention in the theoretical literature is employee turnover. The analysis of employee turnover has a long tradition in labor economics. Many theoretical studies, for instance, use search and matching models to analyze employer changes (e.g., Jovanovic, 1979a, 1979b; Neal, 1999; Sicherman & Galor, 1990). Polachek and Horvath (1977), on the other hand, use life-cycle approach to study job mobility, and migration in particular. Empirical studies have focused, inter alia, on occupational mobility and employer changes and on the wage effects of these career moves (e.g., Booth, Francesconi, & Garcia-Serrano, 1999; Farber, 1994; Parrado, Caner, & Wolff, 2007; Topel & Ward, 1992). However, it is only recently that these ideas have been incorporated into models of careers in firms (e.g., Ghosh, 2007). Waldman (2007) argues that career progression is closely related to voluntary and involuntary turnover decisions and calls for empirical studies to inform theoretical models on the connection of wage and promotion dynamics within a firm and the turnover decision.

We study careers using a large linked employer-employee dataset including over 5,000 firms and more than 3.5 million observations on white-collar employees in the Finnish manufacturing sector over the period of 1981–2006. A novel feature of our dataset is that it allows us to rank jobs into hierarchies that are identical *across* firms. Our article thus adds to the literature by shedding light on the question of how well the observations of the workings of the internal labor markets made in studies focusing on a single firm generalize to a larger set of firms. This also allows us to assess the existing theories in light of results that are not particular to a given firm. We also extend the earlier analysis of career and wage dynamics to cover firm changes as well. Most of the previous studies have either focused on internal labor markets or mobility between firms, and there are only a few papers analyzing promotions in tandem with employer changes (da Silva & van der Klaauw (2011) is an exception).[1] Equipped with a measure of hierarchical levels that is comparable across firms, we are able to provide a broader description of careers than many of the earlier studies on the topic.

We focus on three main sets of issues. First, to provide information on how well the findings of the case studies regarding the workings of internal labor markets generalize to a larger set of firms, we replicate many of the analyses from Baker et al. (1994). These include the following questions: Is there evidence of ports of entry and exit? Are there fast-tracks within firms? Do external hires experience different career development within firms than do incumbents? Second, with our unique data, we can also examine employer changes. Examples of questions investigated in this part are the following: How typical are employer changes? Are employer changes often associated with promotions? What factors contribute to promotions with employer changes? Finally, although promotions and employer changes are important parts of the career process, wages matter as well. Therefore, we also analyze wages and the wage gains of different career events. Here we focus, among other things, on the following issues: How stable are wage differences across hierarchical levels and over business cycles? Are wages convex with respect to the hierarchical level? Are hierarchical levels important determinants of wages? Are there significant wage premiums on promotions?

The structure of the article is as follows. In the second section, we discuss the theoretical research on careers. The third section describes the data. In the fourth section, we analyze the entry into and the exit from the hierarchical levels to examine whether firms restrict movements between internal and external labor markets to certain hierarchical levels, as outlined by Baker et al. (1994). The fifth section focuses on subsequent career development. The sixth section completes our investigation of careers by considering wage determination within firms, and the wage effects of different career moves. Finally, the seventh section summarizes the main findings of the article.

THEORETICAL BACKGROUND

Despite the notable theoretical advances in the analysis of careers during the last two decades, there is still a lack of models that account for all of the empirical regularities of careers within a single framework. Therefore, instead of presenting in detail any particular model of careers, this section discusses several theories that help to understand the different aspects of careers investigated in this article.

We start exploring careers by examining the ports of entry and exit. As discussed, for example, in Baker et al. (1994) and Lazear and Oyer (2004), one of the key elements of internal labor markets is the existence of jobs where most hiring (ports of entry) and separation (ports of exit) take place. By restricting labor movements in and out of the firm to certain jobs, ports-of-entry and ports-of-exit jobs provide insulation to internal labor markets from the competitive market forces. There are several reasons for the existence of ports of entry and ports of exit jobs. One is the various administrative rules used by firms to restrict employees' mobility between jobs. Additionally, firm-specific human capital provides a plausible explanation for ports of entry (e.g., Becker, 1962; Oi, 1962). Jobs higher in the hierarchy may require more firm-specific skills than jobs lower in the hierarchical ranks, in which case workers are hired into less demanding jobs (ports of entry) and climb up the hierarchical ladder after spending sufficient time in the firm to accumulate necessary firm-specific knowledge. If firm-specific human capital plays an important role in career development within firms, then outside recruits should have more general human capital to compete with incumbents (Baker et al., 1994). Yet another reason that might give rise to ports of entry is related to incentives. Lazear and Rosen (1981) and Rosen (1986) present a tournament model of internal labor markets in which wages are attached to jobs rather than to worker characteristics. In this framework, a worker is promoted if he performs better than his co-workers at the same hierarchical level. Otherwise, he remains at his current level. Because not all workers receive promotion, the possibility of receiving one serves as an incentive device. The tournament model thus suggests that jobs at the top of the hierarchy are filled with workers who enter the jobs through internal promotions, whereas new outside recruits are hired into less demanding jobs from which the "tournament" begins.

In the fifth section, we turn to career dynamics after entry into the level. Gibbons and Waldman (1999) develop a model that captures many of the findings in Baker et al. (1994) and other studies on career and wage dynamics. Their model combines worker assignment, human capital acquisition, and learning. Jobs are ranked by the importance of ability, and it is efficient to assign more able workers to more demanding jobs. While performing their jobs, employees acquire general human capital. There is uncertainty about an employee's ability, but it is learned symmetrically over time from realization of production by all firms. In their 2006 paper, Gibbons and Waldman add schooling to this framework. Firms and workers make spot contracts, and workers are paid their expected productivity in advance of production. The productivity of an individual in a given job depends on on-the-job human capital, the level schooling, and random shocks. On-the-job human capital is a function of ability, schooling, and labor market experience. The initial assignment is determined by human capital acquired before entering the labor market. Subsequent career progression is, on the other hand, determined by on-the-job human capital and learning. Expectations of on-the-job human capital can change due to accumulation of work experience or due to updating of beliefs about ability. For example, promotions take place when expected effective ability (a function of ability, schooling, work experience, and prior productivity shocks) exceeds a given threshold. Demotions may also take place if the expectation of ability is revised downwards. This simple model can explain, for instance, why wages and education predict future promotion, why there are promotion fast-tracks, why large wage increases are attached to promotions, why wages are attached to jobs, and why wage distributions overlap across hierarchical levels.

Bernhardt (1995) also develops a model that is able to account for many of the empirical findings of careers. A starting point in Bernhardt's analysis is the paper by Waldman (1984) in which promotions serve as signals of an employee's value, that is, learning about ability is asymmetric. Bernhardt extends Waldman's model, inter alia, by allowing a richer skill development process and considering more than two time periods. Similar to Waldman, in Bernhardt's model, the promotion process is also inefficient. Because promotion reveals information on a worker's ability, employers have incentives not to promote individuals as quickly as is socially optimal, but rather only when the productivity gains resulting from placing a high-ability worker upper in the hierarchy outweigh the value of the employer's private information.

The models presented above base promotion decisions on absolute performance: promotion takes place when expected productivity exceeds some standard. However, promotions can also be based on relative evaluation, as in tournament models of promotion (e.g., Lazear & Rosen, 1981). Indeed, there is evidence that absolute performance is not all that matters for promotion but rather that relative performance also plays a role (DeVaro, 2006).

Thus far, we have discussed models that examine careers within firms. However, many studies show that employer changes are also important in individuals' careers (e.g., Topel & Ward, 1992). Therefore, the models of career dynamics should ideally simultaneously account for both within-firm mobility and employer changes. The number of theoretical studies along these lines is still scarce, but Ghosh (2007) provides one promising example of a paper that attempts to combine internal labor market literature and research on turnover behavior. Ghosh builds on Gibbons and Waldman (1999) and presents a multi-period model with a hierarchical firm structure where workers are assumed to accumulate both specific and general human capital. Furthermore, Ghosh assumes that workers experience disutility from working in a firm, the amount of which workers only learn gradually over time. The accumulation of firm-specific human capital decreases the likelihood of employer changes, while a high realized value of disutility increases turnover. Ghosh's model is able to account for some of the empirical findings concerning the characteristics of internal labor markets, and it also provides predictions about mobility between employers. For example, Ghosh's model predicts that the probability of employer changes decreases with labor market experience, a result that derives from the accumulation of firm-specific human capital.

We end our empirical examination of careers by investigating wages in the sixth section. A central feature of internal labor markets is that wages are attached to jobs. Therefore, one of the issues analyzed in the sixth section is the relative importance of individual characteristics versus job titles as determinants of wages and the contribution of different career tracks for wage growth. Furthermore, we also investigate wage structures within firms. To be more precise, we examine whether wages are convex with respect to hierarchical level. There are several models that predict increasing wage differences between consecutive hierarchical levels as one moves up the hierarchy. The tournament model by Rosen (1986) provides one example. Under the assumption that the effort level remains constant across the rounds of the tournament, Rosen shows that the wage increase resulting from winning the last round is higher compared to the wage gain resulting from winning earlier rounds. In terms of wage growth associated with career moves, much of the literature on career dynamics has focused on analyzing wage changes with promotions. Although these models typically predict wage increases with promotion, the reasons for wage premia differ between models. For example, in Bernhardt (1995), wages increase with promotion both because promotion reveals information about the worker's ability and because job assignment is more efficient due to promotion. In Lazear and Rosen's (1981) tournament model, on the other hand, wages increase with promotion because it provides incentives for workers to exert effort.

DATA

The EK data

This article uses a large linked employee-employer dataset from 1981 to 2006. The data come from the records of the Confederation of Finnish Industries (EK), which is the central organization of employer associations in Finland. Although EK has member firms from many industries, manufacturing has traditionally been the most important sector represented in the data. The firms affiliated with EK represent over two-thirds of the Finnish GDP and over 90% of exports. Of total employment in Finland, the member firms account for approximately 33%. Hence, the data cover a significant share of the Finnish economy as a whole.

Before the data is described in more detail, we provide a snapshot of the wage setting process in general in Finland. Wage setting typically takes place at the sectoral level in the Finnish labor market.[2] The sectoral bargaining can be preceded by coordinating negotiations between central organizations of employers and trade unions. The collective agreements stipulate minimum levels of wages for job complexity and skill levels and minimum wage increases for the industry in question. These sectoral collective agreements typically also bind non-signatory parties (i.e., the contracts are universally binding), which has led to a high coverage rate of collective agreements (around 95%). Naturally, firms and employees may agree to a contract that exceeds these minima set in the collective agreement. Indeed, the wage drift (difference between actual and contractual wage increase) has accounted for roughly 30% of the total wage increases (Vartiainen, 1998). Wage setting is also somewhat freer for managerial employees. Traditionally their wages have been set by individual bargaining, although some are bound by collective agreements.

EK collects the data by sending annual surveys to its member firms. One of the main purposes of the data is to provide information to the central wage negotiations. All member firms, except for the smallest ones in few particular industries, are required to respond to the survey resulting in very low nonresponse rates. Therefore, the non-response bias is practically nonexistent in our data. The data are based on the administrative records of the member firms, which guarantees that all information is accurate and of very high quality. A similar kind of dataset is collected also in Sweden and applied, among others, by Lazear and Oyer (2004).

The EK dataset suits our research purposes well. First, it allows us to follow individuals' careers over a long period of time, up to 25 years.[3] Second, the data enable us to distinguish between many different types of career moves. We can, for example, separate promotions from demotions and within-firm mobility from employer changes. Yet another advantage of our dataset is that it is exceptionally rich. It includes a large set of both employee and firm characteristics and, rather uniquely, some important information on co-workers as well. A more detailed description of the variables used in the article is given in the fifth section.

Although the data contain information on both white-collar and blue-collar workers, we restrict the analysis to full-time, white-collar employees.[4] This is mainly because of the complexities in the occupation classification system in the blue-collar data. Unlike white-collar employees, it is not possible to allocate blue-collar workers systematically to different hierarchical positions based on the job they hold. Furthermore, restricting the sample to full-time workers is of little importance in practice because the share of part-time workers is negligible among white-collar workers, roughly 2% in 2006. Furthermore, there are only small gender differences in this respect. The data include over 3,500,000 observations in total, of which 36.7% are women.[5] The number of individuals is 467,405, with the female share being 39%.

The Hierarchy

Examination of careers where the different career moves are based on the observed changes in a worker's position in the hierarchy sets high demands for the data, especially if the analysis covers career dynamics both inside and between firms. It requires detailed and consistent data on jobs across firms. This is one of the advantages of the EK data over the datasets used in most of the earlier studies on careers. The EK data include 75 different job titles, and the same job titles are in use in every member firm of EK. Therefore, our job classification, to the extent it is in general possible, is comparable across firms. As part of its data-gathering process, EK provides a detailed description of the features of these jobs. For example, there is information on the level of education and work experience required for the job in question, whether the job contains managerial duties and financial responsibilities, whether the operational environment is dynamic and complex, or whether the job is instead composed of more or less repetitive tasks.

We apply the descriptions of jobs to sort them into six hierarchical levels.[6] The top of the hierarchy consists of managerial jobs associated with financial responsibility and administrative duties. Jobs that require a substantial expertise and in which the operational environment is complex are allocated to the second level. The third level also includes expertise jobs associated with varying operational environments, but in which the required level of prior experience is lower than in jobs at the second level. Jobs at the fourth level require a reasonable level of expertise acquired either through formal education or through work experience, but the problems to be solved are less complex than in jobs higher in the hierarchy. The second-to-last level includes jobs for which some prior work experience is needed, but for which the tasks are repetitive in nature. The bottom of the hierarchy consists of routine jobs with low educational requirements involving repetitive and simple tasks.

Of course, not all white-collar workers work in firms with all six levels represented. However, over 82% of observations come from firms having all six levels and 94% of observations are from firms with at least five levels. We also examined the robustness of our results to the number of levels represented at the firm. They proved not to be sensitive in this respect.

Because we observe the hierarchical structures of firms, we are able to define promotion as a transition from a lower hierarchical level to a higher position. This is consistent with the theoretical studies of careers and their definitions of promotions (e.g., Bernhardt, 1995). However, many of the previous studies must have settled for other ways of measuring promotions. One typical approach has been to rely on self-reported evaluation (e.g., McCue, 1996). A major drawback of this measure is that it is subjective. Pergamit and Veum (1999) also show that for a large share of employees, self-reported promotions are not associated with a change in position. Additionally, movement from a job with a lower average wage to a job with a higher average wage has often been interpreted as indicating a promotion (e.g., Lazear, 1992). However, when the relationship between promotions and wage growth is considered, it becomes clear that the use of this measure invites some obvious endogeneity problems.

Before we proceed with describing the resulting hierarchy and how white-collar employees move between levels, we offer two general comments on the hierarchy. First, the CEO and other top management (the executive team) are not included in our hierarchy. Second, it should be noticed that in our article the hierarchical levels are based on job titles and their descriptions without any reference to wages. This diminishes the endogeneity problems related to the examination of the wage effects of level changes compared to the case where hierarchies are constructed using information on average wages of jobs. Finally, because the same job titles and their descriptions are used in every member firm of EK, we can investigate different career moves both within and between firms.

Some descriptive results

Fig. 1 presents the relative size of levels in different years over the period of 1981–2006. As expected, the relative size of levels increases as we move downwards from the top of the hierarchy, except for level six. As described above, this level contains routine tasks, and because white-collar employees are, on average, fairly highly educated, relatively few of them are in level 6 jobs. Another observation from Fig. 1 concerns changes in the structure of the hierarchy over time. The biggest change has occurred in the middle of the hierarchy. The relative size of levels 2 and 3 has increased mainly at the expense of levels 4 and 5. There are two main reasons for these changes. One is the increase in the average level of schooling in Finland over the last two decades. The other is the structural change of the Finnish economy that has

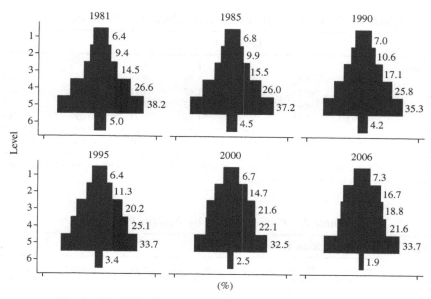

Fig. 1. Size Distribution of Hierarchical Levels (in Percent).

taken place during the observation period, most notably the rapid growth of knowledge-intensive sectors, like the ICT sector.

Table 1 compares a white-collar worker's current hierarchical position to his standing in the hierarchy in the next observation. In line, for example, with Baker et al. (1994), a clear majority of white-collar employees remain at the same level. Table 1 also indicates that promotions are more typical than demotions, although demotions are by no means rare.[7] A similar finding is made by Belzil and Bognanno (2008), Seltzer and Merrett (2000), and Dohmen et al. (2004). Finally, when a white-collar worker is promoted, it is most typical to move up only one hierarchical level at a time.

Several earlier studies have documented a systematic relationship between job transitions and worker's age. For example, da Silva and Van der Klaauw (2011) and Francesconi (2001) show that mobility declines with age, which is consistent with the theoretical model of Polachek and Horvath (1977). This also appears to be the case in our data, as suggested by Table 2, which shows frequencies of different career moves by age.[8] About 88% of white-collar employees younger than 36 years of age neither change an employer nor hierarchical level between two consecutive observations. The

Table 1. Transitions Between Hierarchical Levels (in Percent).

Level t	Level $t+1$						
	1	2	3	4	5	6	N
1	91.88	3.78	1.95	1.59	0.8	0.01	194,391
2	3.29	90.5	3.47	1.62	1.11	0.01	348,407
3	1.12	4.61	89.91	2.33	1.97	0.06	530,243
4	0.91	1.71	3	91.59	2.71	0.09	727,705
5	0.33	0.8	1.91	2.8	93.67	0.49	1,029,208
6	0.03	0.14	0.68	1.29	8.01	89.84	101,699

The table presents all transitions between hierarchical levels (both within and between firms) among those with at least two observations.

Table 2. Career Moves by Age (in Percent).

Age	Same Firm			Firm Changes		
	Same Level	Promotion	Demotion	Same Level	Promotion	Demotion
<26	87.69	5.47	1.98	3.24	1.03	0.58
26–30	86.16	6.08	2.26	3.3	1.4	0.8
31–35	88.26	5.02	2.15	2.88	1.03	0.67
36–40	90.38	3.91	1.95	2.63	0.66	0.46
41–45	91.72	3.03	1.77	2.71	0.43	0.34
46–50	92.74	2.38	1.71	2.66	0.27	0.24
51–55	93.58	1.94	1.68	2.42	0.19	0.19
56–60	94.44	1.62	1.56	2.15	0.13	0.1
>60	95.44	1.33	1.47	1.63	0.06	0.07

The table shows for a particular age category the share of employees experiencing different hierarchical transitions within and between firms. The rows add up to 100.

corresponding figure for those older than 50 years of age is over 93%. This tendency of declining mobility rates with age holds irrespective of the type of career move, although it is most apparent for internal promotions. Table 2 further shows that most of the employer changes are lateral movements without changes in hierarchical position.[9] Finally, the table shows that for older white-collar employees, promotions and demotions are almost equally likely.

Table 3, which draws on Baker et al. (1994), presents descriptive statistics on careers. The upper part of the table investigates the length of careers of those entering a firm during the period of 1981–1995, whereas the lower

Table 3.   Career and Level Characteristics.

Career	Level					
	6	5	4	3	2	1
Number of outside entrants	12,272	83,888	57,565	37,712	21,372	12,419
Percent with 1 year careers	0.31	0.2	0.17	0.16	0.19	0.2
Percent with 2 year careers	0.14	0.12	0.12	0.12	0.13	0.14
Percent with 5–10 year careers	0.21	0.27	0.28	0.29	0.28	0.28
Of which						
Percent holding one title	0.38	0.43	0.47	0.37	0.38	0.36
Percent holding two titles	0.33	0.32	0.29	0.35	0.34	0.34
Percent holding three titles	0.19	0.17	0.16	0.18	0.18	0.2
Percent holding four titles	0.08	0.06	0.06	0.07	0.07	0.08
Percent holding five and more titles	0.03	0.02	0.02	0.03	0.03	0.03
Percent with more than 10 years careers	0.18	0.23	0.25	0.26	0.2	0.19
Of which						
Percent holding one title	0.14	0.17	0.2	0.11	0.13	0.17
Percent holding two titles	0.26	0.3	0.27	0.3	0.29	0.27
Percent holding three titles	0.27	0.25	0.25	0.27	0.27	0.27
Percent holding four titles	0.17	0.15	0.16	0.17	0.16	0.16
Percent holding five and more titles	0.15	0.13	0.12	0.14	0.14	0.14
Average age of new hires (from other firms)	36.29	37.27	38.44	37.23	38.58	39.89
Average work experience (in years) of new hires (from other firms)	16.17	15.18	14.7	11.99	12.87	14.17
Average years of schooling of new hires (from other firms)	11.17	12.55	13.74	15.49	15.98	15.72
Average age of new hires (data entrants)	26.62	30.51	32.28	31.73	34.64	37.39
Average work experience (in years) of new hires (data entrants)	6.69	8.72	9.06	7.21	9.77	12.71
Average years of schooling of new hires (data entrants)	11.42	12.53	13.62	15.12	15.37	14.88
Average age of internal hires	33.66	35.83	36.65	37.18	38.13	38.33
Average work experience of internal hires	13.66	13.72	13.55	12.94	13.2	13.15
Average years of schooling of internal hires	11.1	12.63	13.34	14.48	15.15	15.23

Table 3. (*Continued*)

Career	Level					
	6	5	4	3	2	1
Number of person years in level	123,152	1,232,420	855,698	631,719	427,133	233,603
Percent of entrants into level who are new hires	77	81	72	63	54	52
Exit rate per year (internal exits, %)	5	4	5	5	5	4
Exit rate per year (external exits, %)	2	3	3	3	3	4
Exit rate per year (data exits, %)	12	9	8	7	8	8

The top panel uses only those who entered a firm in 1981–1995. The middle panel uses only those who entered a level either from outside the data or from within a firm between 1981 and 1995. The bottom panel uses all observations in all years.

part, which is analyzed in the fourth section, provides information on the average characteristics of hires into firms together with the rates of external hiring and exit rates across levels. The main observation made from the upper part of Table 3 is that careers within firms are indeed important. Similar to Baker et al. (1994), a significant number of employees spend a long time at a given firm, and they hold many titles during their stay at the firm. For example, of those who enter level 4, 25% spend more than 10 years with the same firm, and 53% of these workers hold three or more titles within the firm.

Overall, the results in Tables 1–3 are well in line with the existing literature on careers. We take this as evidence that our job hierarchy is meaningful.

PORTS OF ENTRY AND EXIT

As discussed in the second section, ports of entry and ports of exit are important elements of internal labor markets. This section examines the patterns of hiring and separations in our data. The lower part of Table 3 presents summary statistics of age, years of schooling, and labor market experience, together with data on the shares of internal and external hires across hierarchical levels. There are three different ways to enter the hierarchical level in the EK data. First, an employee can move into his current level internally, either through promotion or demotion (internal entrant). Second, an employee can be hired into a level outside the firm from another member firm of EK (external entrant). Third, a white-collar worker can be recruited outside the data (data entrant).[10] Although the theory of internal labor market separates only internal hires from those entering the level outside the firm, we further distinguish between the two different groups of external hires. The reason for this is that, as we discuss below, those hired outside the data are quite different from the other external hires in terms of human capital-related characteristics. This might affect the level at which these white-collar workers begin their careers, and how their subsequent careers develop.

In line with the theory of internal labor markets, as we move up the hierarchy, the internal hiring increases in importance. For example, at level 5, internal hires account for 19% of all hires at that level, whereas the corresponding figure at the top of the hierarchy is 48%. However, what is noteworthy in Table 3 is that outside hiring plays such an important role at all levels. Furthermore, external hires are not concentrated at the bottom of the hierarchy, but there is also substantial external hiring at the top of the hierarchy. We thus conclude that the evidence for the existence of ports of entry is weak in Finnish manufacturing. This result supports the findings of Baker et al. (1994) and Lazear and Oyer (2004).[11]

Table 3 also shows that external entrants tend to have more general human capital than internal hires at all levels. White-collar employees entering the firm from another EK member firm are typically older and somewhat more educated than internal hires. This implies that firm-specific human capital is important: external hires must accumulate more general human capital to compete with the internally hired. Also this finding is consistent with Baker et al. (1994). Data entrants, on the other hand, are significantly younger and also typically less educated than other hires at all levels, suggesting that there are some unobserved individual characteristics that are also important in the hiring process.

The bottom of Table 3 examines exits from the hierarchical levels. Following Lazear and Oyer (2004), we break those down into exits within firms (internal exits) and exits from firms. Exits from firms are further divided into two categories: exits to another member firm of EK (external exits) and exits from the data (data exits). Similar to Baker et al. (1994), the evidence for ports of exit is even weaker than that for ports of entry. Internal exit rates are very similar across hierarchical levels without a clear pattern. The same also holds true, to a certain extent, for external exits, although exits from the top of the hierarchy are, in this case, somewhat more common than exits from the bottom of the hierarchy. For the data exits, on the other hand, exit rates decrease as we move up in the hierarchy.

To conclude, Table 3 does not find strong evidence for the existence of ports of entry and ports of exit. It thus seems that external competition plays a role in the functioning of internal labor markets among the firms in Finnish manufacturing. This finding supports the findings of Baker et al. (1994) and Treble et al. (2001). This is also in line with the theory of Gibbons and Waldman (1999, 2006) because in their theory, the key aspects of internal labor markets, firm-specific human capital, and long-term contracts are absent. Strong evidence in favor of internal labor markets would thus not be consistent with their modeling strategy.

CAREERS AFTER ENTRY

Table 3 shows that white-collar employees often spend a long time at a particular firm. Thus, careers within firms are important in Finnish manufacturing. Therefore, in this section we take a closer look at internal labor markets by examining employees' mobility between hierarchical levels and factors affecting mobility. The first part of the section focuses exclusively on career moves within firms, but because mobility between employers is also typical in our data and thus forms an important part of employees' careers, the second part analyzes changes in hierarchical position with employer changes.

Table 4, which also follows the paper by Baker et al. (1994), examines career progression within firms among those who have entered level 4 during the period of 1981–1995.[12] Every worker analyzed in the table has thus had a chance to spend at least 10 years at a firm. We distinguish between internal entrants, entrants from the other member firms, and data entrants. This is because we aim to investigate how outside hires compare with incumbents in terms of subsequent career development. If firm-specific human capital is important to career progression, then we would expect incumbents to fare better than those coming from outside the firm. On the other hand, as Table 3 shows, external hires typically have more general human capital than those hired from inside the firm. This might help external hires to compete with incumbents.

In contrast to Baker et al. (1994), we do not find that hires from outside the firm fare initially better than incumbents. If anything, incumbents are promoted more quickly than external or data entrants in our data. For

Table 4. Career Progress Within Firms, External vs. Internal Hires into Level 4.

Current Level	Statistic	Entrant Type	Level 4 Entrants: Years Since Entering Level 4									
			1	2	3	4	5	6	7	8	9	10
1	% of remaining	Internal entrant		1.8	3.0	3.9	4.8	5.5	6.3	6.9	7.2	7.8
		External entrant		1.5	2.5	3.5	4.3	5.2	5.6	6.2	6.6	7.8
		Data entrant		1.4	2.5	3.9	4.9	5.8	6.8	7.4	8.1	9.1
2	% of remaining	Internal entrant		3.1	5.4	6.7	8.2	9.0	10.2	11.8	13.3	14.0
		External entrant		2.5	4.4	5.9	7.2	8.1	9.7	10.6	12.4	13.8
		Data entrant		2.7	5.0	6.9	8.6	10.4	12.1	13.7	15.0	16.1
3	% of remaining	Internal entrant		5.0	8.3	11.0	12.8	14.2	15.6	16.2	17.0	17.6
		External entrant		4.4	7.9	10.5	12.4	14.0	15.1	15.9	17.2	18.2
		Data entrant		5.2	9.1	12.4	14.7	16.3	17.5	18.2	18.7	18.3
4	% of remaining	Internal entrant	100.0	84.1	74.8	67.9	62.3	58.3	54.0	49.4	45.5	41.3
		External entrant	100.0	88.5	80.3	73.7	68.7	64.2	60.3	56.0	49.5	44.0
		Data entrant	100.0	86.2	75.3	68.4	62.3	57.2	52.9	47.9	43.5	39.4
5	% of remaining	Internal entrant		5.8	8.0	9.8	11.2	12.3	13.1	14.8	16.2	18.2
		External entrant		3.0	4.7	6.1	7.2	8.3	9.0	10.9	13.9	15.8
		Data entrant		4.4	7.8	8.1	9.2	10.0	10.4	12.5	14.6	16.7
6	% of remaining	Internal entrant		0.4	0.5	0.7	0.8	0.7	0.9	1.0	0.9	1.1
		External entrant		0.2	0.2	0.2	0.2	0.3	0.3	0.4	0.4	0.5
		Data entrant		0.2	0.2	0.3	0.3	0.3	0.3	0.3	0.3	0.4

Table 4. (*Continued*)

Current Level	Statistic	Entrant Type	Level 4 Entrants: Years Since Entering Level 4									
			1	2	3	4	5	6	7	8	9	10
	Level (average)	Internal entrant	4	3.9	3.81	3.75	3.69	3.65	3.6	3.56	3.53	3.51
		External entrant	4	3.89	3.81	3.74	3.68	3.63	3.58	3.56	3.53	3.48
		Data entrant	4	3.9	3.82	3.71	3.63	3.56	3.49	3.45	3.42	3.4
	Level (variance)	Internal entrant	0	0.63	0.79	0.89	0.96	1.01	1.06	1.12	1.15	1.19
		External entrant	0	0.55	0.71	0.81	0.88	0.94	0.99	1.04	1.09	1.16
		Data entrant	0	0.57	0.76	0.87	0.95	1.01	1.06	1.11	1.16	1.21
	Exit rate, %	Internal entrant	0.10	0.11	0.11	0.10	0.10	0.10	0.10	0.10	0.10	0.10
		External entrant	0.12	0.12	0.12	0.10	0.11	0.11	0.10	0.11	0.10	0.12
		Data entrant	0.17	0.13	0.13	0.12	0.11	0.11	0.10	0.10	0.11	0.12
	N	Internal entrant	19,843	17,884	15,991	14,290	12,790	11,545	10,367	9,322	8,374	7,496
		External entrant	16,451	14,514	12,831	11,259	10,083	9,006	8,006	7,205	6,446	5,798
		Data entrant	41,122	34,043	29,496	25,553	22,570	20,006	17,889	16,012	14,356	12,840

The table shows career progression of level 4 entrants. The upper panel shows the share of (remaining) employees in a given level by years since entering level 4. The numbers in each column sum up to 100 for internal entrants, external entrants, and data entrants. The lower panel shows the average level, variance, and exit rate by years since entering level 4 for each of the entrant groups.

example, after 2 years since entering level 4, 9.9% of the surviving incumbents have been promoted to levels 1–3, whereas the corresponding figure for external entrants is 8.4%.[13] In addition, in the longer term, a larger share of surviving internal entrants tends to be at higher levels compared to external entrants. However, the gap in promotion rates between the surviving data entrants and incumbents disappears quickly with time. Already, after 2 years since entry into level 4, the fraction of surviving data entrants at higher levels is the same as the corresponding fraction for incumbents. The smooth career progression of data entrants is probably at least partly due to the fact that data entrants are much younger than incumbents or external entrants, and as we know from the previous literature, promotion probability is negatively associated with age.

Table 4 also presents information on exit rates. In line with Baker et al. (1994), exit rates are lower for incumbents than for outside hires during the first years since entry into level 4, although differences in exit rates between the different entrant groups are somewhat lower in our data than in Baker et al. Furthermore, we find that in the longer term, differences in exit rates between incumbents and outside hires become negligible.

Baker et al. (1994) also find that the external entrants have more variability in career outcomes than incumbents. Our results, however, indicate the opposite. As can be seen from the bottom part of Table 4, the variance of level attainment is higher for internal entrants than for outside hires, especially during the first years after entry into level 4. This probably reflects the fact that outside hires have longer work experience. In terms of the Gibbons and Waldman model, labor markets' knowledge of workers' ability increases with work experience and, therefore, experienced workers should move with lower probability after allocation to a given level compared to employees with shorter work experience.

Overall, Table 4 shows that there is significant variation in career development between white-collar employees. For example, some employees are able to move from the lower ranks of the hierarchy to management, whereas some remain stuck at the bottom of the organizational ladder. This invites one to ask further questions about career development within firms. For example, is there evidence of fast-tracks in Finnish manufacturing? What happens to those who experience sluggish career progress? Are they more likely to leave a firm?

Fast-Track Promotions and Exits

These questions are investigated in Table 5, which again draws on Baker et al. (1994). Rows show the time spent at level 5 before promotion to

Table 5. Time to Promotion in Level 5 vs. Promotion and Exit Rates in Level 4.

Years at Level 5	Statistic	Years at Level 4 Before Promotion or Exit									
		1	2	3	4	5	6	7	8	9	10
1	Promotion rate, %	18	16	14	9	8	9	9	7	7	6
	Exit rate, %	17	16	14	12	12	13	10	13	15	12
	N	10,796	7,598	5,296	3,890	2,789	2,192	1,584	1,231	930	2,921
2	Promotion rate, %	14	14	10	8	8	10	9	9	6	5
	Exit rate, %	16	15	13	14	12	14	11	14	12	10
	N	5,769	4,060	3,022	2,010	1,561	1,215	943	767	591	2,168
3	Promotion rate, %	13	12	9	9	6	9	11	6	9	5
	Exit rate, %	12	14	14	12	10	12	11	14	14	9
	N	3,807	2,673	1,928	1,433	1,117	897	732	591	460	1,623
4	Promotion rate, %	13	10	10	9	7	11	8	7	3	4
	Exit rate, %	12	14	12	12	11	11	11	12	11	9
	N	2,477	1,757	1,334	979	757	587	465	366	286	1,085
5	Promotion rate, %	12	6	10	11	6	10	4	8	6	5
	Exit rate, %	13	14	12	12	15	15	11	12	10	8
	N	1,694	1,257	980	728	576	459	350	274	209	797
6	Promotion rate, %	13	8	5	11	7	7	2	5	6	3
	Exit rate, %	13	12	13	17	9	16	9	8	6	10
	N	1,311	977	780	604	442	354	280	238	203	752
7+	Promotion rate, %	9	7	7	7	4	8	3	5	4	3
	Exit rate, %	12	12	12	12	11	9	8	10	10	11
	N	4,110	3,035	2,355	1,784	1,378	1,061	841	689	547	1,349

The table should be read down the columns. For example, employees who were promoted to level 4 after only 1 year at level 5 have an 18% promotion probability during their first year at level 4, whereas for those who spent an additional year at level 5, the promotion rate is 14%.

level 4, whereas columns present promotion and exit rates by different levels of tenure at level 4. To simplify the analysis, we focus on levels 5 and 4, which are the two largest levels measured by employment shares in our data. Furthermore, here, we do not separate between the different entrant groups mainly because the sample size would be too small.

Similar to Baker et al. (1994) and Treble et al. (2001), we find evidence of fast-tracks. Given current tenure at level 4, promotion rates decrease with time spent at level 5. For example, white-collar employees who were promoted to level 4 after only 1 year at level 5 have an 18% promotion probability during their first year at level 4, whereas for those who spent an additional year at level 5 the promotion rate is 14%. Thus, those who are promoted more quickly at level 5 also have better chances of being promoted quickly at level 4.

Baker et al. (1994) and Treble et al. (2001) also find evidence of a phenomenon that they call the fast-track exit effect. Under fast-track exits, individuals promoted quickly have higher exit rates as well. Our results offer some support for the existence of fast-track exits, although exit rates do not vary as strongly by time spent in the previous hierarchical level in our data as they do in Baker et al. and Treble et al. As Table 5 shows, those white-collar employees who were promoted during the first year at level 5 have a 17% exit rate in the first year at level 4 versus 12% for those from whom it took 3 years to get promoted to level 4. One explanation for this phenomenon offered by Baker et al. (1994) is that some high-ability individuals may not find the best possible job for themselves at their current employer, or they are not paid according to their expected marginal product, and therefore, they are more likely to leave the firm. A more detailed analysis shows that most (69%) of the fast-track exits also leave the data. Of those who move to another EK member firm, 26% are promoted, 57% remain at the same level, and 16% are demoted. Thus, there is considerable heterogeneity in career progression for this group. This may reflect differences in reasons for exit. Some may leave the firm, for example, due to downsizing, whereas others may leave for better outside offers.

Promotions, Exits, and Position in Wage Hierarchy

Table 6 continues to examine promotions by showing statistics on white-collar employees' relative wage position within hierarchical levels before and after promotion.[14] It thus gives us further information on what types of employees are promoted. To examine whether there are any differences in

Table 6. Wage Decile Before and After Promotion.

Distribution of Pay for Promotees in Salary Deciles Before and After Promotion: Promotions in Same Firm

Promotion		N	Percentage in Each Salary Decile									
			Bottom	2nd	3rd	4th	5th	6th	7th	8th	9th	Top
Level 6 to level 5	Decile before promotion	5,337	4.8	8.6	8.8	10.9	12.6	7.5	8.6	9	6.9	22.4
	Decile after promotion	5,337	29.2	18.8	12.8	11.5	9.9	6.1	4.7	3.3	1.9	1.8
Level 5 to level 4	Decile before promotion	19,942	4.5	6.1	6.5	9.1	10.4	10.9	12.3	13.6	13.1	13.3
	Decile after promotion	19,942	14	15.9	13.1	12.1	11.1	8.1	7.8	6.5	5.2	6.2
Level 4 to level 3	Decile before promotion	14,303	4.8	6.6	6.8	7.4	9.2	8.8	10.8	12	13.5	20.1
	Decile after promotion	14,303	8.3	12.9	12.9	12.8	12.6	9.5	9.6	8.2	6.1	7.1
Level 3 to level 2	Decile before promotion	16,753	2.3	3.7	5.3	7	9.1	10	12	13.9	15	21.7
	Decile after promotion	16,753	11.5	13.3	12.4	11.9	10.7	8.8	8.7	8.2	6.5	8
Level 2 to level 1	Decile before promotion	7,985	3.3	5.3	7.8	8.8	9.6	8.9	10.6	13.1	13.5	19
	Decile after promotion	7,985	9.6	12.8	12.3	12.3	11.7	8.9	8.6	7.9	5.7	10.2

Distribution of Pay for Promotees in Salary Deciles Before and After Promotion: Promotions in Other Firm

Promotion		N	Bottom	2nd	3rd	4th	5th	6th	7th	8th	9th	Top
Level 6 to level 5	Decile before promotion	671	6.3	11	9.2	12.4	11.8	7.5	7.3	7.9	7.2	19.5
	Decile after promotion	671	24.3	21.6	11.5	12.8	8.6	6.6	6.4	3.3	1.2	3.7
Level 5 to level 4	Decile before promotion	2,799	4.9	6.1	7.1	9.2	10.8	12.1	13.6	12.3	11.4	12.6
	Decile after promotion	2,799	12.7	14.1	12.5	11.1	10.1	8	7.7	7.9	5.8	10.1
Level 4 to level 3	Decile before promotion	2,781	5.8	7.8	7.7	9.4	9.9	9.4	11.3	11.8	10.8	16.1
	Decile after promotion	2,781	6.7	11.8	11.5	12.9	13.7	9.5	9.5	8.3	7.3	8.8
Level 3 to level 2	Decile before promotion	2,599	3.5	6.2	7.5	9.7	10.4	9.4	11.2	11	12.9	18.2
	Decile after promotion	2,599	4.9	10.4	10.7	12.2	12.2	10.3	10.2	8.9	7	13.1
Level 2 to level 1	Decile before promotion	1,271	4.8	10.5	10.5	8.4	10.9	9.7	9.7	11.3	10.5	13.8
	Decile after promotion	1,271	6.7	10.7	11.2	10.2	10.4	8.5	9.1	8.5	7.3	17.4

The table shows the wage decile before and after promotion. The wage deciles are calculated for each firm and hierarchical level.

the relationship between promotions and an individual's position in the wage distribution between internal and external promotions, we separate those who are promoted within a firm from those who are promoted with an employer change.

Table 6 shows that there is a great deal of variation in terms of the wage deciles from which individuals are promoted and to which deciles they end up with after the promotion. Similar to Baker et al. (1994), there is some tendency for those who are promoted to be at the upper end of the wage distribution before promotion and at the lower end of the distribution after promotion. For example, 21.7% of those promoted from level 3 to level 2 come from the highest decile, versus 2.3% from the bottom of the wage distribution. On the other hand, 24.8% of these white-collar employees enter at the lowest two deciles of level 2, whereas only 14.5% go to the highest two deciles. This pattern holds for both internal and external promotions. Nevertheless, some differences in the promotion process can be observed between the two groups of promotees. Most notably, employees who are promoted when changing an employer are more likely to come from the lower wage deciles, but they enter more often at the upper end of the wage distribution than those who are promoted from inside firms. The model of Gibbons and Waldman predicts that most, but not all, of the promotees from a given level should come from the upper end of the wage distribution. This follows because the employees in the upper part of the wage distribution are also closest to the threshold for promotion in terms of on-the-job human capital. However, large positive updates to expected ability lead some employees, who were formerly further away from the threshold, to be promoted.

Following Baker et al. (1994), we also examine exit rates by hierarchical level and wage decile. Matching models would predict that exit rates decrease in the wage deciles, as poor quality employee-employer matches are more likely to be terminated. However, as can be seen from Table 7, this is not what we observe in our data. If anything, exit rates are higher at the top of the wage distribution. This finding is consistent with the results presented by Treble et al. (2001), but in contrast to Baker et al. Treble et al. suggest that there might be promotion bottlenecks within firms that cause some of the high-ability employees to leave the firm.

Regression Model for Promotion

Table 8 examines factors behind promotions by estimating a linear probability model.[15] To allow the explanatory variables to vary between

Table 7. Exit Rates by Hierarchical Level and Wage Decile.

		Exit Rates by Level and Salary Decile: All Exits									
Hierarchical Level	N	Percentage in Each Salary Decile									
		Bottom	2nd	3rd	4th	5th	6th	7th	8th	9th	Top
Level 6	15,864	6.2	10	9.3	10.6	12.9	6.8	8.7	8.2	6.2	21.2
Level 5	163,741	9.5	10.2	9.6	10.1	10.3	9.2	9.6	9.8	9.4	12.3
Level 4	110,078	8.8	10.1	9.9	10.2	10.6	9.2	9.5	9.6	8.9	13.2
Level 3	83,883	8.3	9.9	9.5	10.2	10.5	9	9.6	9.6	9.5	14.1
Level 2	64,532	8	9.5	9	9.7	10.4	8.7	9.3	9.7	9.3	16.4
Level 1	34,830	6.7	9	8.4	9.5	11.2	7.9	8.9	9.4	8.6	20.4

The table shows exit rates from each level by wage decile. The wage deciles are calculated for each firm and hierarchical level.

internal and external promotions, we estimate the model separately for inside promotions and promotions associated with an employer change. The dependent variable for within-firm promotions takes a value of one if an individual moves from a lower hierarchical level to a higher one but stays in the same firm between year t and year $t+1$, and zero otherwise. For the other model, the dependent variable is a dummy that takes a value of 1 if an individual is promoted *and* changes firms between year t and year $t+1$, and zero otherwise.

Our explanatory variables can be grouped into five broad categories. The first category measures an individual's human capital and includes years of education and its square, field of education (nine categories), tenure (four categories), and age (four categories). The second category consists of variables accounting for an individual's earlier career development. We measure prior career with years spent thus far in the current hierarchical level within the same firm and the time spent on the previous hierarchical level within the same firm. Variables controlling for firm characteristics constitute the third category. It includes the number of employees (7 categories) and industry (63 categories). One of the novelties of our study is that we also have data on the characteristics of the co-workers. These characteristics are grouped into the fourth category, which includes years of education, tenure, and gender. If internal promotion competition matters, as in DeVaro (2006), these variables should predict promotion. Finally, we also control for gender, hierarchical level, field of job title, an individual's position in the wage distribution, and year. All explanatory variables are measured at year t.

Table 8. Promotion Estimates.

	OLS		Individual Fixed Effects		Individual and Firm Effects	
	Same Firm	Other Firm	Same Firm	Other Firm	Same Firm	Other Firm
Years of education	0.008***	0.003***	0.001	0.002*	0.003	0.002*
	(0.001)	(0.000)	(0.002)	(0.001)	(0.002)	(0.001)
Years of education squared	−0.014***	−0.006***	0.007	−0.005	0.001	−0.004*
	(0.002)	(0.001)	(0.007)	(0.003)	(0.006)	(0.002)
Tenure						
3–5 years	0.006***	−0.003***	−0.003***	0.008***	−0.004***	0.009***
	(0.001)	(0.000)	(0.001)	(0.000)	(0.001)	(0.000)
6–10 years	0.011***	−0.003***	−0.005***	0.015***	−0.008***	0.016***
	(0.001)	(0.000)	(0.001)	(0.000)	(0.001)	(0.000)
≥11 years	0.015***	−0.003***	−0.014***	0.025***	−0.020***	0.026***
	(0.001)	(0.000)	(0.001)	(0.001)	(0.001)	(0.001)
Age						
30–39 years	−0.013***	−0.002***	0.004***	−0.003***	0.002*	−0.003***
	(0.001)	(0.000)	(0.001)	(0.001)	(0.001)	(0.000)
40–49 years	−0.024***	−0.006***	0.005***	−0.003***	0.003*	−0.003***
	(0.001)	(0.000)	(0.002)	(0.001)	(0.002)	(0.001)
≥50 years	−0.029***	−0.007***	0.001	−0.003***	−0.000	−0.003***
	(0.001)	(0.000)	(0.002)	(0.001)	(0.002)	(0.001)
10th–24th wage percentile	0.006***	0.001***	0.001	−0.001**	0.001	−0.001
	(0.001)	(0.000)	(0.001)	(0.000)	(0.001)	(0.000)
25th–49th percentile	0.015***	0.002***	0.007***	−0.001***	0.006***	−0.001
	(0.001)	(0.000)	(0.001)	(0.000)	(0.001)	(0.000)
50th percentile–74th percentile	0.025***	0.003***	0.017***	−0.001***	0.015***	−0.001
	(0.001)	(0.000)	(0.001)	(0.001)	(0.001)	(0.001)
75th percentile–89th percentile	0.039***	0.004***	0.028***	−0.002***	0.025***	−0.001**
	(0.001)	(0.000)	(0.001)	(0.001)	(0.001)	(0.001)

Table 8. (*Continued*)

	OLS		Individual Fixed Effects		Individual and Firm Effects	
	Same Firm	Other Firm	Same Firm	Other Firm	Same Firm	Other Firm
≥90th percentile	0.056***	0.006***	0.044***	-0.002***	0.041***	-0.001
	(0.001)	(0.000)	(0.002)	(0.001)	(0.001)	(0.001)
Organizational level 3	0.030***	0.006***	0.087***	0.018***	0.092***	0.017***
	(0.001)	(0.000)	(0.001)	(0.001)	(0.001)	(0.000)
Organizational level 4	0.036***	0.010***	0.129***	0.032***	0.140***	0.030***
	(0.001)	(0.000)	(0.002)	(0.001)	(0.001)	(0.000)
Organizational level 5	0.050***	0.012***	0.201***	0.041***	0.211***	0.039***
	(0.001)	(0.000)	(0.002)	(0.001)	(0.001)	(0.001)
Organizational level 6	0.072***	0.017***	0.309***	0.061***	0.324***	0.056***
	(0.002)	(0.001)	(0.004)	(0.002)	(0.003)	(0.001)
Female	-0.005***	-0.002***				
	(0.001)	(0.000)				
Title field: Implementation	-0.011***	0.000	-0.006***	-0.001*	-0.005***	-0.001***
	(0.001)	(0.000)	(0.002)	(0.001)	(0.001)	(0.000)
Title field: Production	-0.002***	0.000*	-0.004***	-0.004***	-0.005***	-0.003***
	(0.001)	(0.000)	(0.002)	(0.001)	(0.001)	(0.000)
Title field: Administration	-0.012***	0.000	-0.010***	-0.003**	-0.011***	-0.003***
	(0.001)	(0.000)	(0.002)	(0.001)	(0.002)	(0.001)
Female share in same job title and firm	0.002	-0.001**	0.012***	0.000	0.011***	0.001
	(0.001)	(0.000)	(0.002)	(0.001)	(0.002)	(0.001)
Mean tenure in same job title and firm	-0.002***	0.000***	-0.004***	-0.000***	-0.004***	0.000**
	(0.000)	(0.000)	(0.000)	(0.000)	(0.000)	(0.000)
Mean level of education at level in same job title and firm	-0.002***	0.000***	-0.005***	-0.001***	-0.005***	-0.001***
	(0.000)	(0.000)	(0.000)	(0.000)	(0.000)	(0.000)
Years at level so far	-0.002***	-0.000***	0.008***	0.000***	0.009***	0.000***
	(0.000)	(0.000)	(0.000)	(0.000)	(0.000)	(0.000)

Years at previous level	0.001***	0.009***	0.001***	0.008***	−0.000***	−0.001***
	(0.000)	(0.000)	(0.000)	(0.000)	(0.000)	(0.000)
Firm size						
51–100	0.002***	−0.001	0.002**	−0.001	0.001*	0.001
	(0.001)	(0.002)	(0.001)	(0.001)	(0.000)	(0.001)
101–200	0.002*	−0.001	0.002***	−0.002*	0.001***	0.002**
	(0.001)	(0.002)	(0.001)	(0.001)	(0.000)	(0.001)
201–500	0.001	0.002	0.001	−0.002	0.000	0.004***
	(0.001)	(0.002)	(0.001)	(0.001)	(0.000)	(0.001)
501–1000	−0.000	−0.001	0.000	−0.004***	0.001	0.008***
	(0.001)	(0.003)	(0.001)	(0.002)	(0.000)	(0.001)
1001–2000	−0.002**	0.003	−0.003***	−0.003**	−0.000	0.009***
	(0.001)	(0.003)	(0.001)	(0.002)	(0.000)	(0.001)
>2000	−0.004***	0.013***	−0.005***	0.002	−0.001***	0.028***
	(0.001)	(0.003)	(0.001)	(0.002)	(0.000)	(0.001)
Observations	1,113,088	1,113,088	1,113,088	1,113,088	1,113,088	1,113,088
R^2			0.018	0.072	0.008	0.033

Notes: (1) Reports coefficients and standard errors for a linear probability model of promotion. (2) Cluster robust standard errors in parentheses in OLS and individual fixed effect models, ***$p<0.01$, **$p<0.05$, *$p<0.1$. (3) Standard errors in the last two columns do not take heteroscedasticity and autocorrelation into account. (4) All columns include field of education dummies (8 categories), firm size dummies (6 categories), industry dummies (63 categories), and year dummies. Tenure is years in the company since hiring; the wage percentiles are calculated for each hierarchical level and firm annually; years at the level so far track the time spent in the current level in the current firm; years at the previous level track the time spent in the previous level in the current firm.

Because promotion probability might be affected by unobserved individual characteristics, which may further be correlated with our explanatory variables, in addition to OLS, we also estimate a fixed effects model, which accounts for time-invariant unobserved individual heterogeneity. Moreover, because firms may apply different standards and rules for promotions, unobserved firm heterogeneity might also matter with respect to promotion probabilities. Therefore, our third model specification includes both individual and firm fixed effects.

Table 8 shows that the level of education is positively associated with both internal and external promotions, which is in line, for example, with the empirical results of Acosta (2010) and the theory of Gibbons and Waldman. Longer tenure with the current employer increases the probability of promotion within the same, but has to opposite effect for promotions to other firms, according to the OLS estimates. In the estimations that control for individual fixed effects and individual and firm effects, the coefficients change sign. Also, this result can be understood in light of the Gibbons and Waldman model, as is discussed below. When it comes to the relationship between age and promotion, the results indicate that individuals older than 50 years of age are less likely to be promoted than those who are between 30 and 39 years of age. Table 8 also shows that the longer an individual has been at his current hierarchical level or was in the previous level, the less likely he is to be promoted. This supports our earlier conclusions about the existence of fast-tracks. The fixed effect results reverse this conclusion: given individual time-invariant heterogeneity, promotion probability is increasing with tenure at the previous and current levels. This is consistent with the Gibbons and Waldman model because, given equal ability, promotion probability depends on education and work experience. Empirically, this means that time-invariant heterogeneity is correlated with both time spent at a level and promotion probability.

Our results regarding the correlation between an individual's position in the wage distribution and promotion probability are in line with Table 6 but in contrast to those presented by Acosta (2010), who investigated promotion dynamics using data from a single US firm. Acosta reports that those at the lower deciles in the distribution of wages by occupational category are more likely to be promoted than those higher in the wage distribution. Our results, on the other hand, show that there is a positive relationship between an individual's position in the wage distribution and promotion probability. This result holds for internal promotions in all three estimation methods.[16] However, accounting for individual fixed effects reverses the results for promotions to other firms. On the other hand, this result is largely statistically insignificant when controlling also for firm effects. All in all, the results show that position in the wage distribution is an important explanatory variable for within-firm promotions, but that it plays a minor role for between-firm promotions.

As expected, promotions are more likely at the bottom of the hierarchy, reflecting the fact that there is more room for promotions at the lower ranks of the hierarchy. We also find that men are more likely to be promoted than women, a result that has been documented in several previous studies (e.g., Blau & Devaro, 2007; McCue, 1996; Pergamit & Veum, 1999; Ransom & Oaxaca, 2005). On the other hand, of the role played by the characteristics of the co-workers, there is little earlier empirical evidence. Our results show that an individual has better chances of being promoted within a firm if his co-workers are less educated with little firm tenure. Somewhat surprisingly, the gender of the colleagues turned out to be unrelated to promotion probability. The characteristics of the co-workers are often also significantly correlated with promotions taking place with employer changes, although with opposite signs. This result is consistent with employees who perceive their promotion probability to be low, searching for alternative employment.

Finally, our estimates show that internal promotions are more common in larger firms. This might indicate that larger firms are more likely to rely on internal labor markets with well-defined career paths than smaller firms (Chan, 1996). When promotions with employer changes are investigated, the firm size effect is less significant, with a less clear-cut pattern.

CAREERS AND WAGES

The importance of hierarchical levels in wage determination and the contribution of promotions to wage growth are central questions in the literature on careers in organizations. Therefore, we end our analysis of careers by taking a closer look at wages. We begin by examining changes in the relative wage structure in Finnish manufacturing over the period of 1981–2006, after which we investigate the relative importance of hierarchical levels versus human capital in accounting for variation in wages. We finish by analyzing wage premiums on different career moves.

Fig. 2 describes the development of mean hourly wages by hierarchical level over time. Mean hourly wages increase with level, although the difference in mean wages is small between levels 1 and 2. More interestingly, real wages have grown in very similar fashion across levels, leaving the relative wage structure practically unchanged during the investigation period. As discussed

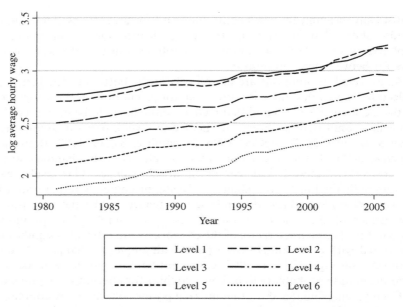

Fig. 2. Mean Hourly Wages by Hierarchical Level for the Period of 1981–2006.

in Baker et al. (1994), this rigidity of wage structure suggests that hierarchical levels play an important role in wage determination.

Fig. 3 examines the variation of wages within hierarchical levels by showing the wage ranges by level. Consistent with Baker et al. (1994) and Treble et al. (2001), we observe wages to increase at an increasing rate with hierarchical level (in the figure, *log* wages increase linearly). However, at level 2, there is a kink in the wage profile, pointing to smaller wage differentials between levels 2 and 1 compared to other levels. This may reflect the fact that our data do not include CEOs and equivalents. Also similar to Baker et al. and Treble et al., we observe substantial wage overlap between levels. For example, employees at the upper quartile of the wage distribution at level 4 have higher wages than employees at the lower quartile at level 1. In Gibbons and Waldman (2006) model, this is driven by education: employees with a high level of education at a lower level may have larger expected output than employees with lower education at a higher level. The variation of wages within levels implies that wages are not only determined by levels but also by other factors. Finally, wage dispersion

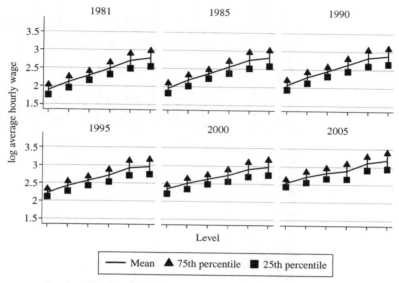

Fig. 3. The Variation of Wages Within Hierarchical Levels.

has generally remained constant in the Finnish manufacturing sector during the last two decades. The top level, however, is an exception: at level 1, wage dispersion increased somewhat between 2000 and 2005.

Following Baker et al. (1994), in Table 9 we examine in more detail the relative importance of human capital versus hierarchical levels in accounting for variation in wages. The first two columns include only human capital-related variables as regressors, the next two columns control only for hierarchical levels, and finally, to illustrate how much the explanatory power increases once human capital variables are added to the model including only level variables, columns 5 and 6 show the results for a combined model. Unlike Baker et al. (1994) and Treble et al. (2001), we find that human capital explains somewhat more of the variance in wages than hierarchical levels. For example, during the period of 2001–2005, human capital variables explained 46.9% of the variance, while hierarchical levels accounted for 43.5% of the variation in wages. We can also observe that the residual variance has increased over time: both human capital variables and hierarchical levels have lost some of their explanatory power during the investigation period, human capital more so than hierarchical levels. Thus, the relative importance of levels has increased over time.[17]

Table 9. Human Capital vs. Hierarchical Level as Determinants of Wage, OLS Regression Results.

	Human Capital, 1981–1985	Human Capital, 2001–2005	Levels, 1981–1985	Levels, 2001–2005	Combined, 1981–1985	Combined, 2001–2005
Years of education	0.106***	0.100***			0.073***	0.067***
	(0.003)	(0.002)			(0.002)	(0.002)
Years of education squared	−0.050***	−0.107***			−0.036***	−0.073***
	(0.011)	(0.007)			(0.008)	(0.006)
Tenure						
3–5 years	0.049***	0.010***			0.041***	0.013***
	(0.001)	(0.001)			(0.001)	(0.001)
6–10 years	0.078***	0.026***			0.063***	0.024***
	(0.001)	(0.002)			(0.001)	(0.001)
≥11 years	0.107***	0.012***			0.086***	0.014***
	(0.002)	(0.002)			(0.001)	(0.001)
Age						
30–39	0.168***	0.191***			0.136***	0.154***
	(0.001)	(0.001)			(0.001)	(0.001)
40–49	0.256***	0.282***			0.202***	0.231***
	(0.002)	(0.002)			(0.001)	(0.002)
≥50	0.255***	0.304***			0.200***	0.250***
	(0.002)	(0.002)			(0.002)	(0.002)

	(1)	(2)	(3)	(4)	(5)	(6)
Female	-0.286***	-0.230***			-0.225***	-0.175***
	(0.001)	(0.002)			(0.001)	(0.001)
Organizational level 1			0.933***	0.751***	0.457***	0.493***
			(0.003)	(0.003)	(0.003)	(0.003)
Organizational level 2			0.836***	0.709***	0.400***	0.465***
			(0.003)	(0.003)	(0.003)	(0.003)
Organizational level 3			0.618***	0.477***	0.266***	0.307***
			(0.003)	(0.003)	(0.002)	(0.003)
Organizational level 4			0.411***	0.355***	0.148***	0.219***
			(0.002)	(0.003)	(0.002)	(0.002)
Organizational level 5			0.228***	0.211***	0.088***	0.131***
			(0.002)	(0.002)	(0.002)	(0.002)
Job titles	No	No	No	No	No	No
Observations	632,694	712,332	632,694	712,332	632,694	712,332
R^2	0.646	0.469	0.528	0.435	0.719	0.574

Notes: (1) The dependent variable is log real hourly wage. (2) Cluster robust standard errors in parentheses, *** $p < 0.01$, ** $p < 0.05$, * $p < 0.1$. (3) Human capital model includes also field of education dummies (eight categories). All models contain firm size dummies (6 categories), industry dummies (63 categories), and year dummies. Tenure is years in the company since hiring. Adding individual and firm effects drastically reduces the coefficients for organizational levels in columns titled "Levels".

The fact that hierarchical levels are less important determinants of wages in our data compared to the datasets used by Baker et al. and Treble et al. can also be observed from the last two columns of Table 9. When we add human capital variables to the specification including only hierarchical levels, there is a considerable increase in the explanatory power, whereas Baker et al. and Treble et al. find only a small increase in R^2 as a result of adding human capital variables to the model. Furthermore, in our data, wages vary significantly more between jobs at the same hierarchical level than what Baker et al. find. They report only a 2% increase in R^2 when hierarchical levels are replaced with job titles, whereas we observe R^2 to increase approximately 25% as a result of using job titles as controls in place of hierarchical levels.[18] These results are quite expected because we study thousands of firms, while Baker et al. and Treble et al. studied only a single firm.

Finally, the parameter estimates for organizational levels increase roughly linearly as we move upwards in the hierarchy. This supports our earlier conclusion about the convex relationship between levels and wages. We also estimated a fixed effect model for hierarchical levels to check whether the convexity result is robust to unobserved individual heterogeneity.[19] The fixed effect estimates confirm the conclusions based on the OLS estimates.

Another way to examine the importance of hierarchical levels as determinants of wages is to investigate wage changes with movements between levels. In the case that wages are strongly attached to hierarchical levels, we should observe significant wage changes with mobility between levels. Many of the earlier studies on the wage effects of changes in the hierarchical position have focused on promotions inside firms (e.g., McCue, 1996; Seltzer & Merrett, 2000). We, however, consider several different career moves. To be more specific, we account for the following set of mobility events: (i) promotion inside the firm, (ii) employer change with promotion, (iii) demotion inside the firm, (iv) employer change with demotion, (v) employer change without a change in the hierarchical level, and (vi) same employer and same hierarchical level (omitted group). The other control variables used in the wage regressions are those used in Table 9. Finally, besides a pooled model, we also estimate the model by previous hierarchical level to allow the wage effects of career moves to depend on one's current position in the hierarchy.

Table 10 shows estimates of salary premiums for different career moves controlling for individual and firm fixed effects. In line with the earlier literature, we find considerable wage returns to promotions. Promotions

Table 10. Return to Career Moves, Fixed Effect Estimates.

Salary Premiums by Type of Transition and Across Levels: Individual and Firm Fixed Effects

	All	Prev. Level 1	Prev. Level 2	Prev. Level 3	Prev. Level 4	Prev. Level 5	Prev. Level 6
Promotion in current firm	0.039***		0.064***	0.056***	0.054***	0.045***	0.030***
	(0.000)		(0.001)	(0.001)	(0.001)	(0.001)	(0.001)
Promotion in new firm	0.057***		0.086***	0.096***	0.084***	0.072***	0.055***
	(0.001)		(0.004)	(0.002)	(0.002)	(0.001)	(0.004)
Demotion in current firm	-0.030***	-0.024***	-0.025***	-0.012***	-0.015***	-0.016***	
	(0.000)	(0.002)	(0.001)	(0.001)	(0.001)	(0.002)	
Demotion in new firm	-0.024***	-0.013***	-0.002	0.007***	0.003	-0.036***	
	(0.001)	(0.003)	(0.002)	(0.002)	(0.001)	(0.005)	
Same level in new firm	0.009***	0.006***	0.011***	0.011***	0.008***	0.005***	0.005**
	(0.000)	(0.002)	(0.001)	(0.001)	(0.001)	(0.001)	(0.002)
Observations	2,709,113	177,478	322,253	489,956	673,030	953,030	93,366

Notes: (1) The dependent variable is log real hourly wage. (2) The table reports coefficients and standard errors (in parentheses), ***$p<0.01$, **$p<0.05$, *$p<0.1$. (3) All columns include the human capital variables from Table 9, firm size dummies (6 categories) and industry dummies (63 categories), and year dummies. The first column additionally includes dummies for the previous hierarchical level.

inside the firm increase wages, on average, by 4%; promotions with an employer change, roughly 1.8 percentage points more. Although promotions are an important source of wage growth, our estimates of the returns to promotion are, however, somewhat lower than those reported by Baker et al. (1994) and Treble et al. (2001). Baker et al. find that promotions increase wages, on average, by 6%, while in the data used by Treble et al., promotions boost wages as much as 12%. On the other hand, our results about the wage effects of demotions inside the firm are close to those presented by Treble et al., who find that within-firm demotions decrease wages, on average, by 2.6%.

The results by previous hierarchical level indicate that there is indeed a lot of variation in the wage premiums on career moves between levels. Similar to Baker et al., we find the returns to promotion increase with level, especially for internal promotions. Further, the wage effects of demotions differ between levels. Demotions inside firms are especially bad news at the top of the hierarchy, whereas the penalties of demotions with employer changes are highest at level 5. Finally, our results show that there is also a small wage gain associated with lateral employer changes at all levels except for level 6.

CONCLUSIONS

We have examined careers of white-collar workers employed in Finnish manufacturing, following the analysis of Baker et al. (1994) quite closely. Our study adds to their paper in two important ways. First, we use a large linked employer-employee dataset including over 5,000 firms instead of personnel records from a single firm. We thus provide insight into how well the findings of Baker et al. generalize to a larger set of firms. Second, our analysis of career and wage dynamics extends beyond firm boundaries to also cover career moves with employer changes. This is made possible by our unique data that allow us to construct job hierarchies that are comparable across firms.

Similar to Baker et al., we do not find strong support for the existence of ports of entry. Although the share of internal hires increases as we move up the hierarchy, outside hiring plays an important role at all hierarchical levels. Also in line with Baker et al., there is even weaker evidence for the ports of exit. When it comes to career development after the entry into a level, some of our results support the findings of Baker et al., while some do not. In contrast to Baker et al., we do not find that outside hires initially do better in the promotion process than incumbents. Quite the contrary, incumbents seem to be promoted more quickly than external hires during the first years after entry into a level. However, incumbents are also demoted more often. Our finding that incumbents have more variable careers after entrance to a given level is at odds with the findings of Baker et al. However, in our data, external hires have more labor market experience, which may explain our result. Perhaps, the smaller variability among external hires is due to the smaller uncertainty about their abilities. If learning is symmetric, as it is in the Gibbons and Waldman model, then longer labor market experience leads to a more precise estimate of ability. With respect to exits from levels, our results resemble those of Baker et al.: also in our data, exit rates are higher for outside hires than for incumbents during the first years after entry.

Further supporting the findings of Baker et al., we find evidence of fast-tracks and fast-track exits. Furthermore, we find, like Baker et al., that there is tendency for the promoted individuals to be at the upper end of the wage distribution before promotion and at the lower end of the distribution after promotion. This result also holds for promotions to other firms. When the analysis is repeated for exits from the levels, Baker et al. fail to find any consistent pattern. In our data, however, exit rates are higher at the top of the wage distribution than at the bottom.

We extended Baker et al.'s analysis of promotion dynamics by estimating linear promotion models for internal and external promotions. The main conclusions from this analysis are as follows: we observe a positive correlation between years of education and the likelihood of promotion. In line with the fast-track hypothesis, we find that promotion probability decreases with the time spent at the current and previous hierarchical levels. However, controlling for employer fixed effects reverses this result. This is consistent with the Gibbons and Waldman model. We also find that individuals higher in the wage distribution at their current hierarchical level are more likely to be promoted than workers who are at the lower deciles in the wage distribution. The characteristics of the co-workers seem to matter as well. An individual has better chances for promotion if his co-workers are less educated with little tenure. This implies that promotions are not only based on some standards but also that employees compete for promotions. Our results thus suggest that future theoretical work should incorporate these aspects of competition to, e.g., the Gibbons and Waldman framework. Interestingly, many of the effects of the different background characteristics on the promotion probability are quite similar for both internal and external promotions.

We ended our analysis of careers by taking a look at wage determination and the role of hierarchical levels in that respect. Similar to Baker et al. (1994), we observe a convex relationship between wages and hierarchical level. There is also substantial wage overlap between hierarchical levels, again in line with Baker et al. This variation of wages within levels indicates that levels do not solely determine wages. A more detailed analysis of the relative importance of hierarchical levels versus human capital in accounting for variation in wages shows that, unlike in Baker et al., human capital explains more of the variance in wages than hierarchical levels. However, this does not mean that levels are unimportant as determinants of wages in our data. For example, during the period of 2001–2005, hierarchical levels accounted for 43.5% of the variation in wages, which is only 3.4 percentage points lower than the corresponding figure for human capital variables. The importance of hierarchical levels can also be seen from the estimation results examining the wage premiums on different career moves. We find significant positive returns to promotions, whereas demotions result in wage losses. This implies that hierarchical levels indeed play an important role in wage determination.

Overall, our findings are quite consistent with those of previous studies on careers based on case studies using data from a single firm. Given that the models of Gibbons and Waldman (1999, 2006) were designed to fit the results in Baker et al. and other studies, it is not surprising that many of our results are consistent with these models. However, not all of the earlier results about the characteristics of internal labor markets are confirmed in our study, suggesting that more research using different datasets from different types of labor markets are clearly needed. Moreover, our results show that for many individuals, moving between employers is an important way to ascend the hierarchical ladder. These results support the recent interest in combining employee turnover and career dynamics within firms in theoretical models.

NOTES

1. Papers investigating internal labor markets were discussed above. Booth et al. (1999), Farber (1994), Munasinghe and Sigman (2004), and Topel and Ward (1992) are examples of studies analyzing employer changes. Booth and Francesconi (2000), Le Grand and Tåhlin (2002), and Pavlopoulos, Fouarge, Muffels, and Vermunt (2007) are, on the other hand, examples of the few studies that have distinguished between intra-firm and inter-firm mobility.

2. More detailed descriptions of the Finnish bargaining system are found in Asplund (2007) and Vartiainen (1998).

3. There might be gaps in the data, e.g., due to spells of unemployment or spells of employment in other sectors.

4. An individual is working full-time if his/her regular weekly working time is over 30 hours.

5. In some cases, the number of observations is lower due to the missing values of certain variables.

6. The number of job titles represented at different levels starting from the top of the hierarchy is as follows: 5 (level 1), 13, 15, 12, 25, and 5 (level 6).

7. Demotions might be, for example, due to job rotation within firms, although there are also other potential reasons for demotions (see, e.g., Bernhardt 1995).

8. Many studies have reported systematic differences in career moves by gender as well. Therefore, we also investigated distributions of career moves separately for men and women. We found significant gender differences in mobility patterns. For example, men are generally more mobile both within firms and between firms than women. Furthermore, men are more likely to be promoted. However, also demotions are more typical for men than for women.

9. We identify employer changes by comparing firm identifiers attached to white-collar employees across years. However, there are some (rare) cases due to business reorganizations where a worker's firm identifier changes, even though a worker does not actually move between employers. To identify a real firm change, we further require that at least 50% of the present co-workers must have changed between years t and $t-1$.

10. This group includes those who come to the labor market for the first time, were previously working for an employer that is not affiliated with EK, or were previously outside the labor market. Unfortunately, the EK dataset does not allow us to distinguish between these different modes of data entry.

11. The share of external hires reported in Table 3 is much higher than the corresponding figure in Baker et al. (1994). This is probably due to the smaller size of firms in our data. In Baker et al., the firm under investigation had over 5,000 management employees in the last observation year, whereas in our data the average size of a firm in 2006 was 90 (calculated as a number of white-collar employees in a firm).

12. We have also made the same analysis for those who have entered level 5 without any changes in the conclusions.

13. The share of internal entrants in levels 3, 2, or 1 two years after entering level 4 is calculated as follows: $5 + 3.1 + 1.8 = 9.9$.

14. Wage deciles are calculated within hierarchical levels and firms for each year.

15. As discussed, for example, by Angrist and Pischke (2009), using the linear probability model instead of a nonlinear one is of little importance, in practice, when the interest is in average marginal effects.

16. Note that even though the coefficients in the columns labeled "other firm" are much smaller, so is the mean of the dependent variable. On average, 4.3% of individuals are promoted at their current firm in any year, whereas 0.6% of individuals earn a promotion concurrently with a change in the firm.

17. We also estimated the models for the period of 1991–1995, and the R^2 for this period falls between the R^2 for years 1981–1985 and 2001–2005.

18. These results are available from the authors upon request.
19. Also the fixed effect estimates are available from the authors upon request.

ACKNOWLEDGMENTS

We thank Juha-Pekka Jokinen for excellent research assistance. Funding from the Finnish Work Environment Fund is gratefully acknowledged.

REFERENCES

Acosta, P. (2010). Promotion dynamics the Peter principle: Incumbents vs. external hires. *Labour Economics, 17*(6), 975–986.

Angrist, J. D., & Pischke, J.-S. (2009). *Mostly harmless econometrics: An empiricist's companion.* Princeton, NJ: Princeton University Press.

Asplund, R. (2007). *Finland: Decentralisation tendencies within a collective wage bargaining system.* Helsinki: The Research Institute of the Finnish Economy.

Baker, G., Gibbs, M., & Holmström, B. (1994). The internal economics of the firm: Evidence from personnel data. *Quarterly Journal of Economics, 109*(4), 881–919.

Baker, G., & Holmström, B. (1995). Internal labor markets: Too many theories, too few facts. *American Economic Review, 85*(2), 255–259.

Becker, G. (1962). Investment in human capital: A theoretical analysis. *Journal of Political Economy, 70*(5), 9–49.

Belzil, C., & Bognanno, M. (2008). Promotions, demotions, halo effects, and the earnings dynamics of American executives. *Journal of Labor Economics, 26*(2), 287–310.

Bernhardt, D. (1995). Strategic promotion and compensation. *Review of Economic Studies, 62*(2), 315–339.

Blau, F. D., & Devaro, J. (2007). New evidence on gender differences in promotion rates: An empirical analysis of a sample of new hires. *Industrial Relations, 46*(3), 511–550.

Booth, A. L., & Francesconi, M. (2000). Job mobility in 1990s Britain: Does gender matter? In S. W. Polachek (Ed.), *Research in Labor Economics: Worker well-being* (Vol. 19, pp. 173–189). New York, NY: Elsevier Science, JAI

Booth, A. L., Francesconi, M., & Garcia-Serrano, C. (1999). Job tenure and job mobility in Britain. *Industrial and Labor Relations Review, 53*(1), 43–70.

Chan, W. (1996). External recruitment versus internal promotion. *Journal of Labor Economics, 14*(4), 555.

da Silva, A. D., & van der Klaauw, B. (2005). *Wage dynamics and promotions inside and between firms. Journal of Population Economics, 24*(4), 1513–1548.

DeVaro, J. (2006). Internal promotion competitions in firms. *RAND Journal of Economics, 37*(3), 521–542.

Dohmen, T. J., Kriechel, B., & Pfann, G. A. (2004). Monkey bars and ladders: The importance of lateral and vertical job mobility in internal labor market careers. *Journal of Population Economics, 17*(2), 193–228.

Farber, H. S. (1994). The analysis of interfirm worker mobility. *Journal of Labor Economics, 12*(4), 554–593.

Francesconi, M. (2001). Determinants and consequences of promotions in Britain. *Oxford Bulletin of Economics and Statistics, 63*(3), 279–310.

Ghosh, S. (2007). Job mobility and careers in firms. *Labour Economics, 14*(3), 603–621.

Gibbons, R., & Waldman, M. (1999). A theory of wage and promotion dynamics inside firms. *Quarterly Journal of Economics, 114*(4), 1321–1358.

Gibbons, R., & Waldman, M. (2006). Enriching a theory of wage and promotion dynamics inside firms. *Journal of Labor Economics, 24*(1), 59–107.

Jovanovic, B. (1979a). Firm-specific capital and turnover. *Journal of Political Economy, 87*(6), 1246–1260.

Jovanovic, B. (1979b). Job matching and the theory of turnover. *Journal of Political Economy, 87*(5), 972–990.

Lazear, E. P. (1992). The job as a concept. In W. J. Bruns, Jr. (Ed.), *Performance measurement, evaluation, and incentives* (pp. 183–215). Boston, MA: Harvard Business School Press.

Lazear, E. P., & Oyer, P. (2004). Internal and external labor markets: A personnel economics approach. *Labour Economics, 11*(5), 527–554.

Lazear, E. P., & Rosen, S. (1981). Rank-order tournaments as optimum labor contracts. *Journal of Political Economy, 89*(5), 841–864.

Le Grand, C., & Tåhlin, M. (2002). Job mobility within and between jobs. *European Sociological Review, 18*(4), 142–151.

McCue, K. (1996). Promotions and wage growth. *Journal of Labor Economics, 14*(2), 175–209.

Munasinghe, L., & Sigman, K. (2004). A hobo syndrome? Mobility, wages, and job turnover. *Labour Economics, 11*(2), 191–218.

Neal, D. (1999). The complexity of job mobility among young men. *Journal of Labor Economics, 17*(2), 237–261.

Oi, W. (1962). Labor as a quasi-fixed factor. *Journal of Political Economy, 70*(6), 538–555.

Parrado, E., Caner, A., & Wolff, E. N. (2007). Occupational and industrial mobility in the United States. *Labour Economics, 14*(3), 435–455.

Pavlopoulos, D., Fouarge, D., Muffels, R., & Vermunt, J. K. (2007). Job mobility and wage mobility of high- and low-paid workers. Schmollers Jahrbuch: Zeitschrift fur Wirtschafts- und Sozialwissenschaften. *Journal of Applied Social Science Studies, 127*(1), 47–58.

Pergamit, M. R., & Veum, J. R. (1999). What is a promotion? *Industrial and Labor Relations Review, 52*(4), 581–601.

Polachek, S. W., & Horvath, F. W. (1977). A life cycle approach to migration: Analysis of the perspicacious peregrinator. In R. Ehrenberg (Ed.), *Research in Labor Economics* (pp. 103–150). Greenwich, CT: JAI Press.

Ransom, M., & Oaxaca, R. L. (2005). Intrafirm mobility and sex differences in pay. *Industrial and Labor Relations Review, 58*(2), 219–237.

Rosen, S. (1986). Prizes and incentives in elimination tournaments. *American Economic Review, 76*(4), 701–715.

Seltzer, A., & Merrett, D. T. (2000). Personnel policies at the Union Bank of Australia: Evidence from the 1888–1900 entry cohorts. *Journal of Labor Economics, 18*(4), 573–613.

Sicherman, N., & Galor, O. (1990). A theory of career mobility. *Journal of Political Economy, 98*(1), 169–192.

Topel, R. H., & Ward, M. P. (1992). Job mobility and the careers of young men. *Quarterly Journal of Economics, 107*(2), 439–479.

Treble, J., van Gameren, E., Bridges, S., & Barmby, T. (2001). The internal economics of the firm: Further evidence from personnel data. *Labour Economics, 8*(5), 531–552.

Vartiainen, J. (1998). *The labour market in Finland: Institutions and outcomes*. Helsinki: Prime
    Minister's Office, Publications Series, 1998/2.
Waldman, M. (1984). Job assignments, signalling, and efficiency. *RAND Journal of Economics*,
    15(2), 255–267.
Waldman, M. (2007). *Theory and evidence in internal labor markets*. MPRA Paper No. 5113.

POSITION-SPECIFIC PROMOTION RATES AND THE "FAST TRACK" EFFECT

Adam Clemens

ABSTRACT

Some positions within a firm consistently lead to promotion with a higher probability than other positions at the same hierarchical level. Therefore, serial correlation of promotion rates is not indicative merely of individuals with high innate ability, but it is also a feature of organizational structure. I describe these positions as "fast jobs" and present a model in which jobholders acquire human capital in these jobs that is more valuable at the next level. Data from a financial services firm confirm that workers in fast jobs are younger than other workers at the same level, and that transfers from fast to slow jobs are common. Thus, the process of grooming workers for advancement is analogous to more aggressive up-or-out systems. This deliberate grooming of some workers for advancement has income inequality implications, as it may reinforce the effect of small biases or small differences in early apparent ability.

Keywords: Internal labor markets; promotion; fast tracks

JEL classifications: M12; M51

Research in Labor Economics, Volume 36, 77–107
Copyright © 2012 by Emerald Group Publishing Limited
All rights of reproduction in any form reserved
ISSN: 0147-9121/doi:10.1108/S0147-9121(2012)0000036007

INTRODUCTION

Studies of career tracks within firms have shown repeatedly that time to promotion is serially correlated, a phenomenon that has been described as a "fast track" effect. This is not surprising, since rapid promotion suggests high innate ability, which, in turn, should predict further promotion. This observation, however, tells us nothing about the role of organizational strategy in career development. It is merely an observation of people being promoted quickly, without reference to specific career tracks. Are these seemingly high-ability individuals seeded randomly throughout the organization, or can their job assignments play a role in their rapid advancement?

The first purpose of this article is to begin to answer these questions by introducing a conceptual distinction between advancement-prone individuals and advancement-friendly positions within a firm. Throughout, I use the term "fast jobs" to indicate positions in an organization that are systematically staffed with workers who subsequently will be promoted at a higher rate than colleagues at the same hierarchical level. Empirically, I show that such positions exist at multiple levels. The data come from the personnel records of the same U.S. financial services firm that was studied in Baker, Gibbs, and Holmstrom (1994a, 1994b), hereafter referred to as "BGH."

The existence of advancement-friendly positions implies that early processes for matching people with responsibilities will affect later outcomes. Ultimately, selecting the right people to groom for advancement will enhance firm performance, and the identity of those who reach the executive suite could depend upon the priorities and biases of lower managers.

The impact of fast jobs on career advancement is difficult to distinguish from the innate ability of the workers, because job assignment is endogenous. Indeed, I find that the marginal impact of fast jobs is weaker after controlling for serial correlation; therefore, the effect of these jobs is related to the observation of people who are promoted quickly. The fact that fast climbers are concentrated in these jobs, however, suggests that there is something unique about these jobs, which plays a role in the firm's strategy.[1]

I offer an interpretation that the unique feature of these jobs is the human capital acquired in them. Workers placed in these jobs tend to be younger and better educated than their peers, suggesting that the firm chooses promising employees early to groom for advancement. The net flow of lateral transfers is from faster to slower jobs, analogous to more aggressive up-or-out systems. I do not find evidence that the effect of these fast jobs is driven by signaling, or by faster learning about the worker's ability.

My empirical analysis is focused on vertical, rather than lateral, movements, and my one-dimensional model does not account for the benefits of diversification. I do find that lateral moves, whether to fast jobs or to "slow jobs" (i.e., jobs with a lower promotion rate), improve a worker's chances for subsequent promotion. Therefore, fast jobs are only one component of the multi-dimensional problem of career progression.

LITERATURE REVIEW

In the seminal study of a firm's personnel records, BGH reports that the probability of a worker's promotion to the next hierarchical level decreases with time spent at the previous level, so that rapid promotions are serially correlated. The authors refer to this phenomenon as a "fast track." This stylized fact is confirmed in the following studies:

- Seltzer and Merrett (2000), a study of the nineteenth-century records of the Union Bank of Australia;
- Treble, van Gameren, Bridges, and Barmby (2001), a study of a British financial-sector firm;
- Dohmen, Kriechel, and Pfann (2004), a study of the Dutch aircraft manufacturer Fokker;
- Gibbs and Hendricks (2004), a study of a large U.S. firm; and
- Chiappori, Salanie, and Valentin (1999), a study that finds momentum in promotions among executives at a French state-owned firm.

There has been some attempt to separate serial correlation from time-invariant unobserved worker heterogeneity. Ariga, Ohkusa, and Brunello (1999) find in a Japanese high-tech manufacturing firm that this serial correlation of promotions remains after controlling for worker fixed effects, and argue that if fast climbing is not purely in the worker's genes, then there are differences in human capital acquisition. Belzil and Bognanno (2008, 2010) examine panel data of executives across many firms and similarly control for worker fixed effects, finding that the remaining serial correlation of promotions is quite heterogeneous, which they interpret as signaling in some circumstances, and a Peter Principle in others. Meyer (1991, 1992) provides theoretical justifications for persistently favoring early winners, from both a perspective of boundedly rational learning and from that of incentive.

Gibbons and Waldman (1999) present a model of career advancement and wage growth fitting several stylized facts. They present promotions in large organizations as being determined by a standard rather than a tournament. The standard is one of effective ability, a function of career experience, which is perfectly observed, and of innate ability, which is revealed over time to the worker and the firm. This model is augmented in Gibbons and Waldman (2006) to allow experience in one position to be less applicable in another, so that optimal allocation depends not only on immediate productivity, but also on the future value of human capital acquired in the current period.

Bernhardt (1995) and DeVaro and Waldman (2007) present an alternative to symmetric learning about worker ability, where job assignment sends signals to competing firms that do not observe productivity but have some information about ability through education. Waldman (1984, 1990) also explores the implications of job assignment as a signal to the labor market. Prendergast (1992) offers yet another alternative, where the firm is better informed than the worker, and where signals can encourage the worker to engage in costly acquisition of firm-specific human capital.

Other papers have examined how fast tracks affect worker entry into the firm. Bretz, Rynes, and Quinn-Trank (2002) show that firms with clear fast tracks have an advantage in attracting high-achievers. Bernhardt and Scoones (1998) show that in the presence of long-term contracts and competition, firm-specific capital accumulation forces the competition for workers to occur in the initial period, when firms cannot exploit asymmetric information about workers, leaving a larger surplus share for the workers.

THEORY

Promotions are traditionally thought of as the outcome of either a tournament or a standard. In a tournament scenario, there are a specific number of jobs to be filled, and there are a larger number of potential candidates who currently occupy lower positions in the organization's hierarchy. Those who show the highest performance – through some combination of effort, ability, and luck – are promoted. In a scenario based on a promotion standard, there is an efficient allocation of the more-able workers to more skill-intensive jobs, and the criteria for promoting one worker are independent of peers. In what follows I focus on the standards approach.

Research has suggested that some firms have a strategic element to promotions, with the potential to generate different outcomes than would a naive tournament or standard. One example of this is Prendergast (1992), which concluded that firms may inefficiently assign talented workers to a difficult job before they are ready. The motivation for doing this is that the difficult job requires the worker to invest in firm-specific human capital, and the worker will not invest without a credible signal that the investment will be rewarded.

A logical implication is that, in an environment with different job titles at the same hierarchical level, the firm could send a credible signal to talented workers without inefficiently promoting them. Instead, placing them in a specific job at the same level as their peers could motivate firm-specific investment. Although not directly addressed in the Prendergast model, this investment should lower the probability of subsequent exit.

Alternatively, Gibbons and Waldman (1999) proposed a simple model of efficient allocation with symmetric information, which I present here. Workers are paid the expected value of their productivity in a given year. The productivity of worker i assigned to job j in time period t is given by

$$y_{ijt} = d_j + c_j(\eta_{it} + \varepsilon_{ijt}) \tag{1}$$

where higher-level jobs have a steeper slope with respect to ability and a lower intercept so that $c_2 > c_1$ and $d_2 < d_1$.

Effective ability η_{it} is increasing in innate ability θ, known to take on one of two values, θ_L and θ_H, and increasing and concave in human capital acquired from experience, x.

$$\eta_{it} = \theta_i f(x_{it}) \tag{2}$$

However, neither innate ability nor effective ability is perfectly observed. Each period, the firm's (and worker's) information about the worker's ability is updated with the worker's normalized output, defined as

$$z_{it} = \frac{y_{ijt} - d_j}{c_j} = \eta_{it} + \varepsilon_{ijt} \tag{3}$$

And a new belief is formed about the worker's innate ability:

$$\theta_{it}^e = E(\theta_i | \theta_{i0}^e, z_{it-x}, \ldots, z_{it-1}) \tag{4}$$

Workers are promoted from job 1 to job 2 when their expected productivity is greater in job 2. This occurs when the belief about their effective ability η_{it}^e is greater than a specific threshold η'. Similarly, workers are promoted to job 3 when $\eta_{it}^e > \eta''$. Promotions are serially correlated because workers with high innate ability are expected to reach η' faster, and to climb from η' to η'' faster.

Gibbons and Waldman (2006) added a forward-looking element to their previous model in order to explain cohort effects. Experience acquired in job 1 has less value in job 2, so that the productivity function for job 2 is

$$y_{i2t} = d_2 + c_2(\theta_i f(x_{i2t} + \alpha x_{i1t} + \varepsilon_{ijt}) \tag{1'}$$

where $\alpha < 1$ is the rate at which experience from job 1 is valued in job 2. Consequently, it may be optimal to assign workers to job 2 even when their expected productivity is higher in job 1, in order to acquire more valuable experience.

A different type of strategic consideration for promotions appears in DeVaro and Waldman (2007). Firms may be able to pay some workers less than their productivity because other firms are less informed about the workers' ability. Promotion sends a signal of high ability to the outside labor market, requiring the firm to raise wages. Since the labor market is better informed about the ability of more educated workers, promoting them is less costly. The authors found that, within the BGH firm, more educated workers were more likely to be promoted and to receive smaller wage increases with their promotions.

Specific jobs could have an effect analogous to education. If the outside labor market observes that workers in a particular job are more likely to be promoted, it could infer that they have higher ability and subsequently bid up their wages. This would make these workers less costly to promote, perpetuating the job's high promotion rate.

Two Jobs at the Same Hierarchical Level

My innovation is to introduce two different level 1 jobs into the Gibbons and Waldman framework. I label these as "Position 1s" and "Position 1f" to designate slow (s) and fast (f) jobs, and to allow the experience gained in them to be of unequal value in the production function for level 2. Experience in the slow job is discounted at rate $\alpha < 1$ upon promotion, as in Gibbons and Waldman (2006), whereas experience in the fast job is not. In addition, I generalize the prior information about ability θ_{i1}^e to include more than education; the firm observes information about new hires that the econometrician does not.

In order for some workers to be allocated in equilibrium to the job that acquires less valuable experience, I assume that it has a compensating higher intercept, d. This could be due to some time and resources being spent on additional training in the fast job. Therefore, workers' immediate productivity is higher in the slow job (1s) than it would be in the fast job (1f), but their long-run value may be increased by placing them in 1f if they are likely to be promoted later. The slope is the same; otherwise, the fast job would be a higher-level job, and there would be motivation to allocate more experienced workers to it.

$$y_{i1ft} = d_{1f} + c_1(\theta_{if}(x_{it}) + \varepsilon_{i1ft}) \tag{5a}$$

$$y_{i1st} = d_{1s} + c_1(\theta_{if}(x_{it}) + \varepsilon_{i1st}) \tag{5b}$$

$$y_{i2t} = d_2 + c_2(\theta_{if}(x_{i2t} + x_{i1ft} + \alpha x_{i1st}) + \varepsilon_{i2t}) \quad d_2 < d_{1f} < d_{1s} \tag{5c}$$

For simplicity, I restrict the model to three periods. In the third period, there is no reason to allocate a worker to a fast job, because, without any remaining future, the only relevant consideration is immediate productivity. Therefore, the relevant problem is

$$V_3 = \max \{d_{1s} + c_1\theta_{i3}^e f(x_s + x_f), d_2 + c_2\theta_{i3}^e f(\alpha x_s + x_f)\} \tag{6}$$

where x_s refers to experience in Position 1s, and x_f refers to experience in either the fast job (1f) or level 2. That is, the expected total value in the third period is equal to expected third-period productivity, which is a function of the job-specific intercept (d_{1s} or d_2), the level-specific slope (c_1 or c_2), the most recent update of perceived ability (θ_{i3}^e), and the relevant experience acquired in previous periods ($x_s + x_f$ or $\alpha x_s + x_f$).

Allocation in the previous periods requires consideration not only of the present production function, but also of the differing continuation values of experience. These depend on time, amount of experience in the slow track, amount of experience in the fast track or second level, and perceived innate ability. Technically, since time and the two types of experience are linearly dependent, one could be omitted from the notation, but I find it more intuitive to denote all three. In the second period, the firm must solve the following:

$$V_2 = \max \{d_{1s} + c_1\theta_{i2}^e f(x_s + x_f) + V_3(x_s + 1, x_f; \theta_{i2}^e), d_{1f} + c_1\theta_{i2}^e f(x_s + x_f)$$
$$+ V_3(x_s, x_f + 1; \theta_{i2}^e), d_2 + c_2\theta_{i2}^e f(\alpha x_s + x_f) + V_3(x_s, x_f + 1; \theta_{i2}^e)\} \tag{7}$$

In each of three possible allocations, the expected value is equal to the expected productivity in the second period – analogous to Eq. (6) – plus a second period expectation of possible value in the third period V_3 expressed as a function of ability and of experience from the first two periods. Note that allocation to Position 1s in period 2 will increase the slow experience x_s

by 1, whereas allocation to Position 1f or to level 2 will increase the fast experience x_f by 1.

I assume that θ_H is not sufficiently high for it to ever be optimal to allocate a worker to level 2 in the first period, so that the first period allocation problem is

$$V_1 = \max \{d_{1s} + c_1 \theta_{i1}^e f(0) + V_2(1,0;\theta_{i1}^e), d_{1f} + c_1 \theta_{i1}^e f(0) + V_2(0,1;\theta_{i1}^e)\} \quad (8)$$

Thus, for each period and each package of experience, there exist threshold values of perceived innate ability that determine optimal placement for that period. Let θ_1' denote the innate ability level that solves $d_{1s} + c_1 \theta_{i1}^e f(0) + V_2(1,0;\theta_{i1}^e) = d_{1f} + c_1 \theta_{i1}^e f(0) + V_2(0,1;\theta_{i1}^e)$; that is, a worker with that perceived innate ability upon hiring is equally valuable in either the fast or slow track in the first period. Similarly, let $\theta_2'(x_s, x_f)$ be the value of θ_{i2}^e that solves $d_{1s} + c_1 \theta_{i2}^e f(x_s + x_f) + V_3(x_s + 1, x_f; \theta_{i2}^e) = d_{1f} + c_1 \theta_{i2}^e f(x_s + x_f) + V_3(x_s, x_f + 1; \theta_{i2}^e)$, noting that the ability level that implies indifference depends on the experience acquired in period one. For promotion, let $\theta_2''(x_s, x_f)$ imply indifference in period 2: $d_{1f} + c_1 \theta_{i2}^e f(x_s + x_f) + V_3(x_s, x_f + 1; \theta_{i2}^e) = d_2 + c_2 \theta_{i2}^e f(\alpha x_s + x_f) + V_3(x_s, x_f + 1; \theta_{i2}^e)$. Finally, the threshold for allocation to level 2 in period 3 (which may or may not be a promotion) is $\theta_3'(x_s, x_f)$ and solves $d_{1s} + c_1 \theta_{i3}^e f(x_s + x_f) = d_2 + c_2 \theta_{i3}^e f(\alpha x_s + x_f)$. Proposition 1 describes the assignment rule.[2]

Proposition 1. Suppose that $\theta_2'(x_s, x_f) < \theta_2''(x_s, x_f)$ so that some workers are optimally allocated to Position 1f in the second period. Then:

(i)   If $\theta_{i1}^e > \theta_1'$, then worker i is assigned to Position 1f in period 1; otherwise, the worker is assigned to Position 1s.

(ii) If $\theta_2'(x_s, x_f) < \theta_{i2}^e < \theta_2''(x_s, x_f)$, then worker i is assigned to Position 1f in period 2, and assigned to 1s if $\theta_{i2}^e < \theta_2'(x_s, x_f)$.

(iii) If $\theta_{i2}^e > \theta_2''(x_s, x_f)$, then worker i is promoted to level 2 in period 2.

(iv) If $\theta_{i3}^e > \theta_3''(x_s, x_f)$, then worker i is assigned to level 2 in period three; otherwise, the worker is assigned to Position 1s.

More-able workers are allocated to level 2 to take advantage of the steeper slope, and, within the lower level, more-able workers are allocated to the fast job because of their greater likelihood of its later advantage being realized.

The greater value of experience in 1f implies a lower threshold for promotion from this position. A worker with less experience in the fast job must compensate with higher innate ability in order to be promoted. Formally:

Proposition 2. $\theta_2''(0,1) < \theta_2''(1,0)$ and $\theta_3''(0,2) < \theta_3''(1,1) < \theta_3''(2,0)$

where $\theta_i''(j,k)$ is the promotion threshold in period i for a worker with j periods of slow experience and k periods of fast experience.

Since a company's ability to learn about a worker's innate ability occurs over time, perceived ability approaches the true values θ_L and θ_H. This creates a motivation to delay placement in the fast job to period 2, when there is greater confidence about whether the worker will be promoted in period three. There is an opposing motivation to allocate workers to the fast track early to acquire more valuable experience, especially if some will be promoted in period 2.

Which of these motivations will dominate depends both on the distribution of beliefs about ability and on the exact parameterization of the productivity function. Therefore, I make two assumptions, which ensure that early allocation to the fast track will optimize the firm's productivity.

Assumption 1. $F_1(\theta_1') < F_2(\theta_2'(1,0)|\theta_{i1}^e < \theta_1')$. That is, the probability of remaining in the slow job in the second period, conditional on having been placed there in the first period, is greater than the unconditional probability of being initially placed in the slow job.

Essentially, the interpretation is that the firm picks some workers whom it initially sees as promising and places them in the fast job, and that it is easier for a worker to appear promising at the start of one's career with no baggage than after already having been passed over for promotion.

Assumption 2. $[F_2(\theta_2''(0,1)) - F_2(\theta_2''(0,1))|\theta_{i1}^e > \theta_1'] < 1 - F_1(\theta_1')$. That is, the probability of remaining in the fast job in the second period, conditional on having been placed there in the first period, is less than the unconditional probability of initially being placed in the fast job.

This seems plausible because there are two ways out of the fast job: (a) workers who have been marked for promotion can accordingly be promoted, or (b) if they do not perform as hoped, they can be relegated to the slow job. The firm first takes a chance on workers and develops them in a fast job, then weeds some out. The following proposition follows from the model and from these two assumptions:

Proposition 3. The average age among workers in Position 1f is lower than among workers in Position 1s.

I place one more condition on the distribution of beliefs F and label it "Assumption 3." Assumption 3. $[F_2(\theta'_2(0,1)|\theta^e_{i1} > \theta'_1)] > 0$, $[F_3(\theta''_3(1,1)|\theta^e_{i2} > \theta'_2(1,0))] > 0$, and $[F_3(\theta''_3(0,2)|\theta^e_{i2} > \theta'_2(0,1))] > 0$.

This condition is necessary in order for placement of workers in the fast job to not irrevocably mark them for promotion. Even with the higher quality of human capital acquired, the firm can change its mind about workers' innate ability and move them to the slow job. This implies that the variance of learning shocks is large enough for some negative shocks to dominate human capital advantages.

Predictions

The existence of multiple job titles at one hierarchical level allows for multiple ways in which promotion rates could systematically differ across jobs. As mentioned above, a fast job could be a signal to the worker, motivating investment in firm-specific human capital. It also could be an unintended signal to the outside labor market, raising the workers' wages and making their subsequent promotion less expensive. In the model I propose, a fast job directly generates human capital more valuable at the next level.

There are two other possible mechanisms that I consider here. First, a fast job could allow the employer to detect the worker's ability with more sensitivity. In this case, workers discovered to be high-ability types are quickly promoted, while others are discovered to be low-ability types and subsequently paid less or forced out. This would imply higher exit rates and a wider variation in annual wage increases (or decreases).

Finally, even if jobs are nominally at the same hierarchical level, one may be more skill-intensive and higher paying than the other. Workers in the better jobs are more able and are closer to the threshold for further promotion. Since, among the observed hierarchical levels in the firm, average age is uniformly increasing with level, it seems reasonable to expect that these de facto higher-level jobs also would be staffed with more experienced workers than other jobs at the same official level.

I list two predictions that follow from my model and four predictions that would logically follow from other mechanisms, but which, in all cases but one, are not inconsistent with my model. Although the empirical verdict on these Alternative Predictions cannot prove or disprove the model, it can help to refine alternative explanations of the systematic difference in promotion rates across jobs.

Model Prediction 1. Jobs will systematically differ in the rate at which workers are promoted out of them. This follows both from higher innate ability in fast jobs (Proposition 1) and a lower promotion threshold (Proposition 2).

Model Prediction 2. Workers in fast jobs will be younger than those in slow jobs at the same hierarchical level. This follows from Proposition 3.

Alternative Prediction 1. (signal to worker). Workers in fast jobs will have lower exit rates.

Alternative Prediction 2. (signal to labor market). Raises accompanying promotion will be smaller, relative to incremental raises, for workers promoted from fast jobs.

Alternative Prediction 3. (more precise learning about ability). Workers in fast jobs will have higher exit rates and/or greater variation in annual wage changes.

Alternative Prediction 4. observed different hierarchical level). Workers in fast jobs will be older than those in slow jobs that appear to be at the same hierarchical level.

If none of the Alternative Predictions hold consistently, then I interpret this as evidence favoring a human capital explanation for varying promotion rates. However, I note that the mechanisms driving promotion may differ across hierarchical levels, functions, or locations within a firm. An alternative explanation may play a role in some promotions, but not in a consistent way throughout the organization.

DATA AND METHODOLOGY

The data come from the personnel records of a U.S. financial services firm described extensively in BGH. There are eight hierarchical levels within the firm, the lower four of which are of similar size; beyond level 4, the hierarchy tapers dramatically. Observations consist of year-end snapshots from 1969 to 1988. Tenure at the firm is only observed for workers entering after 1969, so roughly a quarter of observations are without an entry for tenure. I only observe bonuses, and therefore total compensation, from 1981 onward.

I observe both a job title and the worker's classification into 1 of 20 functions. Together, a title and a function define a job. For each job and each year, I construct a metric of the past rate at which that job led to promotion, which I refer to throughout as the "job promotion rate" and define as the number of promotions from that job in previous years, divided by the total number of observations in that job in previous years.

In Table 1a, for each of the first four hierarchical levels, I summarize this variable both over the whole sample and in the final year, at which point the variable describes the job's average promotion rate over the full sample. Of course, I cannot observe which workers in a given job in 1988 are promoted to a new level in 1989, so the history terminates with promotions out of 1987 jobs.

Among these 1988 values summarizing the whole history, the 25th percentile among level 2 jobs is less than half the 75th percentile, while the 25th percentile is roughly two-thirds the value of the 75th percentile in the other levels.

Table 1b confirms that these differences across job promotion rates differ significantly from 0; within each of the first four levels, the F-statistic associated with job fixed effects has a probability rounded to 0.

Table 1a. Job Promotion Rates.

	N (Workers)	N (Jobs)	Mean	St. Dev.	25th Percentile	Median	75th Percentile
Level 1	16,436	84	0.295	0.125	0.175	0.294	0.367
Level 1, 1988	1,074	41	0.281	0.110	0.233	0.303	0.363
Level 2	16,828	190	0.191	0.114	0.117	0.187	0.263
Level 2, 1988	1,234	120	0.171	0.100	0.118	0.171	0.244
Level 3	16,178	156	0.126	0.063	0.104	0.119	0.139
Level 3, 1988	1,546	98	0.106	0.053	0.084	0.122	0.125
Level 4	13,611	55	0.017	0.021	0.010	0.013	0.021
Level 4, 1988	1,477	28	0.014	0.008	0.010	0.013	0.016

Table 1b. F-Statistic for Job Fixed Effects in Promotion Rate.

	F-test	Probability
Within level 1	$F(84, 16351) = 628.05$	0.00
Within level 2	$F(190, 16637) = 148.86$	0.00
Within level 3	$F(156, 16021) = 94.79$	0.00
Within level 4	$F(55, 13555) = 152.80$	0.00

Table 1c.   Other Summary Statistics.

	N	Mean	St. Dev.	Min.	Max.
Age (Years)	73,787	39.50	9.86	20	71
Education (Years)	62,106	15.50	2.43	12	23
Tenure (Years)	55,402	4.44	3.58	1	19
Female	74,071	0.25	–	–	–
Log total compensation (1988 Dollars)	36,847	10.82	0.41	9.27	13.66
Bonus (%)	36,847	2.70	6.93	0	194
Bonus (%) if >0	8,597	11.58	10.14	0.22	194
Promotion premium	9,062	0.03	0.11	−1.24	0.76

Log promotion premium is defined as arithmetic mean of all log raises in promotion years over employee's career, minus arithmetic mean of all log raises in non-promotion years over employee's career.

In Table 1c, I summarize individual characteristics, as well as some outcomes. The average employee is 39 years old and has about 15 years of education and 4 years of tenure at the firm. A quarter of employees are female. The (geometric) mean wage in 1988 dollars is just under $50,000. I use the geometric mean because my results include changes in log income. The unconditional expected size of a bonus is 2.7 percent of base salary, since often no bonus is given. However, among bonuses actually given, the average size is about 11.6 percent of base salary. For each worker, I construct a promotion premium, which I define as the difference between average log raise in promotion years and average log raise in years when the worker is not promoted. This has an average of about 3 percentage points.

Table 1d shows the number of different jobs. Within each of the first six levels, jobs tend to proliferate over time, although the number of jobs in a level does not grow monotonically. By the end of the sample, there are 120 different jobs within level 2, and 98 within level 3, but there are only 28 in level 4. The number is still lower in the levels beyond 4, with no more than two jobs in level 7.

ESTIMATION RESULTS

Model Predictions

I first establish Model Predictions 1 and 2, then test Alternative Predictions 1–3 (Alternative Prediction 4 does not require a separate test). Table 2

Table 1d. Number of Different Jobs with Observable Past Promotion
Rate.

	Level 1	Level 2	Level 3	Level 4	Level 5	Level 6	Level 7
1970	27	37	19	21	9	2	2
1971	35	48	25	22	8	4	2
1972	28	44	22	21	6	3	1
1973	35	56	25	24	7	4	2
1974	36	53	26	24	9	3	2
1975	36	68	32	29	11	5	2
1976	38	57	33	30	12	6	2
1977	35	61	31	31	18	5	2
1978	36	64	32	32	20	5	2
1979	37	65	35	33	22	4	2
1980	38	67	31	33	22	7	2
1981	40	66	38	32	22	7	2
1982	38	68	38	33	20	7	2
1983	41	73	35	31	19	8	2
1984	40	67	35	29	20	10	2
1985	36	66	32	26	19	13	2
1986	38	78	67	26	19	15	2
1987	40	119	86	29	18	15	2
1988	41	120	98	28	13	16	2

No job has any observed promotion history in 1969.

shows the existence of fast jobs, and Table 3 shows that their effect is not
fully explained by serial correlation of promotions.

In Table 2, I demonstrate that after controlling for observable characteristics, a job's *past* promotion rate is a significant and robust predictor of
promotion for workers currently in the job. There are, indeed, fast jobs. This
is consistent with Model Prediction 1. Since the job promotion rate is a
constructed right-hand-side variable with sampling error, coefficients are
biased toward zero. Since the unit of observation is per person and year, the
estimation automatically places more weight on jobs and on levels that yield
a more precise estimate of the job promotion rate.

Because the worker is the unit of analysis and because I am testing
the effect of an aggregate variable (the past promotion rate from a job,
which the worker shares with others), there is sure to be correlation of
unobservable variables. These factors may be innate, environmental, or
both, but what they have in common is the job in which these workers have

Table 2. Probit Marginal Effects for Promotion.

	Overall	From Level 1	From Level 2	From Level 3	From Level 4
Job promotion rate	23.48%***	42.27%***	24.28%***	10.81%**	7.56%*
	(1.76%)	(3.85%)	(3.45%)	(5.16%)	(4.21%)
Age	−0.46%**	−1.59%***	−0.25%	−0.25%	0.46%**
	(0.18%)	(0.39%)	(0.39%)	(0.41%)	(0.20%)
Age squared	−2.51 e−5	5.95 e−5	−6.74 e−5	−3.60 e−5	−5.65 e−5**
	(2 e−5)	(5 e−5)	(5 e−5)	(5 e−5)	(2 e−5)
Education	1.74%***	1.07%	0.07%	3.60%***	0.29%
	(0.63%)	(1.79%)	(1.42%)	(1.15%)	(0.48%)
Education squared	−0.01%	0.03%	0.04%	−0.06%*	−4.44 e−5
	(0.02%)	(0.06%)	(0.04%)	(0.03%)	(1.3 e−4)
Tenure	1.80%***	8.18%***	2.79%***	1.74%***	−0.11%
	(0.23%)	(0.98%)	(0.54%)	(0.40%)	(0.12%)
Tenure squared	−0.11%***	−0.78%***	−0.23%***	−0.10%***	9.14 e−5
	(0.02%)	(0.12%)	(0.04%)	(0.03%)	(7 e−5)
Controls for gender and year	Yes	Yes	Yes	Yes	Yes
Controls for level	Yes	n/a	n/a	n/a	n/a
Pseudo R^2	0.13	0.07	0.05	0.05	0.05
Observations	40,889	12,483	11,459	9,659	6,861

Errors clustered by employee.
*Significant at 10%; **Significant at 5%; ***Significant at 1%.
The values appearing in parentheses are standard errors of the estimated coefficients.

been placed. They do not affect the validity of the observation that the firm systematically clusters people who will be promoted in certain jobs.

The marginal effect from being in a job with a higher past promotion rate is .23 times the difference in job promotion rate. Within level 1 jobs, this marginal effect is .42, and it gradually declines with level. One standard deviation difference in job-promotion rate within level 1 predicts a little over 5 percentage points higher probability of promotion. Younger workers with more education and more tenure are better candidates for promotion. Although not shown, the job promotion rate during just the first 2 years of the sample has significant predictive power for promotions during any window of the sample.

In Table 3, I examine the BGH finding that odds of promotion increase as time spent in the current level increases, while they decrease as time spent in the previous level increases; that is, more rapid promotions are serially correlated. Both this effect and the effect of the job's past promotion rate are very significant when run simultaneously. The magnitude of each is

Table 3. Probit Marginal Effects for Promotion.

	Without Position Effects	With Position Effects
Time in previous level	−0.87%***	−0.79%***
	(0.30%)	(0.30%)
Job promotion rate	−	11.78%***
		(2.34%)
Time in current level	2.42%***	2.46%***
	(0.27%)	(0.26%)
Age	−0.61%***	−0.51%**
	(0.23%)	(0.23%)
Age squared	5.08 e−6	−6.03 e−6
	(3 e−5)	(3 e−5)
Education	−0.20%	−0.15%
	(0.71%)	(0.71%)
Education squared	0.03%	0.03%
	(0.02%)	(0.02%)
Tenure	0.16%	0.25%
	(0.37%)	(0.37%)
Tenure squared	−0.06%***	−0.06%***
	(0.02%)	(0.02%)
Controls for gender and year	Yes	Yes
Controls for level	Yes	Yes
Pseudo R^2	0.15	0.15
Observations	21,274	21,274

Errors clustered by employee.
*Significant at 10%; **Significant at 5%; ***Significant at 1%.
The values appearing in parentheses are standard errors of the estimated coefficients.

reduced, although more so for the job promotion rate. The marginal impact of one less year at the previous level, declining from 0.9 to 0.8 percentage points, falls well within its confidence interval; the marginal impact of the job promotion rate is roughly cut in half. People who have been climbing quickly are likely to be placed in fast jobs.

Interestingly, education is not significant in Table 3, suggesting that a prior fast climbing rate is a stronger predictor of ability that dominates education. I do not claim to be able to fully isolate value added from innate ability; however, I suggest that a shorter time in the previous level indicates ability, and, therefore, that the remaining effect of the job promotion rate is evidence of value added. This supports the idea that Model Prediction 1 is driven not only by higher ability (Proposition 1) but also by a lower promotion threshold (Proposition 2).

Table 4 shows the demographic characteristics of fast and slow jobs. Workers in fast jobs are younger on average. This is consistent with model

Table 4. Demographic Characteristics of Fast and Slow Job Holders.

	Fast Jobs		Slow Jobs	
	Mean	St. Dev.	Mean	St. Dev.
Age	37.84	9.47	41.06	9.72
Education	15.98	2.42	15.08	2.42
Tenure	4.31	3.48	4.42	3.37

"Fast" is defined as at or above 75th percentile of job promotion rate for its level.
"Slow" is defined as at or below 25th percentile of job promotion rate for its level.

Table 5. Lateral Transfers Between Fast and Slow Jobs.

From Lower to Higher Promotion Rate	From Higher to Lower Promotion Rate
2,310	2,431

These represent at least a 50 percent increase or a 33 percent decrease.

Prediction 2, and contradicts Alternative Prediction 4. To compare summary statistics, I used the sample of workers in the first four levels who are in jobs with promotion rates at or above the 75th percentile for their level, and compared them to workers in jobs at or below the 25th percentile. The fast job workers are about 3 years younger on average, have close to an additional year of education, and have about one-tenth of a year less tenure. This difference is not small; average observed tenure at the firm is only 4.4 years.

Table 5 examines lateral movement between fast and slow jobs and sheds light on what drives the predicted age difference. In order for a transfer to be counted as a relocation (from fast to slow, or vice versa), it must involve a 50 percent increase or a 33 percent decrease in job promotion rate relative to the previous position. Lateral transfers to a job with a lower promotion rate are 5 percent more common (2,431 versus 2,310) than lateral transfers to a job with a higher promotion rate. Therefore, workers in fast jobs are younger and less tenured on average (Model Prediction 2), not only because they are promoted sooner, but also because they are laterally transferred. Lateral transfers may occur for a variety of reasons outside the one-dimensional model, but the net effect is that fast jobs are shedding workers over time, analogous to an "up-or-out" mechanism.

Job promotion rate has a greater effect on younger and more educated workers, the very workers who are more likely to be placed in fast jobs.

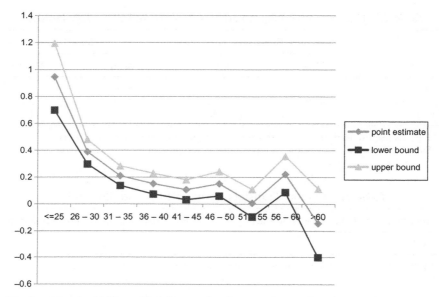

Fig. 1.   Marginal Effect of Job Promotion Rate on Promotion, by Age Bracket, and
Includes Controls for Education, Tenure, Gender, Year, and Level.

Figs. 1 and 2 depict the marginal effects of fast jobs at different age and
education levels.

Fig. 1 shows a clear pattern: the marginal effect of the job promotion rate
is nearly 1 (0.95) among workers aged 25 or younger. It declines sharply
until workers reach their forties, beyond which it becomes more erratic but
stays low. The promotion advantage for workers in fast jobs (Model
Prediction 1) is stronger for those who are also younger (and therefore
satisfying Model Prediction 2 that younger workers will be more common in
fast jobs).

Fig. 2 shows that the impact of the job promotion rate appears to be
larger for college graduates than for workers with only a high school degree
or with some college education. The point estimates for those with a
master's degree or more are lower, but still above those of workers without
bachelor's degrees. The promotion advantage for workers in fast jobs is
stronger for those who are also more educated, and expected on average to
have higher ability (therefore satisfying Proposition 1 that higher ability
workers will be in fast jobs).

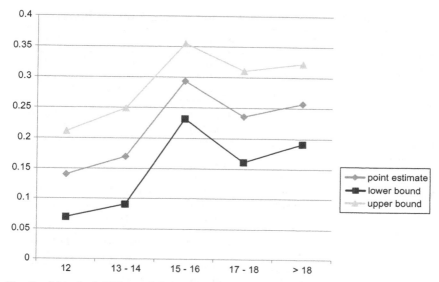

Fig 2. Marginal Effect of Job Promotion Rate on Promotion, by Education Bracket, and Includes Controls for Age, Tenure, Gender, Year, and Level. The Number of Years of Education is Given on Horizontal Axis.

As predicted, some jobs systematically lead to promotion at a higher rate. My model explains this, both through higher average quality of the workers assigned to those jobs, and through more valuable human capital acquired in them. Empirically, people who have been climbing quickly are likely to be placed in these jobs. Workers in fast jobs are younger on average, as predicted. This is partly due to the net flow of lateral transfers from faster to slower jobs. Workers in fast jobs also are more educated, and the job promotion rate has a larger effect on younger and more educated workers.

Alternative Predictions

I next turn my attention to alternative explanations of fast jobs. First, they could be a signal to workers, encouraging them to prepare for promotion by investing in firm-specific human capital. I first test this mechanism by considering a different signal – bonuses. Table 6 shows the effect of discretionary bonuses, as a signal to workers, on exit; Table 7 tests whether a similar mechanism applies to fast jobs.

Table 6. Probit Models of Promotions and Exits on Bonuses.

	Promotions		Exits	
Bonus (%)	0.015***	0.004	−0.005***	−0.006
	(0.002)	(0.014)	(0.002)	(0.017)
	[0.31%]ᵃ	[0.14%]	[−0.10%]	[−0.15%]
Bonus (%) × Age	–	7.78 e−4***	–	−1.69 e−4
		(2.34 e−4)		(2.22 e−4)
		[0.02%]		[−2.54 e−5]
Bonus (%) × Education	–	−0.001	–	4.36 e−4
		(6.35 e−4)		(7.94 e−4)
		[−0.02%]		[8.65 e−5]
Age	−0.015	−0.018*	−0.106***	−0.106***
	(0.010)	(0.010)	(0.009)	(0.009)
	[−0.33%]	[−0.38%]	[−2.24%]	[−2.24%]
Age squared	−1.66 e−4	−1.52 e−4	0.001***	0.001***
	(1.23 e−4)	(1.22 e−4)	(1.04 e−4)	(1.04 e−4)
	[−3.27 e−5]	[−2.99 e−5]	[0.02%]	[0.02%]
Education	0.014	0.015	0.104***	0.104***
	(0.038)	(0.038)	(0.037)	(0.038)
	[0.31%]	[0.35%]	[2.81%]	[2.81%]
Education squared	0.001	0.001	−0.002**	−0.002**
	(0.001)	(0.001)	(0.001)	(0.001)
	[0.02%]	[0.02%]	[−0.07%]	[−0.07%]
Tenure	0.062***	0.064***	−0.015	−0.015
	(0.013)	(0.013)	(0.011)	(0.011)
	[1.30%]	[1.34%]	[−0.63%]	[−0.64%]
Tenure squared	−0.004***	−0.004***	−1.05 e−4	−7.53 e−5
	(9.17 e−4)	(9.31 e−4)	(6.99 e−4)	(6.98 e−4)
	[−0.07%]	[−0.08%]	[0.01%]	[1.49 e−4]
Controls for gender and year	Yes	Yes	Yes	Yes
Controls for position	Yes	Yes	Yes	Yes
Pseudo R^2	0.14	0.14	0.04	0.04
Observations	25,304	25,304	26,829	26,829

Marginal effects (in brackets) from model with level controls rather than job controls indicate effect of this year's discretionary bonus on next year's promotion or exit. Errors clustered by employee.
*Significant at 10%; **Significant at 5%; ***Significant at 1%.
The values appearing in parentheses are standard errors of the estimated coefficients.

Table 6 shows the effect of bonuses on promotion and exit the following year. In all regressions involving bonuses (and not involving job promotion rate), I use fixed effects for each title and function rather than for each

Table 7. Probit Marginal Effects of Fast Tracks for Promotion and Exit.

	Promotions		Exits	
Job promotion rate	23.48%***	45.50%***	5.41%***	3.66%
	(1.76%)	(12.14%)	(1.63%)	(9.83%)
Promotion rate × Age	–	−0.88%***	–	−0.12%
		(0.19%)		(0.14%)
Promotion rate × Education	–	0.51%	–	0.36%
		(0.58%)		(0.48%)
Age	−0.46%**	−0.12%	−2.07%***	−2.02%***
	(0.18%)	(0.19%)	(0.13%)	(0.15%)
Age squared	−2.51 e−5	−4.22 e−5*	0.02%***	0.02%***
	(2 e−5)	(2 e−5)	(2 e−5)	(2 e−5)
Education	1.74%***	1.55%**	3.26%***	3.13%***
	(0.63%)	(0.65%)	(0.55%)	(0.58%)
Education squared	−0.01%	−0.01%	−0.08%***	−0.08%***
	(0.02%)	(0.02%)	(0.02%)	(0.02%)
Tenure	1.80%***	1.90%***	−0.84%***	−0.82%***
	(0.23%)	(0.23%)	(0.17%)	(0.17%)
Tenure squared	−0.11%***	−0.12%***	0.03%***	0.03%**
	(0.02%)	(0.02%)	(0.01%)	(0.01%)
Controls for gender and year	Yes	Yes	Yes	Yes
Controls for level	Yes	Yes	Yes	Yes
Pseudo R^2	0.13	0.13	0.03	0.03
Observations	40,889	40,889	40,980	40,980

Errors clustered by employee.
*Significant at 10%; **Significant at 5%; ***Significant at 1%.
The values appearing in parentheses are standard errors of the marginal effect.

level.[3] Rather than simply being a substitute for promotion, bonuses in this firm seem to work as a credible signal.

Bonuses increase the probability of promotion and decrease the probability of exit, and interaction terms suggest that each effect is stronger for older and less educated workers (although this is only significant for the interaction with age in predicting promotion). This is consistent with a hypothesis that bonuses motivate a worker to make firm-specific invest-ments. Less educated workers are less informed about their own type and, therefore, may be more influenced by signals. This is the pattern we would expect to also hold for fast jobs if Alternative Prediction 1 were true.

Table 7 indicates that, for fast jobs, the relationship between promotion and exit is precisely the opposite. Workers in fast jobs are more likely both to be promoted and to exit, and there is weak evidence that both of these effects are stronger for younger and more educated workers (again, only the age interaction in the promotions model is significant). This contradicts Alternative Prediction 1, and suggests that the effect of fast jobs on promotion prospects is not through worker investment in firm-specific capital. It should be noted, however, that firm-specific capital has long been suspected to play a less important role in this financial services firm than it may play in other firms, since exit continues to occur at a relatively high rate – even among employees with considerable tenure.

Bonuses and job promotion rates have effects of comparable magnitude. While the marginal effects on promotion and exit are roughly 50 times larger in the model with job promotion rates than with bonuses, the average bonus size (as a percentage of base pay) conditional on receiving a bonus is roughly 50 times the average promotion rate in level 2. If job promotion rates were reported as percentages (i.e., multiplied by 100) to scale them the same way as relative bonuses, their marginal effect would be about half the magnitude of the bonus's effect, while their mean would be roughly twice the size.

Although not shown, the effect of the job promotion rate on exit does not follow a consistent pattern across levels. It is positive and significant in level 1, with a marginal effect on the exit rate one-tenth the size of the difference in the job promotion rate, but negative and significant in level 3, with an even larger marginal effect. The impact on exit is positive in levels 2 and 4 but not statistically significant. It is possible that, in the first two levels, fast jobs provide some accelerated learning about the worker that results in either promotion or exit, but, by level 3, this becomes much less important. Therefore, Alternative Predictions 1 and 3 may each have some validity in specific levels or functions within the firm, even if they are not consistent with generalized results.

Another alternative is that, if workers have been promoted at a high rate from a particular job, the outside labor market could see this job as a signal of ability and bid up the associated wage. Workers in this job would then be less expensive to promote.

To test this idea, Table 8 examines whether signaling to the outside labor market reduces the promotion premium. It is slightly smaller for fast jobs, but the difference is not significant. There is no evidence of Alternative Prediction 2. From the standpoint of the human capital acquisition model, workers promoted from slow jobs face a devaluation of their applicable human capital once promoted, which would suggest a smaller promotion raise, but also have just had a positive shock to their perceived innate ability, which would suggest a larger promotion raise.

Bonuses do have a negative effect on the promotion premium, but signaling to the outside market is probably not the explanation, because

Table 8. Least Squares Regression of Log Promotion Premium.

	1	2	3
Job promotion rate	−1.23%	−	−1.35%
	(2.01%)		(1.98%)
Bonus (%)	−	−0.20%**	−0.20%**
		(0.08%)	(0.08%)
Age	−0.21%	−0.19%	−0.22%
	(0.22%)	(0.20%)	(0.22%)
Age squared	2.33 e−5	2.01 e−5	2.44 e−5
	(2.68 e−5)	(2.35 e−5)	(2.66 e−5)
Education	−0.14%	−8.20 e−5	−0.08%
	(0.80%)	(0.92%)	(0.79%)
Education squared	8.48 e−5	4.51 e−5	5.85 e−5
	(0.03%)	(2.98 e−4)	(0.02%)
Tenure	0.76%***	0.86%***	0.88%***
	(0.24%)	(0.24%)	(0.24%)
Tenure squared	−0.04%**	−0.05%***	−0.05%***
	(0.02%)	(0.02%)	(0.02%)
Controls for gender and year	Yes	Yes	Yes
Controls for level	Yes	n/a	Yes
Controls for position	No	Yes	No
Adjusted R^2	0.04	0.06	0.05
Observations	6,818	6,818	6,818
Conditional mean	2.89%	2.89%	2.89%

Errors clustered by employee. Log promotion premium is defined as arithmetic mean of all log raises in promotion years over employee's career, minus arithmetic mean of all log raises in non-promotion years over employee's career.
*Significant at 10%; **Significant at 5%; ***Significant at 1%.
The values appearing in parentheses are standard errors of the estimated coefficients.

bonuses reduce subsequent exit. Rather, it is likely that some workers exert effort in a manner that is appropriate to reward with higher pay in their present job, but that it does not make them more qualified at the next level. This is not an indication of a relationship between bonuses and base salary, because the raises examined here are changes in total compensation, which includes bonuses.

In the process of considering two different signaling mechanisms, I have contrasted the effects of discretionary bonuses and fast jobs. Bonuses reduce the rate of subsequent exit, suggesting that they may encourage workers to invest in the firm; fast jobs do not reduce subsequent exit. Similarly, fast jobs do not reduce the wage premium associated with promotion, as they might if they signaled ability to the outside labor market; interestingly, bonuses do reduce this promotion premium.

Table 9. Probit Marginal Effects on Real Wage Decreases Among Within-Level Wage Changes.

	1	2
Job promotion rate	−12.16%***	−5.80%
	(4.56%)	(4.45%)
Age	–	0.55%*
		(0.31%)
Age squared	–	−1.91 e−5
		(4 e−5)
Education	–	1.41%
		(1.09%)
Education squared	–	−0.04%
		(0.03%)
Tenure	–	1.28%***
		(0.34%)
Tenure squared	–	−0.04%**
		(0.02%)
Control for gender	No	Yes
Controls for year	Yes	Yes
Controls for level	Yes	Yes
Pseudo R^2	0.03	0.05
Observations	17,086	17,086
Conditional mean	0.176	0.176

Errors clustered by employee.
*Significant at 10%; **Significant at 5%; ***Significant at 1%.
The values appearing in parentheses are standard errors of the marginal effect.

If fast jobs offer more precise evaluation of a worker's ability, they should lead both to more promotions and to more wage decreases (adjusted for inflation) or exits. Empirically, fast jobs do lead to exit at some levels, but the effect is not consistent.

Table 9 and Fig. 3 compare annual wage changes to test for differences in how the firm learns about worker ability. Table 9 shows that fast jobs are less likely to lead to real wage decreases; we might expect them to be more likely to lead to real wage decreases if Alternative Prediction 3 were true. Including observable worker characteristics reduces the effect by half (6 percent of the difference in job promotion rates instead of 12 percent) and eliminates the statistical significance. This reduction in wage decreases is not driven directly by promotion, as the sample is restricted to within-level wage changes.

Fig. 3 reveals that the distribution of within-level wage changes resulting from fast jobs (the top quartile) is remarkably similar to slow jobs (the

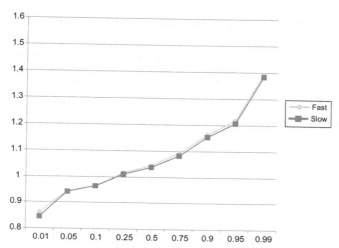

Fig. 3. Distribution of Real Wage Changes (Within Level) Resulting from Fast and Slow Jobs. Percentile of Distribution is Given on Horizontal Axis. "Fast" is Defined as at or above 75th Percentile of Job Promotion Rate for its Level. "Slow" is defined as at or below 25th Percentile of Job Promotion Rate for its Level.

bottom quartile), but uniformly and slightly higher. This contradicts Alternative Prediction 3. The finding that slower jobs are more likely to result in real wage decreases is in fact driven mostly by the second quartile from the bottom.

As a final note, immediate promotion is not the only observed driver of career progression. Lateral transfers of any sort raise the probability of promotion. Table 10 highlights a limitation of the fast-job approach for predicting promotions, by showing the importance of lateral moves.

Controlling for job promotion rate and observable worker characteristics, having been transferred to a slower job increases the probability of promotion by close to 6 percentage points. If the reason for this lateral transfer were always *because* it is to a slower job, this would be illogical and a clear violation of the theory. However, functional assignment in a real firm is a multi-dimensional problem. Some workers may be transferred between functions precisely because they are marked for promotion and are being given a broader view of the firm, and some of the positions they are rotated into may happen to be slow jobs. Lateral transfers to a faster job have a similar effect, although with a smaller magnitude of 4.5 percentage points.[4]

Table 10. Probit Marginal Effects of Lateral Transfers for Promotion.

	1	2	3	4
Lateralled to fasta	4.54%***	6.74%***	1.80%*	4.46%***
	(1.13%)	(1.12%)	(1.06%)	(1.08%)
Lateralled to slowb	3.33%***	4.50%***	5.89%***	5.87%***
	(1.15%)	(1.10%)	(1.22%)	(1.15%)
Current job promotion rate	–	–	36.29%***	22.97%***
			(1.92%)	(1.78%)
Age	–	−0.68%***	–	−0.47%***
		(0.18%)		(0.18%)
Age squared	–	−6.96 e−7	–	−2.32 e−5
		(2 e−5)		(2 e−5)
Education	–	1.70%***	–	1.66%***
		(0.64%)		(0.63%)
Education squared	–	−9.43 e−5	–	−0.01%
		(1.9 e−4)		(0.02%)
Tenure	–	1.32%***	–	1.58%***
		(0.23%)		(0.23%)
Tenure squared	–	−0.08%***	–	−0.10%***
		(0.02%)		(0.02%)
Control for gender	No	Yes	No	Yes
Controls for year	Yes	Yes	Yes	Yes
Controls for level	Yes	Yes	Yes	Yes
Pseudo R^2	0.09	0.13	0.10	0.13
Observations	40,889	40,889	40,889	40,889

Errors clustered by employee.
[a]"Lateralled to fast" indicates that the worker has been moved at some point into her current job from a job at the same level with a promotion rate at least 33 percent lower.
[b]"Lateralled to slow" indicates having been moved into her current job from one with a promotion rate 50% higher.
*Significant at 10%; ***Significant at 1%.
The values appearing in parentheses are standard errors of the marginal effect.

CONCLUSION

This article demonstrates that, within one mid-sized financial services firm, there are persistent and systematic differences in the rate at which jobs lead to promotion. Workers in fast-promotion jobs tend to be younger than their peers at the same hierarchical level. The evidence is consistent with a theory that some positions, referred to as "fast jobs," involve accumulation of human capital that is more valuable at higher-level positions than the experience acquired in "slow jobs." This human capital is unlikely to be strictly firm-specific, since it also can lead to exit. There is no evidence that workers in these jobs are less expensive to promote. Learning about the worker's type appears to operate similarly in fast and slow positions, since the distribution of wage changes is similar.

The firm's strategy for promoting talented workers can lead to unequal advancement among workers. It suggests that the firm identifies workers early on who appear to have high ability, and that it strategically grooms them for advancement. In other words, characteristics or biases that have a small impact in a firm's early assessment could lead to magnified differences in career outcomes. From the firm's perspective, accurately identifying potential well in advance of promotion could be a key driver of efficient allocation and overall productivity.

This firm experienced steady growth and a stable internal structure during the sample period. Future studies must determine whether the same results hold in different industries and different time periods. In particular, the rate at which the firm is able to learn about the worker's ability may be an important factor that drives promotion differences.

NOTES

1. There are any number of unobservable factors that could give certain jobs an advantage (such as location or a strong supervisor), but if these factors are persistent across a 20-year sample, then they are likely to be part of the firm's talent strategy.
2. Appendix A presents the proofs.
3. These results apply only for 1981 through 1988, because I do not observe bonuses before then.
4. Recall that smaller effect of transfers to faster jobs is found after controlling for the job-promotion rate. The total effect of transfer to a fast job is more advantageous than the total effect of transfer to a slow job.

REFERENCES

Ariga, K., Ohkusa, Y., & Brunello, G. (1999). Fast track: Is it in the genes? The promotion policy of a large Japanese firm. *Journal of Economic Behavior and Organization, 38,* 385–402.

Baker, G., Gibbs, M., & Holmstrom, B. (1994a). The internal economics of the firm: Evidence from personnel data. *Quarterly Journal of Economics, 109*(4), 881–919.

Baker, G., Gibbs, M., & Holmstrom, B. (1994b). The wage policy of a firm. *Quarterly Journal of Economics, 109*(4), 921–955.

Belzil, C., & Bognanno, M. (2008). Promotions, demotions, Halo effects and earnings dynamics of American executives. *Journal of Labor Economics, 26*(2), 287–310.

Belzil, C., & Bognanno, M. (2010). The promotion dynamics of American executives. *Research in Labor Economics*, *30*, 189–231.

Bernhardt, D. (1995). Strategic promotion and compensation. *Review of Economic Studies*, *62*(2), 315–339.

Bernhardt, D., & Scoones, D. (1998). Promotion, turnover, and discretionary human capital acquisition. *Journal of Labor Economics*, *16*(1), 122–141.

Bretz, R. D., Jr., Rynes, S. L., & Quinn-Trank, C. (2002). Attracting applicants in the war for talent: Differences in work preferences among high achievers. *Journal of Business and Psychology*, *16*(3), 331–345.

Chiappori, P.-A., Salanie, B., & Valentin, J. (1999). Early starters versus late beginners. *Journal of Political Economy*, *107*(4), 731–760.

DeVaro, J., & Waldman, M. (2007). *The signaling role of promotions: Further theory and empirical evidence*. Mimeo: Cornell University ILR School.

Dohmen, T., Kriechel, B., & Pfann, G. (2004). Monkey bars and ladders: The importance of lateral and vertical job mobility in internal labor market careers. *Journal of Population Economics*, *17*(2), 193–228.

Gibbons, R., & Waldman, M. (1999). A theory of wage and promotion dynamics inside firms. *Quarterly Journal of Economics*, *114*(4), 1321–1358.

Gibbons, R., & Waldman, M. (2006). Enriching a theory of wage and promotion dynamics inside firms. *Journal of Labor Economics*, *24*(1), 59–107.

Gibbs, M., & Hendricks, W. (2004). Do formal salary systems really matter? *Industrial and Labor Relations Review*, *58*(1), 71–93.

Meyer, M. (1991). Learning from coarse information: Biased contests and career profiles. *Review of Economic Studies*, *58*, 15–41.

Meyer, M. (1992). Biased contests and moral hazard: Implications for career profiles. *Annales d'Economie et de Statistique*, *25–26*, 165–187.

Prendergast, C. (1992). Career development and specific human capital collection. *Journal of the Japanese and International Economies*, *6*, 207–227.

Seltzer, A., & Merrett, D. (2000). Personnel policies at the Union Bank of Australia: Evidence from the 1888–1900 entry cohorts. *Journal of Labor Economics*, *18*(4), 573–613.

Treble, J., van Gameren, E., Bridges, S., & Barmby, T. (2001). The internal economics of the firm: Further evidence from personnel data. *Labour Economics*, *8*(5), 531–552.

Waldman, M. (1984). Job assignments, signalling and efficiency. *Rand Journal of Economics*, *15*(2), 255–267.

Waldman, M. (1990). Up-or-out contracts: A signaling perspective. *Journal of Labor Economics*, *8*(2), 230–250.

APPENDIX A: PROOFS

Proof of Proposition 1. (iv) $[d_2 + c_2\theta^e_{i3}f(\alpha x_s + x_f)] - [d_{1s} + c_1\theta^e_{i3}f(x_s + x_f)]$ is increasing in θ^e_{i3} in any scenario where θ''_3 exists. The derivative with respect to θ^e_{i3} is $c_2f(\alpha x_s + x_f) - c_1f(x_s + x_f)$ and, if this is negative, then the full expression is also negative for any possible value of θ^e_{i3}, and the allocation problem is trivial. Therefore, a value of θ^e_{i3} greater than the point of indifference implies that productivity in level 2 is higher.

(iii) Similarly, $[d_2 + c_2\theta^e_{i2}f(\alpha x_s + x_f) + V_3(x_s, x_f + 1; \theta^e_{i2})] - \max\{d_{1s} + c_1\theta^e_{i2}f(x_s + x_f) + V_3(x_s + 1, x_f; \theta^e_{i2}), d_{1f} + c_1\theta^e_{i2}f(x_s + x_f) + V_3(x_s, x_f + 1; \theta^e_{i2})\}$ is increasing in θ^e_{i2}, due to $c_2 > c_1$.

(ii) $[d_{1f} + c_1\theta^e_{i2}f(x_s + x_f) + V_3(x_s, x_f + 1; \theta^e_{i2})] - [d_{1s} + c_1\theta^e_{i2}f(x_s + x_f) + V_3(x_s + 1, x_f; \theta^e_{i2})]$ is increasing in θ^e_{i2} because x_f is worth more in level 2, and it is already shown that likelihood of promotion is increasing in θ^e_{i2} (recalling that θ^e_{i2} is predictive of θ^e_{i3}).

(i) $[d_{1f} + c_1\theta^e_{i1}f(0) + V_2(0, 1; \theta^e_{i1})] - [d_{1s} + c_1\theta^e_{i1}f(0) + V_2(1, 0; \theta^e_{i1})]$ is increasing in θ^e_{i1} because x_f is worth more in level 2, and θ^e_{i1} is predictive of θ^e_{i2} and θ^e_{i3}, both of which increase probability of allocation to level 2. QED

Proof of Proposition 2. Consider the worker with perceived innate ability $\theta^e_{i2} = \theta''_2(0, 1)$. Therefore, if he spent period one in Position 1f, her expected value is equal in job 1f and level 2:

$$d_2 + c_2\theta^e_{i2}f(1) + V_3(0, 2; \theta^e_{i2}) = d_{1f} + c_1\theta^e_{i2}f(1) + V_3(0, 2; \theta^e_{i2})$$

This implies $d_2 + c_2\theta^e_{i2}f(1) = d_{1f} + c_1\theta^e_{i2}f(1)$.

Suppose, however, that she spent period 1 in Position 1s. Then, her expected value in level 2 is $d_2 + c_2\theta^e_{i2}f(\alpha) + V_3(1, 1; \theta^e_{i2})$. This is less than her expected value in job 1f, because

$$[d_2 + c_2\theta^e_{i2}f(\alpha) + V_3(1, 1; \theta^e_{i2})] - [d_{1f} + c_1\theta^e_{i2}f(1) + V_3(1, 1; \theta^e_{i2})]$$
$$= [d_2 + c_2\theta^e_{i2}f(\alpha)] - [d_{1f} + c_1\theta^e_{i2}f(1)]$$
$$= [d_2 + c_2\theta^e_{i2}f(\alpha)] - [d_2 + c_2\theta^e_{i2}f(1)] < 0$$

Therefore, she is below the threshold $\theta''_2(1, 0)$ for promotion from the slow job, and $\theta''_2(0, 1) < \theta''_2(1, 0)$. A similar argument establishes that $\theta''_3(0, 2) < \theta''_3(1, 1) < \theta''_3(2, 0)$. QED

Proof of Proposition 3. Consider the mass of workers in the fast track in period 1 and in period2. The number of workers in Position 1f in the first period, relative to the size of a cohort, is $1 - F_1(\theta'_1)$. The fraction of a cohort in Position 1f in the second period is

$$(1 - F_1(\theta'_1))[F_2(\theta''_2(0,1)) - F_2(\theta'_2(0,1))|\theta^e_{i1} > \theta'_1] + F_1(\theta'_1)$$
$$\times [F_2(\theta''_2(1,0)) - F_2(\theta'_2(1,0))|\theta^e_{i1} < \theta'_1]$$

which, using Assumption 1, is $\leq (1 - F_1(\theta'_1)) \times [F_2(\theta''_2(0,1)) - F_2(\theta'_2(0,1))|$ $\theta^e_{i1} > \theta'_1] + F_1(\theta'_1)[1 - F_1(\theta'_1)]$which, using Assumption 2, is $\leq (1 - F_1(\theta'_1))$ $[1 - F_1(\theta'_1)] + F_1(\theta'_1)[1 - F_1(\theta'_1)] = 1 - F_1(\theta'_1)$.

Therefore, there are at least as many workers in Position 1f in period 1 as in period 2. Since there are no workers in the fast track in period three, the average age of workers in the fast track is at most 1.5, while the average age of workers in the slow track must be at least 1.5, even if all workers are in Position 2 by the third period.   QED

APPENDIX B: MEASUREMENT ERROR IN THE JOB PROMOTION RATE

The key right-hand side variable in this article is a constructed measure of a job's tendency to lead to promotion. There is no direct observation of people marked for rapid advancement or of jobs designed to groom them. Therefore, this quality is observed with noise. The more people who have been in a given position and the longer the job has been observed, the more precisely I can estimate how "fast" it is. Some differences across observed job titles in the rate at which people are promoted out of them is bound to occur even if the actual jobs are identical.

The key question is whether this noise could be correlated with other variables of interest. If not, then the noisy measurement biases estimated coefficients toward zero, and the existence of any observed effect is clear evidence of a real effect. In most regressions run in this article, there is a clear separation between the past and the future. Furthermore, jobs not fitting into any recognized hierarchical level (and therefore incapable of leading to observed promotions) are excluded from the analysis. The rate at which other workers have been promoted from a job in the past predicts future outcomes for the worker. The only way for their success to be correlated with the current worker's is through the job to which they were both matched.

The one exception to this temporal separation is the prediction of workers' promotion premiums over the course of their careers. Their respective raises while in this job lower the difference between their average promotion raise and their average within-level raise. Therefore, noise in the promotion of colleagues in the same job could impact their raises and, therefore, their promotion premium, biasing the result. If a colleague being promoted out of the job implies a new colleague being moved into it as a replacement and earning less, this could leave more room for a raise and bias the promotion premium downward. However, the point of Table 8 is that the impact on promotion premium is not significantly negative, and this possible bias does not endanger that conclusion.

THE EFFECT OF VARIABLE PAY SCHEMES ON WORKPLACE ABSENTEEISM

Konstantinos Pouliakas and Nikolaos Theodoropoulos

ABSTRACT

The effect of variable pay schemes on workplace absenteeism is estimated using two cross-sections of private sector British establishments. Establishments that explicitly link pay with individual performance are found to have significantly lower absence rates. The effect is stronger for establishments that offer variable pay schemes to a greater share of their non-managerial workforce. Matched employer–employee data suggest that the effect is robust to a number of sensitivity tests. Establishments that tie a greater proportion of employees' earnings to variable pay schemes experience lower absence rates. Quintile regressions suggest that the effect is greater among establishments with a higher than average ('sustainable') absence rate. Finally, panel data suggest that a feedback mechanism is present; high absenteeism in the past is correlated with a greater future incidence of individual variable pay schemes, which, in turn, is correlated with lower current absence rates.

Keywords: Performance-related pay; Absenteeism; Incentives

JEL classifications: J22; J33; C21

Research in Labor Economics, Volume 36, 109–157
Copyright © 2012 by Emerald Group Publishing Limited
All rights of reproduction in any form reserved
ISSN: 0147-9121/doi:10.1108/S0147-9121(2012)0000036008

INTRODUCTION

There is increasing interest on the economics of absenteeism. This has been spurred mainly by a growing awareness that the economic and social costs (e.g. sickness benefits, health care, early retirement) of absenteeism are considerable. Estimates of the direct cost of absenteeism for the UK economy, which exclude difficult to quantify effects (e.g. impact on work climate; production bottlenecks) have exhibited an upward trend in recent decades. For example, they have risen from £6 billion per year in the 1980s (Brown & Sessions, 1996) to £11.6 billion in 1993 (Barham & Begum, 2005) and to £17 billion in 2009 (Chartered Institute of Personnel and Development, 2009). In most advanced economies absenteeism is now believed to account for economic losses of approximately 2–3% of Gross Domestic Product, or a typical year's growth (Edwards & Greasley, 2010; EURO-FOUND, 1997). At a policy level the UK and other governments have also become increasingly concerned with the escalating number of people claiming sickness and incapacity benefits, a phenomenon that has overwhelmed social security budgets. For instance, expenditure on sickness and incapacity benefits in 2002 was four-times greater than the respective amount devoted to unemployment insurance (Department for Work and Pensions, 2002).

While economists have focused in the past on elements of the job contract that interact with the cost of absence, such as the basic wage and sick pay replacement rates (Barmby, Orme, & Treble, 1991; Henrekson & Persson, 2004; Johansson & Palme, 1996), an examination of the impact of performance-related pay (PRP) schemes on absence rates has been neglected. The continued prevalence of contingent pay[1] schemes in modern British organizations has been extensively noted (Millward, Stevens, Smart, & Hawes, 1992; Pendleton, Whitfield, & Bryson, 2009). Such schemes have traditionally taken the form of incentives tied to individual (objective or subjective) output (e.g. payment by results, merit pay), collective schemes based on wider measures of performance (e.g. group or workplace bonuses) and more aggregate 'shared capitalist' schemes (e.g. profit-related pay, share-ownership). According to Bryson and Freeman (2010) they are becoming increasingly more common. However, due to data constraints many studies in the past have examined the impact of a catch-all measure of PRP on the absenteeism of specific firms or industries (Brown, Fakhfakh, & Sessions, 1999; Engellandt & Riphahn, 2011; Wilson & Peel, 1991). This has confounded the effect of individual measures of PRP on absenteeism in most cases, and has prohibited the detection of the exact incentive power of dissimilar types of PRP schemes.

This article examines the effect of a wide and heterogeneous set of PRP measures on the absence rates of private sector British firms.[2] It uses data from two cross-sections (1998 and 2004) of the Workplace Employment Relations Survey (WERS), a merged subsample of the 2004 WERS data with the Annual Survey of Hours and Earnings (ASHE) and the 1998–2004 WERS Panel Survey.[3] This permits the investigation of the relationship between a variety of PRP instruments (including their coverage and intensity) and absenteeism. The WERS is a representative dataset of British establishments that covers a wide range of workplace characteristics with which we attempt to comprehensively capture firm heterogeneity. It also permits the matching of employer–employee information when necessary. Given the sparse previous literature on the effects of variable pay schemes on absenteeism, which has typically relied on a narrowly defined population (e.g. a single firm or plants within a firm) there is a clear need for using large nationally representative samples to examine the topic. Despite the shortcomings of the WERS dataset, its questions pertaining to variable pay schemes, workplace absence and numerous firm characteristics provides a particularly rich source of information that allows us to examine the ceteris paribus relationship between absenteeism and PRP. Further, the two cross-sections and the WERS panel data allow us to investigate the relationship at different points in time.

Ceteris paribus, we find that firms that employ PRP schemes tied to the assessment of individual merit and performance have significantly lower absence rates. This negative relation becomes stronger in firms that offer PRP to a greater proportion of their non-managerial workforce, and in those firms where the share of workers' earnings subject to variable pay is greater. A series of sensitivity tests confirm that the inverse relation between PRP and absence is robust to self-selection bias and to the inclusion of a number of significant confounding factors (e.g. administrative measures of earnings and working hours; injury and illness rate of establishments). It is also found to be robust to organization fixed effects, which implies that the negative effect persists even among highly similar establishments that are part of the same organization. Further, quintile regression results suggest that PRP has an asymmetric effect on absence. PRP has a stronger effect on establishments that have an absence rate that exceeds a 'typical' or average level of absence. Finally, evidence of a causal chain of reaction is detected, indicating that firms that suffer from high absence rates in the past are more likely to subsequently adopt individual PRP schemes. The same firms are, in turn, observed to benefit from lower current levels of absenteeism.

The structure of the article is as follows. The second section reviews the hypothesized relation between performance pay and absenteeism, an important indicator of firm performance. The third section describes the data. The fourth section presents the empirical estimates of the absenteeism–PRP relationship, while the fifth and sixth sections engage in a number of important sensitivity and endogeneity tests that exploit the WERS–ASHE and 1998–2004 WERS Panel Surveys, respectively. Finally, the seventh section concludes.

PRP AND ABSENTEEISM

Economists originally viewed the absence phenomenon as a manifestation of labour supply decisions (Allen, 1981). Therefore, greater attention was paid to how hours of work adjust to economic incentives such as wages and statutory sick pay (e.g. Barmby et al., 1991). Several demographic characteristics of workers have also been identified as important predictors of absenteeism, such as being female or of young age (Dione & Dostie, 2007; Vistnes, 1997). Other researchers have examined whether there is a 'disciplining' impact of unemployment on attendance behaviour (Arai & Thoursie, 2005; Barmby, Sessions, & Tremble, 1994; Leigh, 1985). Recently, economists have turned their focus to the demand side of the market, and most notably to firm characteristics that are argued to affect the cost of absence. Typical examples include working time schedules (Brown & Sessions, 1996), unionization (Allen, 1984), 'assembly line' technologies (Coles, Lanfranchi, Skalli, & Treble, 2007; Coles & Tremble, 1996), teamwork (Heywood & Jirjahn, 2004; Heywood, Jirjahn, & Wei, 2008) and firm size (Barmby & Stephan, 2000).

Despite the fact that merit wage increases and attendance bonuses were identified as two 'weapons' that firms can use to raise the penalty of employee absence (Allen, 1981), an examination of the impact of different PRP schemes on absenteeism has been sparse in the literature. According to the standard principal-agent model, firms will attempt to combat moral hazard by conditioning their employees' remuneration to signals of their effort (e.g. the amount of man-hours in the workplace). In equilibrium, firms will be willing to offer incentive pay when its marginal cost is outweighed by the increase in expected revenue, the latter related to a reduced sick wage bill associated with less employee absence. Similarly, workers will be incentivized to improve their attendance behaviour when the marginal gain from not being absent exceeds the marginal cost of effort. This will be determined by the difference between the utility of the overall wage (base salary and bonus pay), on the one hand, and the sum of reservation utility and sick pay, on the other.

Since bonus pay is typically not covered (or partly covered) by the sickness insurance schemes of firms (Barmby et al., 1991), the shadow price of absence is attenuated by the offer of incentive pay. Furthermore, it is expected that diligent or healthier employees will self-select into firms offering PRP (Lazear, 1986, 2000). Due to the greater effort and/or specific traits of those receiving incentive pay, a positive relationship between PRP and earnings/productivity has been documented (Booth & Frank, 1999; Gielen, Kerkhofs, & van Ours, 2010; Seiler, 1984). The gap between contractual and actual hours should therefore be bridged as workers respond optimally to the higher opportunity cost of leisure entailed by PRP. In addition, PRP schemes constitute part of a bundle of managerial innovations, known as High Performance Workplace Practices (HPWPs) (Bloom & Van Reenen, 2010). Since HPWPs are believed to breed greater feelings of employee empowerment and job satisfaction (Bauer, 2004), absenteeism is also expected to be negatively related to PRP via this avenue.

Counter-arguments suggest that the provision of PRP is likely to result in greater absence rates. PRP schemes may undermine valuable teamwork by fostering an individualistic organizational culture that is permeated by envy and free-riding (Holmström, 1979; Milgrom & Roberts, 1992). Moreover, high-powered PRP schemes are believed to heighten the power asymmetry between supervisors and the workforce (Kohn, 1993). Psychological concerns over a potential 'crowding-out' of intrinsic motivation and morale have been raised, with assumed adverse effects on productivity and turnout at work (Frey, 1993; Frey & Jegen, 2001). PRP has also been associated with adverse health outcomes, such as dissatisfaction with work-related stress (Pouliakas & Theodossiou, 2009), an increased incidence of workplace injuries (Bender, Green, & Heywood, 2012; Freeman & Kleiner, 2005) and 'presenteeism' (Chatterji & Tilley, 2002; Skatun, 2003). The latter refers to a greater likelihood of workers becoming chronically ill due to pressure to return back to work earlier than what is required for a healthy recovery. Furthermore, inadequacies in compensation design have been highlighted, such as time inconsistency problems when offering long-term incentives to temporary contract employees (Schnebller & Kopelman, 1983) and perverse reactions to capped bonuses that are stretched over extended qualifying time periods. For instance, workers are found to 'backload' their absence days towards periods in which they anticipate to have already met their targets (Frick, Gotzen, & Simmons, 2008).

The above conflicting hypotheses suggest that there is no theoretical consensus regarding the overall effect of PRP on absenteeism. This ambiguity is also mirrored in the empirical evidence, with some studies confirming the beneficial impact of financial rewards on absence rates (e.g. Dale-Olsen, 2012; Hassink & Koning, 2005; Jacobson, 1989), while others find non-measurable effects (Engellandt & Riphahn, 2011).

DATA SOURCES

Our data are mainly derived from the 1998 and 2004 cross-sections of the Workplace Employment Relations Survey (WERS). Also, a merged subsample of the 2004 WERS data with the Annual Survey of Hours and Earnings (ASHE) and the 1998–2004 WERS Panel Survey are utilized.[4] As in Heywood et al. (2008), only private sector establishments are retained for the purpose of the empirical analysis.[5] In addition, firms that offer PRP solely to managerial employees are dropped from the analysis, since non-managerial workers and executives are likely to be faced with a completely different set of incentive compatibility constraints (Murphy 1999).[6] Moreover, some of the PRP questions in the WERS survey are asked only if non-managerial workers are eligible for the respective instruments.

The WERS Cross-Section Data

The 1998 and 2004 cross-sections are the fourth and fifth instalments of a government funded series of surveys conducted at British workplaces. The previous surveys were conducted in 1980, 1984 and 1990. The sample of workplaces was randomly drawn from the Interdepartmental Business Register (IDBR). This is maintained by the Office for National Statistics (ONS) and is considered to be the highest quality sampling frame of workplaces available in the United Kingdom. The sample is stratified by workplace size and industry and larger workplaces and some industries are overrepresented (Chaplin, Mangla, Purdon, & Airey, 2005). An establishment is defined as comprising the activities of a single employer at a single set of premises, for instance, a single branch of a bank, a car factory or a school. The survey comprises three main sections: the 'Management Questionnaire' (MQ) (face-to-face interviews with the most senior manager with day-to-day responsibility for personnel matters), the 'Worker Representative Questionnaire' and the 'Employee Questionnaire'. All three interview-based questionnaires were conducted using Computer-Assisted Personal Interview (CAPI).

We use data from the MQ as information on absence rates is only available in this part of the survey.[7] Nonetheless, the matched employer–employee element of the data is exploited for the purpose of robustness checks. The 1998 (2004) sample comprises of 2,173 (2,006) establishments, which, after retaining private sector establishments that extend the offer of PRP to the non-managerial workforce, is reduced to 1,192 (1,281).[8] Due to the stratified nature of the survey, the estimates are weighted in order to be representative of the sampling population.

The MQ collected data from managers about the pattern of employee non-attendance in the workplace. The exact question was phrased: '*Over the past 12 months what percentage of work days was lost through employee sickness or absence at this establishment? Please exclude authorized leave or absence, employees away on secondment or courses, or days lost through industrial action*'.[9] This question captures mainly unplanned absence such as casual sick days as well as absence due to employees not turning up to work for some other reason.

Among workplaces where managers were able to provide an answer,[10] the average absence rate in the 1998 (2004) sample equates to a loss of 4.3% (4.6%) of working days per establishment.[11] Fig. 1(a) (1998) and Fig. 1(b) (2004) present the distribution of the absence rate across workplaces. It is evident that there is significant variation of absence rates across establishments in both years. Almost all workplaces reported some degree of absenteeism. Those in the lower decile have a mean absence rate of 1% or below in both waves, while managers in establishments in the highest decile reported that at least 8% (10%) of their work days were lost in 1998 (2004). Zero absence rates account for only 2.1% (4.4%) of the non-missing observations in the 1998 (2004) sample, so there is no excess concentration of responses at the left tail of the distribution. In addition, both distributions are skewed to the right, so the median is lower than the mean. For instance, in the 1998 (2004) sample the median is 3.43 (3.0).

Managers were also asked questions regarding the provision of different forms of variable pay schemes in their workplace. Table A1 provides detailed definitions for the contingent pay variables of interest in the survey. Importantly, the PRP options were specified differently between the 1998 and 2004 waves. To retain consistency in the PRP categories, the following four groups of contingent pay have been constructed following Pendleton et al. (2009); (i) *individual-based PRP*: this is broken down into two constituent parts that include an objective and a subjective component, namely *individual payment by results* (IPBR) and *merit pay* (MP). The former is defined as PRP offered on the basis of measurement of an employee's

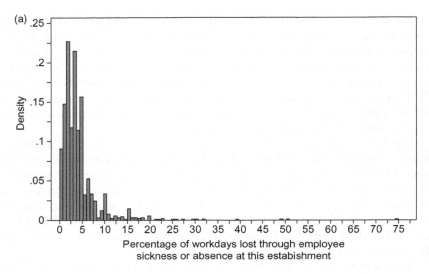

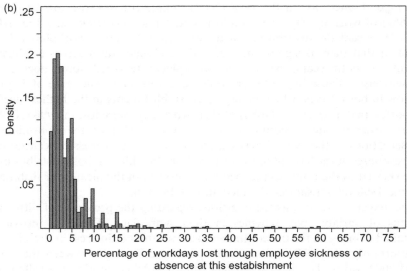

Fig. 1. (a) Workplace Absence Distribution in 1998. (b) Workplace Absence Distribution in 2004. *Note*: The absence question in both waves comes from the management questionnaire and was phrased as follows:

'*Over the past 12 months what percentage of work days was lost through employee sickness or absence at this establishment? Please exclude authorized leave or absence, employees away on secondment or courses, or days lost through industrial action*'.

individual performance or output, whereas the latter captures the subjective evaluation of individual performance by a supervisor or manager (MacLeod & Malcomson, 1998); (ii) *collective payment by results* (CPBR): this refers to PRP determined according to group, workplace or organization-based measures of performance or output; (iii) *profit-related payments or bonuses* (PFRP); and (iv) *employee share ownership* schemes (ESO) (e.g. share incentive plans, save as you earn, company share options).[12]

It is clear from Table 1 (Panel A) that a relatively large number of firms offer PRP of various types in the two waves.[13] About 11–12% of workplaces have IPBR and CPBR schemes in place in 1998, while around 40% utilize PFRP. The incidence of ESO is stable at 18% in both waves. MP is offered by a non-trivial proportion of workplaces (15%) in 2004, while there is also a substantial incidence of IPBR (21%) and CPBR (24%) schemes in that year.

The ASHE–WERS Data

The WERS MQ collects limited information on wages. Even when using the data provided by the Employee Questionnaire, details on hourly and weekly wages are only provided within banded categories. Furthermore, no information is provided in the WERS cross-section data indicating the proportion of employees' pay that is linked to performance measures. In order to overcome these deficiencies, the merged ASHE–WERS dataset has been utilized. This is constructed by combining information on individuals contained within the 2004 ASHE with workplace variables collected from the WERS 2004 MQ. The ASHE has taken place since 2004 and contains data on a 1% sample of British employees, randomly selected on the basis of the last two digits of their national insurance numbers. It is possible to merge the WERS and ASHE datasets on the basis of a combination of enterprise reference numbers and workplace postcodes (Davies & Welpton, 2004). After merging the two datasets, 5,922 individuals remain from 785 matched workplaces, 3,248 (55%) of which are employed in 393 private sector establishments. This sample is characterized by a greater prevalence of workers who are employed in larger workplaces and in certain industries (such as utilities and manufacturing), and is therefore not representative of British establishments as is the original WERS sampling frame. To ensure that the empirical analysis based on this subsample is not biased relative to the original 2004 WERS cross-section design, an appropriate weighting procedure has thus been utilized following Davies and Welpton (2004).[14]

Table 1. Descriptive Statistics (Mean, SD) of Variable Pay Schemes.

	1998	2004
Panel A (WERS)		
MP	0.043	0.150
	(0.202)	(0.358)
IPBR	0.125	0.209
	(0.330)	(0.407)
CPBR	0.108	0.237
	(0.311)	(0.426)
PFRP	0.398	0.334
	(0.490)	(0.472)
ESO	0.184	0.184
	(0.387)	(0.388)
OCB	0.271	—
	(0.445)	
Observations (*N*)	1,192	1,281
Panel B (2004 WERS–ASHE)		
Absence rate	—	0.042
		(0.039)
Mean weekly hours per establishment	—	33.31
		(6.13)
Mean annual gross earnings per establishment	—	24183
		(20220)
Mean hourly earnings per establishment	—	13.14
		(6.14)
Mean incentive intensity per establishment (PRP > 0)	—	0.04
		(0.07)
Observations (*N*)	—	All: 785
		Private sector: 393
Panel C (WERS Panel 1998–2004)		
	1998	2004
MP	0.074	0.531
	(0.261)	(0.500)
	[*r* = −0.172;	[*r* = 0.186;
	p = 0.000]	*p* = 0.000]
IPBR	0.151	0.182
	(0.358)	(0.386)
	[*r* = −0.086;	[*r* = 0.011;
	p = 0.055]	*p* = 0.805]
CPBR	0.146	0.227
	(0.353)	(0.419)
	[*r* = −0.087;	[*r* = −0.069;
	p = 0.052]	*p* = 0.122]
PFRP	0.448	0.434

Table 1. (*Continued*)

	1998	2004
	(0.498)	(0.496)
	[r = −0.039;	[r = 0.030;
ESO	p = 0.381]	p = 0.497]
	0.204	0.179
	(0.403)	(0.383)
	[r = −0.049;	[r = −0.072;
Observations (N)	p = 0.274]	p = 0.107]
	587	587

Note: Means are weighted using establishment weights and can differ from those indicated by the raw data. Standard deviations are in parentheses. '—' implies that the variable is not present. r denotes the Pearson pairwise correlation coefficient between the 1998 absence rate and the respective PRP scheme in each year of the panel [panel weights used]. In Panel B, 785 observations (393 in the private sector) remain after merging the WERS with the ASHE dataset. In Panel C, 587 of the 956 continuing establishments in the 2004 WERS Panel Survey are in the private sector.

The statistical results in Panel B remain Crown Copyright, and should be acknowledged either as such or as 'Source: ONS'.

The ASHE contains information on employees' working hours and earnings obtained by administrative employer records, thus providing accurate measures. It also permits identification of the component of employees' gross annual earnings that is tied to an overall measure of bonus or incentive payments including profit sharing, productivity performance, bonuses, piece-work and commission payments. Almost 20% ($n = 1,137$) of the individuals in the sample are recipients of some form of incentive pay, corresponding to a median of 6% (£1,000) of their annual gross pay. When averaged across establishments, it is evident that about 42% of workplaces offer some form of contingent pay scheme (i.e. there is at least one employee within the firm whose remuneration contains elements of incentive pay). As seen in Table 1 (Panel B), the average proportion of incentive pay in relation to earnings in the sample of firms that have adopted contingent pay schemes is 4%.

The 1998–2004 WERS Panel Survey Data

The 1998–2004 Panel Survey returned to a random selection of the 2,191 workplaces that participated in the 1998 cross-section, with the purpose of investigating the changes that had taken place in those workplaces over the preceding six years. Some 1,479 workplaces from the 1998 wave were selected to be traced for re-interview in 2004, though 1,247 were classified as continuing workplaces. The survey, with a response rate of 77%, yielded an achieved sample of 956 continuing establishments. Unfortunately, no information on absence rates was collected in the 2004 wave. However, the panel survey allows for the identification of the relationship between the absence rate and PRP status of firms in 1998, with the probability that the same firms employed PRP schemes in 2004. This information is used in order to draw inferences about the causal nature of the effect of PRP on absenteeism and the existence of any dynamic interactions between absenteeism and PRP.

An investigation of the dynamic correlations in the raw data reveals that a significant proportion (86%) of firms that had PRP schemes in 1998 continued to use variable remuneration in 2004. Importantly, 47% of firms that did not employ any form of contingent pay in 1998 are observed to do so six years later. Table 1 (Panel C) also indicates an increasing proportion of firms using MP,[15] IPBR and CPBR schemes over time, while there was a slight decrease in the use of more aggregate PFRP and ESO-type incentives. Furthermore, significant correlation coefficients (r) can be observed in Panel C between the absence rate of firms in 1998 and the incidence of variable pay in the same firms in 1998 (negative correlation) and 2004 (positive correlation), suggesting that firms with a high absence rate in the past were more likely to adopt PRP schemes in the future.[16]

EFFECT OF PRP ON ABSENCE RATES

Descriptive Statistics of the PRP–Absenteeism Relationship

Table 2 provides some simple cross-tabulations of the raw data on absence and various types of incentive pay. An independent samples t-test confirms that only MP is associated with significantly lower absence rates in both waves, though IPBR, CPBR and other cash bonuses (OCB) are also conducive to higher workplace attendance rates in the 1998 sample. These results highlight the important and distinct impact that different PRP instruments exert on absenteeism.

Table 2.   Mean of Work Days Lost by Type of Variable Pay Scheme.

	1998			2004		
	Yes	No	t-test	Yes	No	t-test
MP	3.198 (2.439)	4.226 (4.914)	3.086	4.111 (4.869)	4.885 (6.962)	2.189
IPBR	3.409 (2.255)	4.385 (5.225)	4.327	4.845 (5.908)	4.639 (6.716)	0.529
CPBR	3.601 (2.718)	4.328 (5.151)	2.915	4.824 (6.362)	4.642 (6.572)	0.457
PFRP	4.081 (3.735)	4.348 (5.895)	0.909	4.640 (6.506)	4.732 (6.521)	0.251
ESO	4.407 (4.761)	4.098 (4.851)	1.051	5.076 (6.312)	4.522 (6.596)	1.430
OCB	3.769 (3.460)	4.407 (5.340)	2.474	—	—	—

Note: Means are weighted. Standard deviations are in parentheses. '—' implies that the variable is not present.

Effect of Incidence and Coverage of PRP Schemes on Absence

In order to detect the ceteris paribus relation between financial incentives and the absence rate, a number of important determinants of absenteeism are taken into account. As identified in the relevant literature (e.g. Heywood et al., 2008), these include variables describing the *demographic composition of the workforce* (e.g. proportion of employees by gender and age), *firm identity* (e.g. establishment size, region of operation) and *the nature of production* (e.g. industrial sector, shares of occupational groups). Firm characteristics that are related to the labour-leisure tradeoff are also taken into account, such as *working time schedules* (e.g. mean establishment hours of work, whether employees engage in shift work, entitlement to an annualized hours scheme), *contractual flexibility* (proportion of employees on fixed term and part-time contracts) and *economic incentives* (mean establishment earnings, unemployment rate by travel to work area). Furthermore, the context of *industrial relations* (trade union density, presence of joint consultative committees and quality circles) and *occupational health and safety policies* (provision of sick pay in excess of statutory requirements, health and safety committees) are included as controls.

Summary statistics of all explanatory variables of interest are presented in Table A2.

We estimate the following equation using Ordinary Least Squares (OLS):

$$\text{Absence}_j = \beta_0 + \beta_1 \text{PRP}_j + \beta_2 W_j + \beta_3 I_j + \beta_4 R_j + \varepsilon_j \qquad (1)$$

The dependent variable Absence_j indicates the absence rate of establishment j, where $j = 1, \ldots, N$, $\text{PRP}_j = \{\text{IBPR, MP, CPRB, PFRP, ESO, OCB}\}$ captures the offer of various PRP schemes within establishments, W_j summarizes workplace characteristics. Industry and region fixed effects are denoted by I_j and R_j respectively, while ε_j is the establishment-specific error term. OLS coefficients of the effect of PRP on *Absence* will be unbiased provided that $E(\varepsilon_j | PRP_j) = 0$. OLS may nevertheless be inappropriate given that Absence_j is a fractional response variable, in which case Papke and Wooldridge (1996) suggest that a logistic model may be more suitable. However, as no significant differences are detected between the estimates of logistic and OLS models in the analysis, the discussion in the remainder of the article presents the OLS coefficients for simplicity.[17]

Panel A of Table 3 presents estimates of the various PRP schemes on the absenteeism of private sector establishments in Britain for both years of data.[18] It is evident that variable pay schemes that reward individual merit on the basis of subjective appraisals have a significant negative effect on the mean absence rate in both waves. IPBR also has a significant inverse relation to absence in 1998. Specifically, firms which utilize MP and IPBR have a one percentage point lower absence rate in the 1998 data compared to firms without such schemes, ceteris paribus. For a mean absence rate of 4.3% (sample absence mean in 1998), the true effect is equal to -23.3 percentage points $[(-1.0/4.3) \times 100]$, which is a considerable effect. A significant negative effect on absenteeism of 0.8 percentage points is also found with respect to the provision of OCB by firms (i.e. an 18.6 percentage point decrease at the mean).[19] In contrast, there is no evidence of a significant link between absence, CPBR, PFRP and ESO.

Column 2 of Table 3 presents similar results for the 2004 wave. The regression coefficient of MP suggests that establishments that adjust their employees' compensation by subjectively evaluating their performance have a lower number of lost workdays compared to those that do not (by 0.8 percentage points). For a mean absence rate of 4.6% (sample absence mean in 2004), this translates to a decrease of 17.4 percentage points in the mean absence rate $[(-0.8/4.6) \times 100]$. As before, no evidence of a significant relationship between collective or aggregate forms of PRP (CPBR, PRRP, ESO) and absenteeism is found. Importantly, the significant negative

Table 3.   The Effect of Variable Pay Schemes on Absence Rate.

Panel A (WERS)		
Dependent Variable: Workplace Absence Rate	1998	2004
MP	−0.011**	−0.008**
	(0.004)	(0.004)
IPBR	−0.010***	0.005
	(0.003)	(0.004)
CPBR	0.0003	−0.005
	(0.004)	(0.004)
PFRP	−0.005	−0.004
	(0.004)	(0.004)
ESO	−0.0003	0.007
	(0.004)	(0.005)
OCB	−0.008***	—
	(0.003)	
R^2	0.110	0.071
Observations (N)	1,192	1,281

Panel B (WERS)		
Proportion of Non-managerial Employees Received PRP in the Last 12 Months	1998	2004
1−39%	−0.008*	0.004
	(0.004)	(0.007)
40−79%	−0.013***	0.005
	(0.004)	(0.006)
80−100%	−0.012***	−0.011***
	(0.003)	(0.004)
PFRP	−0.0005	−0.004
	(0.004)	(0.004)
ESO	−0.001	0.007
	(0.004)	(0.005)
OCB	−0.008***	—
	(0.003)	
R^2	0.110	0.075
Observations (N)	1,192	1,281

Panel C (2004 WERS–ASHE)		
Proportion of Earnings Tied to PRP (Incentive Intensity)	2004	2004
Mean incentive intensity per establishment	—	−0.138***
		(0.044)
Mean hourly earnings per establishment	−0.076**	−0.066
	(0.037)	(0.047)

Table 3. (*Continued*)

Panel C (2004 WERS–ASHE)

Proportion of Earnings Tied to PRP (Incentive Intensity)	2004	2004
MP	-0.010^*	-0.011^{**}
	(0.005)	(0.005)
IPBR	0.004	0.008
	(0.008)	(0.008)
CPBR	-0.012	-0.011
	(0.010)	(0.009)
PFRP	-0.004	-0.005
	(0.006)	(0.005)
ESO	0.012^*	0.013^{**}
	(0.006)	(0.006)
R^2	0.20	0.22
Observations (N)	390	389

Note: Estimation method is OLS. Estimates are weighted in Panels A and B. In Panel C the weights adjust for the merged ASHE−WERS sample. Robust standard errors are in parentheses. In Panel C the standard errors are also adjusted for clustering of multiple individuals within the same establishment. Levels of significance: ***1%, **5%, *10%. Full controls for Panel A are presented in Table A3, while Panels B and C use the same controls. '—' implies that the variable is not present. The dependent variable has been divided by 100 for expositional purposes. Therefore, the size of the coefficient for MP in 1998 implies that firms with that particular variable pay scheme are likely to have a 1.1% (0.011 × 100) lower absence rate relative to those that do not.
All statistical results in Panel C remain Crown Copyright, and should be acknowledged either as such or as 'Source: ONS'.

coefficient of IPBR in the 1998 data is no longer present in 2004. This could potentially be related to the substantial alteration in the definition of the variable in the 2004 survey, which explicitly identified the components that comprise the separate categories 'payment by results' and 'merit pay'.

The WERS data permits further investigation of the impact of the *coverage* of PRP schemes on absenteeism. Specifically, managers that replied affirmatively to whether their establishment offers individual or collective PRP were subsequently asked to reply to the question: '*What proportion of non-managerial employees at this workplace have received performance related pay in the last 12 months?*'[20] Managers' responses have been grouped into four broad categories: '1–39%', '40–79%' and '80–100%', the omitted category being 'None'. The results of an estimated absence equation that includes variables describing the proportion of workers covered by PRP, instead of its incidence, are displayed in Table 3 (Panel B). The regression coefficients are indicative of the fact that firms with a more extensive coverage of PRP are more likely to experience lower absence rates.[21]

Effect of Proportion of PRP Tied to Earnings: ASHE–WERS Data

As mentioned in section 'The ASHE–WERS Data', the ASHE–WERS dataset allows for identification of the portion of employees' annual gross earnings that comes from bonus or incentive payments (profit sharing, productivity performance, piece-work and commission), although it is not possible to distinguish the latter into its respective components. On the basis of this dataset, the proportion of employees' salaries that is linked to a general measure of incentive pay, henceforth referred to as '*intensity of PRP*', is calculated for the year 2004. The average intensity of PRP per workplace is subsequently computed using the matched employer–employee records.

Using a similar specification as in the 2004 WERS cross-section data, Eq. (1) has been re-estimated on the matched ASHE–WERS subsample, albeit with the addition of the PRP intensity variable and a reliable measure of mean hourly earnings per establishment as separate explanatory variables. The incidence of the various types of incentive schemes provided by firms (e.g. MP, IPBR, CPBR, PRRP, ESO) and all other important determinants of absenteeism (as in Table A3) are controlled for in the regression, whilst the standard errors are adjusted for clustering of employees within the same workplace. In this manner, Panel C of Table 3 indicates that there is a statistically significant negative relationship between the intensity of PRP and absenteeism, ceteris paribus.[22] In particular, a 1 percentage point increase in the average intensity of PRP per establishment is found to be associated with a 14 percentage point decrease on mean absence. This result closely resembles those of Gneezy and Rustichini (2000) and Pouliakas (2010), who have shown that a higher intensity of incentive pay is associated with greater job satisfaction and intrinsic motivation among employees.

SENSITIVITY ANALYSIS

Controlling for Organization Fixed Effects

In the WERS data a number of workplaces constitute units of the *same* organization. To the extent that there is random variation in the use of particular PRP schemes by individual local branches that form part of a larger enterprise, the influence of PRP on absenteeism can hence be explored within a more 'controlled' setting. In particular, identification of the exact workplaces that fall under the umbrella of the same organization permits the examination of the *within-organization* influence of PRP schemes on absenteeism that purges a significant part of any unobserved heterogeneity affecting OLS estimates. In order to pursue this avenue further, the unique IDBR reference numbers of firms contained with the ONS's Virtual Micro-data Laboratory (VML) have been consulted. Cases in which at least two establishments (workplaces) of the WERS sample are local units of the same enterprise (organization) have been identified and retained. This led to a subsample of 305 workplaces that constitute local units of 97 broad organizations, whereby each enterprise contains an average of 3.14 work-places. After confirming that there is significant within-organization varia-tion in the incidence of incentive pay arrangements and in the absence rate,[23] the main absence Eq. (1) has been modified as follows:

$$\text{Absence}_{jo} = \beta_0 + \beta_1 PRP_{jo} + \beta_2 W_{jo} + \beta_3 I_{jo} + \beta_4 R_{jo} + \eta_o + \varepsilon_{jo} \qquad (2)$$

where the subscript 'o' now stands for 'organization' and η_o is the organization fixed effects term, capturing all of the factors that are constant across different workplaces that belong to the same organization. A fixed effects estimator has therefore been used to estimate Eq. (2) using the subsample of the 2004 WERS data described above. The main specification (Eq. (1)) has been retained, albeit with the omission of industry fixed effects since all firms within the same organization belong to the same industry. Importantly, Column 1 of Table 4 shows that the negative influence of MP on absenteeism persists even after controlling for a number of organization-invariant characteristics (e.g. the managerial policies of the headquarters). This finding supports the robustness of the OLS estimates reported in section 'Effect of PRP on Absence Rates'.

Controlling for Earnings and Hours of Work

As predicted by the standard labour-leisure paradigm, reliable estimation of an absence equation hinges critically on correctly identifying variation in earnings and working hours. For this reason, significant attention has been paid to ensuring that the PRP coefficients are robust to the inclusion of reliable measures of earnings and hours in the absence equation. First, the estimation has been replicated by including as controls relevant variables

Table 4. Sensitivity Analysis-Effect of Variable Pay Schemes on Absence Rate.

Dependent Variable: Workplace Absence	Organization Fixed Effects	Self-Selection		Illnesses/Injuries		Teamwork		Job Satisfaction		Subjective Productivity	
	(1)	(2)		(3)		(4)		(5)		(6)	
	2004	1998	2004	1998	2004	1998	2004	1998	2004	1998	2004
MP	-0.035** (-0.015)	-0.010** (0.004)	-0.008** (0.004)	-0.010** (0.004)	-0.009** (0.004)	-0.021** (0.005)	-0.014** (0.004)	-0.005 (0.006)	-0.007 (0.004)	-0.010** (0.004)	-0.008** (0.004)
IPBR	0.018 (-0.020)	-0.009*** (0.003)	0.005 (0.004)	-0.009*** (0.003)	0.005 (0.004)	-0.012** (0.0004)	0.005 (0.004)	-0.009** (0.004)	-0.001 (0.004)	-0.009*** (0.003)	0.005 (0.004)
CPBR	-0.028 (-0.022)	0.0002 (0.003)	-0.004 (0.004)	0.001 (0.004)	-0.005 (0.004)	0.0002 (0.004)	-0.006 (0.004)	-0.001 (0.004)	-0.002 (0.004)	0.001 (0.003)	-0.005 (0.004)
PFRP	-0.021 (-0.016)	-0.005 (0.003)	-0.004 (0.004)	-0.005 (0.004)	-0.004 (0.004)	-0.005 (0.004)	-0.004 (0.004)	-0.007* (0.005)	-0.004 (0.004)	-0.005 (0.004)	-0.004 (0.004)
ESO	0.043 (-0.039)	-0.0004 (0.004)	0.007 (0.004)	-0.0002 (0.004)	0.007 (0.004)	-0.001 (0.004)	0.007 (0.005)	-0.002 (0.004)	0.007 (0.005)	0.0001 (0.004)	0.007 (0.005)
OCB	—	-0.008*** (0.003)	—	-0.009*** (0.003)	—	-0.008** (0.003)	—	-0.007* (0.004)	—	-0.008*** (0.003)	—
Percent of same workforce during last 12 months		-0.005 (0.012)	-0.013 (0.009)								
Percent injury				0.029 (0.036)	-0.002 (0.004)						
Percent illness				0.275** (0.110)	0.091 (0.030)						
Teamwork						-0.007** (0.003)	-0.004 (0.004)				
Teamwork × MP						0.018** (0.008)	0.012* (0.007)				
Teamwork × IPBR						0.004 (0.005)	0.003 (0.006)				

Table 4. (*Continued*)

Dependent Variable: Workplace Absence	Organization Fixed Effects	Self-Selection		Illnesses/Injuries		Teamwork		Job Satisfaction		Subjective Productivity	
	(1)	(2)		(3)		(4)		(5)		(6)	
	2004	1998	2004	1998	2004	1998	2004	1998	2004	1998	2004
Mean satisfaction with influence								−0.017	−0.010		
								(0.016)	(0.009)		
Mean satisfaction with pay								−0.006*	−0.006*		
								(0.003)	(0.004)		
Mean satisfaction with achievement								0.006	0.005		
								(0.006)	(0.008)		
Labour productivity: lot better/better than average										−0.003	−0.001
										(0.003)	(0.004)
R^2	0.268	0.121	0.72	0.144	0.079	0.115	0.074	0.129	0.092	0.111	0.080
Observations (N)	269	1,192	1,281	1,192	1,281	1,192	1,281	944	938	1,192	1,281

Note: Estimation method is OLS. Each column controls for the same variables as reported in Table A3, albeit with the addition of the extra variables as shown in the rows of the table. Robust standard errors are in parentheses. Levels of significance: ***1%, **5%, *10%. '—' implies that the variable is not present. All statistical results in Column 1 remain Crown Copyright, and should be acknowledged either as such or as 'Source: ONS'. Observations in Column 1 are fewer than in the other columns, as the sample is restricted to include only those cases where more than two establishments are part of the same organization. Observations in Column 5 are fewer than in the other columns (except Column 1) as we merge in information from the employee questionnaire. To confirm that the fewer number of observations in Column 5 are not driving the job satisfaction results, we ran the baseline models in these smaller samples. Results did not change.

from the WERS cross-sectional surveys, such as the share of employees within earnings bands and six dummies capturing the share of employees who work overtime hours. Reassuringly, the significant estimates of the PRP variables reported in Table 3 (Panel A) hold (see Column 4 of Tables A4 and A5).

Furthermore, given that the ASHE dataset contains superior information on working hours and earnings that come from administrative sources, the main 2004 absence regression has been replicated on the merged ASHE–WERS subsample. A constructed measure of average gross hourly earnings per establishment has been included as an additional regressor. As can be seen from Table 3 (Column 1 of Panel C), workplaces that offer a higher level of pay per hour to their employees are found to have a significantly lower rate of absence in the order of 7.6 percentage points. Importantly, the statistically significant negative effect of MP on absenteeism persists even after the inclusion of this accurate hourly earnings measure.

Taking Self-Selection into Account

As is well-known from the model of Lazear (1986), the offer of PRP is likely to give rise to a selection issue, whereby more able, diligent and perhaps healthier employees are attracted to such compensation mechanisms. Therefore, it is typically difficult to disentangle whether PRP affects particular outcomes, such as absenteeism, due to its incentive properties or because of self-selection of different types of workers. In order to test whether the negative effect of individual PRP schemes on absenteeism is robust to the selectivity process, a number of additional control variables have been utilized in the analysis. These are used as proxies of the relative churning rate and of the 'quality' of the workforce within establishments. First, a new variable has been included in the specification that captures the extent to which the workforce has remained the 'same' in an establishment during the previous year of the survey. This is constructed after taking into account the proportion of new entrants into the workplace, minus those that left for a specific reason (e.g. dismissed, voluntary resigned, redundant and retired). Although this measure is likely to underestimate the full impact of the selection process over time, it is notable that the negative relationship of the individual PRP variables with absenteeism persists even after taking the variation in the composition of the workforce between establishments into account (see Column 2 of Table 4). Furthermore, an additional test has been undertaken by controlling for whether firms use performance/competency or personality/attitude tests during the recruitment process. As before, the MP and IPBR coefficients remain robust (see Column 5 of Tables A4 and A5).

Controlling for the Incidence of Workplace Illnesses and Injuries

According to Bender et al. (2012), even though piece rates are associated with greater productivity and a positive wage premium, they entail a greater likelihood of workplace injury occurring after controlling for other workplace hazards. Another counterproductive influence of PRP includes the so-called 'presenteeism' phenomenon. Such a process is likely to result in a greater chance of future absence spells (Böckerman & Laukkanen, 2010). In order to take the above issues into account two additional regressors have been added to the specification, which capture the workplace injury and illness rate. Specifically, they measure the proportion of employees that have sustained certain types of injuries (e.g. bone fracture, amputation, loss of sight etc.) or illnesses/disabilities/other physical problems (e.g. skin or respiration problems, stress, musculoskeletal disorders) during working hours in the previous year of the survey. Since the original dependent variable refers to the percentage of workdays lost through *employee sickness* or *absence*, we believe that by controlling for the illness or injury rate one can draw inferences regarding the effect of PRP on the residual component of absence. This residual part of absenteeism should be independent of the state of health and safety of the workforce. Indeed, as shown in Column 3 of Table 4, even after engaging in such an exercise the beneficial attendance effect of MP and IPBR remains unaltered.

Interaction with Teamwork

While the effectiveness of compensation schemes that rely heavily on teamwork hinges critically on the 'silent' constraining effect of peer pressure (Kandel & Lazear, 1992), the evidence of Frick et al. (2008) and Dale-Olsen (2012) suggests that teamwork may be combined with PRP to significantly raise absence rates. This is attributed to the fact that since team production units can cover for absent colleagues without undue disruption in output, workers who anticipate meeting their production targets are likely to free-ride by taking unauthorized absence. It is therefore of interest to examine closely the interrelationship between teamwork, the provision of performance pay and absenteeism. In fact, the positive interaction term

(Column 4 of Table 4) suggests that the sensitivity of absence to PRP is muted in firms with interdependent production.[24] This finding is in line with Brenčič and Norris (2010) and suggests that firms that are dependent on the productive collaborations of workers should exercise caution when deciding whether to implement a PRP scheme as part of a worker attendance plan.

Controlling for Job Satisfaction

In order to examine whether the negative effect of individual PRP on absenteeism is confounded by the job satisfaction of employees, the mean job satisfaction with respect to the facets of pay, influence and achievement has been computed for each workplace, after matching information obtained by the WERS Employee Questionnaire.[25] Table 4 (Column 5) illustrates that the significant effect of MP on absenteeism disappears in both waves once the job satisfaction variables are entered into the absence regressions as separate explanatory variables. Job satisfaction with pay, in particular, has a significant negative association with absenteeism. This suggests that the effect of MP on attendance hinges critically on whether the appraisal process that is linked to wage-setting provokes feelings of satisfaction among employees with respect to their labour market remuneration.

Quintile Regressions

While the OLS estimates of Table 3 show that individual-based PRP schemes are likely to have a negative effect on absenteeism at the mean of the sample, it is interesting to explore the heterogeneity in the coefficients further due to the skewed nature of absenteeism across establishments.[26] On theoretical grounds one would expect that variable pay schemes will exert a dissimilar impact on absenteeism, depending on whether firms have much higher or lower absence rates relative to a mean level of absence. Most firms should be able to tolerate a mean level of absenteeism without experiencing production difficulties. However, levels of absence that exceed this sustainable level may be detrimental to firm performance due to difficulties in carrying out regular productive activities. In contrast, levels that are below the sustainable rate may give rise to problems such as presenteeism, or undue pressure on workers seeking to strike a work–life balance.

Table 5, therefore, contains estimates of quintile regressions that examine the relationship between PRP schemes and absenteeism at five segments of the absence distribution. It is evident that the above a priori hypothesis is

Table 5. The Effect of Variable Pay Schemes on Absence Rate–Quintile Regressions.

	10th Quintile		25th Quintile		50th Quintile		75th Quintile		90th Quintile	
	1998	2004	1998	2004	1998	2004	1998	2004	1998	2004
MP	-0.006**	-0.004***	-0.003	-0.001	-0.004*	-0.005***	-0.011***	-0.006*	-0.017**	-0.008**
	(0.003)	(0.001)	(0.003)	(0.001)	(0.002)	(0.001)	(0.004)	(0.003)	(0.008)	(0.003)
IPBR	0.002	0.002	-0.001	0.001	-0.004*	0.0004	-0.008**	0.003	-0.025***	0.006
	(0.002)	(0.002)	(0.002)	(0.001)	(0.002)	(0.001)	(0.004)	(0.004)	(0.007)	(0.004)
CPBR	-0.002	-0.001	0.001	-0.0003	0.002	-0.001	-0.001	-0.001	0.006	-0.001
	(0.002)	(0.001)	(0.002)	(0.001)	(0.002)	(0.001)	(0.004)	(0.004)	(0.007)	(0.003)
PFRP	0.003**	0.002**	0.001	0.001	0.003	-0.0009*	0.003	-0.0003	-0.012	-0.001
	(0.001)	(0.001)	(0.001)	(0.001)	(0.002)	(0.0006)	(0.003)	(0.003)	(0.007)	(0.003)
ESO	-0.001	0.0003	0.0002	0.002*	-0.001	0.003***	-0.001	0.004	0.012*	0.007**
	(0.002)	(0.0012)	(0.001)	(0.001)	(0.002)	(0.001)	(0.003)	(0.004)	(0.006)	(0.003)
OCB	-0.001	—	0.0003	—	-0.0004	—	-0.002	—	-0.013	—
	(0.001)		(0.001)		(0.002)		(0.002)		(0.006)	
Pseudo R^2	0.136	0.113	0.127	0.104	0.095	0.079	0.073	0.077	0.129	0.119
N	1,192	1,281	1,192	1,281	1,192	1,281	1,192	1,281	1,192	1,281

Note: The other control variables are the same as those reported in Table A3. Full estimates are available upon request. Robust standard errors are in parentheses. Levels of significance: ***1%, **5%, *10%. '—' implies that the variable is not present. For robustness, we also estimated the above regressions by bootstrapping the standard errors using 1,000 replications.

confirmed, since one observes an asymmetric effect of PRP schemes on absenteeism. In particular, it is found that the marginal impact of PRP on the absence rate is larger at the higher rungs of the absence distribution relative to the lower quintiles. This finding is presumably indicative of the greater potential that contingent pay might have for lowering the absence rate of firms experiencing high levels of absenteeism as they return back to the sustainable rate over time. In contrast, the strength of the effect of PRP is likely to be muted in establishments that have absence rates that are already close to some average level.

ENDOGENEITY OF PRP AND ABSENCE

Despite the robustness of the negative MP and IPBR (only in 1998) coefficients in the absence regression, it is possible that endogeneity and reverse causation underlie the significant correlations of the variables. An important criticism regarding the detection of the 'causal' effect of PRP on firm performance is that cross-sectional estimates are likely to mask unobserved firm heterogeneity. This may include dynamic feedback effects of past absence rates and inherent differences in the *trend* of productivity, both of which are correlated with the introduction of PRP schemes by firms and with current absence rates. For instance, it is possible that lower present absence rates may be unrelated to the effect of PRP per se, and reflect, instead, a historically rising trend of productivity that is correlated with the adoption of costly variable pay policies in the first place (Prendergast, 1999). Previously abnormal absence rates that are regressing to the mean may also coincide with the implementation of PRP schemes by specific firms.

In order to address the aforementioned concerns, extra controls capturing the managers' subjective evaluation of current labour productivity within the establishment have been considered (see Column 6 of Table 4). In addition, the 1998 dataset contains the managers' subjective evaluation of whether labour productivity in their establishment has gone up or down compared to five years ago. In all cases no evidence is found to imply that the effect of PRP on absenteeism is somehow modified by the fact that firm productivity or its trend is likely to be correlated with both the adoption of PRP schemes and lower absence rates.

Furthermore, the 1998–2004 WERS Panel Survey has been utilized in order to explore the potential interrelationship between past absence rates of firms and the likelihood that the same firms have employed particular types of PRP schemes in future time periods. In particular, the following equation has been estimated using a probit estimator:

$$\text{PRP}_{04j}^i = \beta_0 + \beta_1 \text{Absence}_{98j} + \beta_2 \text{PRP}_{04j}^l + \beta_3 \text{PRP}_{98j} + \beta_4 X_{04j} + \beta_5 X_{98j} + \beta_6 \Delta_{04-98j} + u_j$$

(3)

where the probability that firms ($j = 1, \dots, N$) are observed to have specific PRP schemes in 2004 $\{i = \text{MP, IPBR, CPBR, PRRP, ESO, OCB}\}$ is regressed against the rate of absence that prevailed in 1998 (Absence_{98}). To obtain an unbiased estimate of β_1 a number of important confounding factors are taken into account, including the incidence of the remaining forms of PRP in the same year (PRP_{04}^l), the historical incidence of PRP in 1998 (PRP_{98}), current and past establishment characteristics (X_{04} and X_{98}) and variables capturing the historical evolution of the firms' financial performance and of management–employee relations since 1998 (Δ_{04-98}).

Results from Eq. (3) are displayed in Table 6A, which includes the marginal effects of the absence and PRP variables of interest.[27] The results indicate that higher levels of past absence are only significantly related to the incidence of *individual-based* PRP (MP and IPBR) in 2004.[28] In Table 6B it is also shown that this positive effect persists even among those firms that did not employ those particular PRP schemes six years earlier. Therefore, there is evidence confirming the existence of an important endogenous feedback mechanism between absenteeism and PRP, with high absence rates in the past inducing the introduction of PRP schemes within establishments in future time periods. This highlights the fact that not including lagged values of absence in the main empirical specification of Eq. (1) is likely to have resulted in underestimation of the true effect of PRP on current rates of absenteeism.[29]

CONCLUSION

Using two cross-sections (1998 and 2004) of the WERS, the matched employer–employee ASHE–WERS dataset and the panel element of the 1998–2004 WERS, the effect of various types of incentive pay on the absence rates of private sector firms is examined. Incentives that are tied to individual performance or output, particularly those that are tightly linked to the subjective evaluation of individual merit, are found to be significantly related to lower absenteeism, ceteris paribus. This effect is stronger in firms that cover a greater proportion of their non-managerial workforce with

Table 6A. Panel Estimates (Probit Model): Effect of Absence Rate and Incidence of Variable Pay Schemes in 1998 on Incidence of Variable Pay Schemes in 2004.

	MP04	IPBR04	CPBR04	PFRP04	ESO04	OCB04
Absence 98	0.041***	0.003**	−0.003	0.002	−0.000	−0.000
	(0.012)	(0.002)	(0.002)	(0.010)	(0.000)	(0.006)
MP 98	0.414***	0.140	−0.027**	0.603***	0.003	0.259*
	(0.065)	(0.118)	(0.011)	(0.085)	(0.005)	(0.145)
IPBR 98	−0.028	0.081	0.220**	0.011	−0.001	−0.023
	(0.137)	(0.068)	(0.101)	(0.139)	(0.001)	(0.052)
CPBR 98	−0.093	−0.017*	0.033	0.109	0.002	0.053
	(0.125)	(0.010)	(0.039)	(0.131)	(0.003)	(0.067)
PFPR 98	0.265***	0.050*	0.003	0.448***	0.003	0.019
	(0.086)	(0.026)	(0.017)	(0.075)	(0.002)	(0.045)
ESO 98	−0.052	−0.006	−0.016	−0.125	0.007	0.048
	(0.106)	(0.011)	(0.013)	(0.102)	(0.007)	(0.055)
OCB 98	0.057	0.002	0.022	0.093	0.000	0.081
	(0.086)	(0.012)	(0.018)	(0.085)	(0.001)	(0.050)
MP 04	—	0.005	0.050**	−0.093	−0.000	0.024
		(0.011)	(0.021)	(0.074)	(0.000)	(0.038)
IPBR 04	−0.108	—	0.509***	0.198	−0.001	−0.028
	(0.120)		(0.101)	(0.142)	(0.001)	(0.047)
CPBR 04	0.320***	0.430***	—	0.161	0.012	−0.035
	(0.098)	(0.097)		(0.110)	(0.012)	(0.045)
PFRP 04	−0.078	0.027	0.023	—	0.004	−0.060
	(0.083)	(0.020)	(0.017)		(0.004)	(0.040)
ESO 04	0.017	−0.017*	0.147**	0.389***	—	−0.084***
	(0.115)	(0.010)	(0.067)	(0.109)		(0.032)
OCB 04	0.085	−0.005	−0.034**	−0.143*	−0.000	—
	(0.083)	(0.011)	(0.014)	(0.076)	(0.001)	
Percentage women 04	0.215	0.031	0.005	−0.244	−0.001	−0.558***
	(0.237)	(0.036)	(0.040)	(0.255)	(0.002)	(0.143)
Percentage part-time 04	−0.239	−0.010	0.008	−0.572**	0.003	0.182
	(0.194)	(0.032)	(0.036)	(0.234)	(0.003)	(0.116)
Percentage union membership 04	0.257	0.033	0.019	−0.324*	0.004	−0.017
	(0.204)	(0.030)	(0.039)	(0.194)	(0.004)	(0.105)
Percentage managers 04	−0.237	−0.045	−0.128	0.004	0.010	−0.127
	(0.467)	(0.099)	(0.101)	(0.460)	(0.011)	(0.238)
Percentage professional staff 04	−1.024***	0.066	0.071	0.480	0.003	0.107
	(0.352)	(0.054)	(0.058)	(0.304)	(0.004)	(0.158)
Percentage technical staff 04	0.440	0.111*	−0.070	0.302	0.005	0.111
	(0.344)	(0.062)	(0.064)	(0.285)	(0.005)	(0.155)

Table 6A. (*Continued*)

	MP04	IPBR04	CPBR04	PFRP04	ESO04	OCB04
Percentage clerical staff 04	0.449	0.146**	−0.142**	−0.228	0.008	0.294**
	(0.309)	(0.070)	(0.067)	(0.289)	(0.008)	(0.148)
Percentage craft and skilled staff 04	0.008	0.109	−0.033	0.419	0.005	−0.244
	(0.337)	(0.071)	(0.060)	(0.332)	(0.006)	(0.173)
Percentage personal and protective staff 04	0.170	0.086*	−0.105**	0.098	0.006	−0.286**
	(0.263)	(0.050)	(0.051)	(0.258)	(0.006)	(0.138)
Percentage operative and assembly staff 04	−0.192	0.133**	−0.058	0.481*	0.006	0.168
	(0.288)	(0.064)	(0.050)	(0.280)	(0.006)	(0.141)
Percentage sales staff 04	−0.285	0.152**	−0.031	0.192	0.008	0.351***
	(0.291)	(0.066)	(0.043)	(0.302)	(0.008)	(0.134)
Log number of employees 04	0.166**	0.035**	0.022	0.256***	0.001	0.067*
	(0.075)	(0.016)	(0.016)	(0.076)	(0.001)	(0.036)
Joint consultative committee 04	−0.136	−0.013	0.029	0.003	−0.001	−0.065**
	(0.093)	(0.009)	(0.025)	(0.079)	(0.001)	(0.032)
Quality circle 04	−0.091	−0.036**	0.053*	−0.104	0.001	0.119**
	(0.086)	(0.016)	(0.030)	(0.075)	(0.001)	(0.049)
Review relative pay rates of different groups 04	0.026	−0.005	−0.004	0.058	0.000	0.175***
	(0.083)	(0.011)	(0.015)	(0.084)	(0.001)	(0.062)
Whether recognized unions 98	0.153	0.020	−0.043**	−0.413***	0.002	0.003
	(0.120)	(0.018)	(0.021)	(0.116)	(0.002)	(0.061)
Log number of employees 98	−0.127*	−0.006	−0.026	−0.251***	0.001	0.011
	(0.077)	(0.013)	(0.016)	(0.078)	(0.001)	(0.037)
Average duration of the normal working week 98	0.004	0.001*	−0.001	−0.002	−0.000	−0.002
	(0.003)	(0.000)	(0.001)	(0.004)	(0.000)	(0.001)
No changes in activity/ takeover/buy-out happened since 98	−0.058	−0.029**	0.011	0.206***	−0.001	−0.049
	(0.076)	(0.012)	(0.015)	(0.078)	(0.001)	(0.035)
Financial performance has improved since 98	−0.149	0.019	−0.030	0.014	−0.000	0.040
	(0.091)	(0.015)	(0.020)	(0.086)	(0.001)	(0.045)
	−0.265**	−0.006	0.009	−0.020	−0.001	−0.021

Table 6A. (*Continued*)

	MP04	IPBR04	CPBR04	PFRP04	ESO04	OCB04
Financial performance same since 98						
	(0.106)	(0.015)	(0.025)	(0.104)	(0.001)	(0.053)
Relations between managers and employees improved a lot since 98	0.166	−0.009	0.037	0.273*	0.038	0.540***
	(0.143)	(0.017)	(0.041)	(0.155)	(0.048)	(0.148)
Relations between managers and employees improved a little since 98	0.404***	−0.008	−0.043**	0.159	0.079	0.372***
	(0.107)	(0.019)	(0.021)	(0.163)	(0.082)	(0.134)
Relations between managers and employees are the same since 98	0.337***	−0.016	−0.020	0.294*	0.018	0.301***
	(0.125)	(0.020)	(0.023)	(0.150)	(0.022)	(0.110)
Industry dummies in 04	Yes	Yes	Yes	Yes	Yes	Yes
Region dummies in 04	Yes	Yes	Yes	Yes	Yes	Yes
Observations (N)	434	434	434	434	434	434

Note: Reported estimates are marginal effects, robust standard errors are in parentheses. Levels of significance: ***1%, **5%, *10%. Regression results are applicable to non-managerial employees in private sector establishments. '—' implies that the variable is not present. The omitted categories are: no PRP scheme in 1998 or in 2004, percentage of routine unskilled occupations, no joint consultative committee in 2004, no quality circles in 2004, no review relative pay rates of different groups in 2004, no recognized trade unions in 1998, changes in activity/takeover/buy-out happened since 1998, financial performance deteriorated since 1998, relations between managers and employees deteriorated since 1998, Yorkshire and Humberside, education sector.

contingent pay policies. A series of sensitivity tests confirm that the negative relation of PRP with absence is robust to selectivity and to the inclusion of administrative measures of earnings and working hours, organization fixed effects and the injury and illness rate of establishments. However, job satisfaction with pay appears to be an important factor that can mediate the positive impact of MP schemes on attendance. High-powered incentives that link a greater share of employee earnings to incentive pay are also found to exert a significant negative influence on absenteeism. Quintile regression results suggest that PRP has an asymmetric effect on absence. We find that

Table 6B.   Panel Estimates (Probit Model): Effect of Absence Rate and Incidence of Variable Pay Schemes in 1998 on Incidence of Variable Pay Schemes in 2004 (Sample of Firms Without Respective Variable Pay Scheme in 1998).

Independent Variables	Dependent Variables					
	MP 04	IPBR 04	CPBR 04	PFRP 04	ESO 04	OCB 04
Absence 98	0.036***	0.00018***	−0.001	0.00001	7.61e–07**	−0.001
	(0.013)	(0.0002)	(0.001)	(0.002)	(1.58e–06)	(0.004)
MP 98	—	0.064***	−0.006**	0.737***	0.0004***	0.039
		(0.068)	(0.003)	(0.265)	(0.001)	(0.085)
IPBR 98	0.011	—	0.131***	0.055	−2.88e–06***	−0.079***
	(0.148)		(0.099)	(0.068)	(7.21e–06)	(0.023)
CPBR 98	−0.093	−0.0004	—	0.027	0.0001	0.301***
	(0.130)	(0.0006)		(0.057)	(0.0002)	(0.123)
PFRP 98	0.298***	0.001	0.004	—	0.0001***	0.094**
	(0.088)	(0.001)	(0.005)		(0.0001)	(0.049)
ESO 98	−0.026	−0.001	−0.002	0.046	—	0.072
	(0.113)	(0.001)	(0.004)	(0.104)		(0.069)
OCB 98	0.040	−0.0004	0.022**	0.178***	4.96e–06	—
	(0.092)	(0.001)	(0.013)	(0.084)	(0.00001)	
MP 04	—	−0.00003	0.007	−0.001	−8.02e–07	0.114***
		(0.0004)	(0.006)	(0.018)	(2.21e–06)	(0.046)
IPBR 04	−0.118	—	0.580***	−0.017	−2.31e–06**	−0.016
	(0.125)		(0.112)	(0.017)	(5.82e–06)	(0.037)
CPBR 04	0.320***	0.696***	—	0.072	0.001***	−0.054
	(0.107)	(0.121)		(0.082)	(0.002)	(0.026)
PFRP 04	−0.107	0.002	0.010**	—	6.65e–06*	−0.090***
	(0.086)	(0.002)	(0.007)		(0.00002)	(0.034)
ESO 04	0.009	−0.004	0.034***	0.917***	—	−0.026
	(0.125)	(0.001)	(0.027)	(0.091)		(0.033)
OCB 04	0.061	−0.0004	−0.008***	−0.051***	−1.73e–06	—
	(0.090)	(0.001)	(0.004)	(0.029)	(4.28e–06)	
Observations (N)	408	359	355	160	280	279

Note: Reported estimates are marginal effects and robust standard errors are in parentheses. Levels of significance: ***1%, **5%, *10%. This specification includes the same controls as those reported in Table 6A. '—' implies that the variable is not present.

PRP has a stronger effect on establishments that have an absence rate above a sustainable level. Moreover, evidence from the 1998 to 2004 WERS Panel survey indicates that an endogenous feedback mechanism is at work, whereby high past absenteeism is related to a greater future incidence of individual PRP in firms, which, in turn, is correlated with lower current rates of absence.

The analysis of this article draws attention to the fact that only certain types of PRP, particularly those that shift the opportunity cost of absence solely onto workers' shoulders, are likely to be beneficial as an absence control tool. However, this conclusion does not imply that PRP is a reward instrument that should be universally utilized by all types of firms to prevent worker non-attendance. Whether PRP is a suitable compensation strategy ultimately depends on the production technology of establishments. For example, it is shown that firms that rely on interdependent production should be wary of using PRP to combat absenteeism, and that the potential of PRP is likely to be greater for firms encountering particularly serious absenteeism difficulties. MacLeod and Malcomson (1998) also emphasize that since subjective MP schemes are largely informal and unenforceable by law, they are subject to the requirement of self-enforcing agreements. These are more likely to be sustainable in less capital-intensive industries, when workers are in short supply and when the cost of having a job vacant is low.

It is also important to point out that due to data limitations it was not possible to adequately control for endogeneity and for dynamic effects in the absence variable using suitable instrumental variable (IV) or panel data estimators in the empirical analysis. Nonetheless, the findings reported on the basis of the WERS panel data highlight the need for future research which will decouple the causal chain of reaction between historical rates of absence, the introduction of PRP schemes by firms and their effect on current levels of absenteeism.

ACKNOWLEDGEMENTS

This work contains statistical data from ONS which is Crown copyright and reproduced with the permission of the controller of HMSO and Queen's Printer for Scotland. The use of the ONS statistical data in this work does not imply the endorsement of the ONS in relation to the interpretation or analysis of the statistical data. This work uses research datasets which may not exactly reproduce National Statistics aggregates.

We thank the sponsors of the Workplace Employment Relations Survey (WERS) – Department for Business Enterprise and Regulatory Reform, ACAS, ESRC and PSI – and the UK Data Archive for access to the WERS data.

We would like to thank the editor Solomon Polacheck and an anonymous referee for constructive comments and suggestions. We are also grateful to T. Barmby, A. Bryson, L. Christofides, J. Forth, C. Pissarides, J. Skatun, I. Theodossiou, A. Zangelidis and seminar participants at the University of Aberdeen Business School, Athens University of Economics and Business, University of Cyprus, Royal Economic Society (Surrey, 2010), IZA Summer Symposium on Labour Economics (2010), the National Institute of Economic and Social Research (NIESR) and the Society of Labor Economists (Vancouver, 2011) for useful comments. Nikolaos Theodoropoulos is grateful to the University of Cyprus for financial support. The usual disclaimer applies.

NOTES

1. We use the terms PRP, variable pay and contingent pay interchangeably.
2. We use the terms establishments, firms and workplaces interchangeably.
3. Belfield and Marsden (2003) utilize the 1998 WERS and the 1990–1998 WERS panel to study performance pay, monitoring and establishment performance. Arrowsmith and Marginson (2011) utilize the 2004 WERS to study variable pay and collective bargaining.
4. The non-publicly available ASHE-WERS dataset was accessed via the Virtual Micro-data Laboratory (VML) of the Office for National Statistics (ONS) in Glasgow. This dataset allowed us to identify establishments that are part of the same organization in the 2004 WERS cross-section data, on the basis of confidential enterprise reference numbers. This permitted the estimation of absence regressions that control for 'organization fixed effects', as described in section 'Controlling for Organization Fixed Effects'.
5. The relative inefficiency of explicit incentives in the public sector is typically attributed to the more complicated nature of performance measurement in state-level jobs, the prevalence of multiple principals, the crucial role of teamwork in public goods production and the important sorting effects due to public service motivation (Burgess & Rato, 2003; Dixit, 2002; Prendergast, 2008; Marsden, 2010). Indeed, the empirical analysis confirmed the absence of any significant PRP effect on worker attendance in the public sector establishments of the WERS data (see Column 1 of Tables A4 and A5).
6. In order to ensure that the empirical estimates are not affected by the greater prevalence of variable pay schemes in financial services relative to other sectors, sensitivity tests have also been undertaken that exclude the financial sector from the sample. The main results hold (see Column 2 of Tables A4 and A5).
7. The survey population for the MQ is all British workplaces barring those in agriculture, hunting and forestry, fishing, mining and quarrying, private households with employed persons and extra-territorial organizations.
8. The response rate in the 1998 (2004) MQ was 80% (64%). Changes in the nature of interest in employment relations led to substantial redesign of the 2004

wave. A major modification was the incorporation of small workplaces (i.e. those employing between five and nine employees). There were also a number of changes to the format of the various survey questions (see Airey, Hales, Hamilton, McKernan, & Purdon, 1999; Kersley et al., 2006).

9. It is acknowledged that this definition of absenteeism does not clarify what constitutes 'authorized' leave, and that the definition of 'authorized' leave may differ across workplaces. Nonetheless, it is believed to be a reliable measure of absence, since managers who responded to the survey were posted an Employee Profile Questionnaire (EPQ) and were requested to have it ready prior to the interview. This interviewing strategy gave managers the opportunity to report the establishment absence rate on the basis of their official registers rather than solely by memory. Thus, it is expected that recall bias is minimized relative to other sources that have used employee reports on absenteeism. The latter have typically been fraught with measurement errors due to the tendency of employees to underreport absence or to count days not scheduled for work as part of their overall absenteeism (Barham & Leonard, 2002).

10. The percentage of missing absence responses in the raw data was 18.5% in 1998 and 17.3% in 2004. It was confirmed that there is no systematic bias in the pattern of non-response using a Heckman-type selection model (e.g. LR tests of independence between outcome and selection equations in 1998 (2004) data: $\chi^2 = 0.01$, p-value: 0.92; ($\chi^2 = 0.04$, p-value: 0.83)). The identifying variable utilized in the selection equation is whether firms keep records of their total costs, since this is expected to be associated with their propensity to keep records on absence, but is not necessarily related to the level of absence. The estimated coefficient of this identifying variable in the first stage of the 1998 (2004) sample is 0.246 (0.237) with a p-value of 0.026 (0.022).

11. Using individual level data from the UK Labour Force Survey (LFS), Ercolani (2006) finds a mean absence rate of 3.19 for 1998 and 2.93 for 2004, respectively. The lower estimates may be due to employee recall bias, or to the fact that the author constructs absence rates by identifying differences between actual and usual hours of work per week that are attributed solely to sickness or injury. The WERS definition, instead, captures a more broad measure of absence.

12. In the 1998 questionnaire there was also an additional option offered to the respondents, which was referred to as 'other cash bonuses' (OCB). Due to the vague nature of this category, it has been included as a separate variable in the 1998 absence regression. The variable MP has also been constructed on the basis of different survey questions between the 1998 and 2004 waves. In particular, MP was not explicitly defined as part of a variable pay scheme in 1998, whereas it was in the 2004 wave.

13. In general, it has been noted that the PRP data show a substantial fall in incidence in the 1998 wave. This is believed to be associated with the substantial revamping of the PRP questions in that survey (Pendleton et al., 2009). More accurate conclusions regarding the trends in variable pay schemes over the years can thus be drawn by examination of the 1998–2004 WERS Panel Survey, since equivalent definitions have been used.

14. This is based on a logistic regression that predicts the probability that the WERS workplaces have matching ASHE records on the basis of firm size, industrial groups, proportion of occupational shares, distribution of earnings groups and

incidence of PRP schemes. The inverse of the predicted values are subsequently used as weights in the absence regressions. Once the above weighting procedure is implemented, comparable estimates are obtained between the WERS-ASHE subsample and the original 2004 WERS data (see Column 6 of Table A5).

15. Millward et al. (1992), using data from previous WERS surveys (1980, 1984 and 1990) and analysing workplaces with 25 or more employees, find that the fraction of workers who received some kind of merit pay was 34% in 1990. We report smaller fractions of workers receiving merit pay since our definition of merit pay excludes managerial employees and also our 1998 (2004) sample also incorporates firms with 10 (5) employees.

16. In particular, for firms that did not have *any* type of PRP in 1998 the Pearson correlation coefficient between the 1998 absence rate and IPBR schemes in 2004 is $r = 0.30$ $(p = 0.01)$, while for MP schemes it is $r = 0.35$ $(p < 0.01)$.

17. A generalized linear model (GLM) was also estimated, which assumes that the logit transformation of *Absence* comes from the family of binomial distributions. This takes into account excess concentration of observations at the boundaries of the permissible interval of responses. The marginal effects and their associated standard errors obtained from the GLM are almost identical to the OLS results reported in Table A3 (see Columns 2 and 4 of Table A3).

18. The regression coefficients of the remaining explanatory variables are found to correspond in most cases with the predictions of prior literature. Due to space considerations they are not discussed in the main text but are reported in Table A3.

19. Given concerns about what are considered to be 'unfair' and exorbitant bonuses offered to CEOs and managers, we investigated further whether the effect of variable pay schemes on absenteeism is compromised if such schemes are only offered to managers or senior officials within the workplace. While no significant interaction effects were found for MP and IBPR, a significant positive interaction was detected for OCB (available upon request). This indicates that the negative impact of cash bonuses on absence is weakened if such financial 'gifts' are not extended to the rest of the workforce, a finding consistent with behavioural theories of motivation (Fehr & Falk, 2002).

20. Managers had to choose between the following categories: 1 'All' (100%), 2 'Almost all' (80–99%), 3 'Most' (60–79%), 4 'Around half' (40–59%), 5 'Some' (20–39%), 6 'Just a few' (1–19%), 7 'None'.

21. Following Pendleton et al. (2009), the possibility that establishments utilize a number of PRP schemes has also been examined. We did this by regressing the number (counts) of simultaneous PRP schemes used by establishments (e.g. 1,2, ... ,6) on the absence rate, the omitted category is no PRP scheme. However, significant evidence in favour of multiple interaction effects is found only in the 1998 wave (see Table A6).

22. An alternative yet more arbitrary specification has also been utilized, whereby the continuous PRP intensity variable has been separated into a number of indicator dummies (e.g. 0%, 1–4%, 4–10%, >10%), roughly corresponding to the frequency distribution of the variable. It is hence confirmed that firms that employ high-powered incentives are significantly more likely to benefit from a lower absence rate relative to those firms that do not employ PRP schemes.

23. For example, the overall variation of MP schemes in the 2004 data is 0.475, the between-organization variation is 0.339 and the within-organization variation is 0.367. Similarly, the overall variability of the absence rate is 0.079, the between-organization variation is 0.047 and the variation between establishments of the same organization is 0.064.

24. It is acknowledged that this effect may be reflecting the endogenous nature of the relationship between PRP and teamwork. Nonetheless, it is not possible to decouple the effects of these two variables within the individual cross-sectional datasets, nor can we use the panel element of the survey for this purpose since we do not observe absence rates in the 2004 wave of the panel survey.

25. These are the only three job satisfaction facets that are the same in the two WERS waves.

26. In addition, sensitivity tests confirm the robustness of the results after dropping outlier observations (e.g. firms with absence rates higher than 20%, see Column 3 of Table A4 and A5).

27. The estimates of the remaining control variables are not discussed due to space constraints but are reported in Table 6A. Appropriate panel weights are used in the estimation of Eq. (3).

28. We also ran an OLS (reverse) regression where we regressed absence in 1998 on PRP schemes in 1998 and 2004, and all the other controls used in Eq. (3). We found a positive and statistically significant relationship between absence in 1998 and merit pay in 2004, which confirms the results presented in Table 6A (see Table A7).

29. It is known by the formula of omitted variable bias that $E(\hat{\beta}_1) = \beta_1 + \gamma b$, where γ is the coefficient of lagged absenteeism in an absence equation such as Eq. (1), and b is the slope of a regression that relates the lagged absence rates with the current incidence of variable pay schemes (e.g. Eq. (3)). Therefore, the estimated negative effect of PRP on current absence, β_1, will be downward-biased when one omits lagged absenteeism in the specification, due to the fact that γ and b are likely to be positive.

REFERENCES

Airey, C., Hales, J., Hamilton, R., McKernan, A., & Purdon, S. (1999). *The workplace employee relations Survey, 1998 (WERS): 1998 technical report (cross section and panel samples)*. London: Social and Community Planning Research.

Allen, S. G. (1981). An empirical model of work attendance. *Review of Economics and Statistics*, *63*, 77–87.

Allen, S. G. (1984). Trade unions, absenteeism and exit voice. *Industrial and Labor Relations Review*, *34*, 207–218.

Arai, M., & Thoursie, P. S. (2005). Incentives and selection in cyclical absenteeism. *Labour Economics*, *12*, 269–280.

Arrowsmith, J., & Marginson, P. (2011). Variable pay and collective bargaining in British retail banking. *British Journal of Industrial Relations*, *49*, 54–79.

Barham, C., & Begum, N. (2005, April). *Sickness absence from work in the UK. Labour market trends* (pp. 149–158). London: Office for National Statistics.

Barham, C., & Leonard, J. (2002, April). *Trends and sources of data on sickness absence. Labour market trends* (pp. 177–185). London: Office for National Statistics.

Barmby, T., Orme, C., & Treble, J. G. (1991). Worker absenteeism: An analysis using microdata. *Economic Journal, 101*, 214–229.

Barmby, T., Sessions, J. G., & Tremble, J. G. (1994). Absenteeism, efficiency wages and shirking. *Scandinavian Journal of Economics, 96*, 561–566.

Barmby, T., & Stephan, G. (2000). Worker absenteeism: Why firm size may matter. *Manchester School, 68*, 568–577.

Bauer T.K. (2004). *High performance workplace practices and job satisfaction: Evidence from Europe*. IZA Discussion Paper, No. 1265, Bonn.

Belfield, R., & Marsden, D. (2003). Performance pay, monitoring environments, and establishment performance. *International Journal of Manpower, 24*, 452–471.

Bender, K. A., Green, C. P., & Heywood, J. S. (2012). Piece rates and workplace injury: Does survey evidence support Adam Smith? *Journal of Population Economics, 25*, 569–590.

Bloom, N., & Van Reenen, J. (2010). Human resource management and productivity. In O. Ashenfelter & D. Card (Eds.), *Handbook of labor economics*.

Böckerman, P., & Laukkanen, E. (2010). What makes you work while you are sick? Evidence from a survey of workers. *The European Journal of Public Health, 20*, 43–46.

Booth, A., & Frank, J. (1999). Earnings, productivity, and performance-related pay. *Journal of Labor Economics, 17*, 447–463.

Brenčič, V., & Norris, J. B. (2010). On-the-job tasks and performance pay: A vacancy-level analysis. *Industrial and Labor Relations Review, 63*, 511–544.

Brown, S., & Sessions, J. G. (1996). The economics of absence: Theory and evidence. *Journal of Economic Surveys, 10*, 23–53.

Brown, S., Fakhfakh, F., & Sessions, J. G. (1999). Absenteeism and employee sharing: An empirical analysis based on French panel data, 1981–1991. *Industrial and Labor Relations Review, 52*, 234–251.

Bryson, A., & Freeman, F. (2010). How does shared capitalism affect economic performance in the United Kingdom?. In D. L. Kruse, R. B. Freeman & J. R. Blasi (Eds.), *Shared capitalism at work: Employee ownership, profit and gain sharing, and broad-based stock options*. Chicago, IL: University of Chicago Press.

Burgess, S., & Rato, M. (2003). The role of incentives in the public sector: Issues and evidence. *Oxford Review of Economic Policy, 19*, 285–300.

Chaplin, J., Mangla, J., Purdon, S., & Airey, C. (2005). The Workplace Employment Relations Survey 2004 (WERS 2004) Technical Report (Cross Section and Panel Surveys), National Centre for Social Research, London.

Chartered Institute of Personnel and Development. (2009). *Absence management 2009*. Retrieved from www.cipd.co.uk

Chatterji, M., & Tilley, C. J. (2002). Sickness, absenteeism, presenteeism and sick pay. *Oxford Economic Papers, 54*, 669–687.

Coles, M., Lanfranchi, J., Skalli, A., & Treble, J. G. (2007). Pay, technology and the cost of worker absence. *Economic Inquiry, 45*, 268–285.

Coles, M. G., & Tremble, J. G. (1996). Calculating the cost of absenteeism. *Labour Economics, 3*, 169–188.

Dale-Olsen, H. (2012). *Sickness absence, performance pay and teams. International Journal of Manpower, 33*, 284–300.

Davies, R., & Welpton, R. (2004). *Linking the annual survey of hours and earnings to the 2004 Workplace Employment Relations Survey: A technical discussion with an illustrative analysis of the gender pay gap.* WERS 2004 Information and Advice Service Technical Paper No. 3. Office for National Statistics, London, UK.

Department of Work and Pensions. (2002). *Pathways to work: Helping people into employment.* Cm 5690. The Licencing Division, HMSO, London, UK.

Dione, J., & Dostie, B. (2007). New evidence on the determinants of absenteeism using linked employer–employee data. *Industrial and Labor Relations Review, 61,* 108–120.

Dixit, A. (2002). Incentives and organizations in the public sector: An interpretative review. *Journal of Human Resources, 37,* 696–727.

Edwards, P., & Greasley, K. (2010). *Absence from work.* Dublin: European Working Conditions Observatory.

Engellandt, A., & Riphahn, R. T. (2011). Evidence on incentive effects of subjective performance evaluations. *Industrial and Labor Relations Review, 64,* 241–257.

Ercolani, M. G. (2006). UK employees' sickness absence: 1984–2005. Department of Economics, DP06-02, University of Birmingham, Birmingham.

European Foundation for the Improvement of Living and Working Conditions (EURO-FOUND). (1997). Preventing absenteeism at the workplace: Research summary. Office for Official Publications of the European Communities, Luxembourg.

Fehr, E., & Falk, A. (2002). Psychological foundations of incentives. *European Economic Review, 46,* 687–724.

Freeman, R. B., & Kleiner, M. M. (2005). The last American shoe manufactures: Decreasing productivity and increasing profits in the shift to continuous flow production. *Industrial Relations, 44,* 307–330.

Frey, B. S. (1993). Does monitoring increase work effort? The rivalry with trust and loyalty. *Economic Inquiry, 31,* 663–670.

Frey, B. S., & Jegen, R. (2001). Motivation crowding theory: A survey of empirical evidence. *Journal of Economic Surveys, 15,* 589–611.

Frick, B., Gotzen, U., & Simmons, R. (2008). The hidden costs of high performance work practices: evidence from a large German steel company. Mimeo.

Gielen, A. C., Kerkhofs, M. J. M., & van Ours, J. C. (2010). How performance related pay affects productivity and employment. *Journal of Population Economics, 23,* 291–301.

Gneezy, U., & Rustichini, A. (2000). Pay enough or don't pay at all. *Quarterly Journal of Economics, 115,* 791–810.

Hassink, W., & Koning, P. (2005). Do financial bonuses to employees reduce their absenteeism: Outcome of a lottery. *Industrial and Labor Relations Review, 62,* 327–342.

Henrekson, M., & Persson, M. (2004). The effects on sick leave of changes in the sickness insurance system. *Journal of Labor Economics, 22,* 87–114.

Heywood, J. S., & Jirjahn, U. (2004). Teams, teamwork and absence. *Scandinavian Journal of Economics, 106,* 765–782.

Heywood, J. S., Jirjahn, U., & Wei, X. (2008). Teamwork, monitoring and absence. *Journal of Economic Behavior and Organization, 68,* 676–690.

Holmström, B. (1979). Moral hazard and observability. *Bell Journal of Economics, 9,* 74–91.

Jacobson, S. L. (1989). The effects of pay incentives on teacher absenteeism. *Journal of Human Resources, 24,* 280–286.

Johansson, P., & Palme, M. (1996). Do economic incentives affect work absence? Empirical evidence using Swedish micro data. *Journal of Public Economics, 59,* 195–218.

Kandel, E., & Lazear, E. P. (1992). Peer pressure and partnerships. *Journal of Political Economy, 100*, 801–817.

Kersley, B. Alpin, K. Forth, J. Bryson, A. Bewley, H. Dix, G. Oxenbridge, S. (2006). *Inside the workplace: findings from the 2004 Workplace Employment Relations Survey.* London, UK: Taylor and Francis Group.

Kohn, A. (1993). *Punished by rewards: The trouble with gold stars, incentive plans, A's, praise, and other bribes.* New York: Houghton Mifflin.

Lazear, E. P. (1986). Salaries and piece rates. *Journal of Business, 59*, 405–431.

Lazear, E. P. (2000). Performance pay and productivity. *American Economic Review, 90*, 1346–1361.

Leigh, J. P. (1985). The effects of unemployment and the business cycle on absenteeism. *Journal of Economics and Business, 37*, 159–170.

MacLeod, W. B., & Malcomson, J. M. (1998). Motivation and markets. *American Economic Review, 88*, 388–411.

Marsden, D. (2010). The paradox of performance related pay schemes: Why do we keep adopting them in the face of evidence that they fail to motivate? In C. Hood, H. Margetts, Perri 6 (Eds.), *Paradoxes of modernization: Unintended consequences of public policy reforms* (pp. 185–202). Oxford, UK: Oxford University Press.

Milgrom, P., & Roberts, J. (1992). *Economics, organizations and management.* Prentice-Hall.

Millward, N., Stevens, M., Smart, D., & Hawes, W. (1992). *Workplace industrial relations in transition.* Aldershot: Darmouth.

Murphy, K. J. (1999). Executive compensation. In O. Ashenfelter & D. Card (Eds.), *Handbook of labor economics.*

Papke, L. E., & Wooldridge, J. M. (1996). Econometric methods for fractional response variables with an application to 401(k) plan participation rates. *Journal of Applied Econometrics, 11*, 619–632.

Pendleton, A., Whitfield, K., & Bryson, A. (2009). The changing use of contingent pay in the modern British workplace. In W. Brown, A. Bryson, J. Forth, & K. Whitfield (Eds.), *The evolution of the modern workplace* (Chap. 11, pp. 256–284). Cambridge, UK: Cambridge University Press.

Pouliakas, K. (2010). Pay enough, don't pay too much or don't pay at all? The impact of bonus intensity on job satisfaction. *Kyklos, 63*, 597–626.

Pouliakas, K., & Theodossiou, I. (2009). Confronting objections to performance pay: The impact of individual and gain-sharing incentives on job satisfaction. *Scottish Journal of Political Economy, 56*, 662–684.

Prendergast, C. (1999). The provision of incentives in firms. *Journal of Economic Literature, 37*, 7–63.

Prendergast, C. (2008). Intrinsic motivation and incentives. *American Economic Review, 98*, 201–205.

Schnebller, G. O., & Kopelman, R. E. (1983). Using incentives to increase absenteeism: A plan that backfired. *Compensation Benefits Review, 15*, 40–45.

Seiler, E. (1984). Piece rate vs. time-rate: The effect of incentives on earnings. *Review of Economics and Statistics, 66*, 363–376.

Skatun, J. D. (2003). Take some days off why don't you? Endogenous sick leave and pay. *Journal of Health Economics, 22*, 379–402.

Vistnes, J. P. (1997). Gender differences in days lost from work due to illness. *Industrial and Labor Relations Review, 50*, 304–323.

Wilson, N., & Peel, M. J. (1991). The impact on absenteeism and quits of profit-sharing and other forms of employee participation. *Industrial and Labor Relations Review, 3*, 454–468.

APPENDIX

Tables A1–A7.

Table A1. Definitions of Variable Pay Schemes.

Whether any employees receive individual-based merit pay (MP)	*1998*: If non-managerial employees have their performance formally appraised and the performance appraisal is directly linked to reviews or changes in individual employees' pay and if the appraisals are carried out by an individual's immediate supervisor or foreman or another manager. *2004*: Do any of the employees at this establishment get paid by results or receive merit pay? Where 'merit pay' is related to a subjective assessment of individual performance by a supervisor or manager (therefore is relevant for non-managerial employees only).
Whether any employees receive individual-based payments by results (IPBR)	*1998*: Do any employees at this establishment receive payments or dividends from individual or group performance-related schemes? Follow-up question asks whether PRP linked to individual, group or team, workplace or organization measures for non-managerial employees. Only the category 'individual performance/output' is retained. *2004*: Do any employees at this establishment get paid by results? Follow-up question asks whether PRP linked to individual, group or team, workplace or organization measures of performance for non-managerial employees. Only the category 'individual performance/output' is retained.
Whether any employees receive group or team, establishment or organization-based payments by results (CPBR)	*1998*: Follow-up question on measures of performance used to determine the amount of PRP used for non-managerial employees. Only the categories 'group or team, workplace or organization' are retained. *2004*: Follow-up question on measures of performance used to determine the amount of performance-related pay used for non-managerial employees. Only the categories 'group or team, workplace or organization' are retained.
Any profit-related payments or bonuses (PFRP) (where workplace is in private trading sector)	*1998*: Do any employees at this workplace receive payments or dividends from any of the following variable pay schemes: profit-related payments or bonuses; deferred profit sharing scheme. *2004*: Do any employees at this workplace receive profit-related payments or profit-related bonuses?

Table A1. (*Continued*)

Any share-ownership schemes with eligible employees (ESO) (where workplace is in private trading sector)	*1998*: Do any employees at this workplace receive payments or dividends from employee share ownership schemes? Eligibility refers to non-managerial employees. *2004*: Does the company operate any of the employee share schemes for any of the employees at this workplace (SIP, SAYE, EMI, CSOP, Other)? Eligibility refers to non-managerial employees.
Other cash bonus (OCB)	*1998*: Do any employees at this workplace receive payments or dividends from any of the following variable pay schemes: other cash bonus.

Note: SIP, Share incentive plan; SAYE, Save as you earn; EMI, Enterprise management incentives; CSOP, Company share option plan; Other, Other employee share scheme.

Table A2. Descriptive Statistics of Control Variables.

Variable	1998	2004
Percentage managers	0.094	0.114
	(0.092)	(0.107)
Percentage professional staff	0.076	0.076
	(0.153)	(0.164)
Percentage technical staff	0.072	0.081
	(0.130)	(0.161)
Percentage clerical and secretarial staff	0.138	0.142
	(0.176)	(0.203)
Percentage craft and skilled service staff	0.137	0.089
	(0.213)	(0.183)
Percentage personal and protective service staff	0.048	0.050
	(0.171)	(0.185)
Percentage operative and assembly staff	0.182	0.127
	(0.277)	(0.242)
Percentage sales staff	0.129	0.180
	(0.249)	(0.297)
Percentage women	0.425	0.444
	(0.278)	(0.285)
Percentage part-time employees	0.227	0.242
	(0.291)	(0.283)
Percentage employees less than 20 years old	0.076	0.106
	(0.116)	(0.159)
Percentage union membership	0.241	0.139
	(0.318)	(0.254)
Number of employees	57.971	26.418
	(213.758)	(88.743)
Between 1 and 24% employees work on fixed term contracts	0.434	0.347
	(0.496)	(0.476)
More than 25% of employees work on fixed term contracts	0.030	0.059
	(0.171)	(0.236)
Sick pay in excess of statutory requirements	0.578	0.494
	(0.494)	(0.500)
Specific health and safety committee	0.164	0.058
	(0.370)	(0.234)
Joint consultative committee/work councils/representative forums	0.214	0.068
	(0.410)	(0.252)
Quality circles/problem solving groups	0.304	0.171
	(0.460)	(0.377)
Shift working for non-managerial employees	0.301	0.210
	(0.459)	(0.408)
Annualized hours for non-managerial employees	0.025	0.032
	(0.157)	(0.176)
Unemployment to vacancy ratio by travel to work area	3.618	3.402
	(1.627)	(2.463)
Observations (N)	1,192	1,281

Note: Means are weighted. Standard deviations are in parentheses. Descriptive statistics on industries and regions are not reported for space considerations but are available upon request.

Table A3. The Effect of Control Variables on Absence Rates (Full Estimates).

Variable	1998		2004	
	(1)	(2)	(3)	(4)
	OLS-Coef.	GLM-ME	OLS-Coef	GLM-ME
MP	−0.011**	−0.010***	−0.008**	−0.008**
	(0.004)	(0.004)	(0.004)	(0.004)
IPBR	−0.010***	−0.009***	0.005	0.005
	(0.003)	(0.003)	(0.004)	(0.004)
CPBR	0.0003	0.001	−0.005	−0.003
	(0.004)	(0.004)	(0.004)	(0.004)
PFRP	−0.005	−0.005	−0.004	−0.005
	(0.004)	(0.003)	(0.004)	(0.003)
ESO	−0.0003	−0.001	0.007	0.007
	(0.004)	(0.004)	(0.005)	(0.004)
OCB	−0.008***	−0.008***	—	—
	(0.003)	(0.003)		
Percentage managers	−0.025	−0.027*	−0.002	0.006
	(0.016)	(0.016)	(0.018)	(0.015)
Percentage professional staff	−0.011	−0.011	−0.033**	−0.030**
	(0.014)	(0.013)	(0.015)	(0.014)
Percentage technical staff	−0.015	−0.017	−0.043***	−0.041***
	(0.012)	(0.011)	(0.015)	(0.013)
Percentage clerical and secretarial staff	−0.024*	−0.021*	−0.024*	−0.020*
	(0.013)	(0.011)	(0.014)	(0.012)
Percentage craft and skilled service	0.006	0.007	−0.023*	−0.020*
	(0.014)	(0.011)	(0.012)	(0.011)
Percentage personal and protective service	−0.015	−0.013	−0.037***	−0.034***
	(0.011)	(0.009)	(0.013)	(0.011)
Percentage operative and assembly staff	0.006	0.005	−0.025*	−0.021**
	(0.015)	(0.011)	(0.013)	(0.010)
Percentage sales staff	0.001	0.001	−0.016	−0.013
	(0.014)	(0.011)	(0.013)	(0.010)
Percentage women	0.028**	0.025***	0.015	0.015
	(0.010)	(0.009)	(0.011)	(0.010)
Percentage part-time employees	−0.009	−0.008	−0.020**	−0.014*
	(0.010)	(0.009)	(0.009)	(0.008)
Percentage employees less than 20 years old	0.039*	0.033**	0.032*	0.021*
	(0.021)	(0.014)	(0.016)	(0.013)
Percentage union membership	0.0003	−0.0001	0.014	0.011
	(0.006)	(0.005)	(0.009)	(0.007)
Log number of employees	−0.001	−0.001	−0.0004	−0.001
	(0.002)	(0.001)	(0.002)	(0.001)

Table A3. (*Continued*)

Variable	1998		2004	
	(1)	(2)	(3)	(4)
	OLS-Coef.	GLM-ME	OLS-Coef	GLM-ME
Between 1 and 24% of employees work on fixed term contracts	0.003	0.003	−0.001	0.001
	(0.003)	(0.003)	(0.004)	(0.004)
More than 25% of employees work on fixed term contracts	0.003	0.002	0.0004	0.001
	(0.012)	(0.009)	(0.011)	(0.011)
Sick pay in excess of statutory requirements	0.011*	0.010**	−0.001	−0.001
	(0.006)	(0.005)	(0.004)	(0.004)
Specific health and safety committee	−0.009***	−0.008***	−0.007	−0.006
	(0.003)	(0.003)	(0.005)	(0.004)
Joint consultative committee/work councils/ representative forums	0.012***	0.012***	0.007	0.007
	(0.004)	(0.003)	(0.005)	(0.005)
Quality circles/problem solving groups	−0.005*	−0.005*	0.002	0.002
	(0.003)	(0.003)	(0.004)	(0.004)
Shift working for non-managerial employees	0.014**	0.013***	0.017***	0.017***
	(0.006)	(0.005)	(0.004)	(0.004)
Annualized hours for non-managerial employees	−0.009**	−0.010***	0.005	0.005
	(0.004)	(0.003)	(0.007)	(0.005)
Unemployment to vacancy ratio by travel to work area	0.0002	0.0004	0.00002	−0.0002
	(0.002)	(0.001)	(0.001)	(0.001)
Industry dummies	Yes	Yes	Yes	Yes
Region dummies	Yes	Yes	Yes	Yes
R^2	0.110	—	0.071	—
Observations (*N*)	1,192	1,192	1,281	1,281

Note: Columns 1 and 3 report OLS coefficient estimates, while Columns 2 and 4 report Marginal Effects (ME) obtained from Generalized Linear Model (GLM) estimation of a logistic transformation of the absence dependent variable. Estimates are weighted. Robust standard errors are in parentheses. Levels of significance: ***1%, **5%, *10%. '—' implies that the variable is not present. Omitted categories: firms without a variable pay scheme, percentage of routine or unskilled workers, zero proportions of employees work on fixed term contracts, employees are not entitled to sick pay in excess of statutory requirements, no specific health and safety committee, no joint consultative committee, no shift working arrangement for non-managerial employees, no annualized time arrangements for non-managerial employees, Yorkshire and Humberside, education sector.

Table A4.   Robustness Checks for WERS 1998.

Independent Variables	Public Sector	Exclude Financial Sector	Drop Firms with Absence Rate Bigger than 20%	Proportion of Earning Bands and Overtime	Personality and Performance Tests
	(1)	(2)	(3)	(4)	(5)
MP	−0.008	−0.012**	−0.006*	−0.009**	−0.010**
	(0.006)	(0.005)	(0.004)	(0.004)	(0.004)
IPBR	−0.006	−0.011***	−0.007***	−0.010***	−0.010***
	(0.004)	(0.004)	(0.002)	(0.003)	(0.003)
CPBR	0.003	0.002	−0.001	0.002	0.001
	(0.005)	(0.004)	(0.002)	(0.004)	(0.004)
PFRP	0.004	−0.005	−0.0004	−0.005	−0.005
	(0.006)	(0.004)	(0.002)	(0.004)	(0.004)
ESO	—	−0.001	−0.001	−0.004	−0.0003
		(0.004)	(0.002)	(0.004)	(0.004)
OCB	−0.003	−0.009***	−0.005**	−0.008***	−0.008***
	(0.004)	(0.003)	(0.002)	(0.003)	(0.003)
Share of employees earning <9k	—	—	—	−0.013	—
				(0.017)	
Share of employees earning <12k	—	—	—	−0.013	—
				(0.012)	
Share of employees earning <16k	—	—	—	−0.003	—
				(0.012)	
Share of employees earning <20k	—	—	—	−0.013	—
				(0.011)	
Share of employees earning <29k	—	—	—	−0.036**	—
				(0.014)	
Share of employees earning >29k	—	—	—	−0.014	—
				(0.015)	
Between 1 and 19% of employees work overtime	—	—	—	−0.0004	—
				(0.008)	
Between 20 and 39% of employees work overtime	—	—	—	−0.007	—
				(0.006)	
Between 40 and 59% of employees work overtime	—	—	—	−0.0003	—
				(0.007)	
Between 60 and 79% of employees work overtime	—	—	—	−0.005	—
				(0.007)	

Table A4. (*Continued*)

Independent Variables	Public Sector	Exclude Financial Sector	Drop Firms with Absence Rate Bigger than 20%	Proportion of Earning Bands and Overtime	Personality and Performance Tests
	(1)	(2)	(3)	(4)	(5)
Between 80 and 99% of employees work overtime	—	—	—	−0.005 (0.007)	—
All employees work overtime (100%)	—	—	—	−0.010 (0.007)	—
Personality or attitude test when filling vacancies	—	—	—	—	0.0004 (0.003)
Performance or competency test when filling vacancies	—	—	—	—	−0.0052* (0.003)
Observations (N)	515	1,116	1,178	1,192	1,192

Note: Estimation method is OLS. The dependent variable is the establishment absence rate in 1998. Full controls are included as in Table A3. Robust standard errors are in parentheses. Estimates of the other control variables are available upon request. Levels of significance: ***1%, **5%, *10%. '—' implies that the variable is not present. The omitted category for the overtime dummies is that none of the employees in the largest occupational group works full time.

Table A5.　　Robustness Checks for WERS 2004.

Independent Variables	Public Sector	Exclude Financial Sector	Drop Firms with Absence Rate Bigger than 20%	Proportion of Earning Bands and Overtime	Personality and Performance Tests	WERS–ASHE
	(1)	(2)	(3)	(4)	(5)	(6)
MP	−0.015 (0.009)	−0.008** (0.004)	−0.005** (0.002)	−0.009** (0.004)	−0.008** (0.004)	−0.009* (0.005)
IPBR	−0.012 (0.012)	0.004 (0.004)	0.004 (0.003)	0.005 (0.004)	0.004 (0.004)	0.004 (0.008)
CPBR	−0.001 (0.010)	−0.010 (0.004)	0.001 (0.003)	−0.003 (0.004)	−0.003 (0.004)	−0.013 (0.010)
PFRP	—	−0.006 (0.004)	−0.001 (0.002)	−0.005 (0.004)	−0.005 (0.004)	−0.003 (0.006)
ESO	—	0.005 (0.005)	0.005* (0.003)	0.007 (0.005)	0.007 (0.004)	0.012* (0.006)
Share of employees earning £4.50 per hour or less	—	—	—	0.020 (0.020)	—	—
Share of employees earning £4.51–£5 per hour	—	—	—	−0.004 (0.011)	—	—
Share of employees earning £5.01–£14.99 per hour	—	—	—	0.010 (0.008)	—	—
Share of employees earning £15 per hour or more	—	—	—	−0.011 (0.011)	—	—
Between 1 and 19% of employees work overtime	—	—	—	0.005 (0.006)	—	—
Between 20 and 39% of employees work overtime	—	—	—	0.013** (0.006)	—	—
Between 40 and 59% of employees work overtime	—	—	—	0.005 (0.006)	—	—
Between 60 and 79% of employees work overtime	—	—	—	0.015* (0.009)	—	—
Between 80 and 99% of employees work overtime	—	—	—	0.004 (0.007)	—	—

Table A5. (Continued)

Independent Variables	Public Sector	Exclude Financial Sector	Drop Firms with Absence Rate Bigger than 20%	Proportion of Earning Bands and Overtime	Personality and Performance Tests	WERS–ASHE
	(1)	(2)	(3)	(4)	(5)	(6)
All employees work overtime (100%)	—	—	—	0.006 (0.008)	—	—
Personality or attitude test when filling vacancies	—	—	—	—	−0.002 (0.004)	—
Performance or competency test when filling vacancies	—	—	—	—	−0.001 (0.004)	—
Observations (N)	398	1,177	1,246	1,281	1,281	390

Note: Estimation method is OLS. The dependent variable is the establishment absence rate in 2004. Full controls are included as in Table A3. Robust standard errors are in parentheses. Estimates of the other control variables are available upon request. Levels of significance: ***1%, **5%, *10%. '—' implies that the variable is not present. The omitted category for the overtime dummies is that none of the employees in the largest occupational group works full time. In the 2004 wave we do not observe the annual remuneration of employees in pay bands as in 1998. Instead, we observe the hourly pay rate of employees. So, the controls for the share of employees within earning bands differ between 1998 and 2004. All statistical results in Column 6 remain Crown Copyright, and should be acknowledged either as such or as 'Source: ONS'.

Table A6. The Effect of Number of Simultaneous Variable Pay
Schemes on Absence Rate.

	1998	2004
One scheme	−0.011	0.008
	(0.007)	(0.006)
Two schemes	−0.013**	0.004
	(0.006)	(0.007)
Three schemes	−0.022***	0.010
	(0.008)	(0.010)
Four schemes	−0.019***	0.013
	(0.006)	(0.014)
Five schemes	−0.021**	−0.009
	(0.009)	(0.013)
Six schemes	−0.032***	—
	(0.009)	
Observations (*N*)	1,192	1,281

Note: Estimation method is OLS. The dependent variable is the establishment absence rate in the respective year. The independent variables are the summation of PRP schemes that are simultaneously employed by each establishment in the respective year. Full controls are included as in Table A3. Robust standard errors are in parentheses. The omitted category is no PRP scheme. Estimates of the other control variables are available upon request. Levels of significance: ***1%, **5%, *10%. '—' implies that the variable is not present. In 2004 we do not observe OCB, this is why there is one less scheme for 2004.

Table A7. Reverse Regression–Absence rate in 1998 on Incidence of Variable Pay Schemes in 1998 and 2004.

Independent Variables	Dependent Variable: Absence Rate in 1998
	PRP Schemes in 1998 and 2004
MP 04	1.541***
	(0.481)
MP 98	1.959
	(1.306)
IPBR 04	0.623
	(1.200)
IPBR 98	−0.525
	(0.668)
CPBR 04	−0.415
	(0.761)
CPBR 98	−0.696
	(0.581)
PFRP 04	−0.067
	(0.497)
PFRP 98	−1.089*
	(0.620)
ESO 04	0.027
	(0.717)
ESO 98	0.461
	(0.580)
OCB 04	−0.247
	(0.710)
OCB 98	−1.116**
	(0.451)
Observations (N)	434

Note: Reported estimates are OLS coefficients and robust standard errors are in parentheses. This specification includes the same controls as those reported in Table 6A. Levels of significance: ***1%, **5%, *10%.

ADVERSE SELECTION AND INCENTIVES IN AN EARLY RETIREMENT PROGRAM [☆]

Kenneth T. Whelan, Ronald G. Ehrenberg, Kevin F. Hallock and Ronald L. Seeber

ABSTRACT

We evaluate potential determinants of enrollment in an early retirement incentive program for non-tenure-track employees at a large university. Using administrative records on the eligible population of employees not covered by collective bargaining agreements, historical employee count and layoff data by budget units, and public information on unit budgets, we find dips in per-employee finances in a budget unit during the application year, and higher recent per employee layoffs were associated with increased probabilities of eligible employee program enrollment. Our results also suggest that, on average, employees whose salaries are lower than we would predict given their personal characteristics and job titles

[☆]Whelan was a PhD student in Policy Analysis and Management at Cornell University and a Research Associate at the Cornell Higher Education Research Institute (CHERI). Whelan passed away unexpectedly in the Fall of 2011 after the completion of this article. He was an important part of our academic community, had a promising career ahead of him, and is dearly missed. This article is dedicated to the three most important people in his life – his wife Jenny and his sons Liam and Miles.

Research in Labor Economics, Volume 36, 159–190
ISSN: 0147-9121/doi:10.1108/S0147-9121(2012)0000036009

were more likely to enroll in the early retirement program. To the extent that employees' compensation reflect their productivity, as it should under a pay system in which annual salary increases are based on merit, this finding suggests that adverse selection was not a problem with the program. That is, we find no evidence that on average the "most productive" employees took the incentive.

Keywords: Cornell University; early retirement; salary; adverse selection; incentives

JEL classification: J32; J33; J63

INTRODUCTION

Cornell University, like many other academic institutions in the United States, was severely affected by the economic downturn and the financial meltdown that began in 2008. In May 2008, the university had projected a balanced operating budget over the next few years. By the fall of 2008 the university realized that these projections were way off. A combination of declining endowments, declining gifts for current operations, declining support from New York State (four of its colleges received some support from the state), increased needs for borrowing to finance ongoing capital projects (because of the failure of projected gift flows for capital construction to materialize), and increasing financial need of its under-graduate students because of declining family incomes left the university with substantial operating budget deficits. The administration quickly understood that corrective actions had to be taken and that the university needed to rethink its cost structure. While layoffs would likely be necessary, because of its role as a major employer in the community in which it was located and its commitment to its employees, Cornell hoped to minimize the number of layoffs that occurred and the administration had the idea of funding a one-time early retirement incentive program for staff to encourage a voluntary reduction in its level of employment.

Our article uses administrative data from Cornell to try to develop an understanding of the factors that led Cornell employees to elect to participate in the program. Our focus is on answering two questions: First, in a decen-tralized large university setting where budget units face different financial situations, did differences in variables related to the financial situations of the units, namely reductions in operating budgets and recent layoff experiences, influence the probability that eligible non-union[1] employees chose to participate in the program? Second, did the program lead to adverse selection, in the sense that people who chose to accept the early retirement offer were those who tended to be of "above average productivity"? If the most productive staff were the ones who tended to accept the early retirement offer, the cost to the university in terms of lost productivity of the departing employees may offset the benefits of the program.[2]

To preview our major findings, we find that employees' probabilities of accepting the early retirement offer were related to the budgetary pressures that they believed that their units faced. Moreover, while we cannot directly observe employee productivity, we can observe if employees were paid below or above average, given their personal characteristics, years of experience at Cornell, and job titles. We find a low value for this relative pay variable is a characteristic of the average employee Cornell chose to layoff in recent years. Furthermore, we find that employees who accepted the early retirement offer, on average, were paid less than we might expect given the above named variables. To the extent that the university's annual merit increase system was working the way it should and relative salaries at the university reflect relative productivities, this suggests that adverse selection did not prove to be a problem. That is, there is no evidence that the "above average ability" employees were most likely to take the early retirement package.

DATA AND METHODS

Program Details

To evaluate the impact of job-related risk factors that may influence non-tenure-track staff's decisions to accept an early retirement program window offer, we use administrative data on all eligible non-union employees ($n = 1083$) for the Staff Retirement Incentive (SRI) program at Cornell University. The SRI was announced to the university community on February 27, 2009 and was made available to all non-tenure-track staff aged 55 or older, with at least 10 years of eligible service at the university as of June 30, 2009, who received less than 25% of their salaries from sponsored research funds.[3] The SRI only required employees leave a benefits eligible position at the university; employees "retiring" under the program were eligible to return to temporary non-benefits eligible positions and, after 3 years, to regular university employment.

The plan's incentives included a taxable lump sum payment equal to 1 year of base pay and a nontaxable contribution to a defined contribution retirement fund of 30% of base pay. Enrollment in the SRI was only available for a fixed amount of time; employees were required to announce their intent to enroll in the program between March 1 and March 30 of 2009. Within this interval of time, there were no additional constraints that would make early or later enrollment desirable.[4] After enrolling, severance with the university from a benefits eligible position was required by June 30, 2009. Staff enrolled in the program received the same benefits provided to all staff retirees, including retiree health insurance coverage.[5]

The SRI was not the only retirement option offered to staff at the time. A Phased Retirement Incentive (PRI), which previously had existed only for tenure-track faculty, was concurrently offered that permitted employees to reduce their working hours to 20 per week for up to 3 years following enrollment. Under this program, salaries would be proportionately reduced, but benefits (such as retirement system contributions) would continue to be based on the employees' full-time salary. Employees could not enroll in both programs and the PRI required supervisor approval, while the SRI did not. These differences could have caused some individuals that would otherwise have accepted the SRI in isolation to accept the PRI when offered together so our results should be seen as conditional on PRI availability. In practice, only two individuals enrolled in the PRI as of June 30, 2009.

Data and Descriptive Statistics

Our analyses make use of data from three sources. Our primary data source consists of administrative records on the universe of non-union individuals eligible for the SRI. These data are typical of what would be available to administrators trying to understand take-up rates for similar incentive programs. Other than salary data, for which we have 10 years for each employee, and the SRI enrollment outcome, all other variables are as of the date the plan became available, March 1, 2009. In this primary data source, we have information on such items as retirement plan in which the individual is enrolled (defined benefit or defined contribution), demographic variables (such as age, gender, race/ethnicity, marital status, and number of dependents currently covered by Cornell's health insurance programs), employment unit (consisting of the 10 colleges and three administrative units), position typical weekly hours of work, job families, pay bands, years employed at Cornell, and years since the last job change within the university. Job families are groupings of job positions by task area (such as Human Resources) or type of position (such as technical or administrative). This variable is tied to job codes and job titles, and has relevance for compensation. Pay bands are defined pay ranges (minimum and maximum) for positions meant to encourage equitable pay across employees with similar expertise or duties. They are set at the university level and restrict management's discretion in setting pay. Higher pay bands typically reflect higher minimum, maximum, and medians for a pay range. Pay bands in our sample fall into two main classifications: "banded" which consists of 18 bands set by the university for staff positions, and "unclassified/academic/ executive" ones in which more flexibility is given to management in setting pay than it had in the "banded" structure.

Our second source of information is on historical employee counts and layoffs. Employee counts are by year as of the end of the fiscal year (FY), June 30, and are at the employment unit (college or administrative unit) level. When per employee variables are computed, the denominator is the prior end of FY employee count. Our layoff data are at the individual level; for much of our analyses they are aggregated up to employment unit FY numbers. When we construct Fiscal Year (FY) 2009 layoff variables we only use layoff numbers through March 2009 and then multiply them by 1.333 to get a projected annual FY number. We do this because layoffs in April, May, and June of 2009 were not observed by SRI applicants before they had to make their decisions by March 31, 2009 to enroll in the program and so we implicitly assume the employee projects that the rate of layoff for the last 3 months of the FY would be the same as in the previous 9 months.

Our third set of data comes from budget reports available to the public on Cornell's website. FY budget reports, which include projections of the next FY's resources and spending, are typically released in May of each year. So, for example, in May 2009, the FY 2010 (July 1, 2009 to June 30, 2010) report was released. This report contained projected unit resources and expenditures for FY 2010. However, it was not released in time for employees considering whether to accept the SRI offer to use this information. While we could have assumed that employees had rational expectations, we instead assumed that they based their projections on likely unit budget changes in FY 2010 on the budget changes that their units had experienced during FYs 2006 through 2009.[6]

In what follows we exclude 3 individuals who held multiple jobs, 3 individuals for whom retirement plan data were missing or who were enrolled in a hybrid defined benefit/contribution retirement plan, and 4 individuals for whom 2006 salary data were missing, for a total of 10 individuals.[7] Our analysis thus uses a sample of 1073 individuals. Approximately one-third of the non-union SRI eligible individuals chose to accept the retirement incentive.

Unfortunately, several potentially important variables are absent from our data. We do not observe dependents, spouses, or partners in our administrative databases, but rather whether dependents, spouses, or partners are covered by the employee's health plan. We also do not observe spousal/partner or employee retirement wealth or health status.[8]

The first column of panel A of Table 1 presents mean values for many of the variables used in this analysis. A relatively small percentage, about 16% of the eligible employees, is covered by a defined benefit pension plan. Most eligible employees were working full time (defined as more than 38 hours per week), were white, and were neither lecturers nor researchers. Eligible employees have an average of 24 years of seniority, which is well above the required 10 years for SRI eligibility, and their years of service varies widely across individuals and has a standard deviation of 8 years. The average age of SRI eligible employees was 60 and 63% were women.

The first column of panel B shows the fraction of SRI eligible individuals employed in different units at the Ithaca campus of the university.[9] These units are the 10 different colleges at Cornell and 3 composite other units that we have created: student services, academic programs, and administration and support.[10] The units have considerable autonomy in making staffing decisions and in deciding how to allocate resources. Furthermore, because funding of the different units comes from a variety of sources, for example, some of the colleges receive some appropriations from New York State and the endowment level per student varies across colleges, the units face different budgetary pressures. To emphasize this point, Fig. 1 displays both budgeted resources and salary expenditures per employee in $10,000, averaged from 2005 to 2008, by unit, with the vertical lines representing two standard error bands around the mean. This figure indicates that there was substantial variation in per employee resources and budgeted salary expenditures among units, with movements between salary and resource levels being very similar across units. The extent of variability in within unit budget amounts for the years 2005 to 2008 differs among the units with the most variability displayed by the Academic Programs (AP) unit for both per employee resources and salary, and the least variability shown by School of Hotel Administration (HOTEL) for resources and by Student Services (SS) for salary.

The variability in resources over time across units comes from the variety of revenue sources the units receive and the variability in each source over time. The units differ in the shares of their revenues coming from tuition, gifts, endowment income, sponsored programs, state and federal

Table 1. Mean Comparisons for Key Explanatory Variables.

Variable	All	Enrolled	Declined	Difference	*t*-stat
Panel A: Socioeconomic					
Age	60.071	61.544	59.352	2.192	8.92***
Years of service	24.437	25.958	23.694	2.264	4.32***
Fulltime	0.893	0.881	0.899	−0.018	−0.9
Non-academic staff	0.828	0.855	0.814	0.041	1.67
Female	0.625	0.645	0.616	0.029	0.92
Asian	0.02	0.009	0.025	−0.016	−1.83
Black	0.021	0.02	0.021	−0.001	−0.1
Hispanic	0.011	0.009	0.012	−0.003	−0.58
Unknown	0.007	0.014	0.003	0.011	2.19*
White	0.942	0.949	0.939	0.01	0.65
Defined benefit plan	0.16	0.188	0.147	0.041	1.7
Spouse or partner on health plan	0.445	0.435	0.451	−0.016	−0.5
Dependent child on health plan	0.235	0.176	0.264	−0.088	−3.18**
Salary 2006–2009 relative change	0.148	0.13	0.156	−0.026	−3.12**
Log 2009 salary	11.022	10.978	11.044	−0.066	−2.29*
Panel B: Employment units					
Student Services (SS)	0.086	0.068	0.094	−0.026	−1.44
Academic Programs (AP)	0.154	0.131	0.165	−0.034	−1.47
Administration and Support (AS)	0.291	0.321	0.276	0.045	1.52
College of Agriculture and Life Sciences (CALS)	0.163	0.168	0.161	0.007	0.28
Architecture, Art, and Planning (AAP)	0.011	0.014	0.01	0.004	0.66
Arts and Sciences (ART)	0.096	0.077	0.105	−0.028	−1.5
Engineering (ENG)	0.029	0.026	0.031	−0.005	−0.45
School of Hotel Administration (HOTEL)	0.012	0.009	0.014	−0.005	−0.75
College of Human Ecology (CHE)	0.029	0.037	0.025	0.012	1.1
School of Industrial and Labor Relations (ILR)	0.038	0.063	0.026	0.037	2.91**
Johnson School (JS)	0.016	0.026	0.011	0.015	1.78
Cornell's Law School (LAW)	0.019	0.011	0.022	−0.011	−1.23
College of Veterinary Medicine (VET)	0.057	0.051	0.06	−0.009	−0.56

P-values indicated by *$p < 0.05$, **$p < 0.01$, ***$p < 0.001$.

appropriations, and allocations from the central administration. In our empirical work we focus on unit level per employee budgeted resources and salary expenditures as the measures that eligible employees may focus on in thinking about the financial pressures that their units face.

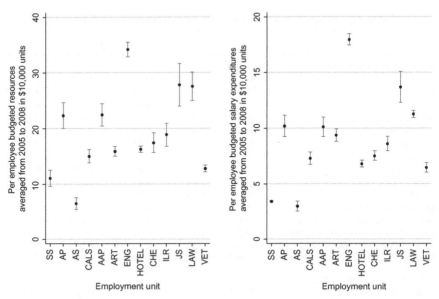

Fig. 1. Depiction of the Variation in Budgeted Per Employee Resource and Salary Levels Among Units: Per Employee Budgeted Resource and Salary Levels are Averaged from 2005 to 2008 in $10,000 Units Graphed Against Employment Units with Two Standard Error Bands Shown in Gray.

The remaining columns of Table 1 display comparisons of means for those eligible employees that enrolled in the SRI and those that declined the retirement incentive offer. Some eligible employees were probably inclined to retire within the interval of time that the SRI required accepted applicants to retire (March 1, 2000–June 30, 2009) independent of the SRI. Their retirement decisions could be motivated by variables such as age, years of service, health, and family considerations, so it is important to control for these variables in our statistical analyses. The comparison of means for those that accepted and declined the retirement incentive sheds light on some of the variables that may prove to be important in our multivariate analyses.

Retirement age incentives appear in government policies and in employee benefit structures. The Internal Revenue Service specifies ages for minimum distributions and penalty-free withdrawal of retirement funds, while the Social Security Administration specifies ages for receipt of full or partial Social Security benefits. Defined benefit pension plan structures also play a role by setting how annual pension benefits levels depend upon years of service, age at retirement, and a measure of average "final" salary. For these reasons we might expect the relationship between SRI enrollment, age, and years of service to be increasing but non-linear. Indeed, Table 1 shows that individuals that enrolled in the SRI are on average 2.19 years older and worked 2.26 more years at Cornell than individuals who turned down the opportunity to accept the retirement incentive offer. Further analyses reported below describe the non-linear relationship.

Having a dependent child on an employee's health plan is associated with not accepting the retirement incentive. This may reflect the age of the employee or that the employee has greater financial responsibilities that reduces the attractiveness of the incentive. Finally, on average, employees who accepted the incentive offer had lower levels of salaries and recent salary growth than employees who did not enroll in the program.

Differences in all of the factors mentioned above across employment units at the university may be responsible for the differences in enrollment rates across employment units observed in panel B of Table 1. For example, while 3.8% of eligible employees were from the School of Industrial and Labor Relations (ILR), 6.3% of the employees who accepted the incentive offer came from this unit. In contrast, while 1.9% of the eligible employees came from Cornell's Law School (LAW), only 1.10% of the employees who accepted the incentive came from this unit. As such, we turn to a multivariate analysis to see if differences in acceptance rates across units still exist after we control for the characteristics of the eligible non-union eligible employees in each unit that are available to us in our data.

Appendix Table A1 presents estimates of a linear probability model of SRI enrollment (Yes = 1, No = 0) as a function of all of the eligible employee characteristics listed in panel A of Table 1 as well as dichotomous variables for the units (panel B) in which the employee was employed.[11] In this model, the continuous age and years of service variables have been converted to 2-year binary indicator variables to allow the effects of age and years of service on the acceptance decision to be nonlinear. The omitted (reference) group in the model is individuals who are white male employees aged 55–56 with 10–15 years of service, who are employed in the Administration and Support (AS) unit. These estimates suggest that in the multivariate context there are no statistically significant differences in the acceptance probabilities associated with employees' full-time/part-time status, academic/nonacademic staff status, race/ethnicity, retirement plan type, or presence of spouse or dependents on the employee's health insurance.

In Fig. 2, we graphically display the coefficients (with two standard error bands) that show the impact of the age, years of service, and employment unit dichotomous variables from appendix Table A1 on the decision to accept the retirement incentive offer. The acceptance probability increases monotonically with age at a decreasing rate until roughly aged 63 and over when it flattens out. The acceptance probability also increases with years of service, with the steepness of the relationship increasing after 30 years of

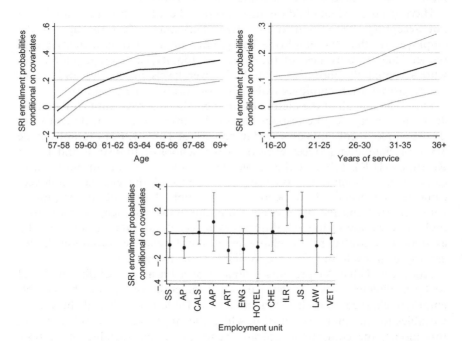

Fig. 2. Coefficients on Age, Years of Service, and Employment Unit Dummies from a Regression of Enrollment in SRI (Yes = 1) on Age, Years of Service, Employment Unit and Other Covariates with Two Standard Error Bands (see the appendix). Age is in Comparison to Those Aged 55–56, Years of Service to 10–15, and Employment Unit to AS.

Employment Unit Codes are as Follows: SS "Student Services," AP "Academic Programs," AS "Administration and Support," CALS "College of Agriculture and Life Sciences," AAP "Architecture, Art, and Planning," ART "College of Arts and Sciences," ENG "Engineering," HOTEL "Hotel Administration," CHE "College of Human Ecology," ILR "Industrial and Labor Relations," JS "Johnson School," LAW "Cornell's Law School," VET "College of Veterinary Medicine."

service. The point estimates suggest that an individual with 36 years of service or more has about a 15 percentage point higher probability of accepting the offer than an individual with 10–15 years of service, all other factors held constant. Presumably many individuals with such long years of service would be contemplating retirement even in the absence of the program.

It is apparent in the bottom panel of the figure that much variation still exists in enrollment probabilities across employment units even after we control for individual's personal characteristics including age and years of service. Relative to the omitted group (AS), employees employed in the academic programs (AP) unit and the College of Arts and Sciences (ART) are less likely to enroll in the SRI, while individuals from the ILR are more likely to enroll in the SRI.[12]

In what follows we try to better understand this heterogeneity of enrollment rates among the employment units that persists even when conditioning on factors such as age, years of service, defined benefit, union status, and family characteristics. Specifically our focus is on individual's perceptions of their risk of being laid off and on whether they are paid less, or more, than average given their personal and job characteristics.

Econometric Framework

We estimate models of the form $y_{ij} = F[\alpha + X_i'\delta + \gamma p_i + \beta z_j] + \varepsilon_{ij}$, where F is a linear model or a logistic transformation, i indexes the individual and j indexes the employment unit. The outcome, y_{ij}, is 1 if individual i in employment unit j enrolled in the SRI and is 0 otherwise. Individual level controls are included in the vector X_i, while p_i is a proxy for a measure of the employee's productivity, and z_j is an employment unit level factor that we hypothesize is associated with SRI enrollment. The vector X_i contains many of the variables found in panel A of Table 1.

In the absence of an observable measure of actual productivity, it is common in the literature to obtain a proxy for productivity by making some comparison of salaries across individuals.[13] If we can identify individuals who are performing roughly the same work and if we believe that the university's merit pay policies lead individuals' salaries to be roughly proportionate to their productivity, then we can use a measure of an individual's "relative" salary as a measure of his or her relative productivity. With our rich administrative data that provides us with information on pay bands, time in most recent position, and functional job categories, we are able to narrowly define groups of potentially substitutable workers and develop relative salary measures.

To construct our relative salary measure, p_i, we first estimate the following equation:

$$s_i = \sum_{k=1}^{n_k} \text{Band}_{ik}\delta_k + \sum_{m=1}^{n_m} \text{Fam}_{im}\gamma_m + X_i'\psi + \eta_i$$

where s_i is the log of 2009 FY salary for individual i. Included on the right-hand side are job band dichotomous variables (Band$_{ik}$, equal to 1 if individual i is in job band k and is 0 otherwise), as well as job family indicators (Fam$_{im}$ equal to 1 if individual i is in job family m and is 0 otherwise). The vector X_i is composed of indicator variables for whether the employee is fulltime and non-academic staff, a continuous variable for years since job entry date, employment unit indicators, and years of service indicators at the same level of aggregation as described in Data and Descriptive Statistics Section.[14]

Our relative salary measure is given by the portion of salary unexplained by this linear equation (the residual); this is normalized by its standard deviation for ease of interpretation. Formally, our proxy for relative salary is estimated as $p_i = p_i^*/\sigma_{p*}$, where $p_i^* = s_i - \sum_{k=1}^{n_k} \text{Band}_{ik}\hat{\delta}_k - \sum_{m=1}^{n_m}$ Fam$_{im}\hat{\gamma}_m - X_i'\hat{\psi}$ and σ_p is the standard deviation of p_i^*.[15] We interpret p_i as the difference in individual's salary from the average salary of her closely substitutable co-workers and we will refer to p_i in what follows as "relative pay."[16]

This relative pay variable is estimated from a first-stage equation; thus, it is subject to sampling variation and its inclusion in the SRI enrollment equation may bias conventional standard errors. Standard errors that do not account for this variation will be smaller than corrected standard errors if the disturbances are uncorrelated; however, if disturbances are correlated the direction is unknown. To show the impact on our standard errors from a bias correction for this variation in the relative pay variable, we also compute standard errors that use the method proposed by Murphy and Topel (2002).

Another statistical issue that we face is the possibility of within employment unit correlation of disturbances. Because we do not observe phenomena such as management style, work environment, peer effects, or promotion structure, it is possible that employees within units are affected in similar ways by these unobservables. Uncorrected, standard errors could be smaller leading us to make incorrect claims about the significance of effects.

A common correction for this is to use the method of Liang and Zeger (1986) which nonparametrically adjusts the covariance matrix to account for clustering as well as heteroskedasticity. The problem with applying this method to our research study is that it relies on group asymptotics and we have only 13 employment units. With a random effects framework, parametric adjustments and Generalized Estimating Equations (GEE) similarly are infeasible with such a small number of groups; however, a corrected GEE covariance matrix by the method of Bias Reduced Linearization (BRL) developed by Bell and McCaffrey (2002) is a possible solution for problems related to the small number of groups. Bell & McCaffrey show, with Monte Carlo methods, that BRL seems to generate statistical tests of the correct size when applied to random effects models with normally distributed errors (Angrist & Lavy, 2009) even when the group size is small.

In practice, we find that the corrections we make for these statistical challenges with either the method of Murphy and Topel or Bell and McCaffrey lead to little adjustments on inference from robust standard errors. However, we do not simultaneously correct for both concerns and it could be argued that the bias from each statistical issue would, if combined, equal more than the sum of the differences we observe individually.

RESULTS

Adverse Selection

Employers relying on a labor force reduction tool that shifts the discretion of exit to the employee need to be confident that the "right" employees choose to enroll. The risk is that highly productive employees would be more likely to opt into the SRI since the probability of obtaining a position elsewhere could be a less risky and a more lucrative prospect for these individuals. If the employer loses highly productive employees, they may also have lost substantial investments in human capital that it has made.

To evaluate if the "right" type of employees enrolled in the SRI, we proceed in two steps. First, we investigate whether a low value of our relative pay variable, the proxy for productivity, is associated with being laid off. Specifically, did the university, when it used the discretionary tool of a layoff, choose to terminate employees with low relative pay?[17] Second, we test for whether low relative pay is associated with the decision to enroll in the SRI.

To accomplish the first step we generate a new relative pay variable constructed from a combination of our SRI non-union eligible population with the population of 177 non-union individuals that suffered layoffs from January 2005 to March 2009. Layoffs for this population are for reasons defined as "lack of funds," "lack of work," or "reorganization." If low relative pay does indicate the "right" type of employee to enroll in the SRI, we would expect that the employees laid off in these prior years were of lower relative pay.[18]

To calculate the relative pay variables on the combination of these two populations a few adjustments are necessary. First, we convert the last annual equivalent salary received by the laid off population into a 2009 equivalent using the between year salary growth rate from our SRI population. Second, we increase the years of service of the laid off population to reflect the amount should they have been employed to 2009.[19] Further, two variables, the statutory/endowed indicator (which we use to distinguish certain pay band differences within the AS and AP units) and the years since job entry date, are not available for our layoff population. Then, to construct this new relative pay variable, p^{new}, we exclude those variables from the regression. We are confident that this does not materially impact a comparison between the new relative pay variable and the relative pay variable calculated exclusively on the SRI non-union eligible population. The correlation coefficient between p^{new} and p conditional on our SRI non-union eligible population is 0.978.

In Fig. 3, we show kernel density plots of p^{new} for the SRI enrollment population and the layoff population using the Epanechnikov kernel with a bandwidth of 0.17.[20] The density for the layoff population is shifted to the left with a mean of -0.29 while the SRI population is centered at 0.05. These means are significantly different with a t-statistic of over 3. There is observably much variation in the relative pay variable among the layoff population.

A possible explanation for this variation is that wide differences existed in how binding the sets of feasible employees under consideration for a layoff were for layoffs that occurred from 2005 to 2009. Although the university has discretion in choosing whom to layoff among workers not covered by a collective bargaining agreement, in effect it may be limited to selecting individuals from a pool attached to a particular project or program. We would anticipate that a reorganization would impose the lowest constraint on its behavior, while it is unclear whether a lack of funds for a position or a lack of work for an employee or group would be more binding on its actions. If funds are truly fungible, a "lack of funds" might actually indicate

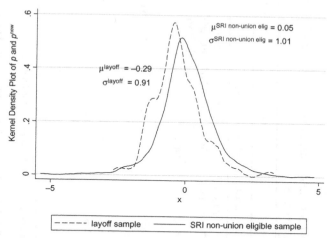

Fig. 3. Kernel Density Plots of the Relative Pay Variable Calculated on the Layoff and SRI Non-Union Eligible Combined Sample Shown for Each Sample Separately.

an unwillingness of the university to make an allocation, perhaps because the set is not actually binding. Alternatively, a "lack of work" could imply an unwillingness of the university to reposition a valued employee, again indicating a non-binding constraint.

A further test then for the validity of the relative pay variable in serving as a proxy for productivity is to see how consistent it is with our expectations about how constrained each of the sets is above. It seems reasonable to assume that when using a layoff the university would want to minimize the average of the productivity lost. If we order the three groups of layoffs by the mean of the relative pay of the individuals laid off in each group, we have [Reorganization (−0.42), Lack of Funds (−0.19), Lack of Work (−0.17)] from low to high. This roughly indicates that the reorganization feasible set is the least binding, consistent with our expectation.

We will now evaluate how SRI enrollment is associated with the characteristic of low relative pay. Using our relative pay variable calculated only on the set of SRI non-union eligible individuals, we estimate linear probability and logit models of SRI enrollment on relative pay and subsets of the variables previously included in the appendix Table A1. The coefficients of the relative pay variable from each of the models are found in Table 2.

Table 2. Coefficients on the Relative Pay Variable from Regressions of SRI Enrollment (Yes = 1) on Relative Pay and Hierarchical Compositions of Covariates.

	(1)		(2)		(3)		(4)		(5)	
	OLS	Logit	OLS	Logit	OLS	Logit	OLS	Logit	OLS	Logit
Relative pay	−0.0332	−0.0331	−0.0336	−0.0336	−0.0339	−0.0343	−0.0337	−0.0341	−0.0322	−0.0296
	(0.0136)*	(0.0138)*	(0.0136)*	(0.0138)*	(0.0136)*	(0.0138)*	(0.0137)*	(0.0139)*	(0.0138)*	(0.0137)*
	[0.0136]		[0.0136]*		[0.0136]*		[0.0136]*		[0.0134]*	
	{0.0134}*		{0.0137}		{0.0135}*		{0.0140}*			
Covariates included in the models above:										
Age, years of service, fulltime and academic staff dummies	Yes		Yes		Yes		Yes		Yes	
Gender and ethnicity			Yes		Yes		Yes		Yes	
Defined benefit					Yes		Yes		Yes	
Family characteristics							Yes		Yes	
Unit dummies and salary change									Yes	

Sample size is 1073. *P*-values indicated by *$p < 0.05$. Robust standard errors shown in parenthesis for OLS with OIM for logit.
Standard errors calculated via Murphy and Topel (1985) are shown in brackets.
Standard errors calculated using the method of biased reduced linearization proposed by Bell & McCaffrey (2002) are shown in curly braces clustering on unit dummies.

The coefficient on relative pay is stable across specifications, ranging from −0.032 to −0.034 with little difference between the OLS and logit marginal effects. Standard error adjustments do not change the conclusions drawn. Our model suggests that a one standard deviation decrease in relative pay is associated with a 3.22% increase in the probability of enrolling in the SRI.[21]

Job-Loss-Related Risk Factors

We suspect that employees consider a distribution of possible future employment durations at the university when deciding whether to enroll in the SRI. Their perceptions of being involuntarily terminated from the university in the future surely influence their decision whether to accept the incentive offer. In the remainder of our article, we include variables that may be indicators of future job-loss risk into the equations that predict whether an individual will enroll in the SRI. Our research design makes use of the variation in layoffs, budgeted resources, and budgeted salary expenditures across employment units at the university from FY 2006 up until the SRI enrollment date of March 31, 2009. Each measure is deflated by the beginning of FY employee count to convert raw layoff and budget change numbers to a per employee number; we believe that these measures will be the ones that employees will focus on when contemplating their likelihood of future layoff.

Of the indicators, layoffs are likely to be the most salient – a co-worker's disappearance would be more troubling and apparent than a change in resources or budgeted salary expenditure. However, layoffs occur very infrequently in the data, approximately 200 between the start of FY 2005 and March 2009. The between unit standard deviation is only 5 per 1000 employees. In contrast, the variation in per employee budgeted resources and salary expenditure is more substantial with a between unit standard deviation of $100,000 for per employee resources and half that for per employee salary expenditures. Of more importance to us, the difference in 2009 and 2008 per employee resources has a standard deviation of $15,000 among employment units while the standard deviation of the difference for salary per employee over the same period is $4000.

However, there are some drawbacks to using per employee budgeted resource or salary expenditure changes. A reduction in resources could indicate a reduction in facility expense or available supplies, or a failure to replace computers or peripherals and not actually suggest any immediate job-loss risk to the employee. In this scenario, it might be that any effect we observe is motivated by a reduction in the quality of the employee's work environment and not from job-loss-related risk as we hypothesize. Our salary expenditure measure reflects the apportioned amount of resources available per employee and if it proves statistically significant, its effect may be directly due to job-loss concerns.

The layoff indicators we use are averages of layoffs per 1000 employees by employment unit across a number of years. Similarly our budgeted resources and salary expenditure measures are changes in per employee amounts in units of $10,000 per employee by employment unit. The unconditional relationship between SRI enrollment probabilities and various indicators of job-loss risk are shown in Fig. 4. In the top-left panel we graph unit SRI enrollment probabilities against the 2006–2009 unit layoffs per 1000 employees. The correlation is clearly positive. Because the observation for the ILR appears to be an outlier, when we conduct multivariate analyses that include the layoff risk variables below, we will experiment with omitting ILR employees from our analyses to see if this omission materially alters any of our conclusions. Our results suggest their omission does not make a difference.

In the right panels we again graph unit SRI enrollment probabilities, but now with either 2009 minus 2008 budgeted resources per employee in $10,000 increments (top) or 2009 minus 2008 budgeted salary expenditures per employee in $10,000 increments (bottom). The correlation of each of these variables across units with the probability that the unit's non-union eligible employees enrolled in the SRI is negative; this suggests that reductions or smaller increases in available per employee resources are associated with SRI enrollment. These raw correlations do not account for the distribution of any of the individual level covariates that also are associated with SRI enrollment. So in the following sections we will estimate the effect of these unit resource variables holding constant the individual level variables, including relative pay.

Layoffs as Indicators

In Table 3 we report linear probability model coefficient estimates and logit model marginal effects for our relative pay and layoff variables in trying to predict SRI enrollment. The models reported in panel A use unit layoffs per 1,000 employees averaged across the years 2006 to 2009. The models reported in panels B and C are similar except that they use 3 and 2 year averages, respectively, for the layoff variables. Column 1 shows the coefficient estimates for relative pay and our various layoff measures, when

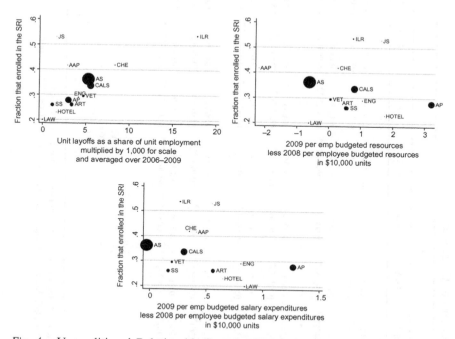

Fig. 4. Unconditional Relationship Between SRI Enrollment (Yes = 1) and Unit Layoffs, Per Employee Salary and Resource Levels. Dot Sizes Are in Proportion to the Size of the Non-Union Eligible Population Employed in That Unit.

Employment Unit Codes are as Follows: SS "Student Services," AP "Academic Programs," AS "Administration and Support," CALS "College of Agriculture and Life Sciences," AAP "Architecture, Art, and Planning," ART "College of Arts and Sciences," ENG "Engineering," HOTEL "Hotel Administration," CHE "College of Human Ecology," ILR "Industrial and Labor Relations," JS "Johnson School," LAW "Cornell's Law School," VET "College of Veterinary Medicine."

we control for employees' age, years of service, full-time/part-time status, and academic/nonacademic position status. Columns 2 through 5 add additional explanatory variables to the models to see how sensitive our relative pay and layoff variables are to their inclusion.

Looking first at the relative pay coefficients, their magnitudes are not significantly different across specifications and not significantly different from the estimates reported in Table 2 from models that exclude the layoff probability variables. Similarly, the coefficients on the layoff variables show little change across specification within each panel. Finally, the effect size on

Table 3. Layoff and Relative Pay Coefficients from Regressions of SRI Enrollment (Yes = 1) on Hierarchical Compositions of Covariates.

	(1) OLS	(1) Logit	(2) OLS	(2) Logit	(3) OLS	(3) Logit	(4) OLS	(4) Logit	(5) OLS	(5) Logit
Panel A: 4-year average										
Relative pay	−0.0334	−0.0329	−0.0336	−0.0333	−0.0338	−0.0335	−0.0334	−0.0331	−0.0329	−0.0298
	(0.0136)*	(0.0136)*	(0.0136)*	(0.0136)*	(0.0136)*	(0.0136)*	(0.0137)*	(0.0137)*	(0.0136)*	(0.0139)*
Per unit layoffs 2009–2006 average	0.0199	0.0191	0.0194	0.0186	0.0187	0.0178	0.0188	0.0179	0.0189	0.0181
	(0.0045)***	(0.0042)***	(0.0046)***	(0.0042)***	(0.0048)***	(0.0043)***	(0.0048)***	(0.0043)***	(0.0048)***	(0.0043)***
Panel B: 3-year average										
Relative pay	−0.0334	−0.0327	−0.0337	−0.0331	−0.0338	−0.0334	−0.0335	−0.0330	−0.0330	−0.0296
	(0.0136)*	(0.0136)*	(0.0136)*	(0.0136)*	(0.0136)*	(0.0136)*	(0.0137)*	(0.0137)*	(0.0136)*	(0.0139)*
Per unit layoffs 2009–2007 average	0.0148	0.0140	0.0145	0.0137	0.0139	0.0131	0.0139	0.0131	0.0140	0.0132
	(0.0035)***	(0.0032)***	(0.0035)***	(0.0032)***	(0.0036)***	(0.0032)***	(0.0036)***	(0.0032)***	(0.0036)***	(0.0032)***
Panel C: 2-year average										
Relative pay	−0.0335	−0.0331	−0.0336	−0.0334	−0.0338	−0.0337	−0.0334	−0.0334	−0.0330	−0.0302
	(0.0136)*	(0.0136)*	(0.0136)*	(0.0136)*	(0.0136)*	(0.0136)*	(0.0137)*	(0.0137)*	(0.0136)*	(0.0139)*
Per unit layoffs 2009–2008 average	0.0145	0.0140	0.0140	0.0135	0.0133	0.0128	0.0134	0.0129	0.0134	0.0129
	(0.0036)***	(0.0033)***	(0.0036)***	(0.0033)***	(0.0037)***	(0.0033)***	(0.0037)***	(0.0033)***	(0.0037)***	(0.0033)***
Covariates included in the models above										
Basic[a]	Yes		Yes		Yes		Yes		Yes	
Gender and ethnicity			Yes		Yes		Yes		Yes	
Defined benefit					Yes		Yes		Yes	
Family characteristics							Yes		Yes	
Salary change									Yes	

Sample size is 1073. Robust standard errors are shown in parentheses for OLS with observed information matrix for logit. *P*-values are indicated by *$p < 0.05$, ***$p < 0.001$.

[a]Basic covariates include age, years of service, fulltime and academic staff dummies.

each layoff variable construction differs little depending on which average we choose. Using the layoff variable constructed from a 4-year average subject to the largest number of covariates (column 5), the coefficient of 0.0181 implies that an increase of 5 layoffs per 1000 employees is associated with a 9 percentage point increase in the probability of enrolling in the SRI. This suggests that employees were responding to perceptions of job-loss risk when deciding to accept the SRI.

Resource Deviations as Indicators
We estimated similar models to those shown in Table 3 with deviations in resources in place of layoffs as potential measures of job-loss risk and the results are presented in Table 4. Panel A includes a variable constructed as the 2009 total budgeted resources per employee less the 2008 total budgeted resources per employee in units of $10,000. Panels B and C contain similar resource measure, with the deviations of the 2009 amounts from 2 and 3 year previous averages, respectively. The effect size diminishes from −0.022 for a 1-year deviation to approximately −0.008 for a deviation from a 3-year average, only significant at the 5% level for the 1-year deviation. This drop in effect size may reflect the limited time horizon employees consider when focusing on previous resource levels. Interpreting the coefficient on the 1-year deviation in resources reported in column 5, a one standard deviation unit increase in resources of $15,000 per employee is associated with a 3.3 percentage point decrease in the probability of enrolling in the SRI. The 1-year budgeted resource deviation provides more support that employees were responding to perceptions of job-loss risk.

Budgeted Salary Expenditure Deviations as a Risk Measure
Our final measure of job-loss risk is reported in Table 5. Here we include three panels as in Table 4 with panel A reporting results based on regressions that include the 2009 per employee budgeted salary expenditures less the 2008 per employee budgeted salary expenditures and the remaining panels report regressions that have a deviation from two or three previous year averages. Similar to the resource measures, the coefficient on the salary measure is consistently significant across specification only in the first panel. Because the movements and levels of the budgeted resources and budgeted salary measures per employee are highly correlated (Fig. 1), we might expect each measure to essentially produce the same impact on employee acceptance of the incentive. Results from panel A suggest that an increase in budgeted per employee salary expenditures of one standard deviation ($4,000 per employee) is associated with a decrease in the probability of

Table 4. Resource and Relative Pay Coefficients from Regressions of SRI Enrollment (Yes = 1) on Hierarchical Compositions of Covariates.

	(1) OLS	(1) Logit	(2) OLS	(2) Logit	(3) OLS	(3) Logit	(4) OLS	(4) Logit	(5) OLS	(5) Logit
Panel A: Deviation from prior year										
Relative pay	-0.0333	-0.0335	-0.0334	-0.0339	-0.0337	-0.0345	-0.0335	-0.0343	-0.0330	-0.0317
	(0.0136)*	(0.0137)*	(0.0136)*	(0.0137)*	(0.0136)*	(0.0137)*	(0.0137)*	(0.0138)*	(0.0136)*	(0.0140)*
Resource 2009 per employee deviation from prior year	-0.0233	-0.0242	-0.0219	-0.0224	-0.0216	-0.0223	-0.0216	-0.0222	-0.0212	-0.0217
	(0.0106)*	(0.0109)*	(0.0106)*	(0.0110)*	(0.0106)*	(0.0110)*	(0.0106)*	(0.0110)*	(0.0106)*	(0.0110)*
Panel B: Deviation from 2-year average										
Relative pay	-0.0332	-0.0333	-0.0334	-0.0338	-0.0337	-0.0345	-0.0335	-0.0343	-0.0331	-0.0315
	(0.0136)*	(0.0137)*	(0.0136)*	(0.0138)*	(0.0136)*	(0.0138)*	(0.0137)*	(0.0138)*	(0.0136)*	(0.0141)*
Resource 2009 per employee deviation from 2-year average	-0.0190	-0.0195	-0.0180	-0.0181	-0.0198	-0.0202	-0.0197	-0.0201	-0.0194	-0.0199
	(0.0130)	(0.0126)	(0.0130)	(0.0127)	(0.0130)	(0.0127)	(0.0131)	(0.0127)	(0.0130)	(0.0127)
Panel C: Deviation from 3-year average										
Relative pay	-0.0332	-0.0332	-0.0335	-0.0337	-0.0338	-0.0344	-0.0336	-0.0342	-0.0332	-0.0314
	(0.0136)*	(0.0138)*	(0.0136)*	(0.0138)*	(0.0136)*	(0.0138)*	(0.0137)*	(0.0139)*	(0.0136)*	(0.0141)*
Resource 2009 per employee deviation from 3-year average	-0.0068	-0.0071	-0.0055	-0.0057	-0.0088	-0.0092	-0.0087	-0.0091	-0.0081	-0.0083
	(0.0109)	(0.0106)	(0.0110)	(0.0106)	(0.0111)	(0.0108)	(0.0111)	(0.0108)	(0.0111)	(0.0108)
Covariates included in the models above										
Basic[a]	Yes		Yes		Yes		Yes		Yes	
Gender and ethnicity			Yes		Yes		Yes		Yes	
Defined benefit					Yes		Yes		Yes	
Family characteristics							Yes		Yes	
Salary change									Yes	

Sample size is 1073. Robust standard errors are shown in parentheses for OLS with observed information matrix for logit. *P*-values are indicated by * $p < 0.05$.

[a]Basic covariates include age, years of service, fulltime and academic staff dummies.

Table 5. Salary Expenditures and Relative Pay Coefficients from Regressions of SRI Enrollment (Yes = 1) on Hierarchical Compositions of Covariates.

	(1) OLS	(1) Logit	(2) OLS	(2) Logit	(3) OLS	(3) Logit	(4) OLS	(4) Logit	(5) OLS	(5) Logit
Panel A: Deviation from prior year										
Relative pay	-0.0333	-0.0336	-0.0334	-0.0339	-0.0337	-0.0344	-0.0334	-0.0341	-0.0329	-0.0317
	(0.0136)*	(0.0136)*	(0.0136)*	(0.0137)*	(0.0136)*	(0.0137)*	(0.0137)*	(0.0137)*	(0.0136)*	(0.0139)*
Salary 2009 per employee deviation from prior year	-0.0918	-0.0950	-0.0881	-0.0901	-0.0834	-0.0859	-0.0837	-0.0860	-0.0830	-0.0846
	(0.0311)**	(0.0326)**	(0.0308)**	(0.0327)**	(0.0311)**	(0.0329)**	(0.0312)**	(0.0329)**	(0.0311)**	(0.0330)**
Panel B: Deviation from 2-year average										
Relative pay	-0.0333	-0.0335	-0.0334	-0.0339	-0.0337	-0.0345	-0.0334	-0.0343	-0.0330	-0.0317
	(0.0136)*	(0.0137)*	(0.0136)*	(0.0137)*	(0.0136)*	(0.0137)*	(0.0137)*	(0.0138)*	(0.0136)*	(0.0140)*
Salary 2009 per employee deviation from 2-year average	-0.0778	-0.0792	-0.0737	-0.0745	-0.0702	-0.0716	-0.0703	-0.0715	-0.0706	-0.0709
	(0.0364)*	(0.0366)*	(0.0362)*	(0.0367)*	(0.0364)	(0.0369)	(0.0365)	(0.0369)	(0.0363)	(0.0369)
Panel C: Deviation from 3-year average										
Relative pay	-0.0332	-0.0332	-0.0335	-0.0337	-0.0338	-0.0344	-0.0336	-0.0342	-0.0332	-0.0314
	(0.0136)*	(0.0138)*	(0.0136)*	(0.0138)	(0.0136)*	(0.0138)*	(0.0137)*	(0.0138)*	(0.0136)*	(0.0141)*
Salary 2009 per employee deviation from 3-year average	-0.0388	-0.0395	-0.0331	-0.0341	-0.0368	-0.0383	-0.0365	-0.0378	-0.0357	-0.0359
	(0.0384)	(0.0371)	(0.0385)	(0.0372)	(0.0386)	(0.0375)	(0.0388)	(0.0375)	(0.0386)	(0.0374)
Covariates included in the models above										
Basic[a]	Yes		Yes		Yes		Yes		Yes	
Gender and ethnicity			Yes		Yes		Yes		Yes	
Defined benefit					Yes		Yes		Yes	
Family characteristics							Yes		Yes	
Salary change									Yes	

Sample size is 1073. Robust standard errors are shown in parentheses for OLS with observed information matrix for logit. P-values indicated by $^*p<0.05$, $^{**}p<0.01$.
[a]Basic covariates include age, years of service, fulltime and academic staff dummies.

enrolling in the SRI ranging from 3.3 to 3.8 percentage points – almost identical to the impact we reported above of a one standard deviation increase in the resource variable. The 1-year budgeted salary expenditure deviation provides further support that employees responded to perceptions of job-loss risk.

Sensitivity Tests
We have found that, on average, individuals with lower relative pay were more likely to accept the offer of the retirement incentive. A subsidiary issue is whether these lower relative pay individuals are more sensitive to the possibility of future layoff and thus more likely to weight such a possibility more heavily in their acceptance decision. Panel A of Table 6 presents estimated coefficients from models that test if this occurs; we estimate models in which we restrict the sample first to people with relative pay above the mean and then with relative pay below the mean. Recalling that the layoff and SRI acceptance rates for ILR were both much higher than for the rest of the university, we further restrict the sample in panel B, excluding employees from ILR, to see if excluding the relatively small number of employees from this unit influences our estimated coefficients.

Effect sizes between panels A and B are very similar, suggesting that our estimated relationships were not driven by the one "outlier" unit. Moreover, we are not able to reject the hypothesis that employees whose relative pay variable is below or above average react differently to layoff probabilities or other measures of unit financial stress in making their decisions whether to accept the retirement incentive offer.

Does One Indicator Dominate?
Finally, in Table 7 we simultaneously include our layoff risk indicator with the resource variable in column 4, and with the salary variable in column 5, to better assess which effect is more important in employees' decisions whether to accept the retirement incentive. The effects of these variables when they were included in the model one at a time are shown in columns 1 through 3 for comparative purposes. The coefficient on the layoff variable changes very little when either the salary or resource variable is also included in the model. In contrast, the salary and resource coefficients are approximately cut in half when the layoff variable is included in the model and their statistical significance is greatly reduced. These findings suggest that the disappearance of co-workers through layoffs (of the increased perception that one's own probability of layoffs will be higher as the result

Table 6. Regression of SRI (Yes = 1) on Models with Layoff, Resource and Salary Change by Relative Pay.

	+ Relative pay <0		Relative pay> = 0		Relative pay <0	
	OLS	Logit	OLS	Logit	OLS	Logit
Panel A: Everyone						
Dependent variable mean	0.3281		0.2832		0.3700	
A.1: Models with layoff						
Layoff per employee 2006–2009 average	0.0190 (0.0049)***	0.0183 (0.0043)***	0.0108 (0.0068)	0.0111 (0.0069)	0.0232 (0.0067)***	0.0222 (0.0059)***
A.2: Models with resources						
Resource 2009 per employee deviation from 2008	-0.0214 (0.0106)*	-0.0211 (0.011)	-0.0060 (0.0147)	-0.0064 (0.0153)	-0.0360 (0.0151)*	-0.0353 (0.0156)*
A.3: Models with salary						
Salary 2009 per employee deviation from 2008	-0.0838 (0.031)**	-0.0828 (0.033)*	-0.0560 (0.0435)	-0.0590 (0.0462)	-0.1032 (0.0452)*	-0.0996 (0.0468)*
Sample size	1073		519		554	
Panel B: Without ILR employees						
Dependent variable mean	0.3198		0.2809		0.3566	
B.1: Models with layoff						
Layoff per employee 2006–2009 average	0.0196 (0.0089)*	0.0193 (0.0088)*	0.0211 (0.0121)	0.0209 (0.0125)	0.0156 (0.0132)	0.0158 (0.0125)
B.2: Models with resources						
Resource 2009 per employee deviation from 2008	-0.0223 (0.0106)*	-0.0218 (0.0109)*	-0.0068 (0.0148)	-0.0073 (0.0153)	-0.0375 (0.0151)*	-0.0364 (0.0153)*
B.3: Models with salary						
Salary 2009 per employee deviation from 2008	-0.0785 (0.0313)*	-0.0763 (0.0328)*	-0.0584 (0.0443)	-0.0611 (0.0464)	-0.0942 (0.0452)*	-0.0887 (0.0461)
Sample size	1032		502		530	

Robust standard errors are shown in parentheses for OLS with observed information matrix for logit. All models contain age, years of service, fulltime and academic staff dummies, gender and ethnicity, defined benefit, family characteristics, and salary change. Not included are relative pay or unit dummies. P-values indicated by * $p<0.05$, ** $p<0.01$, *** $p<0.001$.

Table 7. Regression of SRI (Yes = 1) on Models with Job Loss Indicators Given Individually and in Combination[a].

	(1)	(2)	(3)	(4)	(5)
Panel A: OLS models					
Relative pay	−0.0329	−0.0330	−0.0329	−0.0328	−0.0328
	(0.0136)*	(0.0136)*	(0.0136)*	(0.0136)*	(0.0136)*
Layoff per employee 2006–2009 average	0.0189			0.0178	0.0168
	(0.0048)***			(0.0049)***	(0.0051)***
Resource 2009 per employee deviation from 2008		−0.0212		−0.0125	
		(0.0106)*		(0.0109)	
Salary 2009 per employee deviation from 2008			−0.0830		−0.0465
			(0.0311)**		(0.0329)
Panel B: Logit models					
Relative pay	−0.0298	−0.0317	−0.0317	−0.0303	−0.0304
	(0.0139)*	(0.0140)*	(0.0139)*	(0.0139)*	(0.0139)*
Layoff per employee 2006–2009 average	0.0181			0.0170	0.0160
	(0.0043)***			(0.0044)***	(0.0046)***
Resource 2009 per employee deviation from 2008		−0.0217		−0.0130	
		(0.0110)*		(0.0112)	
Salary 2009 per employee deviation from 2008			−0.0846		−0.0485
			(0.0330)*		(0.0343)

Robust standard errors are shown in parentheses for OLS with observed information matrix for logit. All models contain age, years of service, fulltime and academic staff dummies, gender and ethnicity, defined benefit, family characteristics, and salary change. Not included are unit dummies.

P-values indicated by *$p < 0.05$, **$p < 0.01$, ***$p < 0.001$.

[a]The correlation between the salary and resource indicators is high (0.90). Consequently, they are not included in the same regression.

of previous layoffs) is more relevant in a decision to accept early retirement than strictly financial indicators like resource or salary changes.

CONCLUSION

The Cornell SRI program helped the university to moderate the number of its employees that it subsequently laid off as it tried to restore its economic balance after the economic dislocation of 2008. We have provided evidence that employees' decisions to accept the incentive were conditioned on their perceptions of the economic stress that their units faced. In addition, to the extent that our relative pay variable is a proxy for employees' relative productivity, our results also suggest that adverse selection was not a problem for the university; on average it was the lower relative pay employees who accepted the retirement incentive offer.

ACKNOWLEDGMENTS

We are grateful to Mary Opperman, Vice President for Human Resources at Cornell; Veronica Banks, Manager of Data Analysis at Cornell Benefit Services; Linda Nobles, Senior Benefit Analyst at Cornell, and their staffs for providing us with much of the data used in this study and working with us on the project. CHERI receives financial support from the Andrew W. Mellon Foundation and we are also grateful to the Foundation for its support. We also thank seminar participants at Cornell University, the 2011 WEAI, and the 2011 NBER Summer Institute for helpful comments.

NOTES

1. Non-union refers to Cornell employees whose positions are not covered under a collective bargaining agreement. We restrict our analyses to the non-union population (except for a few falsification tests as we describe below) which represents 84% of those eligible for the retirement incentive. This restriction is imposed because pay increases under Cornell's collective bargaining contracts do not have merit pay components, so relative pay comparisons among union workers will not yield meaningful comparisons of productivity differences.

2. We define above average productivity as those who have positive wage residuals (see details in Econometric Framework Section). Another interpretation, as noted by a referee, is that positive wage residual employees may, in fact, be overpaid so may be

less likely to leave since they cannot recover such wages elsewhere. Another referee noted that some employees may have higher salaries partly as a result of political astuteness. One way to explore this further would be to repeat the analysis for "banded" and "unclassified/academic" employees separately, which we leave for future work.

3. Specific exclusions were made for senior administrators reporting to the president of the university; County-Based Cornell Cooperative Extension Association employees who were paid by the local County Cooperative Extension Associations and not by Cornell; employees at Cornell's Puerto Rico observatory; employees on long-term disability; employees on university leave (who are not guaranteed reemployment rights, and individuals who had submitted voluntary resignation letters prior to March 1).

4. The university had announced that if the number of submitted applicants exceeded the funds available to finance the program, it would base enrollment in the program on applicants' seniority at the university, not the date of their applications. Ultimately, it decided to accept all of the eligible applications. Any submitted application could be withdrawn before the window offer expired. Any individual that received layoff notice while the window was available could still enroll in the program.

5. Of course, there are non-monetary and psychological rewards and costs of retirement at a given time depending on the decisions of co-workers. We do not explore this in the article.

6. In results not shown in this article, we estimated models using FY 2010 budget information to test an assumption of rational expectations. The FY 2010 budget information was not available to the employees prior to accepting the SRI. These models were inconsistent across specification and seldom had precise coefficients.

7. One possibility for missing salary is that the individual was temporarily away from the university that year (for example, a spouse of a faculty member accompanying the faculty member when he or she was on sabbatical). Eligibility for the SRI required 10 years of service, not 10 consecutive years of service.

8. Using the Health and Retirement Survey, Bound, Schoenbaum, Stinebrickner, and Waidmann (1999); Brown (2000), and Dwyer and Hu (2000) showed that higher employee health is negatively correlated with the decision to retire while spousal health has a positive association with retirement probabilities. Stock and Wise (1990) and Samwick (1998) show that the present discounted value of future wealth from retiring at a given date is an important factor in retirement decisions.

9. Cornell also has campuses in New York City and Doha, Qatar. Only Ithaca employees were eligible for the SRI.

10. Employment unit codes are as follows: SS "Student Services," AP "Academic Programs," AS "Administration and Support," CALS "College of Agriculture and Life Sciences," AAP "Architecture, Art & Planning," ART "Arts and Sciences," ENG "Engineering," HOTEL "Hotel Administration," CHE "College of Human Ecology," ILR "Industrial and Labor Relations," JS "Johnson School," LAW "Law School," VET "College of Veterinary Medicine."

11. For comparison purposes, a logit model is also presented in this table; the signs and significance of the coefficients are very similar in the two models. It would be interesting to explore a similar analysis for employees not given the incentive or for workers in units with the incentive but for prior years.

12. The differences in the precision of the estimated coefficients of the employment unit variables are driven largely by differences in sample sizes. Some of the precisely estimated coefficients (e.g., those for Academic Programs (AP) and the College of Agriculture and Life Sciences (CALS)) have over 150 individuals in the eligible population, while some of the imprecisely estimated coefficients (e.g., those for the College of Architecture, Art, and Planning (AAP) and the School of Hotel Administration (HOTEL)) have fewer than 15 individuals in the eligible population.

13. See, e.g., Pencavel (2001), Ashenfelter and Card (2002), Allen, Clark, and Ghent (2004), and Kim (2003).

14. Results are not dependent on this specification. Changing the aggregation cut-points, including age and age squared result in virtually no change in the second-stage coefficient estimates.

15. The standard deviation of the residual is 0.17.

16. This type of argument with respect to a residual of course assumes that the functional form of the model is correctly specified and that no relevant variables are excluded from the analysis.

17. Of course, employees with low relative pay may have been perceived less positively by their supervisors and, therefore, be less happy. We do not explore such psychological explanations in this article.

18. Of course, the low relative pay could also serve as a proxy for something else.

19. Concerned that our method of adjusting the laid off population's salary and years of service could contribute to the distributional differences we observe, we also make the comparison using the following alternative method. Using the historic salary information from our SRI population, we separately compute a value for the relative pay variable for each year an employee was laid off. For example, employees laid off in 2006 will be included in a regression with the SRI population (at their 2006 salary and years of service) to compute a value for the relative pay variable. This method leads to very similar distributional differences between the relative pay variable for the laid off and SRI populations, with the gap in means slightly more dramatic.

20. The bandwidth chosen is the minimum of the optimal bandwidths of each density computed as the bandwidth that would minimize the mean integrated squared error if the data were distributed Gaussian and a Gaussian kernel were used.

21. A final test for interpreting our relative pay variable as a proxy for productivity was to estimate its effect on eligible employees' decisions to accept the retirement incentive offer in a sample of eligible employees who *were* covered by collective bargaining agreements (most of this article is focused on the non-union population, the large majority of staff at Cornell). Inasmuch as these agreements do not provide for merit pay increases, we might expect that the coefficient of the relative pay variable would be statistically insignificantly different from zero when we estimate the relationship between SRI enrollment and relative pay for this sample (if the relationship in the non-union sample is due to relatively low productive non-union employees enrolling in the SRI). While the coefficient for the collective bargaining sample was statistically insignificantly different from zero at the .05 level of significance, it was negative and its absolute magnitude was larger than the similar coefficient from the sample of non-union employees reported in the text. The magnitude of this coefficient in the collective bargaining sample reduces our

confidence somewhat that our relative pay variable is a good proxy for relative productivity in the non-collective bargaining sample.

REFERENCES

Allen, S., Clark, R., & Ghent, L. (2004). Phasing into retirement. *Industrial and Labor Relations Review, 58*(1), 112–127.

Angrist, J. D., & Lavy, V. (2009). The effects of high stakes high school achievement awards: Evidence from a randomized trial. *American Economic Review, 99*(4), 1384–1414.

Ashenfelter, O., & Card, D. (2002). Did the elimination of mandatory retirement affect faculty retirement?. *American Economic Review, 92*(4), 957–980.

Bell, R. M., & McCaffrey, D. (2002). Bias reduction in standard errors for linear regression with multi-stage samples. *Survey Methodology, 28*(2), 169–181.

Brown, C. (2000). Early retirement windows. In O. S. Mitchell, P. B. Hammond & A. M. Rappaport (Eds.), *Forecasting retirement needs and retirement wealth*. Philadelphia, PA: University of Pennsylvania Press.

Dwyer, D., & Hu, J. (2000). Retirement expectations and realizations: The role of health shocks and economic factors. In O. S. Mitchell, P. B. Hammond & A. M. Rappaport (Eds.), *Forecasting retirement needs and retirement wealth* (pp. 274–287). Philadelphia, PA: University of Philadelphia Press.

Kim, S. (2003). The impact of research productivity on early retirement of university professors. *Industrial Relations: A Journal of Economy and Society, 42*(1), 106–125.

Liang, K., & Zeger, S. (1986). Longitudinal data analysis using generalized linear models. *Biometrics, 42*, 121–130.

Murphy, K. M., & Topel, R. (1985). Estimation and inference in two-step econometric models. *Journal of Business and Economic Statistics, 3*(4), 370–379.

Murphy, K. M., & Topel, R. H. (2002). Estimation and inference in two-step econometric models. *Journal of Business and Economic Statistics, 20*(1), 88–97.

Pencavel, J. (2001). The response of employees to severance incentives: The University of California's faculty, 1991–94. *The Journal of Human Resources, 36*(1), 58.

Samwick, A. (1998). New evidence on pensions, social security, and the timing of retirement. *Journal of Public Economics, 70*(2), 207–236.

Stock, J. H., & Wise, D. (1990). Pensions, the option value of work, and retirement. *Econometrica, 58*(5), 1151–1180.

APPENDIX

Table A1. Regression of Enrolled in SRI (Yes = 1) on Socioeconomic Characteristics and Employment Unit Dummies.

	OLS	Logit
Aged 57–58	−0.0199	−0.0277
	(0.0375)	(0.0484)
Aged 59–60	0.1271**	0.1324**
	(0.0438)	(0.0457)
Aged 61–62	0.2242***	0.2156***
	(0.0466)	(0.0450)
Aged 63–64	0.2939***	0.2791***
	(0.0551)	(0.0512)
Aged 65–66	0.3010***	0.2832***
	(0.0664)	(0.0586)
Aged 67–68	0.3321***	0.3165***
	(0.0873)	(0.0780)
Aged 69 +	0.3749***	0.3453***
	(0.0955)	(0.0781)
Years of service 16–20	0.0167	0.0184
	(0.0459)	(0.0470)
Years of service 21–25	0.0400	0.0409
	(0.0421)	(0.0435)
Years of service 26–30	0.0580	0.0608
	(0.0430)	(0.0434)
Years of service 31–35	0.1180*	0.1157*
	(0.0515)	(0.0487)
Years of service 36 +	0.1829**	0.1615**
	(0.0614)	(0.0537)
Fulltime	−0.0148	−0.0051
	(0.0513)	(0.0472)
Non-academic staff	0.0550	0.0604
	(0.0404)	(0.0429)
Female	0.0157	0.0196
	(0.0304)	(0.0300)
Asian	−0.1804*	−0.2202
	(0.0776)	(0.1248)
Black	0.0233	0.0228
	(0.0966)	(0.0943)
Hispanic	−0.0195	−0.0097
	(0.1417)	(0.1356)
Unknown	0.3602	0.3140
	(0.2015)	(0.1620)

Table A1. (*Continued*)

	OLS	Logit
Defined benefit plan	−0.0096	−0.0068
	(0.0507)	(0.0481)
Spouse or partner on health plan	0.0031	0.0048
	(0.0296)	(0.0288)
Dependent child on health plan	−0.0226	−0.0238
	(0.0330)	(0.0370)
SS	−0.0995	−0.0970
	(0.0534)	(0.0542)
AP	−0.1234**	−0.1191**
	(0.0438)	(0.0453)
CALS	0.0047	0.0063
	(0.0496)	(0.0487)
AAP	0.0923	0.0984
	(0.1507)	(0.1249)
ART	−0.1478**	−0.1445**
	(0.0532)	(0.0553)
ENG	−0.1346	−0.1319
	(0.0826)	(0.0858)
HOTEL	−0.1162	−0.1133
	(0.1029)	(0.1326)
CHE	0.0124	0.0137
	(0.0963)	(0.0822)
ILR	0.2280**	0.2120**
	(0.0850)	(0.0729)
JS	0.1648	0.1445
	(0.1165)	(0.1039)
LAW	−0.1055	−0.1043
	(0.0982)	(0.1117)
VET	−0.0518	−0.0434
	(0.0671)	(0.0681)
Salary 2006–2009 relative change	−0.2086*	−0.3144*
	(0.1029)	(0.1517)
Log 2009 salary	−0.0934*	−0.0866*
	(0.0376)	(0.0368)
Constant	1.2053**	
	(0.4133)	

Sample size is 1073. Robust standard errors are shown in parentheses for OLS with observed information matrix for logit.
Employment unit codes are as follows: SS "Student Services," AP "Academic Programs," CALS "College of Agriculture and Life Sciences," AAP "Architecture, Art, and Planning," ART "Arts and Sciences," ENG "Engineering," HOTEL "School of Hotel Administration," CHE "College of Human Ecology," ILR "School of Industrial and Labor Relations," JS "Johnson School," LAW "Cornell's Law School," VET "College of Veterinary Medicine."
P-values indicated by *$p<0.05$, **$p<0.01$, ***$p<0.001$.

THE MENTAL COST OF PENSION LOSS: THE EXPERIENCE OF RUSSIA'S PENSIONERS DURING TRANSITION

Penka Kovacheva and Xiaotong Niu

ABSTRACT

In this article we investigate the impact of the 1996 pension crisis in Russia on several measures of subjective well-being (SWB). Using a difference-in-difference strategy and an individual fixed-effects model, we find that an exogenous shock to the redistribution system has a significant negative effect on the SWB of pensioners who fail to receive their pensions. The effect differs across aspects of life evaluation; the shock has a significant negative effect on current life satisfaction (LS), whereas it has no effect on self-assessed health. The effect of the shock extends to non-pensioners who live with pensioners in arrears: they experience an equally strong and significant decline in LS even after accounting for personal income. In addition, we find that the pension crisis leads pensioner households to neither receive more nor send less money to extended family, thus leaving these households to bear alone the entire monetary cost. Lastly, we find suggestive evidence that the crisis, despite being a purely monetary shock, affects well-being in ways that go beyond

Research in Labor Economics, Volume 36, 191–240
Copyright © 2012 by Emerald Group Publishing Limited
All rights of reproduction in any form reserved
ISSN: 0147-9121/doi:10.1108/S0147-9121(2012)0000036010

the monetary size of pension loss. Policies aimed to fully compensate for such disruptions in the redistribution system would need to take these externalities into account.

Keywords: Subjective well-being; pension crisis; income shocks; transition economies

JEL classifications: D12; I31; I38; P29

INTRODUCTION

There is a growing literature on the correlates and determinants of subjective well-being (SWB) (Kahneman & Krueger, 2006). In particular, the effects of income on SWB have received a lot of attention, especially in the context of developed countries.[1] Fewer studies have analyzed this relationship in the context of transition economies, and most of the existing studies have not identified an exogenous source of variation in income.[2] In transition economies, the public redistribution system can be a source of idiosyncratic income shocks for the household.[3] An important policy question is how the instability of social programs affects welfare as measured by SWB. Our results show that an adverse shock to the Russian pension system leads to a significant decline in measures of SWB and that the non-pecuniary cost of the shock is substantial.

This article exploits an episode of instability in the Russian pension system. In Russia, the elderly are a particular vulnerable group financially because most of them have no other personal source of income and live with few other employed adults. We investigate the impact of the 1996 pension crisis in Russia on several measures of SWB of pensioners and non-pensioner members of their households. In 1996, an uncertain political climate prior to the presidential elections of that year led to declines in economic output and in tax collection (the latter due to widespread tax exemptions granted before the elections). This resulted in a large decline in tax revenues relative to pension entitlements in most regions. The pension system experienced a significant funding crisis and many adults eligible for pensions were not paid in 1996. Nevertheless, the crisis was a one-time shock – the economy stabilized soon after the election and the pension system was restored in

1997. Still, the short-term impact of the crisis was severe: poverty rates doubled among affected pensioners (Jensen & Richter, 2003).[4]

Our results show that the crisis significantly reduces life satisfaction (LS) of the affected pensioners. The availability of other measures of life evaluation in the data allows us to study which aspects of life are affected by the crisis. In particular, while self-assessed health (SAH) is not affected by the experience of pension arrears, pensioner's expectations for future LS and future economic welfare and self perceptions of relative societal power are significantly lowered. There are also spillover effects to non-pensioners living in the same households with affected pensioners. Their reported LS declines just as strongly as the pensioners who are directly affected.

In addition, we find that the effect of the crisis is heterogeneous with respect to gender and expectations prior to the crisis. Male pensioners experience a greater decline in almost all measures of SWB. The crisis also has a stronger negative impact on those individuals – both pensioners and non-pensioners – who had more positive expectations about their future prior to the crisis.

Our study also looks at potential spillover effects from the crisis beyond households with affected pensioners. We find no evidence of inter-household coping mechanisms to the pension crisis: the affected households neither give less nor receive significantly more money from extended family and friends during the crisis.

Lastly, we find some suggestive evidence that an institutional disruption in the pension system has non-pecuniary costs that extend beyond the income shock from the loss of pension income. We base this claim on several findings. First, our estimates of the effect of the crisis are 10 times larger than the predicted effect of a one-off income decline equal to the average pension size. Second, we find that non-pensioner household members report loss in LS equal to that of the pensioners directly affected by the crisis even when we control for the former's personal income. Third, we find no evidence that the magnitude of the crisis effect rises significantly with the number of pensioners in arrears in the household, which is what we would expect if the cost of the crisis were purely monetary. Finally, we find that the crisis has negative effects even on objective measures of well-being – immediate memory recall – for both pensioners and non-pensioners.

We contribute to the literature in several ways. First, our study establishes the causal effect of income on SWB using an exogenous shock to the redistribution system. Transition economies provide a fruitful context for studying such income shocks. During the 1990s, these economies experienced large and exogenous variations in incomes, which offer insights to many general economic questions. For example, Frijters, Haisken-DeNew, and Shields (2004a), Frijters, Haisken-DeNew, & Shields (2004b), Frijters, Haisken-DeNew, & Shields (2005) use the exogenous income variation between East and West Germany following reunification to study the effects of household income on LS (Frijters et al., 2004a, 2004b) and on health outcomes (Frijters et al., 2005). Similar to our findings, these studies find that rising household income is important for explaining rising LS in East Germany, and it is less important for explaining variation in health outcomes. Yet, the income shock in these studies is different in nature from ours. German reunification led to a steady increase in household income in East Germany, whereas the Russian pension crisis caused a one-time large decline in income. Another study which also focuses on Russia is Frijters, Geishecker, Haisken-DeNew, and Shields (2006). That article examines how LS was affected by large swings in real household income that occurred in the late 1990s. Given the very large size of these income swings, the authors argue that they can be treated as exogenous shocks. Our contribution to this literature is that we analyze the effects of income on a level more disaggregate than the household – we are able to separately identify the effects of income loss when it is personally incurred and the effects of income loss when it is incurred only indirectly through shared household resources.

Second, unlike the studies cited above, our study explicitly exploits the fact that the pension income shock is due to an institutional failure. As a result, we can investigate whether there is any non-pecuniary cost to SWB apart from the monetary amount of pension loss. Such shocks to the redistribution systems might account for why cross-country studies find that individuals living in transition economies are much unhappier than would be predicted by their income levels (Deaton, 2008). Our study on the impact of a pension crisis on SWB provides some understanding into the causes of dissatisfaction with life in Russia, an economy in transition.

Third, our study provides an analysis on a richer set of SWB measures in addition to the measure of LS, which is the most frequently used in the literature. These additional measures of SWB provide information on different dimensions of welfare and can provide a deeper understanding of the effects of the pension crisis on overall life evaluation. In particular, the literature has emphasized the importance of relative income in determining SWB (Clark, Frijters, & Shields, 2008). Our data include several direct measures of self-assessed position in society: economic, respect, and power rankings. These measures allow us to assess the effect of an income shock on one's perceived position relative to others in society.[5] Our data also include measures of expectations. According to the traditional life cycle theory of consumption, one-time income shocks should have a smaller effect on utility than permanent shocks because of the opportunity for inter-temporal consumption smoothing. In hindsight, we know that the pension crisis was a one-time shock. However, if the pension-eligible adults thought that the crisis would persist into the future, the pension crisis could have a large effect on expected permanent income, which might translate into a large income effect of the pension crisis on LS.

Fourth, our study builds on the literature of household resource allocation (Behrman, 1995). Previous empirical studies have shown that household members share resources,[6] but it is unclear whether such monetary spillovers translate into spillovers of LS. If there is an intra-household response to the public crisis and we focus only on affected pensioners, we would underestimate the societal impact. We address this issue by looking at the effect of the pension crisis on the SWB of other individuals who are only indirectly affected by living together with pensioners who are directly affected. In addition, the crisis might affect other households linked to pensioner households through extended family networks. In Russia, such extended family networks are important source of informal monetary transfers, especially during the transition period. In particular, Kuhn and Stillman (2004) find that pensioners in Russia give substantial monetary transfers to their adult children. Unfortunately, we cannot identify adult children who are not living with their pensioner parents in our data. However, we have information on the amount of monetary transfers sent and received by each household in our sample and we analyze the impact of pension arrears on these transfers.

Fifth, our study provides evidence supporting the theory of expectations being the reference point that determines preferences. In particular, we look at whether the crisis has a differential effect on SWB for groups with different pre-crisis expectations. Reference-dependent preferences in consumer theory suggest that utility is affected not only by the actual amount of resources but also by the amount of resources relative to a reference point. The reference point has been traditionally modeled as the status quo (Samuelson & Zeckhauser, 1988). More recently, Köszegi and Rabin (2006) develop a model of consumer behavior in which the reference point is the rational expectations formed in the recent past about future outcomes. Laboratory experiments provide evidence in support of rational expectations as the reference point (Ericson & Fuster, 2011). If it is expectations rather than the status quo that matter, we would expect those with higher pre-crisis expectations to experience a greater decline in SWB after controlling for household income. Indeed, this is what we find in our analysis.

The remainder of the article is organized as follows. The second section discusses the data and the measures of SWB used in the study. The third section describes the pension crisis of 1996. The fourth section presents the estimation strategy and addresses some identification issues. The fifth section reports the main estimates of the effect of pension arrears on the SWB of affected pensioners and non-pensioners living in households with affected pensioners. The sixth section discusses additional considerations and results from related objective measures of well-being. Lastly, the seventh section concludes with a discussion of policy implications.

DATA

The sample we use comes from Phase II of the Russia Longitudinal Monitoring Survey (RLMS),[7] a panel data of Russian households that started in 1994. Phase II data are collected in 1994, 1995, 1996, 1998, and annually starting in 2000. About 4,000 households were first interviewed in 1994. Each household is given a household questionnaire. In addition, individual questionnaires are given to all members of the household except the very young and the very old. Households that move out of their original dwellings are not followed in subsequent rounds and new households are added to the survey to maintain sample size and representation. However, given low migration and moderate non-response rates, sample attrition has been modest (Heeringa, 1997) and especially so for older demographic groups that are the focus of our study.[8]

In our main analysis we focus on the first three survey rounds: 1994, 1995, and 1996.[9] Each round is administered in the last 3 months of the calendar year – October through December. The 1996 survey is the first survey collected after the pension crisis started earlier that year. In our study we exploit the panel nature of the data, which allows us to track affected individuals before and after the crisis. Pension eligibility in Russia is defined by age: all women over the age of 55 and all men over the age of 60 are eligible for pension receipts. Our sample consists of all pension-eligible adults in 1996 and other members of their households. The individual surveys include information on income and pension receipts in the past 30 days. We define an age-eligible pensioner as being in pension arrears if he or she did not receive any pension income in the last 30 days.

We analyze several measures of SWB. In the survey, respondents are asked to assess their overall LS and health status on a five-point scale in which 1 is "very bad" and 5 is "very good." We refer to these variables as measures of LS and SAH. We also look at the effect of the crisis on other aspects of life evaluation. The survey asks respondents to place themselves on a nine-step Cantril (1965) ladder for perceived economic, power, and respect rankings in society. The English-translated question on perceived economic ranking is as follows:

> And now, please, imagine a 9-step ladder where on the bottom, the first step, stand the poorest people, and on the highest step, the ninth, stand the rich. On which step are you today?

This measure is referred to as the Welfare Ladder Question (WLQ) in the literature. The English-translated question on perceived power ranking is as follows:

> And now, please, imagine a 9-step ladder where on the bottom, the first step, stand people who are completely without rights, and on the highest step, the ninth, stand those who have a lot of power. On which step are you?

This measure is referred to as the Power Ladder Question (PLQ) in the literature (Lokshin & Ravallion, 2005). Lastly, the question on perceived respect ranking is as follows:

> And now, another 9-step ladder where on the lowest step, are people who are absolutely not respected, and on the highest step stand those who are very respected. On which step of this ladder are you?

This measure is referred to as the Respect Ladder Question (RLQ).

In the data there is also a set of measures reflecting one's outlook on future economic welfare and future LS (both measured on a five-point ordinal scale). The question about future economic welfare asks "How concerned are you about the possibility that you might not be able to provide yourself with the bare essentials in the next 12 months?" where an answer of 1 is "very concerned" and an answer of 5 is "not at all concerned." The question about future LS asks "Do you think that in the next 12 months you and your family will live better than today or worse?" where an answer of 1 is "much worse" and an answer of 5 is "much better."

Table 1 presents characteristics of our sample of pensioners and non-pensioners in 1994 and 1995, the two pre-crisis years. Over 70% of our pensioner sample is female. This is probably due to the much lower life expectancy of Russian men than Russian women and the lower age cut-off for pension eligibility for women. Pensioners who experience pension arrears during the 1996 crisis are similar to those in non-arrears in the years prior to the crisis in terms of age, gender, rates of marriage, unemployment, disability, and household composition. Both groups also transfer similar

Table 1. Pre-Crisis Demographic Characteristics by Pension Arrears Status During the 1996 Crisis.

	Non-arrears		Arrears	
	Mean	St. Error	Mean	St. Error
(a) Pensioners				
Female	0.709	0.014	0.737	0.020
Married	0.590	0.015	0.588	0.022
College degree	0.139	0.010	0.082	0.012
High school diploma	0.427	0.015	0.366	0.022
Years of age (in 1995)	65.293	0.243	64.831	0.363
Disabled	0.029	0.005	0.018	0.006
Unemployed	0.815	0.012	0.847	0.016
Pension income in bottom decile (dummy)	0.130	0.010	0.218	0.019
Household income (excluding pensions) (000's)	2.059	0.120	1.495	0.123
Net monetary transfers from extended family (000's)	−0.279	0.074	−0.239	0.159
Number of kids < 7 years old in household	0.115	0.011	0.122	0.018
Number of youths 7–18 years old in household	0.164	0.014	0.161	0.021
Number of adults in household	0.744	0.032	0.737	0.048
Number of pensioners in household	1.502	0.019	1.492	0.026
Rural area	0.230	0.013	0.437	0.022
N	1089		490	
(b) Non-pensioner household members who live with a pensioner				
Female	0.470	0.021	0.403	0.029
Married	0.594	0.020	0.604	0.029
College degree	0.207	0.017	0.119	0.019
High school diploma	0.787	0.017	0.734	0.027
Years of age (in 1995)	35.133	0.526	34.874	0.774
Disabled	0.029	0.007	0.050	0.013
Unemployed	0.380	0.020	0.388	0.029
Personal income (000's)	2.230	0.136	1.455	0.129
Household income (excluding pensions) (000's)	5.143	0.248	3.498	0.231
Net monetary transfers from extended family (000's)	−0.117	0.047	−0.273	0.368
Number of kids < 7 years old in household	0.272	0.022	0.388	0.040
Number of youths 7–18 years old in household	0.535	0.029	0.496	0.043
Number of adults in household	2.122	0.041	2.133	0.056
Number of pensioners in household	1.052	0.024	1.191	0.034
Rural area	0.176	0.016	0.439	0.030
N	581		278	

Note: The pre-crisis demographic characteristics in bold are those that are statistically different at the 5% level between the group in arrears and the group not in arrears. All income and monetary transfers are measured in 1000's of June 1992 rubles and calculated as the average of the two pre-crisis years, 1994 and 1995.

(positive) amounts of money to their extended families. The biggest difference between the groups is that the former are almost twice as likely to live in a rural area – close to 44% versus 23%. This difference likely accounts at least partially for the former's lower education and income. We observe the same patterns by arrears status among the non-pensioners living in pensioner households. In addition to the above differences, those in arrears are slightly more likely to live in households with more young children and pensioners. In the next section, we describe the pension crisis and analyze in more detail the determinants of arrears status.

THE PENSION CRISIS OF 1996[10]

The old-age pension system in Russia is administered by the state pension fund, the Pension Fund of Russia (PFR). Pension receipt is based on age eligibility and not on current employment status. There are also provisions for early retirement and early pension receipt for serious medical conditions or work in hazardous conditions.[11] Until the pension reform in 2002, the PFR was financed mainly from payroll taxes from employers and, to a very small extent, from the government budget. In 1996 the uncertain political climate before the results of the July presidential elections triggered a decline in economic output. That decline was also accompanied by a decline in tax collection due to weaker tax enforcement and various tax exemptions given out in connection to the elections. As a result, the pay-as-you-go pension system experienced a serious shortage of revenues relative to entitlements. This funding crisis caused a sudden increase in the percentage of pensioners not receiving their pensions. Fig. 1 shows the trend in pension arrears over the years. The rate of arrears was under 10% in 1994 and 1995. It jumped to more than 30% during the crisis in 1996 and went back down afterwards.

The pension system in Russia is largely decentralized. Regional pension funds collect local payroll taxes and local pension offices disburse pensions out of these revenues. Any revenue surplus is sent to the central pension fund which distributes it to those regional funds which have more regional entitlements than regional tax revenues. Such decentralization can potentially lead to regional differences in the severity of the crisis. If this were the case, we would worry that the estimated effect is capturing the differences between administrative regions. Table 2 presents the fraction of age-eligible pensioners in arrears by eight main geographical regions.[12] The

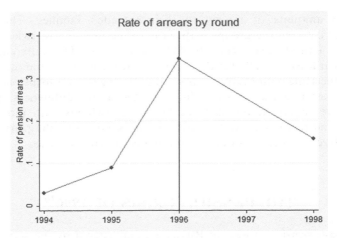

Fig. 1. Time Trend in the Rate of Pension Arrears. *Notes:* The Figure Plots the Fraction of Age-Eligible Pensioners in Arrears by Survey Round.

incidence of pension arrears was widespread during the crisis. Except for the metropolitan region, which includes Moscow and St. Petersburg, all other regions experienced sizable increase in pension arrears during the crisis. Not only was the crisis widespread, but its impact on individuals was potentially considerable. Pension income is very important for pensioner households. In 1995, pension income represented 74.6% of the total household income for pensioner households in our RLMS sample.

The reason for the pension crisis is obvious: there was not enough in the pension fund to pay off all obligations. Less obvious is how administrators dealt with the fund shortage. Instead of lowering the pension amount for every eligible pensioner, resources were used to meet obligations for a subset of eligible adults. Fig. 2 shows the average amount of pension receipt in the sample by survey round. All pensions are converted in June 1992 rubles. We see that the average pension amount among the non-arrears is comparable in 1995 and 1996, whereas the average amount among all pensioners drops sharply in this period due to increase in the number of arrears.

Since only some pensioners were paid, what were the selection criteria? We estimate a linear probability model where the outcome variable is whether a pensioner is in arrears in 1996. We want to see which pre-crisis

Table 2.   Rates of Pension Arrears by Region Before and After the 1996
Crisis.

	1995		1996	
	Mean	St. Error	Mean	St. Error
Metropolitan: Moscow and St. Petersburg cities (both donor districts)	0.027	0.163	0.031	0.015
Northern and Northwestern (contains one donor district: Komi Republic)	0.057	0.232	0.327	0.048
Central and Central Black-Earth (only debtor districts)	0.091	0.288	0.285	0.023
Volga-Vaytski and Volga Basin (only debtor districts)	0.078	0.269	0.365	0.027
North Caucasian (only debtor districts)	0.142	0.349	0.526	0.032
Ural (only debtor districts)	0.080	0.271	0.302	0.033
Western Siberian (contains one donor district: Khanty-Mansi Oblast)	0.232	0.423	0.515	0.039
Eastern Siberian and Far Eastern (contains one donor district: Primorsky Krai)	0.000	0.000	0.309	0.038
Overall	0.090	0.006	0.345	0.011

Note: Based on authors' own calculation using the RLMS. In parentheses we indicate whether the given geographical region contains administrative pension districts which were net donors of pension revenues during the 1996 pension crisis. In italics are those regions that do *not* experience a statistically significant increase at the 5% level in the rate of arrears between 1995 and 1996.

characteristics can predict arrears status in 1996. There were official guidelines suggesting that priority is given to those with low income, the unemployed, and the single. Some regions also gave priority to the old and the disabled. Nevertheless, these guidelines were neither well, nor universally followed. As Table 3 shows, the probability of arrears during the crisis is not associated with pre-crisis household income in any region. Low pension income and being unemployed prior to the crisis are also not universal determinants of arrears status, with only a couple of regions showing a statistically significant negative association for at most one of these characteristics. Moreover, in several regions these variables are associated with arrears status in the direction opposite of the one predicted by the priority criteria. Neither are any of the other pre-crisis individual or household characteristics systematically related to arrears status.[13]

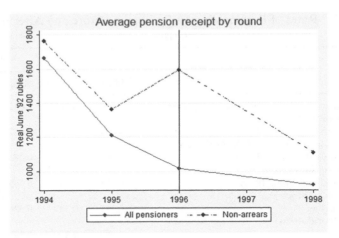

Fig. 2. Time Trend in the Amount of Pension Receipt. *Note*: The Solid Line Plots the Average Real Pension Income Among All Age-Eligible Pensioners by Survey Round. The Dotted Line Plots the Average Real Pension Income Among Those Who Actually Receive Their Pensions by Survey Round.

EMPIRICAL STRATEGY

Main Estimates

We employ a difference-in-difference (DD) approach to study the effect of pension arrears on SWB. In particular, we compare the change in the measures of SWB before and after the pension crisis for our treatment and control groups. Our pensioner sample consists of all individuals who are eligible for pensions in 1996 and who did not experience pension arrears in any year before the crisis. Our non-pensioner sample consists of all adult individuals who are living in the same household with at least one member of the pensioner sample. Within the pensioner sample we define the treatment group as those individuals who do not receive their pensions during the 1996 crisis and the control group as those individuals who do receive their pensions during the crisis. Within the non-pensioner sample we define the treatment group as adult individuals living with pensioners who are in arrears during the crisis and the control group as adult individuals living with pensioners who are not in arrears. The identifying assumption is that in the absence of the crisis, there would be

Table 3. Pre-Crisis Determinants of Pension Arrears During the 1996 Crisis by Region.

	Region 1	Region 2	Region 3	Region 4	Region 5	Region 6	Region 7	Region 8
Pre-crisis levels								
Female	0.037	0.033	0.073	0.019	-0.058	0.044	-0.081**	0.059
	(0.034)	(0.103)	(0.045)	(0.045)	(0.072)	(0.026)	(0.017)	(0.025)
Married	-0.077	0.028	-0.015	-0.027	-0.025	-0.028	0.052	-0.068
	(0.048)	(0.193)	(0.066)	(0.082)	(0.203)	(0.126)	(0.074)	(0.100)
College	0.057	0.043	0.124	-0.001	-0.238*	-0.169	-0.359*	0.013
	(0.012)	(0.051)	(0.086)	(0.056)	(0.085)	(0.110)	(0.106)	(0.212)
High School	0.044*	0.015	0.091	-0.097	-0.153*	0.070	-0.035	-0.221
	(0.005)	(0.023)	(0.085)	(0.091)	(0.060)	(0.049)	(0.106)	(0.130)
Age	0.015	-0.202	-0.026	-0.037*	-0.000	-0.018	-0.004	-0.080
	(0.012)	(0.042)	(0.042)	(0.017)	(0.031)	(0.092)	(0.042)	(0.121)
Age squared (/100)	-1.137	16.591	1.863	2.447*	-0.186	0.332	0.131	5.251
	(0.916)	(2.919)	(2.933)	(1.073)	(2.300)	(6.536)	(3.382)	(8.781)
Disabled	-0.125	0.207	-0.010	-0.410**	0.117	-0.296	-0.230	-0.078
	(0.024)	(0.212)	(0.128)	(0.136)	(0.138)	(0.175)	(0.352)	(0.066)
Unemployed	0.041**	0.006	0.108	-0.018	0.074	0.053	-0.103*	-0.270
	(0.002)	(0.126)	(0.072)	(0.057)	(0.071)	(0.082)	(0.352)	(0.181)
Pension in bottom decile (dummy)	0.274	-0.223	0.236**	0.013	0.046	0.060	-0.131**	-0.115**
	(0.101)	(0.122)	(0.083)	(0.059)	(0.099)	(0.137)	(0.033)	(0.022)
Other household income	0.003	0.009	-0.004	-0.011	-0.006	0.007	-0.008	-0.003
	(0.001)	(0.011)	(0.005)	(0.014)	(0.013)	(0.005)	(0.010)	(0.002)

Table 3. (Continued)

	Region 1	Region 2	Region 3	Region 4	Region 5	Region 6	Region 7	Region 8
Number of 0–7 year olds in household	0.023	−0.040	0.114	−0.133	−0.052	−0.051	0.266***	−0.032
	(0.050)	(0.138)	(0.079)	(0.097)	(0.025)	(0.138)	(0.019)	(0.096)
Number of 7–18 year olds in household	−0.007	−0.044	0.000	−0.050	0.037	−0.051	−0.033	0.118
	(0.015)	(0.015)	(0.047)	(0.056)	(0.079)	(0.091)	(0.031)	(0.089)
Number of adults in household	−0.008	0.035	−0.018	−0.012	0.061*	0.002	−0.033	−0.036
	(0.014)	(0.027)	(0.019)	(0.055)	(0.023)	(0.024)	(0.023)	(0.049)
Number of pensioners in household	0.034	0.062	−0.059	−0.045	−0.018	0.085	−0.009	0.095
	(0.012)	(0.053)	(0.046)	(0.064)	(0.087)	(0.084)	(0.027)	(0.070)
Rural area	–	0.503*	0.082	0.139	−0.107	0.107	0.354*	0.215
		(0.050)	(0.089)	(0.147)	(0.086)	(0.157)	(0.112)	(0.264)
N	125	88	369	337	205	198	123	134
R^2	0.154	0.403	0.082	0.060	0.057	0.087	0.254	0.126

Note: Reported are coefficients from linear probability models of pension arrears status in 1996 on pre-crisis characteristics. Standard errors are given in parentheses. Standard errors are clustered at the district-year level. All models also include a constant. Income is measured in 1000's of June 1992 rubles. *** $p < 0.01$, ** $p < 0.05$, * $p < 0.1$.

no differential time trends in the measures of SWB between treatment and control groups.

Fig. 3 plots the time trend of all seven measures of SWB for the pensioner sample. These figures can be viewed as presentations of simple DD models without any controls. In the pre-crisis period – 1994–1995, pensioners who would go in arrears during the 1996 crisis report almost identical levels and trends in LS as those pensioners who would not go in arrears during the crisis (Fig. 3(a)). The two groups also report very similar expectations for future LS and future economic welfare in the pre-crisis period (Fig. 3(b) and (c)). Immediately after the 1996 crisis, however, the former group experiences sizable declines in all three of these measures while the latter

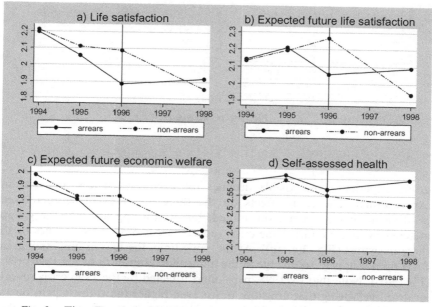

Fig. 3. Time Trends in Measures of Subjective Well-Being for Pensioners.
Note: The Figures Plot the Trends in All SWB Measures for the Pensioner Sample.
The Solid Lines Represent Individuals in Pension Arrears During the 1996 Crisis,
and the Dotted Lines Represent Individuals Not in Arrears During the Crisis. For
Measures Plotted in (a)–(d), the Scale of Responses Is 1 to 5 and for Measures
Plotted in (e) and (f) the Scale Is 1 to 9.

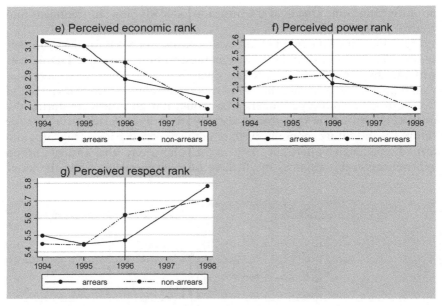

Fig. 3. (Continued)

group experiences no visible declines (or even experiences increases in expectations). The crisis effects on the three measures of self-perceived position in society seem more muted, but it still appears that the group affected by arrears during the crisis reports larger post-crisis declines in all three measures (Fig. 3(e)–(g)). At the same time, the two groups' trends in SAH do not appear to diverge in the immediate aftermath of the 1996 crisis (Fig. 3(d)). Note that by 1998, pensioners affected by the 1996 crisis report levels of well-being that are close to (or even higher than) those pensioners who were unaffected by the 1996 crisis. However, as mentioned before, the 1998 reports of well-being are *after* the severe financial crisis of that year and so this apparent convergence might be a product of the larger financial crisis and not necessarily evidence that the pension crisis effects were short-lived.

The decentralized nature of the pension system implies the possibility of differential effects of the crisis across regions. In addition, the official guidelines that determine priority of pension receipts could also induce differences between the treatment and control groups. To guard against such potential problems, we control for pre-crisis characteristics and differential trends across regions. Even if the treatment, or arrears status, is randomly assigned, the inclusion of these additional controls improves the precision of our estimates. The DD regression model is given by

$$y_{it} = \beta_0 + \beta_1 Arrears_i + \beta_2 Arrears_i \times Year1996_t + \beta_3 Year1995_t \\ + \beta_4 Year1996_t + \gamma' Z_{it} + \varepsilon_{it} \tag{1}$$

where y_{it} is the SWB measure of individual i at time t ($t = 1994, 1995, 1996$), $Arrears_i$ is an indicator variable for the treatment group that equals 1 if the individual does not receive his or her pension during the pension crisis of 1996, $Year1995_t$ and $Year1996_t$ are indicator variables for 1995 and 1996, and Z_{it} is a vector of exogenous demographic and pre-crisis socioeconomic characteristics, which are likely to be correlated with both arrears status and SWB. These controls are as follows: age and age squared, indicators for female, married, high school graduate, college graduate, residing in rural area; indicators for pre-crisis disability status, pre-crisis unemployment status, low pre-crisis pension, pre-crisis total household income[14] excluding pensions and pre-crisis number of household members in ages 0–6, 7–17, pre-pension age adults, and pensioners. We also include a set of indicators for the eight main geographical regions (see Table 2 for classification) as well as their interactions with $Year1995_t$ and $Year1996_t$, to control for both permanent and time-variant regional differences.

We estimate Eq. (1) by OLS and cluster the standard errors at the level of administrative pension district-year.[15] The coefficient of interest, β_2, gives the effect of the pension crisis on the measures of SWB. Namely, it is the difference in the post-crisis change of SWB between treatment and control groups. This identification is valid if there are no other factors besides those accounted for in Z_{it} that differentially affect the trends in SWB of treatment and control groups.

We then proceed by adding individual fixed effects to the DD specification. The regression equation now becomes

$$y_{it} = \beta_0 + \beta_1 Arrears_i \times Year1996_t + \beta_2 Year1995_t + \beta_3 Year1996_t \\ + \gamma' Z_{it} + I_i + \varepsilon_{it} \tag{2}$$

where I_i are the individual-specific effects. The rest of the variables are defined in the same way as in Eq. (1), except that we have removed all time-invariant characteristics and Z_{it} now includes a linear and quadratic term in age and interactions between the indicators for geographical region and survey year. Standard errors are clustered at the administrative pension district level. In this specification, the coefficient of interest is β_1, which gives the within-person effect of the pension crisis. This specification is more conservative than the DD specification because it allows us to additionally control for any unobservable (permanent) individual characteristics that might be correlated with both arrears status and measures of SWB. This is our preferred specification for all subsequent analysis.

Channels of the Pension Crisis

Eqs. (1) and (2) give us the estimated effect of the pension crisis on SWB. We now proceed to explore the channels through which the pension crisis affects SWB. By definition, being in pension arrears during the crisis has a negative income effect on household resources. Yet, post-crisis household income excluding pensions is possibly endogenous with respect to arrears status: pensioners in arrears might go back to the labor force, or other non-pensioner household members might increase their labor supply to compensate for the pension loss. Similar endogeneity concerns apply to the post-crisis net monetary transfers from extended family and friends and to the post-crisis household composition. To separate the income effect of being in arrears from these possible household responses to the crisis, we include the following additional controls, measured at their post-crisis levels: total household income excluding pensions (as a linear and quadratic term), net monetary transfers from extended family and friends, and number of household members by age group (defined above).

Even though the pension crisis manifested itself as an income shock, it might also have had a non-pecuniary cost on SWB. In particular, we hypothesize that such an income shock which originates from an institutional failure reduces well-being in ways that are not captured fully by the size of the pension loss. To test this, we estimate Eq. (2) by splitting the treatment group in two subgroups based on the intensity of treatment. We separately measure the effect of arrears for households who lost two or more pensions in the crisis and for households who lost exactly one pension in the crisis. If the crisis cost is experienced only in monetary terms, then the former group must experience a significantly greater decline in SWB.

Exploiting the rich set of SWB measures in our dataset, we also examine the possibility that the pension crisis affects other aspects of SWB which capture relative life evaluation, where the relation can be with respect to others in society or with respect to one's future self. To test this, we estimate the effect of pension arrears on the three measures of self-perceived relative standing in society (WLQ, PLQ, and RLQ) and the two measures of future expectations (for LS and economic welfare) using the econometric model as specified in Eqs. (1) and (2).

To further study the heterogeneity of the crisis effect, we estimate the effects separately for female and male pensioners. We also test the hypothesis that the pre-crisis expectation for the future is the relevant reference point that determines how the crisis impacts SWB. To do this we perform separate estimation for two groups that differ in their pre-crisis expectations. In our data we have two measures of expectations, expectations about future LS and future economic welfare, where each is defined on a 1 to 5 scale. We sum the two measures of expectations to obtain one measure of overall expectation measured on a 2 to 10 scale. We then take the average of this overall expectation in the two pre-crisis years: 1994 and 1995. Those individuals with an overall pre-crisis expectation measure of 4 or less are defined as having a low pre-crisis outlook and those with an expectation measure greater than 4 are defined as having a high pre-crisis outlook. The outcomes of interests are LS, SAH, and self-perceived rankings in the society (WLQ, PLQ, and RLQ). We estimate Eq. (2) separately for the group of low and the group of high pre-crisis outlook for the future.

Intra-Household and Inter-Household Externalities

To see whether the adverse effects of the pension crisis extend beyond the pensioners directly affected, we study the effects of the crisis on SWB for the sample of non-pensioners who live in households with pensioners. We use the same strategy as in our analysis of the sample of pensioners. For the main results we estimate Eqs. (1) and (2), where in the DD estimates without individual fixed effects we add pre-crisis personal income as an additional control. This allows us to estimate the effect of the crisis separately from any other potential effects due to differences in personal pre-crisis resources between our treatment and control groups.

We then include as additional controls post-crisis measures such as personal income and household income excluding pensions (as linear and quadratic terms), net monetary transfers from family and friends, and household composition. In this way we separate the income effect of pension loss from possible compensating responses by other household members.[16] In particular, we test whether living with a pensioner in arrears affects one's well-being separately from the current level of personal resources and whether the size of the effect rises with the number of pensioners in arrears. We also explore two additional dimensions of heterogeneity: we examine whether the effect of arrears differs by gender and by the level of pre-crisis expectations for the future. All these analyses are performed in same way as described above in the case of pensioners.

In addition, we attempt a test of whether the crisis impact extends even further into society beyond pensioner households to other households of extended family and friends. Because those latter households cannot be identified in the survey, we cannot directly test the effect of the crisis on measures of SWB for those households. Instead, we test whether households linked by familial or social ties to pensioners in arrears are affected by the pension crisis through changes in the monetary transfers being sent or received by them. We estimate the household-level equivalent of the individual fixed effect specification in Eq. (2):

$$
\begin{aligned}
y_{ht} = \beta_0 + \beta_1 Arrears_h \times Year1996_t + \beta_2 Year1995_t + \beta_3 Year1996_t \\
+ \gamma' Z_{ht} + I_h + \varepsilon_{ht}
\end{aligned}
\tag{3}
$$

where we use the following set of outcomes: indicators for whether pensioner household h gives or receives monetary transfers to extended family and friends (the extensive margin), and the amounts of money given or received by pensioner household h (the intensive margin). In the vector of controls Z_{ht} we include interactions between geographical region and year, a linear and quadratic term for household income (excluding pensions), and the previously defined measures of household composition. I_h represents the household fixed effects. The coefficient of interest is β_1, which captures the effect of the crisis on the frequency and level of monetary transfers being sent or received by pensioner households.

Specification Checks

In this section we present some specification checks on our identification strategy. The identification of the causal effect relies on the exogeneity of the crisis. First, we want to test whether the pension crisis was indeed unexpected. If the affected individuals had prior knowledge about the crisis, they might have adjusted their behavior to alleviate the effect of pension arrears prior to 1996. In such a case the post-crisis change in SWB would be underestimating the crisis impact. To find out if this is a cause of concern, we examine the difference between treatment and control groups in their last pre-crisis reports of expectations about future economic welfare and future LS.[17] We estimate the following model using data from 1995 – the last year before the crisis:

$$y_{i1995} = \beta_0 + \beta_1 Arrears_i + \gamma' Z_{i1995} + \varepsilon_{i1995} \qquad (4)$$

where y_i is one of the two measures of expectations, future LS and future economic welfare; $Arrears_i$ is an indicator equal to 1 if the individual is affected by the crisis in the following year 1996; and Z_{i1995} is the same set of controls defined further above. Given this specification, β_1 captures the difference in future expectations between our treatment and control groups 1 year before the crisis. A coefficient of zero would suggest that the 1996 pension crisis is not anticipated by those who are subsequently affected by it. Our results confirm that pensioners in arrears had no different pre-crisis expectations than pensioners not in arrears (if anything, the former had higher expectations). Non-pensioners in arrears had slightly lower pre-crisis expectations, but the difference is only marginally significant and only in the case of future LS (Table 4(a)). We interpret this as evidence that the crisis was unexpected for the pensioners who are affected by it personally. We cannot claim this with the same level of certainty for the non-pensioners who lived with these pensioners. However, any prior adjustment in expectations would mean that the results reported in the fifth section underestimate the crisis effects for the non-pensioner sample.

The validity of our strategy also depends on the assumption that there is no pre-existing difference in time trends between treatment and control groups. We examine this assumption by adding a separate pre-crisis time trend for the group in arrears and for the group in non-arrears:

$$y_{it} = \beta_0 + \beta_1 Arrears_i \times Year1995_t + \beta_2 Arrears_i \times Year1996_t$$
$$+ \beta_3 Year1995_t + \beta_4 Year1996_t + \gamma' Z_{it} + I_i + \varepsilon_{it} \qquad (5)$$

where all variables are defined in the same way as in Eq. (2). In this specification, the coefficient β_1 measures potential pre-crisis trend difference between treatment and control groups. We would reject the DD assumption if this coefficient were nonzero. The estimates are given in Table 4(b) and (c). All pre-crisis trend differences are economically and statistically insignificant for pensioners and, except for one marginally significant coefficient, for non-pensioners.

Table 4. Specification Checks.

(a) Pre-crisis levels of future expectations[a]

	Future Life Satisfaction		Future Economic Welfare	
	(1) Pensioners	(2) Non-Pensioners	(3) Pensioners	(4) Non-Pensioners
Arrears	0.018 (0.054)	−0.187* (0.097)	0.050 (0.063)	−0.046 (0.093)
N	1,579	859	1,579	859
R^2	0.011	0.124	0.060	0.117

	Life Satisfaction (1)	Self-Assessed Health (2)	Future Life Satisfaction (3)	Future Economic Welfare (4)	Economic Rank (5)	Power Rank (6)	Respect Rank (7)
(b) Pre-crisis trends for pensioners[b]							
Arrears × Year1995	−0.017 (0.070)	−0.029 (0.027)	0.056 (0.079)	0.053 (0.091)	0.115 (0.103)	0.066 (0.126)	−0.171 (0.167)
N	4,687	4,687	4,687	4,687	4,687	4,687	4,687
R^2	0.032	0.018	0.024	0.031	0.027	0.022	0.022
(c) Pre-crisis trend for non-pensioners[c]							
Arrears × Year1995	0.036 (0.140)	−0.031 (0.076)	−0.196* (0.112)	0.031 (0.110)	0.081 (0.158)	0.250 (0.188)	0.051 (0.227)
N	1,693	1,693	1,693	1,693	1,693	1,693	1,693
R^2	0.106	0.216	0.124	0.108	0.109	0.076	0.055

[a]Reported are selected coefficients from OLS models specified in Eq. (4) with standard errors clustered at district-year. *** $p < 0.01$, ** $p < 0.05$, * $p < 0.1$.
[b]Reported are selected coefficients from OLS models with individual fixed effects specified in Eq. (5). *** $p < 0.01$, ** $p < 0.05$, * $p < 0.1$.
[c]Reported are selected coefficients from OLS models with individual fixed effects specified in Eq. (5). *** $p < 0.01$, ** $p < 0.05$, * $p < 0.1$.
Standard errors are given in parentheses.

RESULTS

The Effect of the Crisis on SWB of Pensioners

Table 5 presents the estimates from Eq. (1) for the pensioner sample. The odd-numbered columns contain the baseline model – the simple DD estimator without any controls – and the even-numbered columns contain the richer model that includes the vector of controls Z_{it}. The top row in the table gives the estimates of the crisis effects – the estimated coefficients on the interaction between arrears status and the crisis year 1996. Comparing the baseline and the richer model, we see that the inclusion of demographic and socioeconomic characteristics makes little difference to the estimated effect of the crisis. The crisis has a significant effect on pensioners' LS: on the five-point scale of LS, the crisis causes a decline of about .16 points. The crisis has even larger effects on expectations for the future: we estimate that both expectations for future LS and future economic welfare decline by about .22–.23 points (on a five-point scale).

At the same time we find no significant effect on pensioners' subjective measure of health and small negative effects on pensioners' self-perceived relative rankings in society. One exception is the self-perceived power ranking that shows a marginally significant decline. Other determinants of SWB are as expected: married individuals, more educated individuals, and those with higher pre-crisis household income tend to have higher levels of SWB, whereas those with low pre-crisis pensions, the unemployed, and the disabled tend to have lower levels of SWB.

To put the magnitude of these estimates in a context, we compare the estimated effects of the crisis with the effects of some of the demographics. In particular, the crisis effect on LS is comparable to the effect of being unemployed or (in absolute value) the effects of being married or having a college degree. Note in particular that for all SWB measures the coefficient on arrears status during the 1996 crisis is close to 10 times as large in absolute value as the coefficient on pre-crisis household income. Household income is measured in 1000s of June 1992 rubles, whereas an average pension in 1995 is around 1300 June 1992 rubles (Fig. 2). A rough estimate shows that the loss of around 1300 rubles in the pension crisis appears to exert 10 times as large (in absolute value) an effect on well-being as having extra 1000 rubles in household income. We consider this suggestive evidence that the pension crisis imposes a very large non-pecuniary cost for affected pensioners.[18]

Table 5. The Effect of the 1996 Crisis on SWB of Pensioners (DD Specifications).

	Life Satisfaction		Self-Assessed Health		Future Life Satisfaction		Future Economic Welfare	
	(1)	(2)	(3)	(4)	(5)	(6)	(7)	(8)
Arrears × Year1996	-0.167*	-0.159*	-0.014	-0.023	-0.224**	-0.219**	-0.241***	-0.229***
	(0.087)	(0.086)	(0.050)	(0.048)	(0.100)	(0.093)	(0.085)	(0.076)
Year1995	-0.115**	-0.168	0.043	0.069***	0.063	-0.125	-0.139**	-0.113
	(0.057)	(0.182)	(0.029)	(0.022)	(0.191)	(0.191)	(0.065)	(0.190)
Year1996	-0.131*	-0.183	0.004	-0.010	0.136*	0.038	-0.140**	-0.129
	(0.069)	(0.121)	(0.040)	(0.027)	(0.071)	(0.162)	(0.066)	(0.120)
Arrears	-0.034	0.003	0.033	0.041*	0.012	0.004	-0.042	0.025
	(0.050)	(0.049)	(0.020)	(0.022)	(0.045)	(0.042)	(0.057)	(0.046)
Female		-0.046		-0.164***		0.017		-0.244***
		(0.033)		(0.025)		(0.031)		(0.037)
Married		0.114**		-0.078**		0.122**		0.128**
		(0.049)		(0.032)		(0.048)		(0.059)
College		0.126**		0.142***		0.013		0.331***
		(0.054)		(0.029)		(0.055)		(0.062)
High school		0.056		0.083***		-0.013		0.111**
		(0.040)		(0.025)		(0.043)		(0.055)
Age		0.027		-0.004		0.064***		-0.045
		(0.031)		(0.018)		(0.023)		(0.031)
Age squared (/100)		-1.310		-1.386		-4.072**		4.422**
		(2.269)		(1.306)		(1.622)		(2.204)
Disabled pre-crisis		-0.043		-0.406***		-0.062		-0.282***
		(0.096)		(0.058)		(0.086)		(0.076)
Unemployed pre-crisis		-0.210***		-0.166***		-0.037		-0.100**
		(0.045)		(0.027)		(0.042)		(0.050)
Low pension pre-crisis		-0.138***		-0.092***		-0.086**		-0.126***
		(0.045)		(0.034)		(0.043)		(0.047)

	Economic Rank		Power Rank		Respect Rank	
	(9)	(10)	(11)	(12)	(13)	(14)
Arrears × Year1996	-0.166 (0.118)	-0.148 (0.111)	-0.209 (0.130)	-0.208* (0.117)	-0.177 (0.183)	-0.131 (0.149)
Year1995	-0.100 (0.084)	-0.091 (0.095)	0.104 (0.089)	-0.164** (0.081)	-0.021 (0.170)	-0.050 (0.185)
Year1996	-0.132 (0.090)	-0.072 (0.100)	0.101 (0.093)	-0.081 (0.067)	0.162 (0.169)	0.548*** (0.185)
Arrears	0.052 (0.068)	0.075 (0.058)	0.156** (0.071)	0.174*** (0.064)	0.028 (0.106)	0.061 (0.086)
Female		-0.048 (0.045)		-0.043 (0.047)		0.087 (0.059)
Married		0.274*** (0.072)		0.048 (0.058)		0.241*** (0.084)
College		0.487*** (0.077)		0.380*** (0.091)		0.677*** (0.128)
High school		0.394*** (0.067)		0.305*** (0.071)		0.384*** (0.085)
Age		0.001 (0.036)		0.000 (0.035)		0.099* (0.059)
Age squared (/100)		0.592 (2.547)		0.376 (2.485)		-7.324* (4.288)
Hhold income pre-crisis		0.019*** (0.006)	0.003 (0.002)	0.007 (0.006)		0.021*** (0.006)
Rural		0.068 (0.044)	-0.010 (0.029)	0.117*** (0.044)		0.056 (0.054)
N	4,687	4,687	4,687	4,687	4,687	4,687
R^2	0.008	0.052	0.133	0.019	0.010	0.065

Table 5. (*Continued*)

	Economic Rank		Power Rank		Respect Rank	
	(9)	(10)	(11)	(12)	(13)	(14)
Disabled pre-crisis		0.078		0.061		0.012
		(0.130)		(0.120)		(0.200)
Unemployed pre-crisis		−0.259***		−0.263***		−0.277***
		(0.054)		(0.065)		(0.084)
Low pension pre-crisis		−0.287***		−0.127**		−0.356***
		(0.068)		(0.057)		(0.087)
Hhold income pre-crisis		0.028***		0.010*		0.004
		(0.010)		(0.006)		(0.011)
Rural		0.182***		0.193**		−0.074
		(0.062)		(0.076)		(0.100)
N	4,687	4,687	4,687	4,687	4,687	4,687
R^2	0.003	0.085	0.003	0.047	0.001	0.062

Note: Reported are selected coefficients from OLS models specified in Eq. (1) with standard errors clustered at district-year. Standard errors are given in parentheses. Income is measured in 1000's of real rubles. Low pension pre-crisis is defined as having a pension income in the bottom decile of the pre-crisis pension income distribution. *** $p<0.01$, ** $p<0.05$, * $p<0.1$.

The finding of substantial effects on LS and future expectations and no effect on SAH goes in line with our understanding of the former being flow quantities influenced by current levels of income and the latter being a stock quantity mostly unaffected by current levels of income. More surprising is our finding of a statistically insignificant effect on the pensioners' self-perceived economic ranking in society. One possible explanation might be that there was widespread decline in economic welfare during 1996 (as we describe earlier) and hence pensioners' *relative* economic standing in society was uninfluenced.

Results from our preferred specification that includes individual fixed effects are presented in Table 6. They confirm all our findings from the specification without fixed effects, and most of the crisis effects are even larger and more precisely estimated. In particular, the crisis effect on pensioners' LS is slightly larger (a decline of more than .18 points) and is now statistically significant at the 5% level. The self-perceived power ranking in society is also significant at the 5% level – the crisis causes a decline of about .19 points on the nine-point power scale. Moreover, the estimates change only imperceptibly when we include controls for post-crisis measures such as total household income other than pensions, net monetary transfers from extended family and friends, and household composition. This suggests that allowing for a response to the crisis through other income sources or other household members has little to no effect on pensioners' experience of the crisis. In fact, we find little evidence of such response as discussed further below.

Table 7 shows how the size of the crisis effect depends on the total size of pension income lost, measured by the number of pensioners in arrears. The odd-numbered columns show the estimates of the crisis effect when the crisis affects only one pensioner in the household and the even-numbered columns show the estimates when the crisis affects two or more pensioners in the household. These results demonstrate that the crisis effect does not rise substantially with the number of household pensions lost in the crisis. In fact, LS, the self-perceived economic, and the self-perceived respect rankings all decline slightly less among pensioners in arrears when they are not the only ones in the household with lost pensions. For any of the measures, we cannot reject the hypothesis that losing just one pension in the household is as costly to SWB as losing more. We consider this another piece of suggestive evidence that the cost of the crisis cannot be fully measured with the loss of pension income.

Tables 8 and 9 examine other potential sources of heterogeneity in the effects of the crisis. In particular, we find that males and females report

Table 6. The Effect of the 1996 Crisis on SWB for Pensioners (Individual Fixed-Effect Models).

	Life Satisfaction		Self-Assessed Health		Future Life Satisfaction		Future Economic Welfare	
	(1)	(2)	(3)	(4)	(5)	(6)	(7)	(8)
Arrears × Year1996	−0.187**	−0.183**	−0.024	−0.022	−0.262***	−0.256***	−0.236***	−0.236***
	(0.078)	(0.077)	(0.054)	(0.055)	(0.075)	(0.076)	(0.058)	(0.057)
Controls for income, transfers, and hhold composition	No	Yes	No	Yes	No	Yes	No	Yes
N	4,687	4,687	4,687	4,687	4,687	4,687	4,687	4,687
R^2	0.028	0.033	0.013	0.015	0.015	0.024	0.026	0.031

	Economic Rank		Power Rank		Respect Rank	
	(9)	(10)	(11)	(12)	(13)	(14)
Arrears × Year1996	−0.128	−0.128	−0.188**	−0.185**	−0.176*	−0.170
	(0.088)	(0.088)	(0.088)	(0.088)	(0.101)	(0.102)
Controls for income, transfers, and hhold composition	No	Yes	No	Yes	No	Yes
N	4,687	4,687	4,687	4,687	4,687	4,687
R^2	0.022	0.026	0.018	0.021	0.020	0.021

Note: Reported are selected coefficients from OLS models with individual fixed effects specified in Eq. (2). Standard errors are given in parentheses. The even-numbered columns contain controls for current household income (excluding pensions), net transfers from extended family and friends, and household composition. *** $p < 0.01$, ** $p < 0.05$, * $p < 0.1$.

Table 7. The Effect of the 1996 Crisis on SWB of Pensioners by Number of Household Arrears.

	Life Satisfaction		Self-Assessed Health		Future Life Satisfaction		Future Economic Welfare	
	(1) Only one in arrears	(2) Two or more in arrears	(3) Only one in arrears	(4) Two or more in arrears	(5) Only one in arrears	(6) Two or more in arrears	(7) Only one in arrears	(8) Two or more in arrears
Arrears × Year1996	-0.204** (0.083)	-0.167* (0.096)	-0.043 (0.057)	0.006 (0.062)	-0.222** (0.084)	-0.323*** (0.098)	-0.172** (0.076)	-0.345*** (0.106)
N	3,643	3,773	3,643	3,773	3,643	3,773	3,643	3,773
R^2	0.028	0.024	0.012	0.017	0.016	0.017	0.024	0.022

	Economic Rank		Power Rank		Respect Rank	
	(9) Only one in arrears	(10) Two or more in arrears	(11) Only one in arrears	(12) Two or more in arrears	(13) Only one in arrears	(14) Two or more in arrears
Arrears × Year1996	-0.175* (0.097)	-0.041 (0.122)	-0.130 (0.091)	-0.307** (0.139)	-0.256* (0.145)	-0.030 (0.173)
N	3,643	3,773	3,643	3,773	3,643	3,773
R^2	0.021	0.021	0.012	0.019	0.020	0.023

Note: Reported are selected coefficients from OLS models with individual fixed effects specified in Eq. (2). Standard errors are given in parentheses. In the odd-numbered columns the treatment group is restricted to pensioners who are the only ones in arrears in the household. In the even-numbered columns the treatment group is restricted to pensioners who have at least one other pensioner in arrears in the household besides themselves. In all cases, the control group is pensioners who are not in arrears. *** $p<0.01$, ** $p<0.05$, * $p<0.1$.

Table 8. The Effect of the 1996 Crisis on SWB of Pensioners by Gender.

	Life Satisfaction		Self-Assessed Health		Future Life Satisfaction		Future Economic Welfare	
	(1) Men	(2) Women	(3) Men	(4) Women	(5) Men	(6) Women	(7) Men	(8) Women
Arrears × Year1996	−0.281** (0.104)	−0.147 (0.091)	−0.012 (0.086)	−0.024 (0.056)	−0.328*** (0.115)	−0.238*** (0.082)	−0.208* (0.109)	−0.246*** (0.059)
N	1,333	3,354	1,333	3,354	1,333	3,354	1,333	3,354
R^2	0.040	0.039	0.060	0.020	0.040	0.023	0.041	0.032

	Economic Rank		Power Rank		Respect Rank	
	(9) Men	(10) Women	(11) Men	(12) Women	(13) Men	(14) Women
Arrears × Year1996	−0.203 (0.190)	−0.103 (0.094)	−0.396** (0.176)	−0.107 (0.102)	−0.039 (0.188)	−0.210 (0.138)
N	1,333	3,354	1,333	3,354	1,333	3,354
R^2	0.049	0.032	0.029	0.027	0.043	0.023

Note: Reported are selected coefficients from OLS models with individual fixed effects specified in Eq. (2). *** $p < 0.01$, ** $p < 0.05$, * $p < 0.1$. Standard errors are given in parentheses.

Table 9. The Effect of the 1996 Crisis on SWB of Pensioners by Pre-Crisis Expectations.

	Life Satisfaction		Self-Assessed Health	
	(1) Low Outlook	(2) High Outlook	(3) Low Outlook	(4) High Outlook
Arrears × Year1996	−0.156 (0.095)	−0.225* (0.113)	0.009 (0.060)	−0.080 (0.069)
N	2,832	1,855	2,832	1,855
R^2	0.030	0.064	0.019	0.033

	Economic Rank		Power Rank		Respect Rank	
	(5) Low Outlook	(6) High Outlook	(7) Low Outlook	(8) High Outlook	(9) Low Outlook	(10) High Outlook
Arrears × Year1996	−0.059 (0.132)	−0.228 (0.200)	−0.067 (0.123)	−0.352** (0.143)	−0.062 (0.147)	−0.363** (0.173)
N	2,832	1,855	2,832	1,855	2,832	1,855
R^2	0.024	0.053	0.032	0.038	0.031	0.026

Note: Reported are selected coefficients from OLS models with individual fixed effects specified in Eq. (2). *** $p < 0.01$, ** $p < 0.05$, * $p < 0.1$. Standard errors are given in parentheses.

different experiences of the crisis along different aspects of life evaluation. The pension crisis causes somewhat greater declines in LS and self-perceived power ranking in society among male than among female pensioners. The two measures of future expectations, on the other hand, show little difference between the genders. We find that pre-crisis expectations also influence how pensioners experience the crisis. In particular, the crisis causes a greater decline in all measures of SWB for those pensioners who had higher pre-crisis expectations. We believe this finding lends some support to the theory that prior expectations, and not just the current status quo, matter for experienced utility.

The Effect of the Crisis on SWB of Non-Pensioners

The crisis effect is not limited to the pensioners personally affected. We find that even non-pensioners experience worsening in SWB as a result of living in the same households with pensioners in arrears (Tables 10 and 11). For

Table 10. The Effect of the 1996 Crisis on SWB of Non-Pensioners (DD Specifications).

	Life Satisfaction		Self-Assessed Health		Future Life Satisfaction		Future Economic Welfare	
	(1)	(2)	(3)	(4)	(5)	(6)	(7)	(8)
Arrears × Year1996	−0.249**	−0.224**	0.063	0.054	0.129	0.090	−0.141	−0.137
	(0.111)	(0.105)	(0.110)	(0.073)	(0.177)	(0.132)	(0.112)	(0.103)
Year1995	−0.073	0.127	0.051	0.009	0.054	−0.024	−0.049	−0.062
	(0.077)	(0.091)	(0.055)	(0.144)	(0.079)	(0.058)	(0.083)	(0.053)
Year1996	−0.085	0.291***	0.037	−0.021	0.020	0.132	−0.054	−0.053*
	(0.073)	(0.090)	(0.047)	(0.098)	(0.072)	(0.167)	(0.084)	(0.030)
Arrears	0.011	0.044	0.004	−0.027	−0.110	−0.085	−0.106*	−0.087
	(0.072)	(0.068)	(0.055)	(0.039)	(0.069)	(0.061)	(0.061)	(0.057)
Female		−0.072		−0.248***		−0.135***		−0.150***
		(0.044)		(0.028)		(0.037)		(0.042)
Married		0.158***		0.041		0.061		−0.010
		(0.045)		(0.032)		(0.046)		(0.054)
College		0.147***		0.111***		0.094		0.013
		(0.056)		(0.035)		(0.060)		(0.077)
High school		0.051		0.028		0.057		−0.006
		(0.039)		(0.032)		(0.046)		(0.051)
Age		−0.105***		0.008		−0.028**		−0.095***
		(0.013)		(0.007)		(0.012)		(0.012)
Age squared (/100)		11.602***		−3.473***		0.322		10.235***
		(1.683)		(0.917)		(1.612)		(1.560)
Disabled pre-crisis		−0.029		−0.972***		−0.191*		0.106
		(0.101)		(0.084)		(0.107)		(0.117)
Unemployed pre-crisis		−0.224***		0.019		0.064		−0.116**
		(0.050)		(0.031)		(0.043)		(0.048)
Personal income pre-crisis		−0.003		−0.015***		0.008		0.020**
		(0.010)		(0.005)		(0.006)		(0.009)

	Economic Rank		Power Rank		Respect Rank	
	(9)	(10)	(11)	(12)	(13)	(14)
Arrears × Year1996	−0.207 (0.183)	−0.236 (0.150)	−0.250 (0.243)	−0.215 (0.174)	−0.413* (0.244)	−0.348* (0.205)
Year1995	−0.036 (0.084)	−0.004 (0.088)	0.134 (0.118)	0.184 (0.279)	−0.149 (0.123)	−0.101 (0.257)
Year1996	0.091 (0.109)	0.561*** (0.163)	0.296** (0.122)	0.712** (0.287)	0.023 (0.164)	0.798*** (0.197)
Arrears	0.043 (0.086)	0.032 (0.082)	0.143 (0.120)	0.083 (0.098)	0.020 (0.126)	−0.038 (0.117)
Female		0.012 (0.058)		−0.106* (0.061)		0.161** (0.063)
Married		0.283*** (0.073)		0.091 (0.077)		0.183** (0.087)
College		0.397*** (0.100)		0.554*** (0.116)		0.495*** (0.113)
High school		0.235*** (0.071)		0.160** (0.075)		0.229*** (0.079)
Age		−0.120*** (0.016)		−0.092*** (0.018)		−0.070*** (0.021)
Age squared (/100)		13.001*** (2.126)		8.929*** (2.428)		9.289*** (2.631)
Hhold income pre-crisis		0.025*** (0.007)	0.005 (0.003)	0.012** (0.005)		0.021*** (0.006)
Rural		−0.036 (0.064)	0.124*** (0.043)	−0.102 (0.067)		0.062 (0.061)
N	2,524	2,524	2,524	2,524	2,524	2,524
R^2	0.007	0.104	0.210	0.125	0.006	0.098

Table 10. (*Continued*)

	Economic Rank		Power Rank		Respect Rank	
	(9)	(10)	(11)	(12)	(13)	(14)
Disabled pre-crisis		-0.203		-0.347**		0.098
		(0.154)		(0.151)		(0.234)
Unemployed pre-crisis		-0.240***		-0.250***		-0.424***
		(0.059)		(0.073)		(0.102)
Personal income pre-crisis		0.013		0.013		0.007
		(0.011)		(0.012)		(0.010)
Hhold income pre-crisis		0.034***		0.003		0.021*
		(0.010)		(0.010)		(0.011)
Rural		0.073		0.038		-0.026
		(0.079)		(0.096)		(0.103)
N	2,524	2,524	2,524	2,524	2,524	2,524
R^2	0.001	0.107	0.004	0.081	0.004	0.074

Note: Reported are selected coefficients from OLS models specified in Equation (1) with standard errors clustered at district-year. Standard errors are given in parentheses. Income is measured in 1000's of real rubles. *** $p < 0.01$, ** $p < 0.05$, * $p < 0.1$.

Table 11. The Effect of the 1996 Crisis on SWB of Non-Pensioners (Individual Fixed-Effect Models).

	Life Satisfaction		Self-Assessed Health		Future Life Satisfaction		Future Economic Welfare	
	(1)	(2)	(3)	(4)	(5)	(6)	(7)	(8)
Arrears × Year1996	-0.224***	-0.204**	0.055	0.060	0.082	0.086	-0.109	-0.101
	(0.078)	(0.084)	(0.050)	(0.051)	(0.101)	(0.097)	(0.075)	(0.072)
Controls for income, transfers, and hhold composition	No	Yes	No	Yes	No	Yes	No	Yes
N	2,524	2,524	2,524	2,524	2,524	2,524	2,524	2,524
R^2	0.030	0.049	0.020	0.028	0.016	0.026	0.012	0.030

	Economic Rank		Power Rank		Respect Rank	
	(9)	(10)	(11)	(12)	(13)	(14)
Arrears × Year1996	-0.157	-0.134	-0.170	-0.161	-0.242	-0.226
	(0.098)	(0.102)	(0.140)	(0.136)	(0.181)	(0.193)
Controls for income, transfers, and hhold composition	No	Yes	No	Yes	No	Yes
N	2,524	2,524	2,524	2,524	2,524	2,524
R^2	0.033	0.045	0.023	0.034	0.037	0.044

Note: Reported are selected coefficients from OLS models with individual fixed effects specified in Eq. (2). Standard errors are given in parentheses. The even-numbered columns contain controls for current personal and household income (excluding pensions), net transfers from extended family and friends, and household composition. *** $p < 0.01$, ** $p < 0.05$, * $p < 0.1$.

non-pensioners we find that living with a pensioner in arrears during the crisis causes a large and statistically significant decline in LS. In fact, we estimate a decline of over .20 points on the five-point LS scale, which is slightly larger (though statistically indistinguishable) than the decline among pensioners. The strong crisis effect on the LS of non-pensioners is quite robust to the inclusion not only of post-crisis household income and household composition, but also of post-crisis personal income. That the decline in LS is unaffected by the level of personal resources is again suggestive of some non-pecuniary cost of the pension crisis. The other measures of SWB appear to be affected less for non-pensioners, except for the three self-perceived rankings in society. These SWB measures exhibit large declines for non-pensioners but are measured much more imprecisely than in the larger pensioner sample. The self-perceived respect ranking shows the largest decline among the three measures and is also statistically significant at the 10% level (in the specification without individual fixed effects).

Similar to pensioners, we also find that the decline in SWB for non-pensioners does not rise substantively with the number of pensioners in arrears in the household (Table 12). Although the decline in LS is somewhat larger for non-pensioners who lost more than one pension in the household, the decline in self-perceived respect ranking is somewhat larger for non-pensioners who lost exactly one pension in the household. In fact, consistent with our findings for pensioners, the decline in each SWB measure is statistically indistinguishable between the group who lost several pensions in the household and the group who lost only one pension in the household.

Non-pensioners also show heterogeneity in their experiences of the crisis based on gender and pre-crisis expectations. Table 13 presents estimated effects of the pension crisis by gender. Unlike pensioners, the significant decline in LS among non-pensioners appears to be largely driven by women. The effect of pre-crisis expectations, however, is consistent across the pensioner and non-pensioner sample: non-pensioners who had higher pre-crisis expectations for the future also report greater decline in LS after the crisis (Table 14).

Our results indicate that the pensioner household cannot be analyzed as a homogenous unit when we examine the effect of the pension crisis. Pensioners and non-pensioners show similarities in the effect of the crisis on some aspects of SWB (LS) but differences in others (future expectations). And even in those aspects of well-being where the crisis affects the two groups similarly, we find that women and men experience the crisis differently.

Table 12. The Effect of the 1996 Crisis on SWB of Non-Pensioners by Number of Household Arrears.

	Life Satisfaction		Self-Assessed Health		Future Life Satisfaction		Future Economic Welfare	
	(1) Only one in arrears	(2) Two or more in arrears	(3) Only one in arrears	(4) Two or more in arrears	(5) Only one in arrears	(6) Two or more in arrears	(7) Only one in arrears	(8) Two or more in arrears
Arrears × Year1996	−0.183* (0.095)	−0.264* (0.134)	0.056 (0.056)	0.090 (0.077)	−0.032 (0.118)	0.206 (0.170)	−0.130 (0.101)	−0.149 (0.169)
N	1,667	2,008	1,667	2,008	1,667	2,008	1,667	2,008
R^2	0.031	0.035	0.024	0.027	0.023	0.024	0.018	0.016

	Economic Rank		Power Rank		Respect Rank	
	(9) Only one in arrears	(10) Two or more in arrears	(11) Only one in arrears	(12) Two or more in arrears	(13) Only one in arrears	(14) Two or more in arrears
Arrears × Year1996	−0.004 (0.113)	−0.489** (0.188)	−0.199 (0.160)	−0.219 (0.240)	−0.219 (0.214)	−0.055 (0.278)
N	1,667	2,008	1,667	2,008	1,667	2,008
R^2	0.038	0.035	0.033	0.035	0.043	0.050

Note: Reported are selected coefficients from OLS models with individual fixed effects specified in Eq. (2). Standard errors are given in parentheses. In the odd-numbered columns, the treatment group is restricted to non-pensioners who live with only one pensioner in arrears. In the even-numbered columns, the treatment group is restricted to non-pensioners who live with more than one pensioners in arrears. In all cases the control group is non-pensioners who live with no pensioners in arrears. *** p<0.01, ** p<0.05, * p<0.1.

Table 13. The Effect of the 1996 Crisis on SWB of Non-Pensioners by Gender.

	Life Satisfaction		Self-Assessed Health		Future Life Satisfaction		Future Economic Welfare	
	(1) Men	(2) Women	(3) Men	(4) Women	(5) Men	(6) Women	(7) Men	(8) Women
Arrears × Year1996	−0.165 (0.127)	−0.238** (0.111)	0.111* (0.062)	0.008 (0.072)	0.057 (0.116)	0.142 (0.130)	−0.198* (0.101)	0.030 (0.131)
N	1,399	1,125	1,399	1,125	1,399	1,125	1,399	1,125
R^2	0.058	0.077	0.026	0.058	0.030	0.054	0.048	0.053

	Economic Rank		Power Rank		Respect Rank	
	(9) Men	(10) Women	(11) Men	(12) Women	(13) Men	(14) Women
Arrears × Year1996	−0.123 (0.113)	−0.144 (0.151)	−0.248 (0.187)	−0.058 (0.154)	−0.148 (0.207)	−0.303 (0.249)
N	1,399	1,125	1,399	1,125	1,399	1,125
R^2	0.072	0.052	0.048	0.057	0.046	0.079

Notes: Reported are selected coefficients from OLS models with individual fixed effects specified in Eq. (2). *** $p < 0.01$, ** $p < 0.05$, * $p < 0.1$. Standard errors are given in parentheses.

Table 14. The Effect of the 1996 Crisis on SWB of Non-Pensioners by Pre-Crisis Expectations.

	Life Satisfaction		Self-Assessed Health	
	(1) Low Outlook	(2) High Outlook	(3) Low Outlook	(4) High Outlook
Arrears × Year1996	−0.148	−0.255**	0.061	0.061
	(0.122)	(0.097)	(0.053)	(0.081)
N	1,335	1,189	1,335	1,189
R^2	0.069	0.085	0.053	0.038

	Economic Rank		Power Rank		Respect Rank	
	(5) Low Outlook	(6) High Outlook	(7) Low Outlook	(8) High Outlook	(9) Low Outlook	(10) High Outlook
Arrears × Year1996	0.008	−0.298*	0.042	−0.416*	−0.228	−0.174
	(0.131)	(0.169)	(0.205)	(0.238)	(0.204)	(0.270)
N	1,335	1,189	1,335	1,189	1,335	1,189
R^2	0.071	0.080	0.046	0.076	0.056	0.067

Notes: Reported are selected coefficients from OLS models with individual fixed effects specified in Eq. (2). *** $p < 0.01$, ** $p < 0.05$, * $p < 0.1$. Standard errors are given in parentheses.

Robustness Checks

In this section, we describe a series of robustness checks to establish that our results are not sensitive to changes in the baseline specification we pick. All results are available upon request.

The first robustness check we perform is to test whether our results depend on the assumption that SWB is measured on a cardinal scale – an underlying assumption in our linear regression models. Our results are qualitatively robust to estimating ordered probit models,[19] which do not assume a cardinal scale.

The second check is to recode each measure of SWB by collapsing them into binary 0-1 variables. For LS, SAH, and the two measures of future expectations, we recode as 1 answers that are above 3 on the original 1 to 5 scales. As described in the second section, answers above 3 correspond to strictly positive reports of current well-being or future expectations. For the three measures of societal rankings, we recode as 1 all answers that are

Table 15. The Effect of the 1996 Crisis on Objective Measures of Well-Being.

	Home Production (1)	Meat (2)	Sugar (3)	Lending (4)
(a) Household expenditure ratios[a]				
Arrears × Year1996	0.018*	−0.011	−0.017**	−0.023**
	(0.010)	(0.012)	(0.008)	(0.009)
N	3,000	3,000	3,000	3,000
R^2	0.054	0.023	0.029	0.011

	Immediate Memory Recall		Delayed Memory Recall	
	(1) Pensioners	(2) Non-pensioners	(3) Pensioners	(4) Non-pensioners
(b) Cognitive measures[b]				
Arrears × Year1996	−0.043*	−0.208*	−0.043	0.043
	(0.024)	(0.118)	(0.031)	(0.101)
N	2,874	931	2,662	913
R^2	0.027	0.164	0.019	0.051

	Received Any (1)	Given Any (2)	Amount Received (3)	Amount Given (4)
(c) Household transfers from extended family and friends[a]				
Arrears × Year1996	−0.018	−0.028	−0.050	−0.043
	(0.025)	(0.036)	(0.108)	(0.081)
N	3,636	3,636	3,636	3,636
R^2	0.023	0.038	0.021	0.064

[a]Reported are selected coefficients from OLS models estimated at the household level with household fixed effects as specified in Eq. (3). Standard errors are given in parentheses.
[b]Reported are selected coefficients from OLS models with individual fixed effects specified in Eq. (2). Memory measures are coded as 0-1 binary variables. The digit 1 corresponds to having remembered more than half of the words in the list that the respondent is asked to memorize. These questions are asked in 1995 and 1996 (not in 1994) of respondents above the age of 54.
*** $p < 0.01$, ** $p < 0.05$, * $p < 0.1$.

above 4 on the original 1 to 9 scales. As described in the second section, these answers correspond to reports of higher than average societal ranking. These alternative specifications produce the same qualitative results as the main specifications reported in the previous sections.

Table 16. Duration of the Effect of the 1996 Crisis.

	Life Satisfaction	Self-Assessed Health	Future Life Satisfaction	Future Economic Welfare	Economic Rank	Power Rank	Respect Rank
	(1)	(2)	(3)	(4)	(5)	(6)	(7)
(a) Pensioners[a]							
Arrears × Year1998	0.054	0.023	0.095	0.039	0.016	−0.135	−0.020
	(0.065)	(0.041)	(0.081)	(0.061)	(0.092)	(0.082)	(0.135)
N	5,855	5,855	5,855	5,855	5,855	5,855	5,855
R^2	0.038	0.022	0.027	0.043	0.039	0.022	0.017
(b) Non-pensioners[b]							
Arrears × Year1998	0.005	0.033	0.377***	0.246***	0.122	0.114	0.045
	(0.085)	(0.082)	(0.101)	(0.077)	(0.163)	(0.134)	(0.207)
N	3,183	3,183	3,183	3,183	3,183	3,183	3,183
R^2	0.043	0.028	0.038	0.028	0.046	0.028	0.032

*** $p < 0.01$, ** $p < 0.05$, * $p < 0.1$.
[a] Reported are selected coefficients from OLS models with individual fixed effects specified in Eq. (6).
[b] Reported are selected coefficients from linear probability models specified in Eq. (6) with standard errors clustered at district-year. Standard errors are given in parentheses.

The third type of robustness checks we run is to test our sample selection. In our main analysis we exclude pensioners (and their non-pensioner household members) who report arrears in any year other than 1996 when the pension crisis occurred. The first check we do is to add these individuals to our sample and consider them part of our control group. We treat these individuals as controls because we are interested in the effect of the 1996 pension crisis and not in the general effect of failing to receive a pension. The second sample check we do is to expand our definition of pensioners to include people who receive early pensions due to early retirement because of serious illnesses or work in dangerous occupations. Once again, the main qualitative conclusions are robust to all of these robustness checks.

ADDITIONAL CONSIDERATIONS

In this section, we consider in turn the effects of the crisis that (1) go beyond measures of SWB, (2) go beyond pensioner households, and (3) go beyond the immediate aftermath of the crisis.

In this article, we find that the pension crisis has a significant negative effect on several aspects of life evaluation both for the directly affected pensioners and for the other non-pensioner members of their households. Is this effect also mirrored in changes in the objective conditions of their lives? Jensen and Richter (2003) focus on the implications of the crisis on health-related measures of well-being. They find that pension crisis leads to a significant reduction in caloric intake, but has a more muted and varied response in terms of health outcomes. For example, medication use and doctor visits decline significantly for men but not for women, and physical limitations rise only marginally for men and not at all for women. These marginally significant effects on objective health reports are consistent with the insignificant effects we find on subjective health reports.

A possible explanation for the overall insignificant effect on health might be found in the changing composition of household expenditures. As mentioned earlier, Jensen and Richter (2003) show that the crisis reduces calorie intake. We explore this further. In particular, we find that households affected by the crisis spend a smaller share on meat and sugar and a larger share on home-grown produce, with the changes in the latter two shares being both economically and statistically significant (Table 15(a)).[20] It is possible that these changes in consumption patterns exert some positive effect on health that partially counters the negative effect from the loss of pension income.

Another health-related aspect of well-being that is relevant for the pension-aged is cognitive ability and particularly memory. Our interest in analyzing this aspect of well-being also lies in the suggestive evidence we reported earlier that the cost of the crisis is not entirely explained by the income loss from pension arrears. If some of the non-pecuniary cost is stress-related, it might be reflected in measures of memory. The RLMS includes tests of immediate memory recall and delayed memory recall. In the first set of tests, after reading 10 words, the interviewer asks each respondent to recall as many words as possible. The immediate memory recall is measured by the number of words the respondent could recall immediately. After asking several other questions, the interviewer again asks the respondent to recall those 10 words. The delayed memory recall is measured by the number of words the respondent could recall after responding to several other questions. We code those measures as 0-1 binary variables where 1 stands for having correctly memorized more than half of the words on the list. We find that the crisis has negative effects on both immediate and delayed memory recall for pensioners and an even larger negative effect on immediate memory recall for non-pensioners (Table 15(b)). While the effects on delayed memory are statistically insignificant, the negative effects on immediate memory recall are significant at the 10% level for both pensioners and non-pensioners.[21] These results are in line with the previously discussed evidence in favor of non-pecuniary costs from the pension crisis.

Overall, it appears that the crisis affected both objective and subjective measures of well-being, although the effects on the latter seem stronger. It is plausible that the measures of SWB capture elements of *experienced* utility which are not measured by objective circumstances. We believe that the inclusion of SWB measures in the analysis of the pension crisis paints a more complete picture of the consequences of such adverse events on the individuals personally affected and on the other members of their households.

The second theme we explore in this section is whether the monetary impact of the crisis extends beyond the pensioner households to other family members and friends linked through an informal network of inter-household monetary transfers. Our estimates of Eq. (3) show that the pension crisis does not have a statistically significant effect on neither the frequency nor the size of monetary transfers in the network of extended family and friends; the income shock from the crisis appears to be borne entirely by pensioner households (Table 15(c)). These results are surprising because pensioners experience a significant monetary loss due to the pension crisis. One possible explanation might be that the pensioners made prior commitments, so that we do not observe immediately an inter-household response to this crisis. Alternatively, if the pensioners' social network consists primarily of people who are also affected by the pension crisis, that would diminish the scope for inter-household insurance.[22]

The last theme we explore is the impact of the crisis beyond the immediate aftermath. In monetary terms the pension crisis was a one-time shock. Most pensioners went back to receiving their pensions in 1998, the first survey done after 1996, and the average pension adjusted for inflation is constant across survey rounds. Yet, does this necessarily imply that SWB would return to its pre-crisis level once individual income recovers? Unfortunately, establishing the long-term effects of the pension crisis is problematic given that the first survey after 1996 is collected after the 1998 financial crisis. Hence, the interpretation of results which include the 1998 survey year relies on the assumption that the financial crisis does not differentially impact our treatment and control groups. We present these results with this caveat in mind.

We estimate the effect of the crisis after 1996 as follows:

$$y_{it} = \beta_0 + \beta_1 Arrears_i + \beta_2 Arrears_i \times Year1996_t + \beta_3 Arrears_i \times Year1998_t$$
$$+ \beta_4 Year1995_t + \beta_5 Year1996_t + \beta_6 Year1998_t + \gamma' Z_{it} + I_i + \varepsilon_{it} \qquad (6)$$

where we add an indicator for 1998 and its interaction with arrears status; all remaining variables are defined in the same way as in Eq. (2). The coefficient of interest is β_3, which captures the difference in time trend between arrears and non-arrears groups in 1998, two years after the pension crisis. The estimates of this coefficient are given in Table 16. None of them are statistically significant for the pensioner sample. For the non-pensioners, the only two estimates that are statistically significant – the effects on future expectations – are in fact positive (Tables 16). In other words, the trend in SWB over 1994–1998 is no worse for individuals affected by the 1996 pension crisis – either directly as pensioners in arrears or indirectly as living with pensioners in arrears. As mentioned above, this short-lived effect could well be a result of the 1996 pension crisis being swamped by the larger 1998 financial crisis. This particular timing casts doubt on whether the short-lived effects we find here can be generalized to other shocks to the redistribution system. We cannot dismiss the possibility that had the financial crisis not occurred, the pension crisis effect would have persisted for longer.[23]

DISCUSSION AND CONCLUSIONS

In this study we find that an exogenous shock to the redistribution system has a significant negative effect on the SWB of pensioners who were eligible for pensions but failed to receive them. The effect on well-being is stronger than predicted if the cost of the crisis were just the one-off monetary cost of pension loss. In particular, we find that pensioners' expectations for the future decline significantly and that the overall decline in SWB is just as strong for those who lose exactly one pension in the household as for those who lose more. The societal impact extends to non-pensioner members of these households. The reported decrease in well-being for non-pensioners remains unchanged even after accounting for their post-crisis personal income. In addition, mental well-being – measured by objective memory tests – also appears to decline by greater extent for individuals affected by the crisis – both pensioners and non-pensioners. One interpretation of all these results is that the pension crisis has a broader non-monetary effect on well-being. Such an effect has been documented for other life events such as unemployment (Luechinger, Meier, & Stutzer, 2010). Indeed, our estimates show that being in pension arrears (regardless of whether experienced by oneself directly or by another household member) causes a decline in well-being of a similar size as that of being unemployed.

In conclusion, pensioner households appear to have borne the full monetary burden of pension loss caused by the 1996 crisis. We find no evidence of significant increase of monetary flows from extended family and friends. Within these pensioner households, we document effects on well-being that are consistent with significant additional non-pecuniary costs from the instability of the redistribution system. The crisis impact extends beyond the pensioners directly affected to the non-pensioners who live with them. Any public policies aimed to fully compensate for such disruptions in the redistribution system would need to be devised in ways that take these externalities into account.

ACKNOWLEDGMENTS

The authors are grateful for valuable comments and suggestions by Konstantinos Tatsiramos (the editor), two anonymous referees, Anne Case, Angus Deaton, Henry Farber, Alan Krueger, Cormac O'Grada, Andrew

Shephard, conference participants at the 2011 Joint Workshop FORS, University of Lausanne and IDSC of IZA on Redistribution and Well-Being, Lausanne, Switzerland, and seminar participants at the Center for Health and Well-Being, Princeton University, Princeton, New Jersey.

NOTES

1. For recent reviews, see Frey and Stutzer (2002), Di Tella and MacCulloch (2006), and Stutzer and Frey (2010).

2. An exception is a study on lottery winnings and measures of SWB (Gardner & Oswald, 2007). That article examines the effects of an exogenous positive income shock, whereas our study focuses on the effects of an exogenous negative income shock. Our analysis can reveal potentially different insights given experimental evidence that losses are felt more keenly than gains (Kahneman, Knetsch, & Thaler, 1991).

3. The literature has also studied wage arrears in transition economies, another source of income loss that is rare in developed countries but widespread in transition economies. Earle and Sabirianova (2002, 2009) examine wage arrears in Russia using a framework that combines information on firms, workers, and local labor markets. According to these studies, wage arrears persisted for long periods throughout the 1990s and were the result of endogenous decisions by firms and workers. Hence, unlike pension arrears during the 1996 crisis, these episodes of wage arrears do not provide an exogenous source of income variation.

4. A study closely related to ours is Jensen and Richter (2003). That study analyzes the same pension crisis as we do but uses a different empirical approach and examines different outcomes of interest. In particular, Jensen and Richter (2003) treat equally all individuals in a pensioner household, whereas we allow for a differential treatment on pensioners directly affected and on non-pensioners indirectly affected by living with pensioners. In addition, whereas our focus is on the effects on various aspects of subjective well-being, their focus is on health-related inputs (incomes and calories) and outcomes (use of health services and medications). Jensen and Richter (2003) find significant effect on poverty rates and calorie intake but a more muted and varied effect on health reports and medication use. More details on the comparison between their results on objective health and our results on subjective well-being can be found in the sixth section.

5. Lokshin and Ravallion (2005) find a significant cross-sectional relationship between household and personal income and perceived power in the context of Russia.

6. In particular, in developing countries, pension income has been found to have a significant effect on the entire household and its members: pension receipt in South Africa changes household composition by increasing labor migration of prime-age household members (Ardington, Case, & Hosegood, 2009) and improves the health of children in the household (Duflo, 2003).

7. The source of our data is the "Russia Longitudinal Monitoring Survey, RLMS-HSE," conducted by Higher School of Economics and ZAO "Demoscope" together

with Carolina Population Center, University of North Carolina at Chapel Hill and the Institute of Sociology RAS. We gratefully acknowledge these institutions for giving us access to the data.

8. The survey also includes a community questionnaire that collects extensive data for each survey site. For more details on the survey design, see http://www.cpc.unc.edu/projects/rlms-hse/project

9. In the sixth section, we present additional analysis on the long-term effect of the pension crisis using data from the fourth survey round which took place in October 1998–January 1999. We exclude data from 1998 (or later rounds) from our main analysis due to the difficulty in separating the effect of the 1996 pension crisis from the effect of the 1998 financial crisis which started before data was collected in 1998. Although we have no particular reasons to believe that the financial crisis – a country-wide shock – should affect differently our treatment and control groups, we also have no means of testing this assumption.

10. The description of the pension crisis in this section relies heavily on Jensen and Richter (2003). Interested readers can find more details in that study.

11. We exclude the group of early retirees from our main analysis because of sample selection issues. The effect of the crisis might be heterogeneous along the dimensions of personal or household characteristics that also determine early retirement. Since we do not observe the reasons for early retirement, we cannot adequately control for this potential heterogeneity in effect. Nevertheless, as discussed in the sixth section, our results are robust to including early retirees in the sample.

12. The administration of the pension system is done at a more disaggregated regional level – in 1996 there were 89 administrative districts in Russia that collected taxes and disbursed pensions independently of each other. Thirty-two of these districts are included in the RLMS sample but the small number of observations does not allow us to present separate estimates at the district level. In Table 2, we show how the eight geographical regions map to these administrative districts based on their debtor or donor status in 1996, as defined by the PFR. Among the 32 districts included in the RLMS, only 5 were donor districts in 1996. Two of those districts map directly into the metropolitan region, and the other three are each subsumed into the following three regions: Northern and Northwestern, Western Siberian and Eastern Siberian, and Far Eastern. The remaining four geographical regions consist only of debtor districts.

13. When we estimate this model for all regions combined (with regional dummies to allow for regional level differences), we find that the only statistically significant determinant of arrears status is living in a rural area.

14. All income measures in subsequent analysis are deflated to June 1992 rubles, using the CPI index provided by the RLMS survey team.

15. In the fifth section, we demonstrate that our results are robust to alternative specifications such as an ordered probit which, unlike the OLS model, does not assume that the measures of SWB are cardinal. We use OLS as our preferred specification because the magnitudes of the effects estimated from this model are easier to interpret and because adding individual fixed effects in ordered probit models poses additional technical difficulties. In addition, Ferrer-i-Carbonel and

Frijters (2004) show that OLS models perform very similarly to ordered probit models for measures of SWB.

16. As discussed before, by including these post-crisis measures we face the possibility that they are endogenous with respect to arrears status.

17. As described in the second section, the questions about future expectations only ask about the future 12 months, which is why we use the 1995 reports to see if the 1996 crisis was anticipated.

18. One reason might be that pensioners experience any loss of pension income more strongly that gains in household income – note that the coefficient on low pre-crisis pension is also much larger than the coefficient on pre-crisis household income (excluding pensions). Another reason is indicated by the significant crisis effects on future expectations. Namely, it might be that pensioners expected the crisis to last and so the crisis effects are large because they incorporate expected future pension losses. However, further investigation of the source of this non-pecuniary cost is beyond the scope of this article.

19. As discussed previously, the ordered probit model does not allow for a straightforward inclusion of individual fixed effects. Hence, we test the cardinality assumption by estimating ordered probit models without fixed effects and compare the results with the results from OLS models without fixed effects (the latter are given in Tables 5 and 10).

20. We find no significant change (both economically and statistically) in any other category of expenditure shares. All results are available upon request.

21. Unfortunately, these cognitive measures were asked only in 1995 and 1996 (and not in 1994) and were asked only for individuals aged 55 and above. It is possible that the power of the statistical tests is affected by the smaller sample size.

22. Also consistent with the hypothesis of limited scope for insurance is the lack of significant increase in the amount formally borrowed through loans or credits (results available upon request). It appears that the only insurance channel available during crisis was decreasing the share of household resources formally lent to others (Table 15(b)).

23. Jensen and Richter (2003) find that pensioners in arrears in 1996 have a higher rate of mortality in 1998 but it is uncertain whether even this effect can be attributed to the pension crisis alone – it might well be that it was the double shocks from the 1996 pension crisis and the 1998 financial crisis that led to higher mortality in 1998.

REFERENCES

Ardington, C., Case, A., & Hosegood, V. (2009). Labor supply responses to large social transfers: Longitudinal evidence from South Africa. *American Economic Journal: Applied Economics, 1*(1), 22–48.

Behrman, J. (1995). Intrahousehold distribution and the family. In M. R. Rosenzweig & O. Stark (Eds.), *Handbook of population and family economics*. Amsterdam: North-Holland.

Cantril, H. (1965). *The pattern of human concern*. New Brunswick: Rutgers University Press.

Clark, A., Frijters, P., & Shields, M. (2008). Relative income, happiness and utility: An explanation for the Easterlin Paradox and other puzzles. *Journal of Economic Literature, 46*(1), 95–144.

Deaton, A. (2008). Income, health, and well-being around the world: Evidence from the Gallup World Poll. *Journal of Economic Perspectives, 22*(2), 53–72.

Di Tella, R., & MacCulloch, R. (2006). Some uses of happiness data in economics. *Journal of Economic Perspective, 20*(1), 25–46.

Duflo, E. (2003). Grandmothers and granddaughters: Old-age pensions and intrahousehold allocation in South Africa. *World Bank Economic Review, 17*(1), 1–25.

Earle, J. S., & Sabirianova, K. Z. (2002). How late to pay? Understanding wage arrears in Russia. *Journal of Labor Economics, 20*(3), 661–707.

Earle, J. S., & Sabirianova, K. Z. (2009). Complementarity and custom in wage contract violation. *Review of Economics and Statistics, 91*(4), 832–849.

Ericson, K. M. M., & Fuster, A. (2011). Expectations as endowments: Evidence on reference-dependent preferences from exchange and valuation experiments. *Quarterly Journal of Economics, 126*(4), 1879–1907.

Ferrer-i-Carbonel, A., & Frijters, P. (2004). How important is methodology for the estimates of the determinants of happiness?. *The Economic Journal, 114*(497), 641–659.

Frey, B. S., & Stutzer, A. (2002). What can economists learn from happiness research?. *Journal of Economic Literature, 40*(2), 402–435.

Frijters, P., Geishecker, I., Haisken-DeNew, J. P., & Shields, M. A. (2006). Can the large swings in Russian life satisfaction be explained by ups and downs in real incomes?. *Scandinavian Journal of Economics, 108*(3), 433–458.

Frijters, P., Haisken-DeNew, J. P., & Shields, M. A. (2004a). Investigating the patterns and determinants of life satisfaction in Germany following reunification. *Journal of Human Resources, 39*(3), 649–674.

Frijters, P., Haisken-DeNew, J. P., & Shields, M. A. (2004b). Money does matter! Evidence from increased real incomes in East Germany following reunification. *American Economic Review, 94*(3), 730–741.

Frijters, P., Haisken-DeNew, J. P., & Shields, M. A. (2005). The causal effect of income on health: Evidence from German reunification. *Journal of Health Economics, 24*(5), 997–1017.

Gardner, J., & Oswald, A. J. (2007). Money and mental wellbeing: A longitudinal study of medium-sized lottery wins. *Journal of Health Economics, 26*(1), 49–60.

Heeringa, S. G. (1997). Russia Longitudinal Monitoring Survey (RLMS) sample attrition, replenishment, and weighting in rounds V–VII. Retrieved from http://www.cpc.unc.edu/projects/rlms-hse/project/samprep.pdf

Jensen, R. T., & Richter, K. (2003). The health implications of social security failure: Evidence from the Russian pension crisis. *Journal of Public Economics, 88*(1), 209–236.

Kahneman, D., Knetsch, J. L., & Thaler, R. H. (1991). Anomalies: The endowment effect, loss aversion, and status quo bias. *Journal of Economic Perspectives, 5*(1), 193–206.

Kahneman, D., & Krueger, A. B. (2006). Developments in the measurement of subjective well-being. *Journal of Economic Perspectives, 20*(1), 3–24.

Köszegi, B., & Rabin, M. (2006). A model of reference-dependent preferences. *Quarterly Journal of Economics, 121*, 1133–1165.

Kuhn, R., & Stillman, S. (2004). Understanding interhousehold transfers in a transition economy: Evidence from Russia. *Economic Development and Cultural Change, 53*(1), 131–156.

Lokshin, M., & Ravallion, M. (2005). Rich and powerful? Subjective power and welfare in
    Russia. *Journal of Economic Behavior and Organization, 56*(2), 141–172.
Luechinger, S., Meier, S., & Stutzer, A. (2010). Why does unemployment hurt the employed?
    Evidence from the life satisfaction gap between the public and the private sector. *Journal
    of Human Resources, 45*(4), 998–1045.
Samuelson, W., & Zeckhauser, R. (1988). Status quo bias in decision making. *Journal of Risk
    and Uncertainty, 1*, 7–59.
Stutzer, A., & Frey, B. S. (2010). Recent advances in the economics of individual subjective
    well-being. *Social Research, 77*(2), 679–714.

CAN LONG-TERM COHABITING AND MARITAL UNIONS BE INCENTIVIZED?

Audrey Light and Yoshiaki Omori

ABSTRACT

In this study, we ask whether economic factors that can be directly manipulated by public policy have important effects on the probability that women experience long-lasting unions. Using data from the 1979 National Longitudinal Survey of Youth, we estimate a five-stage sequential choice model for women's transitions between single with no prior unions, cohabiting, first-married, re-single (divorced or separated), and remarried. We control for expected income tax burdens, Aid to Families with Dependent Children (AFDC) or Temporary Assistance for Needy Families (TANF) benefits, Medicaid expenditures, and parameters of state divorce laws, along with an array of demographic, family background, and market factors. We simulate women's sequences of transitions from age 18 to 48 and use the simulated outcomes to predict the probability that a woman with given characteristics (a) forms a first union by age 24 and maintains the union for at least 12 years, and (b) forms a second union by age 36 and maintains it for at least 12 years. While non-policy factors such as race and schooling prove to have important effects on the predicted probabilities of long-term unions, the policy factors have small and/or imprecisely estimated effects; in short,

Research in Labor Economics, Volume 36, 241–283
Copyright © 2012 by Emerald Group Publishing Limited
All rights of reproduction in any form reserved
ISSN: 0147-9121/doi:10.1108/S0147-9121(2012)0000036011

we fail to identify policy mechanisms that could potentially be used to incentivize long-term unions.

Keywords: Marriage; cohabitation; divorce; public policy

JEL classifications: J12; H4

INTRODUCTION

Family formation in the United States changed dramatically over the last four decades: marriage rates declined, divorce rates rose sharply before leveling off, and cohabitation among unmarried couples became increasingly common. These patterns have been carefully documented (Bumpass & Lu 2000; Bumpass, Sweet, & Cherlin, 1991; Cherlin, 1992; Smock, 2000; Stevenson & Wolfers, 2007), but researchers continue to seek a better understanding of the behavioral mechanisms by which individuals choose their marital status. To what extent does family background affect these choices? To what extent are they financial decisions? What types of "shocks" prompt individuals to revise past decisions and either enter into or dissolve relationships? In the face of rapid social change, we must continually refine our answers to these questions – particularly if incentives to choose one marital status over another are to be used as policy tools for improving the welfare of families. From elimination of the income tax "marriage penalty" to no-fault divorce laws to welfare reform, policy initiatives that address the link between marriage and well-being require a solid understanding of the forces that drive union-forming decisions.

In this study, we provide new evidence on the determinants of union formation by asking whether a range of economic factors that can be directly manipulated by public policy have important effects on the probability that women experience long-lasting unions. We use data from the 1979 National Longitudinal Survey of Youth (NLSY79) to estimate a multi-stage choice model that follows single, 18-year-old women as they transition into and out of each cohabiting union and marriage over the next three decades. Our covariates include expected income tax burdens, maximum allowed state Aid to Families with Dependent Children (AFDC) or Temporary Assistance for Needy Families (TANF) benefits, average state Medicaid expenditures and parameters of state divorce laws, along with a broad array of market, family background, demographic, and marital history variables. We use parameter estimates from the choice models to simulate women's union-related histories from age 18 to age 48. These simulated outcomes allow us to predict the probability of any long-term path of interest; we choose to focus on the probability that (a) an 18-year-old enters her *first* cohabiting union and/or marriage by age 24 and maintains it for at least 12 years; and (b) a 30-year-old divorcée forms a *new* union by age 36 and maintains it for at least 12 years. By assigning our sample members alternative sets of covariate values, we can assess the effects of various policy interventions on the likelihood of each long-term outcome. We also compare estimated "marginal effects" of policy factors to the estimated effects of race, schooling, market characteristics, and other factors that are not directly controlled by policy.

Elements of our analytic strategy have been seen in earlier research, but our approach is noteworthy for incorporating the following features. First, we depart from the existing literature in an important way by assessing the effect of each observed factor on the predicted probability of getting married and *staying* married or, more generally, forming a union via marriage *or* cohabitation and maintaining it for the long-term. Most researchers who study determinants of cohabitation, marriage, and divorce focus on the probability of a transition in the "next period" undertaken by individuals who are currently single (e.g., Blackburn, 2000; Lundberg & Rose, 2003; Xie, Raymo, Goyette, & Thornton, 2003) *or* cohabiting (e.g., Lichter, Qian, & Mellott, 2006; Smock & Manning, 1997; Wu & Pollard, 2000) *or* married (e.g., Friedberg, 1998; Whittington & Alm, 1997; Wolfers, 2006). Most of what we know about union formation and dissolution comes from such short-term estimates, yet they are inherently limited if our goal is to understand who marries for the first time and does *not* divorce, or cohabits and then marries and *remains* married, etc. – a goal that requires us to estimate each stage of the decision-making process and use sequences of "next period" transition probabilities to compute long-term probabilities. By moving the focus from year-to-year transitions to long-term paths (i.e., long-term sequences of year-to-year transitions), we are able to determine which policy and non-policy interventions are effective in promoting the formation of long-term unions.[1]

Second, we control for a number of economic policy factors simultaneously, along with demographic and family background factors (e.g., race, ethnicity, religion, living arrangements at age 14), skill factors (ability test scores, schooling attainment), and market factors (county racial and gender composition, unemployment rates). A small number of recent studies also incorporate an array of policy variables (Blau & van der Klaauw, 2010; Eissa & Hoynes, 2000b; Light & Omori, 2007, 2012), but the more typical approach is to focus on the effects of tax policy (cites) *or* welfare policy (cites) *or* divorce laws (cites) (Alm & Whittington, 1999; Whittington & Alm, 1997), welfare policy (Bitler, Gelbach, Hoynes, & Zavodny, 2004; Ellwood & Bane, 1985; Grogger & Bronars, 2001), or divorce laws (Friedberg, 1998; Nakonezny, Shull, & Rodgers, 1995; Wolfers, 2006) on marriage-related transitions. We learn not only whether each of these policy variables "matters," but how their estimated effects on women's marital transitions compare to each other and to the estimated effects of factors that policy-makers cannot directly manipulate.

Third, we focus on economic factors that are exogenous to marriage-related decisions. For example, we control for *expected* state income tax burdens rather than *actual* tax burdens, and for the generosity of states' welfare benefit rather than individuals' past or current welfare recipiency. By eliminating endogenous variation in employment, earnings, and other factors that can depend on marital status, we are able to isolate the "true" effects of economic incentives on union formation. Identification is aided by our reliance on state-level policies which, unlike federal laws, generate within-year variation in the data; in the absence of within-year variation, we would be unable to separate effects of policy from aging and duration effects.

Our approach reveals that despite often having nontrivial effects on a woman's likelihood of entering a marriage or cohabiting union, policy factors are largely unimportant when it comes to the probability of entering a union and maintaining it for several years. For example, setting each state's maximum AFDC benefit to an atypically low level (equal to the 10th percentile in the benefit distribution) increases by 18% the predicted probability that an 18-year-old woman marries in the next 6 years, but her predicted probability of marrying and *staying* married for at least 12 years increases by only 9%. Moreover, because marriages substitute for cohabiting unions, this extreme policy intervention accounts for a mere 1% increase in her predicted probability of forming and maintaining *any* union. The elimination of unilateral divorce is predicted to increase the probability of entering and maintaining a long-term first union by 7% despite lowering the predicted probability of union entry. Other policy factors that we consider have trivial effects on the predicted probability of a long-term first union. In contrast, the estimated effects on long-term unions of such factors as race, schooling attainment, and cognitive achievement are economically significant. When we extend our simulations to *second* unions entered into by 30-year-old women, we find that the estimated effects of policy factors are imprecisely estimated. In summary, we identify several demographic and background characteristics that substantially increase the predicted probability that a woman will cohabit or marry and stay with her partner for at least 12 years – but we find no avenues through which policy can reliably be used to incentivize long-term unions.

BACKGROUND

In estimating multi-stage discrete choice models for transitions into and out of cohabiting and marital unions, we control for a wide array of covariates to account for marital histories, policy and market factors, family background and demographic factors, and cognitive skill and schooling attainment. In the fourth section, we describe each covariate and present summary statistics for our stage-specific samples. In this section, we focus on the subset of factors that can, in principle, be readily manipulated by public policy to "incentivize" long-term unions by affecting the costs or benefits associated with each marital option. We explain how these policy-related economic factors are expected to influence union-forming decisions, and we briefly summarize existing empirical evidence on the importance of these key factors.

Welfare Benefits

The now-defunct AFDC program provided cash benefits to low-income, single mothers in the United States and, in some instances, to two-parent families where one parent was not biologically related to the children. Other two-parent families received no benefits unless a parent's unemployment status made them eligible for AFDC-UP. Thus, the program imposed a "marriage tax" insofar as nonmarital fertility would typically increase cash benefits and marital fertility would not. For many years, this marriage penalty was reinforced by the fact that Medicaid eligibility was tied directly to AFDC eligibility. However, reforms introduced in the late 1980s and 1990s increased Medicaid income eligibility beyond the limit set by AFDC, while also eliminating the requirement that children live with a single or cohabiting parent to be eligible for Medicaid. The Personal Responsibility and Work Opportunity Reconciliation Act of 1996 replaced AFDC with TANF. Under this program, states increased eligibility for two-parent families, reduced the generosity of benefits (in part by imposing time limits), and operated welfare-to-work programs. Each component of TANF is predicted to make marriage a more attractive option than it was under

AFDC programs, although welfare-to-work programs could also discourage marriage by making women more economically independent (Oppenheimer, 2000).[2]

Regardless of which regime we consider, welfare programs in the United States provide cash benefits that are tied to varying degrees to the recipient's marital status. Moreover, benefit levels – and, therefore, the gaps in expected benefits between married and unmarried women – vary dramatically across states. Table 1 shows the maximum AFDC or TANF payment available for a family of four in 1985, 1995, and 2005 in select states.[3] In 1985, the least generous states (Mississippi, Alabama, and Tennessee) paid between $201 and $260 per month (in 1996 dollars), while the median state (Maryland) paid $552 and the most generous state (Alaska) paid $1,118. A comparison of the 1985, 1995, and 2005 distributions suggests that cross-state variation dominates cross-year variation during this observation period, and that states tend to maintain their rankings over time. Similar cross-state variation is seen for average Medicaid expenditures for a family of four. This cross-state variation in the "cost" of marriage, as well as the additional variation caused by policy changes over time, is one avenue by which we can assess the effect of economic factors on union formation.

Numerous researchers have exploited cross-state and cross-year variation in benefit levels to assess the empirical effects of AFDC, TANF, and Medicaid on union formation. As expected, studies of the AFDC-marriage link generally find that increased benefit levels decrease the likelihood that

Table 1. Maximum AFDC or TANF Benefits Available in Select States, in 1985, 1995, and 2005.

Rank	1985 (AFDC)		1995 (AFDC)		2005 (TANF)	
	State	Amount	State	Amount	State	Amount
1	Mississippi	$201	Mississippi	$147	Mississippi	$163
2	Alabama	$202	Alabama	$198	Tennessee	$189
3	Tennessee	$260	Tennessee	$231	Texas	$189
26	Maryland	$552	Maryland	$460	New Jersey	$409
49	Wisconsin	$890	Vermont	$747	California	$723
50	California	$958	Hawaii	$877	Alaska	$859
51	Alaska	$1,118	Alaska	$1,047	Minnesota	$869

Note: Dollar amounts shown are maximum; monthly benefits available for a family of four in the given state-year, divided by the implicit price deflator for gross domestic product (base year = 1996). See the fourth section for data sources.

single women marry (Blackburn, 2000; Grogger & Bronars, 2001; Hoynes, 1997; Schultz, 1998; Winkler, 1994) and increase the likelihood of divorce (Ellwood & Bane, 1985; Hoffman & Duncan, 1995). Moffitt, Reville, and Winkler (1998) demonstrate that a surprisingly high percent of AFDC recipients cohabit, presumably because they are not penalized for monetary contributions made by unmarried partners. Bitler et al. (2004) find that the transition from AFDC to TANF caused fewer marriages but also less divorce, while Kaestner and Kaushal (2005) find little effect of TANF on marriage rates. These conflicting results are consistent with the fact that TANF programs simultaneously encourage marriage by increasing eligibility for married women and discourage marriage by promoting female employment. Yelowitz (1998) observes that the theoretical effect of Medicaid expansion on marriage rates is similarly ambiguous, but provides empirical evidence that the net effect of increased eligibility on entry into marriage is positive. Schultz (1998) finds that increased Medicaid and AFDC generosity decrease the probability of marriage while Decker (2000), using data from 1965 to 1972, provides evidence that marriage probabilities declined when Medicaid was introduced. While a great deal has been learned about the effects of welfare benefits on union formation, cohabiters' transitions have been largely overlooked in this literature.[4]

Income Taxes

A husband and wife in the United States who earn similar levels of taxable income often face a different federal tax burden than they would face if unmarried. A marriage penalty arises when the standard deduction for a married couple is less than twice the standard deduction for a single filer (e.g., $6,550 versus $3,900 in 1995). Similarly, a married couple in which one partner earns all or most of the taxable income generally receives a marriage bonus by using the larger standard deduction. The Economic Growth and Tax Relief Reconciliation Act of 2001, the Jobs and Growth Tax Relief Reconciliation Act of 2003, and the Working Families Tax Relief Act of 2004 reduced or eliminated the "marriage penalty" for many couples, particularly in the lower tax brackets. However, state income tax obligations continue to vary with marital status across the income distribution because many states impose a tax penalty or bonus due to differential standard deductions. Moreover, because states vary dramatically in their income tax rates and allowable deductions, the difference between the tax owed by a given couple if single or cohabiting and the tax

248 AUDREY LIGHT AND YOSHIAKI OMORI

owed if married can vary across states even in the absence of a marriage penalty or bonus.[5]

To illustrate how state income tax burdens vary with marital status, in Table 2 we summarize the taxes owed by a hypothetical couple in three states in 1985, 1995, and 2005, assuming one partner earns $35,000 and the other earns $20,000 in inflation-adjusted dollars. We also assume this couple has no other taxable income, no itemized deductions, and no dependents.

Table 2. State Income Tax Obligations in Select States, in Tax Years 1985, 1995, and 2005.

	Earned Income	Filing Status	1985		1995		2005	
			Tax	Rate[a]	Tax	Rate[a]	Tax	Rate[a]
			Minnesota					
a	$20,000	single	$1,015	7.8	$816	6.0	$710	5.4
b	$35,000	single	$2,303	9.5	$1,974	8.0	$1,715	7.1
c	$55,000		$3,318		$2,790		$2,425	
d	$55,000	joint	$3,671	9.2	$3,017	8.0	$2,598	7.1
d−c			*$353*		*$227*		*$173*	
			California					
a	$20,000	single	$238	5.0	$357	4.0	$324	4.0
b	$35,000	single	$1,252	9.0	$1,405	9.3	$1,291	8.0
c	$55,000		$1,490		$1,762		$1,615	
d	$55,000	joint	$1,304	7.0	$1,592	6.0	$1,466	6.0
d−c			*−$186*		*−$170*		*−$149*	
			Texas					
a	$20,000	single	$0	0	$0	0	$0	0
b	$35,000	single	$0	0	$0	0	$0	0
c	$55,000		$0		$0		$0	
d	$55,000	joint	$0	0	$0	0	$0	0
d−c			*$0*		*$0*		*$0*	

Note: Dollar amounts are deflated by the implicit price deflator for gross domestic product (base year = 1995); corresponding nominal income for rows *a* and *b* are $14,618 and $25,581 in 1985, and $24,369 and $42,646 in 2005. Each individual couple is assumed to have no taxable income other than earned income, no itemized deductions, and no dependents. Row *c* shows the total tax bill for a cohabiting couple with the assumed income levels, while row *d* shows the couple's tax bill if married and filing jointly. The difference between rows *d* and *c* is the tax penalty (if positive) or bonus (if negative) associated with marriage. Tax obligations are calculated using version 9 of Internet TAXSIM available at http://www.nber.org/~taxsim/.
[a]Marginal state income tax rate.

We focus on one state (Minnesota) that imposes a marriage penalty, one state (California) that has a marriage bonus, and one state (Texas) that is marriage neutral by virtue of having no state income tax. If this couple lives in Minnesota in 1985, they owe $3,318 in state income tax if they are single or cohabiting, and $3,671 if they are married and filing jointly; in other words, this couple faces a "marriage penalty" of $353 above and beyond any penalty imposed by federal law. Because Texas has no state income tax, this couple will owe the same amount (zero) regardless of marital status. In California, they will pay $186 more in state income tax if they are single than if they are married ($1,490 versus $1,304) – that is, they will face a marriage bonus.[6] Comparable figures for 1995 and 2005 indicate a considerable degree of stability in the tax obligations in California and, of course, Texas, but a reduction in the tax obligations and marriage penalties in Minnesota due to declining marginal tax rates.

In a seminal study of the marriage-tax link, Alm and Whittington (1999) control for individuals' federal income tax burdens in modeling transitions into marriage and find that the "marriage tax" is associated with a slight decrease in the probability that women marry. While most studies in this vein examine the effect of taxes on transitions into marriage (Alm & Whittington, 1995a, 1995b; Brien, Lillard, & Stern, 2006; Lopez-Laborda & Zarate-Marco, 2004), Whittington and Alm (1997) find that tax policy that penalizes married couples also has a small, positive effect on the probability of divorce. Eissa and Hoynes (2000b) find that income tax penalties have a small, imprecisely estimated, negative effect on transitions from cohabitation to marriage, but this transition has received far less attention in the literature than transitions between single and married. Moreover, most existing studies rely on federal tax laws, which only vary over time, and many compute income tax burdens on the basis of *actual* (endogenous) earnings rather than predicted earnings. Our analysis relies on cross-state variation in tax law to isolate the effect of income tax obligations from the effects of aging, and we assign all sample members an identical, median incomes (for themselves and their hypothetical partners) to abstract from all individual-specific variation in income and family size.

Divorce and Property Division

When the decision is made to dissolve a union, married couples are governed by state laws regarding grounds for divorce, the determination of alimony, and the division of property. Every state in the United States except New York allowed no-fault divorce by the mid-1980s, and most introduced unilateral divorce as well. No-fault divorce refers to a legal environment in which the petitioner is not required to establish that his/her spouse was guilty of adultery, cruelty, or other forms of marital misconduct. Unilateral divorce is a form of no-fault divorce that does not require the mutual consent of both spouses. The near-universal adoption of no-fault divorce does not imply that divorce is granted with equal ease in every state: states differ with respect to separation requirements preceding the granting of no-fault divorce, the need for mutual consent, and the laws governing alimony and property division. No state has explicit laws stating how unmarried, cohabiting couples should divide their property upon dissolving their union, although courts are often willing to grant "palimony" to unmarried partners if the couple has a written or implied agreement concerning property settlements. In short, legal protection varies significantly across states for both married and unmarried couples.

Based on data from Friedberg (1998), Table 3 identifies 31 states that granted unilateral divorce without separation requirements in 1985, 1995, and 2005, as well as an additional 15 states that granted unilateral (no fault) divorce after a mandatory separation.[7] Separation requirements – which generally range from six months to three years – can substantially raise the cost of divorce to the point that some individuals establish fault (if allowed by state law) to circumvent the waiting period.

There is considerable disagreement in the literature over whether unilateral and no-fault divorce affects divorce decisions. Peters (1986, 1992) applies the Coase theorem to argue that couples offset the direct

Table 3. Summary of State Laws Governing Divorce in 1985, 1995, and 2005.

Divorce Law	States
Unilateral divorce, no separation requirement	AL, AK, AZ, CA, CO, CT, FL, GA, HI, ID, IN, IA, KS, KY, ME, MA, MI, MN, MT, NE, NV, NH, NM, ND, OK, OR, RI, SD*, TX, WA, WY (n = 31)
Unilateral divorce, mandatory separation requirement	DC, IL*, LA, MD, MO, NJ, NC, OH, PA*, SC, UT*, VT, VA, WV, WI (n = 15)
No unilateral divorce	AR, DE, MS, NY, TN (n = 5)

*Denotes states known to have changed their divorce regime during the observation period used for this analysis (1979–2008). No state changed its regime between 1985 and 2005.
Note: Data are based on Friedberg (1998) and additional sources detailed in the fourth section of this article.

effects of unilateral divorce via contracting. Allen (1992) questions her assumption that utility is perfectly transferable among spouses. Mechoulan (2006) observes that couples who marry prior to the adoption of no-fault or unilateral laws are unable to arrange the appropriate contingent contract unless they have perfect foresight about impending changes in the law. From an empirical standpoint, it is difficult to pin down a causal effect of divorce law on divorce decisions. Bougheas and Georgellis (1999), Ellman and Lohr (1998), Friedberg (1998), and Nakonezny et al. (1995) differ in the time periods considered, whether short-term or long-term effects are estimated, and how divorce outcomes are measured. A recent study by Wolfers (2006) suggests that the introduction of unilateral divorce had a small, short-lived (positive) effect on divorce rates. Although voices in the policy arena are currently calling for a return to "fault" divorce as a means of lowering divorce rates in the United States, the literature has yet to establish whether such a switch would significantly affect divorce decisions. Moreover, we lack evidence on the extent to which divorce law affects entry into marriage and, in particular, the decision to marry rather than cohabit.

ESTIMATION

Choice Model

Our goal is to model all stages of the union-forming process with a series of stage-specific discrete-choice models. Our data allow us to follow every woman in our sample from her initial spell of being single (with no prior marriage or cohabitation) through first cohabitation spells, first marriages, second single spells, second cohabitation spells, and so forth. Due to limited sample sizes for cohabitation spells and marriages beyond the first, however, we collapse what for some women would be a 12-stage model into the following, five-stage process: In stage 1, single women with no prior marriages or cohabiting unions decide on a period-by-period basis whether to stay single, cohabit, or marry. Women who choose cohabitation advance to stage 2, where they decide on a period-by-period basis whether to continue cohabiting, dissolve their union, or marry. Anyone who chooses to marry in stage 1 or stage 2 advances to stage 3, where they decide on a period-by-period basis whether to maintain that first marriage or divorce. Women who terminate *any* marriage or cohabiting union enter stage 4 (an aggregate "re-single" stage), where they again decide on a period-by-period basis whether to stay single, cohabit, or marry. If women in stage 4 choose to cohabit they reenter stage 2, which consists of *all* (not just first-time) cohabitation spells. Women in stage 2 or 4 who remarry move to stage 5, which consists of *all* second and subsequent marriages.

We assume that in each period – defined as a 1-year interval – individuals choose the stage-specific alternative that maximizes expected utility. We assume the expected utility of alternative *j* for individual *i* in stage *g* at time *t* can be expressed as a linear function of various observed and unobserved factors. That is

$$V^j_{igt} = \beta^j_g X^j_{igt} + \varepsilon^j_{igt} \quad \text{for } j = s, c, m \text{ and } g = 1, 2, 3, 4, 5 \tag{1}$$

where X^j_{igt} represents observed factors (current spell duration, policy factors, demographic controls, etc.) and ε^j_{igt} represents unobserved factors affecting the value of alternative *j*. Note that in stages 3 and 5, which correspond to first and subsequent marriages, alternative *c* (cohabitation) is unavailable because married women must divorce (i.e., choose alternative *s*) before cohabitation becomes an option. The model allows observed factors to vary across individuals, over time (within and between stages), and across alternatives although, in principle, many factors (race, religion, highest grade completed) are time-invariant for each woman. The parameters (β) describing the effects of covariates on expected utility are allowed to vary across stages because relative income tax burdens, divorce laws, and many other factors are likely to have a different effect on the value of being single than on the value of cohabitation or marriage.

We assume the residuals (ε) are drawn from an extreme value distribution, which means the transition probabilities that form the likelihood function have a logistic structure. We compute standard errors that account for inter-temporal correlations among the residuals for a given woman in a given stage, but we assume independence across alternatives and across stages. Thus, we independently estimate multinomial logits for stages 1 (single with no prior unions), 2 (cohabiting), and 4 (single with prior unions), and binomial logits for stages 3 and 5 (first and subsequent marriages).[8]

We conclude this section by previewing a number of empirical issues related to the estimation of our five-stage model, all of which are clarified further in the fourth section. First, every woman in our sample begins the sequential choice process in stage 1 (single with no prior unions) at a uniform, exogenously determined point in the lifecycle (age 18). Second, each woman contributes between 2 and 30 person-year observations to the sample used for estimation. (As detailed in the fourth section, we use data for 1979–2008, but a woman who reaches age 18 later than 1979 and/or drops out of the survey prior to 2008 contributes fewer than 30 annual observations to the sample.) Third, the number of observations a woman contributes to each stage – and, more generally, the number of stages she enters – is strictly a function of her union-forming behavior. A woman who forms a first union at age 19 contributes only one observation to the stage 1 sample before moving to stage 2 (cohabitation) or stage 3 (first marriage), while a woman who remains single throughout the observation period contributes as many as 30 observations to the stage 1 sample. While the latter woman appears *only* in stage 1, a woman who marries, divorces, and remarries appears in stage 1 (single with no prior unions), stage 3 (first marriage), stage 4 (single with prior unions), and stage 5 (second and subsequent marriages). A woman with multiple cohabiting and marital partners not only appears in all five stages, but can appear in stage 2 (cohabitation), stage 4 (single with prior unions), and stage 5 (second and subsequent marriages) multiple times.

Simulation

After estimating the five binomial or multinomial logit models described above, we use our parameter estimates to simulate each woman's union-forming history from age 18 to 48. The idea is to simulate the 31-year sequence of marital statuses (e.g., SSSSCCMSSSM...MMMM) for a large sample of women, define a dummy variable that indicates whether each simulated sequence conforms to a particular long-term path of interest, and use the mean and standard deviation of that dummy variable as our predicted probability. Specifically, we simulate each woman's history for each of 150 random draws from the estimated distribution of the parameter estimates, thus accounting for the point estimates for β_g^j in Eq. (1) as well as their standard errors.[9]

A key step in conducting the simulations is to decide which covariate values to use. We begin with a baseline simulation in which we assign each woman her initial, actual value for each element of X – that is, the value prevailing at $t = 1$ (age 18) and $g = 1$ (stage 1). As we simulate each period-by-period transition from age 18 to 48, we update marital history covariates (duration of current spell, number of prior cohabitations, etc.) each period to reflect the simulated outcomes while holding all other covariates constant at their initial value. By relying on actual covariate values observed at $t = 1$, we can simulate each woman's path from age 18 to 48 regardless of whether she is observed at every age.[10] We conduct additional simulations after assigning each woman identical values for *select* covariates. For example, in one simulation each woman is assigned an identically "low" AFDC benefit equal to the 10th percentile in the overall distribution, while in another simulation each woman is assigned a race/ethnicity of nonblack, non-Hispanic. For each simulation in which a single covariate or set of covariates is assigned a uniform value, all other covariates are assigned the initial, actual value as in the baseline simulation described above. This series of simulations allows us to identify the "marginal effect" of a given covariate (or set of covariates) on the predicted probability of following any long-term path of interest.

Once we obtain $N \cdot 150$ (where N is the number of women in our sample), simulated outcomes from age 18 to 48 for each set of assigned covariate values, the second key step is to define the long-term paths of interest. We consider one long-term path for first unions, and a similarly defined path for second unions. From a starting point of being single with no prior unions at age 18, any woman who enters cohabitation or marriage by age 24 and remains with the same partner for at least 12 years meets our definition of a long-term first union. From a starting point of separating from a first partner at age 30, any woman who enters a new (cohabiting or marital) union by age 36 and maintains the union for at least 12 years meets our definition of a long-term second union. We choose these two paths because they meet a number of desirable criteria: First, by considering unions entered within 6 years of the starting point, we avoid focusing on unions formed at unusually young ages; our paths include first unions formed as late as age 24 and second union formed as late as age 36. Second, by using identical 6-year entry intervals and 12-year durations for both first and second unions, we ensure that our predicted probabilities are comparable across paths. Third, 12-year durations are the longest we can consider over a 30-year observation period without introducing considerable overlap between first and second unions.[11]

In presenting these predicted long-term probabilities in the fifth section, we report both entry probabilities (e.g., the probability of forming a first union by age 24) and joint probabilities (e.g., the probability of forming a first union by age 24 and maintaining it for at least 12 years). In addition, we disaggregate each entry probability and joint probability by the type of union (cohabitation versus marriage). For example, we report the probability of cohabiting by age 24, the probability of marrying by age 24, and the probability of forming any union by age 24, which is the sum of the two preceding probabilities.

In Table 4, we provide several examples of simulated sequences of marital outcomes to illustrate our calculations. Row 1 shows a simulation in which the woman remains single at age 24; because she is not predicted to cohabit

Table 4. Examples of Simulated Sequences of Marital Outcomes.

	C by Age 24	M by Age 24	Maintain 12+ Years	18	19	20	21	22	23	24	25	26	27	28	29	30	31	32	33	34	35	36
1	N	N	–	S	S	S	S	S	S	S	S	S	S	S	S	S	S	S	S	S	S	S
2	N	Y	Y	S	M	M	M	M	M	M	M	M	M	M	M	M	M	M	M	M	M	M
3	Y	N	N	S	S	S	C	C	C	C	C	C	C	S	S	S	S	S	S	S	S	S
4	Y	Y	Y	S	S	S	C	C	M	M	M	M	M	M	M	M	M	M	M	M	M	M

	Re-S at age 30	C by age 36	M by age 36	18	19	20	21	22	23	24	25	26	27	28	29	30	31	32	33	34	35	36
5	Y	N	N	S	M	M	M	M	M	M	M	M	M	M	M	S	S	S	S	S	S	S
6	Y	N	Y	S	S	S	S	S	S	S	M	M	M	M	M	S	S	S	S	S	M	M

Note: These mock simulated outcomes (shown only to age 36) illustrate cases where the woman is predicted to enter a first cohabiting union by age 24 (C by age 24), enter a first marriage by age 24 (M by age 24), maintain a first union for at least 12 years (maintain 12 + years), enter a second union via cohabitation by age 36 (C by age 36), or enter a second union via marriage by age 36 (M by age 36). The column titled "Re-S at age 30" identifies simulated outcomes where the individual becomes "re-single" by separating from a first partner at age 30.

(C) or marry (M) by age 24, simulated outcomes beyond age 24 are irrelevant to the computation of first-union probabilities. Row 2 shows a simulated path that leads to marriage (M) at age 19, while both paths in rows 3–4 lead to cohabitation (C) at age 21. If these four cases were to represent our sample of $N \cdot 150$ simulations, our predicted probabilities of cohabiting by age 24, marrying by age 24, and cohabiting or marrying by age 24 would be 0.50, 0.25, and 0.75, respectively. The simulations in row 2 and 4 reveal unions that last beyond 12 years; in the latter case, the cohabiting union converts to marriage at age 23 and endures at least to age 36. Based on these examples, the predicted, joint probability of experiencing a long-term first union formed via cohabitation is 0.25, and the comparable probability for a first union formed via marriage is also 0.25. Rows 5–6 in Table 4 show two simulated sequences in which the woman separates from her first partner at age 30, so both sequences would be used to calculate probabilities related to second unions. In this two-observation sample, the probability of entering a second union via marriage by age 36 is 0.50.

DATA

Sample Selection

Our primary data source is the NLSY79. The survey began in 1979 with a sample of 12,686 individuals born in 1957–1964. The original sample is 60% nonblack, non-Hispanic, 25% black, and 15% Hispanic, and roughly 50% male. Respondents were surveyed annually from 1979 to 1994 and biennially thereafter; we use data for survey years 1979 through 2008.[12]

In selecting a sample for our analysis, we begin by eliminating the 6,403 NLSY79 respondents who are male. We confine our attention to women because they (and their children) tend to be the focus of marriage-related public policy. Next, we eliminate 3,424 female respondents whose 18th birthdays occur more than 9 months before the 1979 interview date, who drop out of the survey before their 18th birthday, or who marry or cohabit before their 18th birthday. These selection rules produce a sample of 2,859 women born in 1960–1964 who are single (never married, never cohabited) when first observed. We use the age 18 cutoff in order to initialize stage 1, to the extent possible, on the basis of an exogenous factor (age) rather than self-determined events such as observed first unions. Ideally, we would initialize stage 1 when each woman starts making union-forming decisions, but this occurs prior to the start of the survey for many women, given that individuals can cohabit long before they can legally marry. Among the 2,859 women who are observed from their 18th birthdays onward and who are single at that starting date, we eliminate another 98 individuals because key variables are missing. The remaining sample consists of 2,761 women, 29% of whom are black and 17% of whom are Hispanic.

We construct an annual observation for each of these individuals from the year they are age 18 until the year of their last interview. For each person-year observation, we identify the respondent's marital status as single, cohabiting, or married, and we determine which new status, if any, she transitions to during the succeeding 12 months. If a woman is single at the time of the 1990 and 1991 interviews, for example, we must ensure that no marriage or cohabitation takes place between interviews in order to identify the observation as "single-to-single" (SS). Similarly, if she reports herself as cohabiting in 1990 and 1991, we must make sure she is with the same partner to classify the observation as "cohabiting-to-cohabiting" (CC) rather than "cohabiting-to-single" (CS). To associate each person-year observation with a transition type, we use all available information on marriage, cohabitation, and divorce. NLSY79 respondents report their marital status at each interview, and they also provide a complete event history of the dates when each marriage begins and ends. From 1990 onward, dates for cohabitation spells are reported as well. Although start and end dates for cohabitation spells are not reported prior to 1990, we know whether the respondent is cohabitating at the time of each interview, and we also have identifier codes for each cohabiting partner. If a respondent is cohabiting in two successive interviews but with different partners, we will correctly identify the CS transition. Similarly, when a respondent divorces and remarries between interviews there is no danger of treating her as continuously married; the transition will be correctly identified as "married-to-single" (MS).[13]

We use information on marital status and transitions to divide the sample of person-year observations into five stage-specific samples, summarized in Table 5. The stage 1 sample contains 20,810 observations for all 2,761 women in our sample; each woman is in stage 1 from age 18 until she forms a first union, or until she is last interviewed. The stage 2 sample consists of 4,721 observations for 1,292 women in cohabiting unions. Due to the relatively small number of cohabiting unions observed in the data, we do not restrict this stage to first cohabiting spells. The stage 3 sample contains 25,566 observations for 2,178 women in their first marriages. The sample for stage 4 contains 10,850 observations corresponding to second and subsequent "re-single" spells experienced by 1,492 women who were previously cohabiting and/or married, while the stage 5 sample contains

Table 5. Sample Sizes by Stage.

Stage	Stage Definition	Number of Women	Number of Observations
1	Single, no prior unions	2,761	20,810
2	Cohabiting	1,292	4,721
3	First marriages	2,178	25,566
4	Single, prior unions	1,492	10,850
5	Second to fourth marriages	724	6,092
All		2,761	68,039

Note: Each woman starts in stage 1 at age 18, and contributes one observation per year to the stage 1 sample until she moves to stage 2 by cohabiting, moves to stage 3 by marrying, or is last interviewed. More generally, each woman appears in between one and five stages between age 18 and her last interview, and contributes a total of 2 to 30 person-year observations to the total, five-stage sample.

6,092 observations for 724 women in second, third, and fourth marriages. We emphasize that the women appearing in stages 2–5 are a subset of the 2,761 women in stage 1. A woman can remain in stage 1 throughout the observation period if she never forms a union or, at the other extreme, she can appear in all five stages (with multiple spells in stages 2, 4, and 5) if she has multiple partners during the observation period. Each woman contributes between 2 and 30 observations to the five-stage sample. A woman must turn age 18 prior to her 1979 interview and remain in the survey through 2008 to contribute 30 observations; women who are born later or who drop out of the survey contribute fewer observations.

Covariates

The multi-stage, discrete choice model described in the third section assumes that on an annual basis, each woman chooses the available marital status that yields the greatest expected utility. In light of this assumed decision-making process, we control for covariates that are likely to affect the cost and benefit associated with being single, cohabiting, and marrying. While many of our covariates are time-invariant from age 18 onward, for time-varying variables we use the value that prevails during the calendar year associated with the given person-year observation for estimation because contemporaneous values (as opposed to lagged or lead values) are likely to best represent the woman's current assessment of the value of each status.

We group our extensive set of covariates into four categories: marital history variables, policy and market factors, demographic and family background factors, and skill factors. We discuss the variables within each category in turn; summary statistics for each covariate for the stage 1–3 samples are reported in Table 6.

In each stage-specific model, we control for a number of marital history variables. The probability of a union-related transition has been shown to change dramatically with current spell duration, in part because couples invest in union-specific capital (Bennett, Blanc, & Bloom, 1988; Lichter et al. 2006; Lillard, Brien, &Waite, 1995). We allow for duration dependence with a measure of current spell duration in years and its square; it is clear from the estimates in Table 7 that the degree of duration dependence differs dramatically by stage, but extensive experimentation revealed that more flexible functional forms are unnecessary. In select stages, we also control for the age at which the current spell began, the number of prior cohabitation spells, the number of prior marriages, and an indicator of whether the woman cohabited with her husband prior to the current marriage. These are not included in all stages because, for example, all spells in stage 1 are initialized at age 18, while the number of prior marriages is uniformly zero in stage 1 and the stage 3 sample of first marriages.

To control for potential welfare benefits, we include measures of the maximum, monthly AFDC or TANF benefit available for a family of four, divided by the implicit price deflator for gross domestic product (GDP), and the average Medicaid expenditure for a family of four, divided by the consumer price index (CPI) for medical care. We use 1996 as the base year for both price indices. Both measures are specific to the state of residence and calendar year corresponding to the person-year observation, and are independent of the woman's income, household composition, and eligibility.[14]

To measure the expected income tax penalty or bonus associated with marriage, we begin by associating every person-year observation in a given stage with a uniform measure of expected earnings for women in that stage, and a uniform measure of expected earnings for a hypothetical, male partner of women in that stage. These two earnings measures are the median, predicted earnings obtained by estimating stage-specific, gender-specific earnings models with data reported by *all* NLSY79 respondents who are at least 18 years old and whose current marital status corresponds to the given stage (single with no prior unions, cohabiting, first marriage, etc.).[15] After merging these median earnings variables into our (women only) samples, we then use the calendar year and state of residence corresponding to each person-year observation to compute the woman's expected state income tax

Table 6. Summary Statistics for Stage 1, Stage 2, and Stage 3 Samples.

Covariates	Stage 1		Stage 2		Stage 3	
	Mean	S.D.	Mean	S.D.	Mean	S.D.
Marital history						
Spell duration, years	6.82	6.78	2.27	3.16	8.41	6.14
Spell duration squared, years	92.60	151.78	15.16	43.78	108.40	133.02
Age when spell began	18.00	0	27.69	6.62	23.63	4.35
Number of prior cohabitation spells	–		.50	.80	.36	.61
Number of prior marriages	–		.43	.63	–	
1 if cohabited with spouse before marriage	–		–		.26	
Policy and market factors						
Maximum monthly AFDC/TANF benefit, $100s[a]	4.93	2.88	4.18	3.28	3.28	3.09
Average Medicaid expenditure, $100s[a]	3.50	1.70	2.80	2.00	2.42	2.09
State income tax marriage penalty, $100s[a]	.46	1.17	.38	1.09	.28	1.17
1 if unilateral divorce, no separation	.50		.55		.53	
1 if unilateral divorce, mandatory separation	.28		.26		.29	
Percent same race in county	52.27	32.43	56.26	32.76	60.03	31.31
Percent men in county	48.44	1.28	48.79	1.31	48.84	1.24
County unemployment rate	7.78	3.31	7.03	3.09	6.73	3.04
Background and demographic factors						
1 if black	.42		.25		.23	
1 if Hispanic	.16		.22		.19	
1 if foreign born	.06		.05		.07	
1 if lived with single mother, age 14	.23		.23		.15	
mother and stepfather, age 14	.07		.11		.08	
mother and father, age 14	.63		.57		.71	
Mother's highest grade completed	10.94	3.16	10.59	2.94	10.92	3.10
1 if access to reading materials, age 14	.89		.89		.90	
1 if child born before age 18	.06		.09		.02	
1 if Baptist	.33		.27		.26	
Catholic	.32		.38		.38	
Other Christian	.20		.20		.21	
Other religion	.11		.09		.12	
1 if attends church more than one times per month	.23		.20		.22	
More than one times per week	.45		.35		.47	
Traditional values score	1.83	1.64	1.99	1.70	1.81	1.65

Table 6. (*Continued*)

Covariates	Stage 1		Stage 2		Stage 3	
	Mean	S.D.	Mean	S.D.	Mean	S.D.
Skill factors						
AFQT percentile score	41.02	28.98	36.66	27.20	46.42	27.63
1 if final highest grade completed < 12	.07		.17		.05	
= 13–15	.27		.23		.27	
≥ 16	.28		.12		.27	
Spouse's highest grade completed	–		12.23	2.38	13.24	2.61
Number of observations	20,810		4,721		25,566	
Number of women	2,671		1,292		2,178	

Note: Covariates also includes missing value indicators for mother's highest grade completed and AFQT score; stage-specific sample means are used to replace missing values.
[a]Medicaid expenditures are divided by the consumer price index for medical care, and welfare and income tax variables are divided by the implicit price deflator for gross domestic product; the base year is 1996.

burden, assuming she and her (real or hypothetical) partner have no dependents and no other taxable income. We first assume each median couple is married and filing jointly, and we then assume they are single or cohabiting and filing separately.[16] The expected income tax liability if married net of the expected liability if non-married is our measure of the state income tax marriage penalty or bonus.

Within each stage, variation in our income tax variable depends *entirely* on state of residence and calendar year; because we assign every woman the identical median income for herself and her hypothetical partner, our tax variable is independent of the woman's (and her partner's) actual income, as well as family size, schooling, and any other factors that affect income tax liabilities. Our measure varies considerably both within and across years because we rely on state income tax policies rather than federal laws. We use state rather than federal income tax codes because the latter contains no within-year variation, which means we would be unable to separate variation in expected (federal) income tax obligations from aging and union duration effects, given the narrow range of birth years in our sample. Table 6 reveals that the stage 1 mean of our state tax variable (deflated by the implicit price deflator for GDP, using 1996 as the base year) is $46, with a standard error of $117. We are not arguing that cohabitation, marriage, and divorce decisions are driven by costs of this magnitude. Instead, we rely on the fact that variation in this exogenous measure is representative of variation in women's actual (federal and state) income tax obligations.

Our policy variables also include two measures of state laws governing divorce. As discussed in the second section, virtually all states allow some form of no-fault divorce during our observation period, so we instead control for whether they grant unilateral divorce (no-fault divorce without mutual consent) with and without separation requirements. Table 6 shows that 50% of the stage 1 observations are contributed by women living in states with unilateral divorce (without separation requirements), while another 28% of observations correspond to states that grant no-fault or unilateral divorce after a period of mandatory separation; Table 3 shows which states fall into each category.[17] In light of evidence presented in Friedberg (1998) and Iyvarakul, McElroy, and Staub (2011), we experimented with a more extensive set of variables to distinguish between no-fault and unilateral divorce, to identify the length of mandatory separations, and to identify whether fault can be established as grounds for divorce. None of our experiments had a substantive effect on the findings reported in the fifth section, although some yielded estimated coefficients that are smaller in magnitude than what we obtain with a simple, two-variable classification of divorce law.

Our five policy-related covariates – each of which is intended to capture a potential economic incentive to marry, cohabit, or divorce – capture cross-state and, to a lesser extent, cross-year differences in state policies and laws governing transfers, income taxes, and laws. We rely heavily on cross-state variation in these policy variables because we follow women born within a five-year window from age 18 forward and, therefore, would be hard-pressed to separate aging and union duration effects from any cross-year changes in policy.[18] Given our reliance on cross-state variation, our claims that each variable is strictly exogenous relies on the assumption that women do not choose their state of residence *in conjunction with their marital status* to lower divorce costs, reduce income taxes, or increase welfare or Medicaid benefits.

In addition to our policy variables, we include three contextual variables that represent characteristics of sample members' marriage markets: the percent of the respondent's county population that is male, the percent of the county population that is the same race/ethnicity (black, Hispanic, or other) as the respondent, and the county unemployment rate. All three variables are constructed by merging county-level data from the City and

County Data Book (collected by the U.S. Census Bureau) with the NLSY79 data, using county of residence indicators from the NLSY79 Geocode file.[19] Variables such as these have also been used by Lichter, LeClere, & McLaughlin (1991) and Lichter, McLaughlin, & Ribar (2002)) and others.

To control for demographic factors and family influences that might affect union formation, we use an extensive array of time-constant variables, all of which are reported in 1979. This includes dummy variables indicating whether the woman is black or Hispanic, whether she was born outside the United States, and whether she lived with a single mother, a mother and stepfather, or both biological parents at age 14; any living arrangement that did not include the mother forms the omitted group. We also control for each sample member's mother's highest grade completed, and for an indicator that "reading materials" (magazines, newspapers, and/or a library card) were available in the woman's household at age 14. To account for the presence of children while satisfying our desire to rely on covariates that are exogenous to the union-forming process, we control for whether any children were born to the respondent prior to the start of stage 1 (i.e., before age 18). Our background measures also include dummy variables indicating the woman's reported religion (with no religion as the omitted category) and frequency of church attendance, and a measure of how "traditional" her views are. We construct a traditional values measure by summing the number of times she agrees or strongly agrees with seven statements about family, including "a woman's place is in the home, not in the office or shop," and "women are much happier if they stay at home and take care of their children." Traditional values scores range from zero to seven.

Our remaining covariates measure labor market skills and, as such, serve as exogenous measures of earnings potential. These measures include each woman's "final" highest grade completed (as of age 35) and scores on the Armed Forces Qualifying Test (AFQT). AFQT scores are derived from scores on the Armed Services Vocational Aptitude Battery, which was administered to NLSY79 respondents in 1980. We regress percentile AFQT scores on a set of birth-year dummies and use the residual as the age-adjusted score; unadjusted percentile scores are reported in Table 6. Our measure of highest grade completed is arguably endogenous to the union-forming process, yet we include it because our key findings prove to be robust to whether we use actual highest grade completed, predicted highest grade completed, or high school graduation status at age 18. In stages where a partner is present (stages 3, 4, and 5), we also control for the spouse's or cohabiting partner's highest grade completed as a measure of his earnings potential.

FINDINGS

Estimated Coefficients for Year-to-Year Transitions

Table 7 contains estimated parameters for all five stages of our choice model. Before turning our attention to the predicted probabilities obtained by using the parameter estimates in Table 7 to simulate long-term outcomes, we assess the signs of select covariates.

Table 7 reveals that increased AFDC or TANF benefits are associated with fewer transitions into marriage (S to M) and more transitions into cohabitation (S to C) among single women in stages 1 and 4, as well as fewer transitions to marriage (C to M) among cohabiters in stage 2 (although not all coefficients are statistically distinguishable from zero at conventional significance levels). These patterns indicate that exogenous decreases in AFDC/TANF benefits might induce single women to marry, but union formation will not necessarily increase if these S to M transitions are offset by fewer S to C transitions. Moreover, we find that increased benefits are associated with a decreased probability of divorce among women in first and subsequent marriages (stages 3 and 5) – which is consistent with evidence in Bitler et al. (2004) that transitions from AFDC to TANF led to less divorce – so exogenous decreases in benefits will not necessarily promote long-term unions even if they induce more women to marry.[20] This simple assessment of the signs of the estimated AFDC/TANF coefficients in Table 7 highlights the fact that multi-stage computations of the probabilities of experiencing long-term unions can conflict with single-stage computations of the probabilities of entering unions.

Unilateral divorce laws prove to be associated with increased divorce probabilities among first-married women (stage 3) and remarried women (stage 5), although estimates in the latter model lack precision. Surprisingly, unilateral divorce is associated with increased entry into marriage among single women with no prior unions (stage 1) and cohabiting women (stage 2), but with decreased entry into marriage among "re-single" women in stage 4 (although most divorce-related parameter estimates lack precision). These patterns highlight the fact that we cannot fully assess effects of divorce laws on the decision to divorce without simultaneously considering the preceding decision to marry (Mechoulan, 2006).

Table 7 also reveals that the estimated coefficients for family background, demographic, and skill-related measures are consistent with patterns that are well established in the literature. Blacks and women who were raised by a single mother appear to have lower probabilities than others of entering

Table 7. Binomial and Multinomial Logit Estimates for Stages 1-5.

Covariate	Stage 1 (Single, No Prior Unions)				Stage 2 (Cohabiting)			
	S to C		S to M		C to M		C to S	
	Coeff.	S.E.	Coeff.	S.E.	Coeff.	S.E.	Coeff.	S.E.
Marital history								
Constant	-5.757	1.491	-2.953	1.270	-.485	1.923	-1.436	1.668
Spell duration	.108	.023	.066	.019	-.113	.038	-.242	.032
Spell duration squared/10	-.070	.013	-.071	.011	-.024	.04-	-.059	.024
Age began spell	—	—	—	—	-.020	.012	-.075	.011
Number of prior cohabitation spells	—	—	—	—	-.199	.133	-.207	.100
Number of prior marriages	—	—	—	—	.027	.090	.027	.083
Policy and market factors								
Maximum monthly AFDC/TANF benefit	.039	.018	-.063	.015	-.009	.023	.006	.019
Average Medicaid expenditure	-.055	.042	-.019	.028	.090	.034	-.045	.033
State income tax marriage penalty	.051	.029	-.030	.028	-.019	.042	.018	.036
1 if unilateral divorce, no separation	.033	.105	.049	.082	.161	.131	.059	.113
1 if unilateral divorce, mandatory separation	.015	.112	.160	.087	.016	.137	.029	.121
Percent same race in county	-.006	.002	-.001	.002	-.002	.003	-.001	.002
Percent men in county	.093	.029	.031	.025	-.018	.039	.061	.033
Unemployment rate in county	-.017	.011	.003	.009	.014	.016	-.007	.014
Background and demographic factors								
1 if black	-1.180	.186	-.930	.147	-.711	.230	.001	.191
1 if Hispanic	-.679	.185	-.180	.154	-.420	.220	-.007	.203

AUDREY LIGHT AND YOSHIAKI OMORI

Table 7. (*Continued*)

Covariate	Stage 1 (Single, No Prior Unions)				Stage 2 (Cohabiting)			
	S to C		S to M		C to M		C to S	
	Coeff.	S.E.	Coeff.	S.E.	Coeff.	S.E.	Coeff.	S.E.
1 if foreign born	−.232	.165	.110	.126	−.161	.225	−.084	.179
1 if lived with single mother, age 14	−.360	.150	−.162	.146	−.323	.174	.217	.139
Mother and stepfather, age 14	−.086	.178	.057	.172	−.011	.190	.231	.163
Mother and father, age 14	−.594	.141	.020	.134	−.017	.153	−.023	.133
Mother's highest grade completed	.021	.015	−.021	.012	.020	.020	.047	.016
1 if access to reading materials, age 14	−.021	.132	.018	.114	−.077	.187	−.131	.124
1 if child born before age 18	−.199	.119	−.202	.104	−.135	.103	−.054	.095
1 if Baptist	−.343	.181	.235	.179	−.223	.220	−.083	.211
Catholic	−.317	.183	−.038	.179	−.031	.213	−.170	.200
Other Christian	−.344	.181	.103	.179	.230	.213	−.033	.201
Other religion	−.384	.200	.260	.186	.148	.249	.126	.222
1 if attends church more than one times per month	.071	.094	.065	.086	.081	.122	−.029	.112
More than one times per week	−.214	.088	.145	.072	.207	.109	.033	.092
Traditional values score	−.053	.024	.001	.019	−.093	.031	.011	.026
Skill factors								
AFQT score	.001	.002	−.001	.001	.003	.002	−.002	.002
1 if final highest grade completed <12	.481	.136	−.342	.137	−.090	.147	−.276	.118
= 13–15	−.188	.095	−.235	.080	.151	.117	−.143	.100
≥16 +	−.687	.110	−.545	.089	.160	.155	.000	.143
Spouse's highest grade completed	—		—		.067	.023	−.007	.018
Log likelihood	−8512.36				−3827.83			
Number of observations	20,810				4,721			
Number of women	2,761				1,292			

266

Covariate	Stage 3 (First Marriages) M to S		Stage 4 (Single, Prior Unions) S to C		Stage 4 (Single, Prior Unions) S to M		Stage 5 (2nd⁺ Marriages) M to S	
	Coeff.	S.E.	Coeff.	S.E.	Coeff.	S.E.	Coeff.	S.E.
Marital history								
Constant	−.227	1.661	−3.763	1.725	−5.314	2.446	3.478	2.488
Spell duration	.077	.023	−.145	.030	−.146	.036	.026	.039
Spell duration squared/10	−.053	.011	.011	.020	−.006	.021	−.041	.022
Age began spell	−.056	.012	−.062	.010	−.109	.014	−.170	.018
Number of prior cohabitation spells	.293	.091	.054	.048	−.200	.076	.256	.094
Number of prior marriages	—	—	−.140	.069	−.058	.092	.218	.216
1 if cohabited with spouse before marriage	−.230	.128	—	—	—	—	−.342	.164
Policy and market factors								
Maximum monthly AFDC/TANF benefit	−.039	.020	.016	.020	−.063	.029	−.067	.038
Average Medicaid expenditure	.010	.033	−.034	.030	−.069	.047	−.014	.057
State income tax marriage penalty	−.007	.033	−.033	.040	−.092	.067	−.030	.066
1 if unilateral divorce, no separation	.350	.078	−.143	.114	−.242	.149	.063	.192
1 if unilateral divorce, mandatory separation	.153	.108	−.058	.122	−.244	.165	.287	.206
Percent same race in county	−.001	.002	.002	.002	−.005	.003	−.005	.004
Percent men in county	−.033	.032	.078	.034	.138	.048	.012	.048
County unemployment rate	.000	.012	.013	.010	.003	.019	−.010	.019
Background and demographic factors								
1 if black	.004	.163	−.538	.176	−.822	.238	.505	.291
1 if Hispanic	−.177	.178	.140	.184	−.527	.248	−.296	.315
1 if foreign born	−.236	.169	−.382	.215	−.076	.214	−.682	.399
1 if lived with single mother, age 14	.383	.161	−.008	.155	−.055	.216	−.116	.255
Mother and stepfather, age 14	.150	.188	.119	.181	.297	.248	−.217	.261
Mother and father, age 14	.052	.155	.072	.145	.190	.198	−.034	.226
Mother's highest grade completed	.028	.015	.012	.010	.006	.022	−.013	.028

Table 7. (Continued)

Covariate	Stage 3 (First Marriages) M to S		Stage 4 (Single, Prior Unions) S to C		Stage 4 (Single, Prior Unions) S to M		Stage 5 (2nd+ Marriages) M to S	
	Coeff.	S.E.	Coeff.	S.E.	Coeff.	S.E.	Coeff.	S.E.
1 if access to reading materials, age 14	.177	.123	.045	.131	.418	.204	−.509	.202
1 if child born before age 18	−.217	.084	−.080	.081	−.009	.111	−.266	.127
1 if Baptist	.075	.199	.030	.191	−.051	.335	−.048	.370
Catholic	−.031	.204	−.071	.194	−.049	.333	.180	.381
Other Christian	.128	.204	.045	.188	−.141	.339	−.304	.371
Other religion	.131	.211	−.134	.207	−.015	.346	−.122	.394
1 if attends church more than one times per month	−.146	.099	.042	.105	.164	.146	−.215	.184
More than one times per week	−.140	.082	−.139	.091	.291	.126	−.086	.145
Traditional values score	−.038	.022	.030	.026	.040	.033	.001	.039
Skill factors								
AFQT score	−.007	.002	.003	.001	−.000	.003	.001	.003
1 if final highest grade completed <12	.169	.141	.109	.128	−.015	.180	−.084	.249
= 13–15	−.036	.089	−.188	.104	−.067	.131	.169	.149
≥16+	−.243	.118	−.289	.142	.143	.169	−.126	.217
Spouse's highest grade completed	−.049	.017	—		—		—	
Log likelihood	−3676.28		−4,518.84				−1377.97	
Number of observations	25,566		10,850				6,092	
Number of women	2,178		1,492				724	

Note: Each stage includes missing value indicators for mother's highest grade completed and AFQT score; stage-specific sample means are used to replace missing values. Standard errors account for non-independence of residuals across observations for the same person.

marriage and cohabitation via any route (S to C, S to M, and C to M). Women who attend church on a weekly basis or who have traditional values are predicted to be less likely than others to cohabit or divorce, especially in early stages. Higher schooling levels are associated with an increased probability of marrying in stages 2 and 4 but a decreased probability of marrying in stage 1, given that college-educated women tend to marry relatively late; higher schooling attainment is also associated with a decreased probability of divorce (stages 3 and 5).

Predicted Probabilities of Long-Term Unions

Our primary goal is to learn whether each factor of interest – especially those factors that can potentially be manipulated by public policy – has an economically significant effect on the probability of forming a union within a given age interval, and maintaining that union for at least 12 years. Because these inferences cannot be made by examining each short-term transition probability, we turn to the results of our long-term simulations.

To compute the estimates in Tables 8 and 9, we use our stage 1 sample of 2,761 single women with no prior unions, and simulate their outcomes from ages 18 to 48 as described in the third section. Table 8 shows the predicted probability that 18-year-old women form a first union in the next 6 years (i.e., by age 24) as well as the joint probability of forming that first union and maintaining it for the next 12 years. Thus, these predictions are based on simulated outcomes from age 18 to a maximum age of 36. Table 9 shows the predicted probability that 30-year-old women enter a second union within 6 years (i.e., by age 36) conditional on having terminated a prior union at age 30. It also provides the joint probability of entering a second union as just described and maintaining it for at least 12 years. The predicted probabilities summarized in Table 9 are from the same simulations used for Table 8, but use outcomes for the entire age range (18–48). As described in the third section, we perform a baseline simulation (reported in row 1 of Tables 8 and 9) in which all women are assigned their actual, initial values for each covariate; all time-varying covariates aside from marital history variables (current spell duration, number of prior spells, etc.) are held constant throughout the simulation. The estimated "marginal effects" summarized in rows 2–13 of Tables 8 and 9 are based on subsequent simulations in which each woman is assigned an identical value for the given covariate or set of covariates indicated in Tables 8 and 9.

Table 8. Predicted Effects of Covariates on Probabilities of Entering and Maintaining First Unions (Starting Point Is Age 18 with No Prior Unions).

Assigned Covariate Values	Probability of Entering First Union by Age 24			Probability of Entering First Union by Age 24 and Maintaining it for 12+ Years		
	C	M	M or C	C	M	M or C
1. Predicted probabilities using actual values for all covariates[a]	.228 (.001)	.367 (.001)	.595 (.001)	.081 (.001)	.202 (.002)	.283 (.002)
Increment to predicted probability in 1 due to[b]						
2. AFDC/TANF benefit at 10th percentile	−.038 (.001)	.066 (.001)	.029 (.001)	−.016 (.001)	.019 (.001)	.003 (.001)
3. Medicaid expenditure at 10th percentile	.010 (.001)	.003 (.001)	.013 (.001)	.000 (.001)	.002 (.001)	.002 (.001)
4. Income tax penalty at 10th percentile	−.003 (.001)	.004 (.001)	.001 (.001)	−.001 (.001)	.001 (.001)	.000 (.001)
5. No unilateral divorce	−.002 (.001)	−.012 (.001)	−.014 (.001)	.006 (.001)	.014 (.001)	.020 (.001)
6. Percent same sex/race at 90th percentile	−.014 (.001)	.005 (.001)	−.009 (.001)	−.005 (.001)	.012 (.001)	.006 (.001)
7. Nonblack, non-Hispanic	.067 (.001)	.047 (.001)	.115 (.001)	.027 (.002)	.017 (.001)	.044 (.001)
8. Lived with mother and father at age 14	−.035 (.001)	.014 (.001)	−.021 (.001)	−.011 (.001)	.004 (.001)	−.007 (.001)
9. Mother's highest grade completed = 16+	.027 (.000)	−.034 (.001)	−.007 (.001)	−.003 (.001)	−.033 (.001)	−.036 (.001)
10. No child born prior to age 18	.002 (.001)	.002 (.001)	.004 (.001)	.000 (.001)	−.001 (.001)	−.001 (.001)
11. AFQT score at 90th percentile	.014 (.001)	−.016 (.001)	−.002 (.001)	.021 (.001)	.023 (.002)	.044 (.001)
12. Highest grade completed = 16+	−.067 (.001)	−.056 (.001)	−.123 (.001)	−.017 (.001)	−.010 (.001)	−.027 (.001)
13. Traditional values score at 90th percentile	−.056 (.001)	.068 (.001)	.012 (.001)	−.019 (.001)	.052 (.001)	.033 (.001)

[a] Row 1 is based on simulated outcomes for a sample of 2,761 women with no prior unions. Each woman's history from age 18 to 48 is simulated 150 times, using actual covariate values and a random draw from the estimated parameter distributions in Table 7. The left three columns are predicted probabilities of entering a first union by age 24 via cohabitation (C), marriage (M), or either; the right three columns are predicted joint probabilities of entering and maintaining those unions for at least 12 years; standard errors are in parentheses.

[b] Rows 2–13 show the *increment* to the predicted probability shown in row 1 obtained by assigning each woman the specified covariate value(s) and using actual values for all nonspecified covariates; standard errors of the differences are in parentheses.

Table 9. Predicted Effects of Covariates on Probabilities of Entering and Maintaining Second Unions (Starting Point Is Separated from First Partner at Age 30).

Assigned Covariate Values	Probability of Entering Second Union by Age 36			Probability of Entering Second Union by Age 36 and Maintaining it for 12+ Years		
	C	M	M or C	C	M	M or C
1. Predicted probabilities using actual values for all covariates[a]	.391 (.005)	.162 (.004)	.553 (.006)	.221 (.005)	.107 (.003)	.328 (.005)
Increment to predicted probability in 1 due to[b]						
2. AFDC/TANF benefit at 10th percentile	-.021 (.039)	.014 (.032)	-.007 (.040)	-.021 (.032)	-.003 (.026)	-.024 (.039)
3. Medicaid expenditure at 10th percentile	.003 (.044)	.017 (.020)	.020 (.042)	-.032 (.036)	.004 (.025)	-.028 (.040)
4. Income tax penalty at 10th percentile	.003 (.044)	.036 (.030)	.039 (.040)	-.023 (.108)	.009 (.005)	-.014 (.082)
5. No unilateral divorce	.009 (.045)	.019 (.034)	.028 (.046)	.026 (.040)	.009 (.031)	.035 (.045)
6. Percent same sex/race at 90th percentile	.075 (.045)	-.022 (.029)	.057 (.044)	.053 (.042)	-.035 (.026)	.018 (.044)
7. Nonblack, non-Hispanic	.007 (.002)	.031 (.003)	.038 (.003)	.011 (.005)	-.014 (.006)	-.003 (.004)
8. Lived with mother and father at age 14	-.013 (.044)	-.013 (.031)	-.026 (.047)	.017 (.040)	-.026 (.029)	-.009 (.045)
9. Mother's highest grade completed = 16+	.013 (.002)	.001 (.003)	.014 (.002)	-.011 (.003)	.003 (.003)	-.008 (.003)
10. No child born prior to age 18	.057 (.044)	-.049 (.029)	.008 (.046)	.073 (.040)	-.053 (.027)	.020 (.044)
11. AFQT score at 90th percentile	.004 (.044)	.009 (.034)	.013 (.047)	.031 (.040)	-.004 (.029)	.027 (.044)
12. Highest grade completed = 16+	-.044 (.054)	.022 (.042)	-.022 (.055)	-.078 (.045)	.017 (.037)	-.061 (.053)
13. Traditional values score at 90th percentile	-.071 (.042)	.052 (.034)	-.019 (.043)	-.049 (.035)	.015 (.027)	-.034 (.040)

[a]Row 1 is based on simulated outcomes for a sample of 2,761 women with no prior unions. Each woman's history from age 18 to 48 is simulated 150 times, using actual covariate values and a random draw from the estimated parameter distributions in Table 7. The left three columns are predicted probabilities of entering a second union by age 36 via cohabitation (C), marriage (M), or either, *conditional on separating from a first partner at age 30*; the right three columns are predicted joint probabilities of entering and maintaining those unions for at least 12 years.

[b]Rows 2–13 show the *increment* to the predicted probability shown in row 1 obtained by assigning each woman the specified covariate value(s) and using actual values for all nonspecified covariates; standard errors of the differences are in parentheses.

Focusing first on Table 8, the top row reveals that 23% of 18-year-old, single women are expected to enter into cohabitation by age 24, while 37% are expected to move directly into marriage.[21] Adding these numbers together reveals that women in our sample have a 60% chance of forming a first union by age 24. While cohabitation is not the modal form of entering a first union by age 24, it is common enough to raise the probability of union formation by 23 percentage points, or by 62% relative to the "marriage only" probability of 0.37. The right-most columns of Table 8 show that women in our sample are predicted to have a 8.1% chance of cohabiting by age 24 and remaining with their partner for at least 12 years (including cases where the cohabiting couple marries within the 12-year interval), a 20.2% chance of marrying by age 24 and remaining married for at least 12 years and, therefore, a 28.3% chance of forming and maintaining a union of either type. We can infer from these estimates that unions entered via cohabitation have a 36% chance of surviving for 12 years (0.081/0.228), while unions entered via marriage have a 55% chance of surviving. Cohabitation is not as likely as marriage to lead to a long-term union, but because it is such a common form of entry it ultimately raises the probability of experiencing a "long-term" first union by 8 percentage points, or by 40% relative to the "marriage only" probability. In short, cohabitation proves to make a larger contribution to long-term union formation than analysts might infer by focusing on cohabiters' relatively high annual rates of dissolution.[22]

Before proceeding to the estimated effects of alternative policy and non-policy factors, we emphasize that the predicted probabilities of experiencing a long-term union entered by cohabitation or marriage (reported in the right-most columns of Tables 8 and 9) constitute our "bottom line" estimates. Although an assessment of the benefits to marriage and cohabitation is beyond the scope of our analysis, there is little reason to believe that cohabitation is less preferred than marriage when the focus is on long-term unions. Most evidence on the relative merits of marriage is based on the fact that cohabiting unions tend to be quite short (Bumpass et al. 1991; Lichter et al. 2006); when long-term unions are analyzed, however, marriage is not necessarily more beneficial than cohabitation (Willets, 2006).

In rows 2–13 of Table 8, we show how each predicted long-term probability in row 1 changes when we re-run the simulations after assigning each sample member the identical value for one or more select covariates. To assess the role of welfare availability, we set the maximum, monthly AFDC/TANF benefit to an amount ($261 in 1995 dollars) that would place each state's generosity in the 10th percentile of the stage 1 distribution. This intervention causes the predicted probability of marrying by age 24 to increase by 0.066, and it causes the predicted probability of marrying by age 24 and remaining married for at least 12 years to increase by 0.019. These estimated effects represent increases in the baseline (row 1) marriage probabilities of 18% and 9%, respectively. However, the same hypothetical policy intervention is predicted to *decrease* the probability of entering a first union via cohabitation by 0.038 and *decrease* the probability of entering and maintaining a cohabiting union by 0.016; both increments represent a 17–20% reduction in the baseline estimates seen in row 1. In total, this dramatic policy intervention – which, needless to say, could directly harm the well-being of eligible women and their children independent of any effects it might have on union formation – is predicted to increase the probability that women experience long-term, first unions by a mere one-third of a percentage point.

As small as the estimated effect of AFDC/TANF benefits on long-term first unions proves to be, the policy interventions considered in rows 3 and 4 of Table 8 have even smaller estimated effects. When Medicaid expenditures are set at the 10th percentile value, the predicted probability of forming a union increases by 1.3 percentage points, and the predicted probability of forming and maintaining a union increases by only 0.002. Setting the income tax penalty at the 10th percentile value (which amounts to a marriage bonus of $47) causes a slight substitution in entry probabilities away from cohabitation toward marriage, but ultimately has a trivial effect on the predicted joint probability of entering and maintaining a first union. Row 5 of Table 8 reveals that the elimination of unilateral divorce has a somewhat larger effect than the welfare and tax interventions: The elimination of unilateral divorce is predicted to lower the probability of entering a union of any type by 0.014 and to raise the probability of entering and maintaining a union of any type by 0.02. This is the biggest "bottom line" effect seen in rows 2–5 of Table 8, yet an increment of 0.02 represents only a 7% increase relative to the baseline probability of 0.283 shown in row 1.

In summary, all of our assumed policy interventions prove to be "marriage enhancing," but none has an economically important effect on the predicted probability that young women experience long-term first unions. Many of these factors have a sizeable, statistically significant effect on the predicted probability of making select year-to-year transitions, but "adding up" those predicted, year-to-year transition probabilities over successive periods (and especially across stages of the model) reveals that each policy intervention has a trivial effect on long-term outcomes. We emphasize that our predicted long-term probabilities are a function of underlying short-term probabilities and, therefore, represent the same underlying decision-making.

Turning to rows 6–13 of Table 8, several factors that cannot be readily manipulated by policy prove to have substantial effects on the predicted probability of a long-term union. For example, women who are "white" (nonblack and non-Hispanic) are predicted to be 6.7 percentage points (29%) more likely than the women in the baseline (row 1) simulations to cohabit, 4.7 percentage points (13%) more likely to marry, and 4.4 percentage points (16%) more likely to form a union of either type and maintain it for at least 12 years. This finding is consistent with widespread evidence (seen in Table 7) that white women are far less likely than blacks to cohabit and marry.

Table 8 also reveals relatively large estimated marginal effects for AFQT scores (row 11) and traditional values (row 13). Setting each woman's AFQT score to the 90th percentile in the overall distribution leads to a 1.6 percentage point decrease in the predicted probability of marrying by age 24, but a nearly offsetting increase in the predicted probability of cohabiting. This intervention leads to a 4.4 percentage point increase in the predicted probability of forming any union and maintaining it for at least 12 years because unions entered via cohabitation and marriage tend to last longer when women have high AFQT scores. A very different pattern is seen among women with traditional values: Women who score at the 90th percentile on this scale (which corresponds to agreeing or strongly agreeing with four out of seven statements about traditional family values) are 6.8 percentage points more likely than the typical woman to marry by age 24, and 5.2 percentage points more likely to marry and stay married for at least 12 years. However, a high traditional value score has an opposite-signed effect on the predicted probability of cohabiting, so the bottom line is that these women are only 1.2 percentage points more likely form a first union, and only 3.3 percentage points more likely to form and maintain a first union.

Among the remaining "interventions" considered in Table 8, we find that a favorable marriage market (row 6) and living with both parents at age 14 (row 8) are predicted to drive women away from cohabitation toward marriage, but to an economically insignificant degree. Similarly, not bearing a child prior to age 18 (row 10) proves to have a trivial effect on the predicted probability of entering or maintaining a first union. Setting either the mother's highest grade completed or the woman's own highest grade completed equal to 16+ years (rows 9 and 12) lowers the predicted probability of experiencing a long-term first union, but this effect operates solely through a decreased probability of union entry – for example, in row

12 we see that college-educated women are 6.7 (5.6) percentage points less likely than the typical woman to cohabit (marry) by age 24. Although both schooling variables – which are exogenous predictors of women's earnings potential – are considered favorable to union formation in general, these findings are consistent with the notion that they promote unions at later ages.

Table 9 presents the same predicted probabilities as Table 8, but now the focus is on second unions formed by women who dissolve a previous cohabitation or marriage at age 30. The estimates in row 1 of Table 9 differ from what is seen in Table 8 in a number of ways. First, the predicted probability of forming *any* union within 6 years is lower for women when they are 30 and divorced/separated than it was when they were 18 with no prior unions: we estimate that the former have only a 55% chance of entering a second union by age 36 (Table 9), whereas the latter have a 60% chance of entering a first union (Table 8). Second, the predicted probability of cohabiting in the next 6 years is much higher at age 30 than at age 18 and, in fact, cohabitation is the modal form of entry into second unions: in row 1 of Table 9, we see that the predicted probability of cohabiting by age 36 is 0.391 (versus 0.228 in Table 8), which is 2.4 times greater than the predicted probability of marrying by age 36. Third, second unions are predicted to be more likely than first unions to last for at least 12 years. Dividing each joint probability by its corresponding entry probability, we see that second unions that begin via cohabitation have a 57% chance of being long-lasting (versus 36% in Table 8), while unions that begin with marriage have a 66% chance of lasting for 12+ years (versus 55% in Table 8). Fourth, the patterns seen in entry probabilities carry over to joint probabilities: 30-year-old "divorcées" are more likely to enter and maintain a cohabiting union than they were as 18-year-olds (0.221 versus 0.081), less likely to enter and maintain a marriage (0.107 versus 0.202) and, adding up the predicted probabilities, more likely to enter and maintain a union of either type (0.328 versus 0.283).

Turning to the estimated incremental effects shown in rows 2–13 of Table 9, one overarching pattern is immediately apparent: with few exceptions, the "marginal effects" in Table 9 are estimated much less precisely than their counterparts in Table 8, and most are statistically indistinguishable from zero at conventional significance levels. Even though some of the point estimates in Table 9 are larger than what is seen in Table 8, our primary conclusion is that we identify *no* policy factor that could reliably be used to incentivize long-term second unions among women in their 30s. Row 5 of Table 9 reveals that elimination of unilateral divorce is predicted to raise the probability of forming and maintaining a second union by 0.035, which represents a 11% boost relative to the baseline estimate in row 1. However, the large standard error precludes us from pointing to this factor (or any other factor considered in rows 2–5) as a potentially useful policy tool for promoting long-term second union formation.

CONCLUDING COMMENTS

Current and recent U.S. public policy can be characterized as pro-marriage. Examples include the Economic Growth and Tax Relief Reconciliation Act of 2001, the Jobs and Growth Tax Relief Reconciliation Act of 2003, and the Working Families Tax Relief Act of 2004, all of which changed federal tax law to provide "marriage penalty" relief; the 1996 Healthy Marriage Initiative, in which numerous federal programs provide services to help couples sustain their marriages; and Covenant Marriage laws passed in Arkansas, Oklahoma, and Louisiana that allow married couples to limit the grounds by which they can be divorced. Many social scientists have taken a pro-marriage stance in their research by arguing that marriage enhances a range of important outcomes. Prominent examples include Waite (1995) and Waite and Gallagher (2000).

In our view, discussion about union formation will benefit from additional information on two issues. First, social scientists should continue to learn whether marriage (or cohabitation) causes various outcomes rather than simply being correlated with them. Progress has been made in assessing the causal effects of marriage and cohabitation on wages (Cornwell & Rupert, 1997; Gray, 1997; Korenman & Neumark, 1991; Loh, 1996; Stratton, 2002), family income (Light, 2004), and selected child outcomes (Levine & Painter, 2000), but much "pro-marriage" evidence continues to be based on cross-sectional correlations. Second, if the promotion of marriage is judged to be desirable, we should learn more about how marriage decisions can be influenced – that is, we should identify factors that can be *manipulated* by public policy and that *causally* increase the probability that individuals will get married and stay married. Without taking a stand on whether such policy is desirable, we contribute evidence on this second issue.

We consider a range of policy factors that can potentially be used to incentivize long-term unions: AFDC/TANF benefits, Medicaid expenditures, income tax laws, and divorce laws. While the effects of these factors on union formation have been studied before, we are able to compare their estimated effects side by side, and use simulations to determine whether policy interventions can be expected to promote long-term unions. We identify one policy intervention (lowering maximum AFDC/TANF benefits in all states to the 10th percentile value) with a nontrivial effect on the predicted probability that young women *enter* a first marriage by age 24, but this intervention has a near-zero effect on the predicted probability of forming a first union and *maintaining* it for at least 12 years. Another intervention (the elimination of unilateral divorce) raises the predicted probability of entering and maintaining a long-term first union by 2 percentage points (7% relative to the baseline probability) despite lowering the predicted probability of union entry. All policy interventions that we consider have imprecisely estimated effects on the likelihood that women form second unions by age 36 and maintain them for at least 12 years. At the same time, we find that factors that are not easily controlled by public policy, such as race, schooling, and the presence of children, are often predicted to be important determinants of long-term unions. In short, we fail to identify policy mechanisms that could potentially be used to incentivize long-term unions.

NOTES

1. Blau and van der Klaauw (2010), Gemici and Laufer (2010), Keane and Wolpin (2010), and van der Klaauw (1996) are examples of existing studies that model sequential transitions into and out of unions rather than focusing on a single stage of the process. However, their emphasis is on jointly modeling union formation and other outcomes (labor supply, fertility, etc.) rather than identifying determinants of long-term unions. To our knowledge, our earlier studies (Light & Omori 2007, 2012) are the only ones prior to this study to model multiple stages of the union-forming process *and* use the multi-stage estimates to predict probabilities of entering and maintaining long-term unions. In Light and Omori (2007), we focus on transitions into and out of first unions, and compute long-term probabilities analytically. In Light and Omori (2012), we use the same model and simulation procedure as in the current study, but do not examine effects of alternative policy interventions.

2. See Bitler et al. (2004), Blank (2002), Hoynes (1997), Moffitt (1990, 1992), and Yelowitz (1998) for additional details on each program's characteristics and predicted effects on union formation.

3. These calendar years are chosen because they span the observation period used in our analysis (1979–2008).

4. Lichter et al. (2006) and Manning and Smock (1995) identify the effects of *actual* (endogenous) welfare receipt, rather than exogenous potential benefits, on cohabiters' transitions.

5. Additional details on the relevant tax laws and theoretical effects of taxes on marriage decisions can be found in Alm, Dickert-Conlin, and Whittington (1999), Chade and Ventura (2005), Eissa and Hoynes (2000a), and Feenberg and Rosen (1995).

6. A marriage penalty arises in Minnesota in part federal taxable income (adjusted for federal standard deductions) is considered taxable income, so the federal penalty carries through to the state. A marriage bonus arises in California because it imposes tax on the federal adjusted gross income (which does not reflect the differential federal standard deduction), while also using a lower tax rate for married couples filing jointly than for single taxpayers.

7. As detailed in the fourth section, we examined a number of additional data sources to establish that no states changed categories subsequent to 1996, which is approximately when Friedberg's data were collected.

8. We assume errors are independent across alternatives and stages because alternative specifications posed identification problems. Following Cameron and Heckman (2001) and Light and Omori (2007), we attempted to characterize the errors in (1) as $\varepsilon_{igt}^j = \alpha_g^j \phi_i + v_{igt}^j$, where α_g^j are eight alternative- and stage-specific factor-loadings to be estimated, and ϕ_i represents time-invariant unobservables drawn from a standard normal distribution. We successfully estimated a three-stage version of this dependent model in Light and Omori (2007), but encountered identification problems in our five-stage model – problems that can presumably be skirted by expanding to a two-factor loading model and imposing exclusion restrictions as in Heckman, Humphries, Urzua, and Veramendi (2011), although that computationally demanding extension is beyond the scope of the current study. Blau and van der Klaauw (2010) achieved identification in a single-stage, eight-alternative model by assuming the ϕ_i are drawn from a discrete distribution with only two support points. We replicated the Blau and van der Klaauw error structure with a three-stage model and found the estimates to be highly sensitive to the number of support points; the use of two support points yielded estimates that are virtually identical to what we obtain with an "independence of irrelevant alternatives" assumption.

9. Angeles, Guilkey, and Mroz (2005), Blau and van der Klaauw (2010), and Light and Omori (2012) use a similar simulation method.

10. Our sample members were born in 1960–1964 and our longitudinal data are from survey years 1979–2008, so relatively few respondents are observed to age 48. In addition, for variables that are not collected in an event history format, we face occasional unknown covariate values due to missed interviews.

11. In a related paper (Light & Omori, 2012), we consider four alternative durations for first unions: 8, 12, 18, and 24 years. While the probability of entering a union by a given age is invariant to the duration considered, we show that the predicted probability of maintaining a union *conditional* on entering the union falls with duration, as does the predicted joint probability (i.e., the product of the entry and conditional probabilities). However, we find that estimated effects of covariates on the joint probability are largely invariant to the duration considered.

12. The NLSY79 is not only well-suited to our analysis, but to our knowledge is the *only* U.S. survey that will support our requirements for (a) a large sample of respondents who are followed from age 18 into their late 40s; (b) detailed information on transitions into and out of cohabitation and marriage; and (c) a host of covariates plus geographic identifiers needed to match to state-level policy variables.

13. Because information on marriage and cohabitation is collected in an event history format, we can identify each sample member's marital status on an annual basis, regardless of whether she was interviewed each year. In particular, we can fill in odd-numbered years from 1995 onward when the NLSY79 switched to biennial interviews.

14. These variables are from Robert Moffitt's welfare benefit database ben_dat.txt that is available, along with documentation, at http://www.econ.jhu.edu/People/Moffitt/datasets.html; the Urban Institute's welfare rules database available at http://www.urban.org/toolkit/databases/index.cfm; and Kaiser Foundation reports available at http://www.kff.org/.

15. The dependent variable is the log of total earnings reported for the prior year. Covariates are the year-specific implicit price deflator for personal consumption expenditure; year-specific per capita income in the respondent's county; the year-specific unemployment rate in the respondent's county; a quartic in age; age-adjusted AFQT scores; dummy variables for the respondent's highest grade completed (0–11, 12, 13–15, or 16+), and dummy variables indicating whether the respondent is black and Hispanic.

16. State income tax obligations are computed with version 9 of Internet Taxsim, available at http://www.nber.org/~taxsim/.

17. We base our classification on data reported in Friedberg (1998). We also examined state-level data available at abanet.org as well as numerous state-specific websites to determine whether any states changed regimes during the latter part of our observation period (1996–2008).

18. Because of this cohort effect, we cannot control for any policies that arose relatively late in the 30-year observation period, such as covenant marriage laws (enacted in several states around 2000), state-level earned income tax credits (which were rare prior to the late 1990s), and TANF-specific rules (introduced in 1996 and later). For the stage 1 model in particular, these variables play the role of "late first union" indicators and cause significant changes in the estimated duration coefficients.

19. City and County Data Books do not provide annual observations, so we use the value for the year that is closest in time to each person-year observation in our sample.

20. The same patterns are seen with respect to changes in the income tax marriage penalty, given that the estimated coefficients for the income tax and AFDC/TANF variables have identical signs for all but one transition (S to C transitions in stage 4).

21. To clarify, 22.8% of simulated paths from age 18 to 24 have the form SC*, SSC*, SSSC*, SSSSC*, SSSSSC*, or SSSSSSC*, where an asterisk represents the fact that simulated outcomes beyond the initial single-to-cohabiting transition are irrelevant for this computation. Similarly, 36.7% have simulated paths of the type SM*, SSM*, SSSM*, etc.

22. See Light and Omori (2012) for a more extensive analysis of the role of cohabitation in the formation of long-term unions.

ACKNOWLEDGMENTS

This research was funded by a grant to Light from the National Science Foundation (grant SES-0415427) and a grant to Omori from the Japan Society for the Promotion of Science (Grant-in-Aid for Scientific Research (B)16530169); we thank both agencies for their generous support. We also thank Taehyun Ahn and Ranajoy Ray-Chaudhuri for excellent research assistance and three anonymous referees for helpful comments.

REFERENCES

Allen, D. W. (1992). Marriage and divorce: Comment. *American Economic Review, 82*, 679–685.

Alm, J., Dickert-Conlin, S., & Whittington, L. A. (1999). Policy watch: The marriage penalty. *Journal of Economic Perspectives, 13*(3), 193–204.

Alm, J., & Whittington, L. A. (1995a). Income taxes and the marriage decision. *Applied Economics, 27*, 25–31.

Alm, J., & Whittington, L. A. (1995b). Does the income tax affect marital decisions? *National Tax Journal, 48*, 565–572.

Alm, J., & Whittington, L. A. (1999). For love or money? The impact of income taxes on marriage. *Economica, 66*, 297–316.

Angeles, G., Guilkey, D. K., & Mroz, T. A. (2005). The effects of education and family planning programs on fertility in Indonesia. *Economic Development and Cultural Change, 54*, 165–201.

Bennett, N. G., Blanc, A. K., & Bloom, D. E. (1988). Commitment and the modern union: Assessing the link between premarital cohabitation and subsequent marital stability. *American Sociological Review, 53*, 127–138.

Bitler, M. P., Gelbach, J. B., Hoynes, H. W., & Zavodny, M. (2004). The impact of welfare reform on marriage and divorce. *Demography, 41*, 213–236.

Blackburn, M. L. (2000). Welfare effects on the marital decisions of never-married mothers. *Journal of Human Resources, 35*, 116–142.

Blank, R. M. (2002). Evaluating welfare reform in the United States. *Journal of Economic Literature, 40*, 1105–1166.

Blau, D. M., & van der Klaauw, W. (2010). What determines family structure? *Economic Inquiry*. doi: 10.1111/j.1465-7295.2010.00334.x

Bougheas, S., & Georgellis, Y. (1999). The effect of divorce costs on marriage formation and dissolution. *Journal of Population Economics, 12*, 489–498.

Brien, M. J., Lillard, L. A., & Stern, S. (2006). Cohabitation, marriage, and divorce in a model of match quality. *International Economic Review, 47*, 451–494.

Bumpass, L. L., & Lu, H.-H. (2000). Trends in cohabitation and implications for children's family contexts in the United States. *Population Studies, 54*, 29–41.

Bumpass, L. L., Sweet, J. A., & Cherlin, A. (1991). The role of cohabitation in declining rates of marriage. *Journal of Marriage and the Family, 53*, 913–927.

Cameron, S. V., & Heckman, J. J. (2001). The dynamics of educational attainment for black, Hispanic, and white males. *Journal of Political Economy, 109*, 455–499.

Chade, H., & Ventura, G. (2005). Income taxation and marital decisions. *Review of Economic Dynamics, 8,* 565–599.

Cherlin, A. J. (1992). *Marriage, divorce, remarriage.* Cambridge, MA: Harvard University Press.

Cornwell, C., & Rupert, P. (1997). Unobservable individual effects, marriage and the earnings of young men. *Economic Inquiry, 35,* 285–294.

Decker, S. L. (2000). Medicaid, AFDC and family formation. *Applied Economics, 32,* 1947–1956.

Eissa, N., & Hoynes, H. (2000a). Explaining trends in the tax-transfer cost of marriage: Demographics vs. tax reform? *National Tax Journal, 53,* 683–713.

Eissa, N., & Hoynes, H. (2000b, December). Tax and transfer policy, and family formation: Marriage and cohabitation. Unpublished paper.

Ellman, I. M., & Lohr, S. L. (1998). Dissolving the relationship between divorce laws and divorce rates. *International Review of Law and Economics, 18,* 341–359.

Ellwood, D. T., & Bane, M. J. (1985). The impact of AFDC on family structure and living arrangements. In R. G. Ehrenberg (Ed.), *Research in labor economics* (Vol. 7, pp. 137–207). Greenwich, CT: JAI Press.

Feenberg, D. R., & Rosen, H. S. (1995). Recent developments in the marriage tax. *National Tax Journal, 48,* 91–101.

Friedberg, L. (1998). Did unilateral divorce raise divorce rates? Evidence from panel data. *American Economic Review, 88,* 608–627.

Gemici, A., & Laufer, S. (2010, April). Cohabitation and marriage. New York University Department of Economics. Unpublished paper.

Gray, J. S. (1997). The fall in men's return to marriage: Declining productivity effects or changing selection? *Journal of Human Resources, 32,* 481–504.

Grogger, J., & Bronars, S. G. (2001). The effect of welfare payments on the marriage and fertility behavior of unwed mothers: Results from a twins experiment. *Journal of Political Economy, 109,* 529–545.

Heckman, J. J., Humphries, J.E., Urzua, S., & Veramendi, G. (2011, October). *The effects of educational choices on labor market, health, and social outcomes.* University of Chicago Human Capital and Economic Opportunity working paper no. 2011–002.

Hoffman, S. D., & Duncan, G. J. (1995). The effect of income, wages, and AFDC benefits on marital disruptions. *Journal of Human Resources, 30,* 19–41.

Hoynes, H. W. (1997). Does welfare play any role in female headship decisions? *Journal of Public Economics, 65,* 89–117.

Iyvarakul, T., McElroy, M. B., & Staub, K. (2011, March 2011). *Dynamic optimization in models for state panel data: A cohort panel data of the effects of divorce laws on divorce rates.* Unpublished manuscript.

Kaestner, R., & Kaushal, N. (2005). Immigrant and native responses to welfare reform. *Journal of Population Economics, 18,* 69–92.

Keane, M. P., & Wolpin, K. I. (2010). The role of labor and marriage markets, preference heterogeneity and the welfare system in the life cycle decisions of white, black, and Hispanic women. *International Economic Review, 41,* 851–892.

Korenman, S., & Neumark, D. (1991). Does marriage really make men more productive? *Journal of Human Resources, 26,* 282–307.

Levine, D. I., & Painter, G. (2000). Family structure and youth outcomes: Which correlations are causal? *Journal of Human Resources, 35,* 524–549.

Lichter, D. T., LeClere, F. B., & McLaughlin, D. K. (1991). Local marriage markets and the marital behavior of black and white women. *American Journal of Sociology, 96*, 843–867.

Lichter, D. T., McLaughlin, D. K., & Ribar, D. C. (2002). Economic restructuring and the retreat from marriage. *Social Science Research, 31*, 230–256.

Lichter, D. T., Qian, Z., & Mellott, L. M. (2006). Marriage or dissolution? Union transitions among poor cohabiting women. *Demography, 43*, 223–240.

Light, A. (2004). Gender differences in the marriage and cohabitation income premium. *Demography, 41*, 263–275.

Light, A., & Omori, Y. (2007, August). Economic incentives and family formation. Unpublished paper.

Light, A., & Omori, Y. (2012, April). Determinants of long-term unions: Who survives the "Seven Year Itch"? Unpublished paper.

Lillard, L. A., Brien, M. J., & Waite, L. J. (1995). Premarital cohabitation and subsequent marital dissolution: A matter of self-selection? *Demography, 32*, 437–457.

Loh, E. S. (1996). Productivity differences and the marriage wage premium for white males. *Journal of Human Resources, 31*, 566–589.

Lopez-Laborda, J., & Zarate-Marco, A. (2004). To marry or not to marry: Tax is the question. *Public Budgeting and Finance, 24*(3), 98–123.

Lundberg, S., & Rose, E. (2003). Child gender and the transition to marriage. *Demography, 40*, 333–349.

Manning, W. D., & Smock, P. J. (1995). Why marry? Race and the transition to marriage among cohabitors. *Demography, 32*, 509–520.

Mechoulan, S. (2006). Divorce laws and the structure of the American family. *Journal of Legal Studies, 35*, 143–174.

Moffitt, R. A. (1990). The effect of the U.S. welfare system on marital status. *Journal of Public Economics, 41*, 101–124.

Moffitt, R. A. (1992). Incentive effects of the U.S. welfare system: A review. *Journal of Economic Literature, 30*, 1–61.

Moffitt, R. A., Reville, R., & Winkler, A. (1998). Beyond single mothers: Cohabitation and marriage in the AFDC program. *Demography, 35*, 259–278.

Nakonezny, P. A., Shull, R. D., & Rodgers, J. L. (1995). The effect of no-fault divorce law on the divorce rate across the 50 states and its relation to income, education, and religiosity. *Journal of Marriage and the Family, 57*, 477–488.

Oppenheimer, V. K. (2000). The role of economic factors in union formation. In L. J. Waite (Ed.), *Ties that bind: Perspectives on marriage and cohabitation* (pp. 283–301). New York, NY: Aldine de Gruyter.

Peters, H. E. (1986). Marriage and divorce: Informational constraints and private contracting. *American Economic Review, 76*, 437–454.

Peters, H. E. (1992). Marriage and divorce: Reply. *American Economic Review, 82*, 686–693.

Schultz, T. P. (1998). Eroding the economic foundations of marriage and fertility in the United States. *Structural Change and Economic Dynamics, 9*, 391–413.

Smock, P. (2000). Cohabitation in the United States: An appraisal of research themes, findings, and implications. *Annual Review of Sociology, 26*, 1–20.

Smock, P. J., & Manning, W. D. (1997). Cohabiting partners' economic circumstances and marriage. *Demography, 34*, 331–341.

Stevenson, B., & Wolfers, J. (2007). Marriage and divorce: Changes and their driving forces. *Journal of Economic Perspectives, 21*, 27–52.

Stratton, L. S. (2002). Examining the wage differential for married and cohabiting men. *Economic Inquiry, 40,* 199–212.

van der Klaauw, W. (1996). Female labour supply and marital status decisions: A life-cycle model. *Review of Economic Studies, 63,* 199–235.

Waite, L. J. (1995). Does marriage matter? *Demography, 32,* 483–507.

Waite, L. J., & Gallagher, M. (2000). *The case for marriage.* New York, NY: Doubleday.

Whittington, L. A., & Alm, J. (1997). Till death or taxes do us part: The effect of income taxation on divorce. *Journal of Human Resources, 32,* 388–412.

Willets, M. C. (2006). Union quality comparisons between long-term heterosexual cohabitation and legal marriage. *Journal of Family Issues, 27,* 10–127.

Winkler, A. E. (1994). The determinants of a mothers choice of family structure: Labor market conditions, AFDC policy, or community mores. *Population Research and Policy Review, 13,* 283–303.

Wolfers, J. (2006). Did unilateral divorce raise divorce rates? A reconciliation and new results. *American Economic Review, 96,* 1802–1820.

Wu, Z., & Pollard, M. S. (2000). Economic circumstances and the stability of nonmarital cohabitation. *Journal of Family Issues, 21,* 303–328.

Xie, Y., Raymo, J. M., Goyette, K., & Thornton, A. (2003). Economic potential and entry into marriage and cohabitation. *Demography, 40,* 351–368.

Yelowitz, A. S. (1998). Will extending Medicaid to two-parent families encourage marriage? *Journal of Human Resources, 33,* 833–865.

INDIAN ENTREPRENEURIAL SUCCESS IN THE UNITED STATES, CANADA, AND THE UNITED KINGDOM

Robert W. Fairlie, Harry Krashinsky,
Julie Zissimopoulos and Krishna B. Kumar

ABSTRACT

Indian immigrants in the United States and other wealthy countries are successful in entrepreneurship. Using Census data from the three largest developed countries receiving Indian immigrants in the world – the United States, the United Kingdom, and Canada – we examine the performance of Indian entrepreneurs and explanations for their success. We find that business income of Indian entrepreneurs in the United States is substantially higher than the national average and is higher than for any other immigrant group. Approximately half of the average difference in income between Indian entrepreneurs and the national average is explained by their high levels of education while industry differences explain an additional 10 percent. In Canada, Indian entrepreneurs have average earnings slightly below the national average but are more likely to hire employees, as are their counterparts in the United States and the

Research in Labor Economics, Volume 36, 285–318
ISSN: 0147-9121/doi:10.1108/S0147-9121(2012)0000036012

United Kingdom. The Indian educational advantage is smaller in Canada and the United Kingdom, contributing less to their entrepreneurial success.

Keywords: Entrepreneurship; immigration; Indian migrants

JEL Classifications: L26; J15

INTRODUCTION

Entrepreneurs contribute to economic growth by creating new industries, increasing productivity through competition, identifying viable new technologies, working efficiently and intensively, and creating jobs (Haltiwanger, Jarmin, & Miranda, 2010; SBA, 2010; OECD, 2005). Based on cross-country data, however, van Stel, Carree, and Thurik (2005) find that although the relationship between entrepreneurship and growth is positive for developed countries, it is negative for developing countries. They speculate that the negative association may in part be due to low levels of human capital of entrepreneurs in developing countries.

The case of India is particularly interesting because Indian immigrants in the United States are highly successful in entrepreneurship. The average net business income of Indian entrepreneurs is $84,080, significantly higher than the national average of $52,086. This success is particularly striking given the low per capita income of Indians in their home country – only $2,644 even after adjusting for purchasing power parity. Immigrants from countries where the per capita income is much higher than in India, including Taiwan, Korea, Greece, Germany, and England, have substantially lower entrepreneurial earnings in the United States than Indian entrepreneurs. In fact, Indian immigrants have the highest average net business income of all immigrant groups in the United States. The evidence on Indian immigrants' entrepreneurial achievement in other wealthy countries such as the United Kingdom and Canada is less conclusive, but also suggestive of success. In both countries, Indian entrepreneurs are more likely to hire employees than the national average.

More than 1 million Indians have migrated to the United States, making it the largest receiving country in the world. The United Kingdom, with half a million Indian immigrants, and Canada, with roughly a third of a million, are the next two largest receiving countries in the developed world. While many of these immigrants seek employment in established firms in the host nations, many also become entrepreneurs, especially in technology-laden fields. Twenty-five percent of engineering and technology companies started in the United States during the past decade were founded by immigrants many of whom are from India (Wadhwa, Saxenian, Rissing, & Gereffi, 2007). These firms had $52 billion in sales and hired 450,000 workers in 2005. Previous research also indicates that immigrant entrepreneurs have made important contributions to high-tech regions such as Silicon Valley (Saxenian, 1999, 2000). Engineers from China and India run roughly one quarter of all technology businesses started in Silicon Valley.

Little research has attempted to identify the sources of the relatively strong economic performance of businesses owned by immigrants from India in the United States and other industrialized countries. Although previous research using data from various countries provides some evidence on the success of Indian entrepreneurs – see Mar (2005), Fairlie and Robb (2008), Kalnins and Chung (2006), Clark and Drinkwater (2000, 2006), Li (2001), Ley (2006), Johnson (2000), and Singh (2004) for a few recent studies – a comprehensive analysis has not been performed.

Do observable characteristics explain their success, or is there a country-specific effect at work? One hypothesis, echoing the view of van Stel et al. (2005), is that high levels of education contribute to the success of Indian entrepreneurs. That is, the exodus of highly educated workers or "brain drain" from India may be responsible for entrepreneurial success in these developed countries, although surprisingly this question has not been studied in the previous literature. Another potential explanation is that Indian entrepreneurs concentrate in high earnings industries, which also has not been studied. We address these questions in the article.

Moreover, a systematic exploration of Indian entrepreneurs in developed countries would be a useful first step in understanding if observable characteristics such as human capital can explain much of this success, the role of complementary inputs and institutions in determining entrepreneurial success, the contribution of immigrant groups to entrepreneurship and growth in developed countries, and the corresponding loss, if any, to the home countries. Given the above-mentioned gap in the current literature, providing a systematic description of Indian entrepreneurial success based on large datasets from three different countries, undertaking a decomposition analysis to understand the explained and unexplained differences in their success relative to the reference group (native-born whites), and motivating issues for future research based on such an examination are the initial steps we take in this article.

We take a broad geographical and industrial approach to examine the performance of Indian entrepreneurs. In particular, we use Census data from the United States, the United Kingdom, and Canada to provide the first analysis of entrepreneurship among Indian immigrants in the three largest receiving developed countries.[1] The sample sizes for all three Censuses are extremely large and allow us to examine business performance among Indian entrepreneurs in the three countries. In fact, these are the only nationally representative micro-datasets with large enough sample sizes to conduct a focused analysis on Indian entrepreneurs.

Even though differences in data across the three countries preclude us from pooling the data, examining the success of Indian entrepreneurs across a range of industrialized countries is likely to shed light on whether similar observable traits of entrepreneurs are responsible for their performance or whether country-specific factors above and beyond these traits are primarily responsible. Using decomposition techniques, we find that education explains nearly half of the difference in business income between Indian entrepreneurs and U.S. born white entrepreneurs (which approximates the national average) and sectoral choice explains another one-fifth of the difference. Once other observable characteristics such as gender, age, and marital status are included, nearly three-quarters of the difference can be explained. In Canada, Indian entrepreneurs have average earnings slightly below the national average but they are more likely to hire employees, as are their counterparts in the United States and the United Kingdom. The Indian educational advantage is smaller in Canada and the United Kingdom, partly contributing to lower relative entrepreneurial success in these countries. These results are similar in the sense they suggest that most of the Indian entrepreneurial success can be explained by observable differences that are a priori plausible rather than recourse to an India-specific effect. However, the magnitude explained by observables differs across the three countries.

It would of course be useful to understand more conclusively if the success of Indian immigrants stems from positive selection of Indian entrepreneurs into these countries or from an Indian advantage in entrepreneurship. Unfortunately, we cannot study this directly without data on Indians who remain in India. But, the differences in the results summarized above can shed some light on this. If Indian entrepreneurial advantage were the main factor, the outcomes of success would have been similar in all three countries. Instead, Indian entrepreneurs are most successful in the United States, and the observed characteristics explain most of their success there when compared to that in Canada and the United Kingdom. These differences could arise because Indian entrepreneurs select into these countries differently, or because the countries differ in factors complementary to entrepreneurial success. The higher educational advantage of Indian entrepreneurs relative to natives in the United States appears to suggest that there could be selection differences across countries. However, we find that the differences in returns to education we observe for entrepreneurs across countries are similar to differences in returns for salaried workers. This suggests country factors also matter.

The rest of this article proceeds as follows. In the next section we discuss the data sources for the three countries. The third section presents descriptive statistics on the performance of Indian entrepreneurs in the United States, Canada, and the United Kingdom. In the fourth section, we analyze the causes of Indian entrepreneurial success in each of the three countries using decomposition techniques. The fifth section concludes.

DATA

For the analysis, we use the 2000 U.S. Census of Population Public Use Microdata (PUMS) 5-Percent Samples (14.1 million observations), the 2001 United Kingdom Census 3-Percent Sample from the Individual Anonymised Records (1.6 million observations), and the 2001 Canada Census Public Use Microdata File (PUMF) of about 2.7 percent of the population (approximately 800,000 observations). The Census samples from each country are representative of the entire population in the country, resulting in representative samples of all immigrant groups residing in each country at the time of the surveys.[2] Our analysis sample for the United Kingdom, however, includes only England and Wales. In all Censuses, information on birth country, ethnicity, and immigration status is provided and used to define Indian and other Asian immigrant groups.[3]

For all Censuses we define business owners from the class of worker question for the main job activity in the survey week. In the United States, the questions asked allow us to identify as self-employed business owners all owners of unincorporated, incorporated, employer, and non-employer businesses although we cannot distinguish between the latter two. In Canada, the main job question allows us to identify as business owners all owners of unincorporated and incorporated businesses with and without paid help.[4] In the United Kingdom, the main job question allows us to identify as business owners self-employed workers with employees and those without employees.

The U.S. and Canadian Censuses report business income allowing us to measure the performance of Indian and other businesses. In the U.K. Census, business income is not publicly available. We distinguish between employer businesses (which have employees) and non-employer businesses as an alternative measure of performance. The Canadian Census also allows for the identification of employer businesses.

For all countries, we restrict the samples to include individuals ages 25–64. We exclude young workers to identify completed schooling and older workers because of the complication with retirement decisions.[5] We also exclude individuals who are not currently working and who do not report working at least 15 hours per week.[6] Although side-businesses are already ruled out because of the focus on business ownership for the main job activity, these restrictions exclude all small-scale business activities. However, agricultural industries are included in all analyses.[7]

Educational distributions are not perfectly comparable across the three countries because of differences in educational systems. To make comparisons across countries, we focus on the percent of the prime-age workforce that has a college degree. In the U.K. Census, education is reported as highest qualification obtained and translated into one of five levels such that levels 4 and 5 represent a college education or higher.[8] Indians may obtain their education abroad or in the host country. Unfortunately, the Census data from all three countries do not provide evidence on where the education was obtained. However, since Indians who have graduated from the leading colleges are the ones more likely to emigrate, the loss of information on the source of education and therefore the quality of such education is not likely to be severe.[9]

THE SUCCESS OF INDIAN ENTREPRENEURS

The United States

More than 1 million immigrants from India reside in the United States according to estimates based on the 2000 Census. The only source countries with more immigrants in the United States are Mexico (9.3 million), the Philippines (1.5 million), and Germany (1.2 million). The rate of business ownership is not substantially higher among Indian immigrants than the national average. Estimates from the Census indicate that 10.9 percent of the Indian immigrant workforce owns a business compared with 10.1 percent of the total workforce in the United States (Fairlie,

Zissimopoulos, & Krashinsky, 2010). The rate of business ownership is the same as the rate for all Asian immigrants of 10.9 percent. The interesting difference between Indian immigrants and the national average is not in business ownership rates, but is in the relative success of these businesses. The businesses owned by Indian entrepreneurs are very successful on average when compared to all businesses and other Asian immigrant-owned businesses.

Table 1 reports estimates of net business income by group in the United States. Indian entrepreneurs earn $84,080 per year on average. This is roughly 60 percent higher than the national average income of business owners ($52,086).[10] Indian entrepreneurs also earn more on average than all other Asian immigrants, whose average earnings are $48,708.[11] Table 2 reports estimates of business income for detailed immigrant groups. It can be seen that Indian entrepreneurs have the highest business income among all 44 listed immigrant groups in the United States.[12] Indian entrepreneurs are more successful on average than entrepreneurs even from wealthy countries such as Canada, the United Kingdom, Germany, the Netherlands, and Ireland. In most cases, Indian entrepreneurs earn $20,000 more than entrepreneurs from these countries, which is remarkable given that the GDP per capita of India is less than one-tenth of that of the European Union, even after adjusting for purchasing power parity. Indian entrepreneurs are also by far the highest earning entrepreneurs from any country in Asia.

The finding of superior performance among Indian entrepreneurs is consistent with estimates from other data sources. The only other nationally representative dataset with information on the race of a business owner and a large enough sample size for examining the performance of Indian entrepreneurs is the Survey of Business Owners (SBO), and its earlier version the Characteristics of Business Owners (CBO).[13] Estimates from these sources provide evidence that Indian-owned businesses have higher profits and hire more employees than the average for all firms

Table 1. Business Outcomes by Country of Origin.

Immigrant Group	Net Business Income	N
U.S. Total	$52,086	534,194
All Asian immigrants	$54,208	17,093
Indian immigrants	$84,080	2,684

Note: The sample consists of all business owners ages 25–64.
Source: U.S. Census 2000.

Table 2. Net Business Income for Detailed Immigrant Groups.

Source Country	Net Business Income	Sample Size
India	84,080	2,684
Iran	77,452	1,473
Egypt	69,707	352
Canada	68,795	2,208
Lebanon	66,500	512
Israel	65,499	632
Iraq	64,201	311
Hungary	63,283	311
United Kingdom	63,278	414
Pakistan	61,701	621
Greece	61,021	881
Other Asian	60,981	665
Philippines	59,990	1,634
Taiwan	59,192	1,085
England	58,672	1,238
Germany	57,877	1,750
Netherlands	57,706	353
Argentina	56,523	469
Russia	55,749	617
Japan	55,192	775
Romania	54,496	368
France	52,184	419
Italy	51,809	1,457
Ireland	51,512	510
Cuba	50,868	2,070
Nigeria	48,811	319
Portugal	48,561	480
Korea	48,074	4,015
Ukraine	46,177	454
China	45,815	2,481
Poland	43,801	1,228
Haiti	41,156	378
Peru	36,887	604
Jamaica	36,714	780
Vietnam	34,862	2,253
Colombia	34,375	1,116
Nicaragua	32,624	349
Brazil	31,237	675
Ecuador	29,906	491
Mexico	28,153	11,008
Dominican Republic	27,716	828
El Salvador	27,481	1,383
Honduras	24,545	367
Guatemala	23,419	774

Note: (1) The sample consists of all business owners ages 25–64. (2) All immigrant groups with a sample size of 300 or more are reported.
Source: U.S. Census 2000.

(Fairlie & Robb, 2008). Indian firms are also substantially less likely to close than are all firms.[14] The only exception is that Indian firms are found to have similar levels of total sales as the national average. Business-level data thus confirms the findings from individual-level data on the success of Indian entrepreneurs.

Indian-owned businesses are distributed over all industries but are concentrated in different industries than the national average (see Table 3). Two of the most important differences are that Indian entrepreneurs are less likely to be located in agriculture and construction. The construction industry comprises 17.4 percent of all businesses in the United States; however, only 1.8 percent of Indian entrepreneurs are located in this industry. Indian firms are also less likely to concentrate in professional services and other services. Indian entrepreneurs are more likely than business owners as a whole to concentrate in retail trade, education, health and social services, and arts, entertainment, and recreation. Although sample sizes make it difficult to carefully examine detailed industries, we find that the three most common industries for Indian immigrant entrepreneurs are offices of physicians (15.2 percent), traveler accommodation (9.0 percent), and grocery stores (6.5 percent).

Table 3. Industry Distribution of Indian Immigrant Businesses.

	U.S. Total	Indian Immigrants
Agriculture and mining	5.8%	1.0%
Construction	17.4%	1.8%
Manufacturing	4.6%	3.3%
Wholesale trade	3.3%	5.6%
Retail trade	10.1%	21.1%
Transportation	3.8%	5.5%
Information	1.6%	0.7%
FIRE	7.6%	5.7%
Professional services	18.5%	13.8%
Education, health, and social services	10.5%	22.9%
Arts, entertainment, and recreation	5.9%	14.5%
Other services	10.8%	4.0%
Sample size	534,194	2,684

Note: (1) The sample consists of individuals ages 25–64 who own a business with 15 or more hours worked per week. (2) All estimates are calculated using sample weights provided by the Census.
Source: U.S. Census 2000.

Canada and the United Kingdom

Are Indian entrepreneurs also more successful in Canada and the United Kingdom? Table 4 reports average business outcomes for Indian and Asian immigrants and all entrepreneurs in Canada and the United Kingdom. In Canada, Indian entrepreneurs earn slightly less than the average income among all entrepreneurs ($28,580 versus $30,296).[15] In the Canadian Census, information on whether the business has employees (employer firms) is also available. Employment may represent a rough proxy for business success. Employment rates are highly correlated with sales, profits, and survival rates (U.S. Census Bureau, 1997, U.S. Census Bureau, 2006). Firms with more employees are less likely to fail, have higher sales, and have higher profits on average. Examining this information, we find that 48.4 percent of Indian entrepreneurs hire employees. This is higher than the national average of 42.4 percent.

Unfortunately, earnings data are not available in the U.K. Census; therefore, we focus on employment as an indicator of a business owner's achievement. Indian entrepreneurs are substantially more likely to hire employees (53.6 percent compared to the national average of 37.1 percent).

In summary, Indian entrepreneurs are more successful when compared to the national average in Canada and the United Kingdom as measured by percentage who hire employees, but slightly less so if income is used as a measure for Canada.

Table 4.   Business Outcomes by Country of Origin.

Immigrant Group	Net Business Income	Canada		United Kingdom	
		Percent Employer Firms	N	Percent Employer Firms	N
Total	$30,296	42.4%	39,933	37.1%	84,439
All Asian Immigrants	$24,301	51.4%	2,652	54.5%	3,002
Indian Immigrants	$28,580	48.4%	539	53.6%	1,111

Note: The United Kingdom includes England and Wales only. For the United Kingdom, "Asian immigrants" group is defined by country of birth and self-reported ethnicity and does not include all persons born in Asia and residing in the United Kingdom. For example, it does not include ethnic British born in India.

Sources: Canada Census 2001 and U.K. Census 2001.

The industry distributions for Canada and the United Kingdom are reported in Tables 5 and 6, respectively. For Indian business owners in Canada, patterns in industrial concentration relative to the overall population of business owners are similar to those found in the United States. Indians are less likely than the national average to own businesses in agricultural or construction industries, but are more likely to own businesses in the transportation industry. The most common industries for Indian entrepreneurs are transportation (20.4 percent), retail trade (14.8 percent), business services (14.1 percent), and health services (12.2 percent) in Canada.

Similarly, in the United Kingdom the major difference between the industry distribution for Indian entrepreneurs and all entrepreneurs are the lower concentrations of Indian business owners in agriculture and construction (Table 6). Indian entrepreneurs in the United Kingdom are highly concentrated in wholesale and retail trade with 41.9 percent in this industry compared to only 16.1 percent overall. Indian firms are also more concentrated in transport, storage and communication, and health and social work than the national average. Indian businesses in the United Kingdom are clearly more concentrated in specific industries than in the

Table 5. Industry Distribution of Indian Immigrant Businesses.

	Canada Total	Indian Immigrants
Agriculture and mining	12.7%	3.0%
Construction	13.1%	4.5%
Manufacturing	5.0%	5.0%
Wholesale trade	3.9%	5.4%
Retail trade	12.0%	14.8%
Transportation	4.8%	20.4%
Communication	1.0%	0.6%
FIRE	3.9%	5.0%
Business services	15.8%	14.1%
Government services	0.1%	0.0%
Education, health, and social services	10.6%	12.2%
Accommodation, food, and beverages	4.4%	6.3%
Other services	12.8%	8.7%
Sample size	39,933	539

Note: (1) The sample consists of individuals ages 25–64 who own a business with 15 or more hours worked per week. (2) All estimates are calculated using sample weights provided by the Census.
Source: Canada Census 2000.

Table 6.   Industry Distribution of Indian Immigrant Businesses.

	U.K. Total	Indian Immigrants
Agriculture, hunting, and forestry	5.7%	0.0%
Fishing	0.1%	0.0%
Mining and quarrying	0.1%	0.1%
Manufacturing	8.9%	7.5%
Electricity, gas, and water supply	0.3%	0.2%
Construction	20.1%	7.8%
Wholesale and retail trade; repair of motor vehicles	16.1%	41.9%
Hotels and restaurants	5.3%	5.2%
Transport, storage, and communication	6.7%	10.8%
Financial intermediation	2.2%	2.3%
Real estate, renting and business activities	17.2%	9.0%
Public administration and defense; compulsory social security	0.8%	0.5%
Education	2.3%	1.4%
Health and social work	6.3%	10.1%
Other community, social, and personal service activities	7.8%	3.1%
Private households employing domestic staff	0.1%	0.1%
Extra-territorial organizations and bodies	0.0%	0.0%
Sample size	84,439	1,111

Note: (1) The sample consists of individuals ages 25–64 who own a business with 15 or more hours worked per week. (2) The United Kingdom includes England and Wales only. For the United Kingdom, "Asian immigrants" group is defined by country of birth and self-reported ethnicity and does not include all persons born in Asia and residing in the United Kingdom. For example, it does not include ethnic British born in India.
Source: U.K. Census 2001.

United States and Canada, which may contribute differently to their relative success.

EXPLANATIONS FOR THE SUCCESS OF INDIAN ENTREPRENEURS

What factors contribute to the success of Indian entrepreneurs? One hypothesis is that Indian entrepreneurs are highly educated and this human capital contributes to their business success. We report group differences in education levels and other characteristics in Table 7. We switch to comparing Indian entrepreneurs to native-born white entrepreneurs (instead of the

Table 7.   Mean Education and Characteristics among Indian and White
Entrepreneurs.

	United States		Canada		United Kingdom	
	Indians	Whites	Indians	Whites	Indians	Whites
College graduate	68.3%	34.6%	50.0%	25.4%	35.8%	21.4%
Female	25.7%	31.1%	26.6%	31.8%	27.7%	24.8%
Ages 25–29	4.3%	5.8%	5.0%	5.1%	2.6%	6.4%
Ages 45–59	47.1%	44.6%	43.3%	44.2%	46.1%	44.3%
Ages 60–64	5.6%	7.5%	6.9%	6.3%	5.6%	7.5%
Married	91.3%	75.5%	91.6%	72.2%	90.6%	66.3%
Agriculture	0.9%	6.5%	1.4%	11.7%	0.1%	6.3%
Construction	1.8%	18.2%	4.3%	13.6%	6.8%	21.1%
Sample size	2,684	432,399	418	30,171	1,825	78,016

Note: (1) The sample consists of the self-employed business owners ages 25–64. (2) The United Kingdom includes England and Wales only. For the United Kingdom, "Asian immigrants" group is defined by country of birth and self-reported ethnicity and does not include all persons born in Asia and residing in the United Kingdom. For example, it does not include ethnic British born in India.
Sources: U.S. Census 2000, Canada Census 2001, and U.K. Census 2001.

national average) in order to create mutually exclusive categories for the regression and decomposition analysis that follow.

In all three countries, Indian entrepreneurs are more likely to be college graduates than native-born white entrepreneurs.[16] Mean levels for the national average are very similar to those reported for native-born whites. More than two-thirds of Indian entrepreneurs in the United States are college graduates, and half of all Indian entrepreneurs in Canada are college graduates, which is double the rate for native-born whites or the national average in both countries.[17] In the United Kingdom, just over one-third of Indian entrepreneurs are college educated, and while this fraction is lower than those in the United States and Canada, it is still higher than the percent of college-educated native-born whites (21 percent). Indian entrepreneurs in all three countries are also much more likely to be married than native-born whites. The differences in other characteristics such as sex and age between Indian immigrant entrepreneurs and native-born white entrepreneurs are generally small.

Employing a multivariate regression model, we assess the contribution of human capital in the entrepreneurial success of Indian immigrants in each country, investigate other determinants of business performance, and use a

decomposition technique to examine the relative importance of the determinants.[18] We estimate the same regression model (except for the outcome
variable, which is log business income and/or employment) separately for
each country. As mentioned above, since not all outcome variables are
available for the three countries, we are unable to pool the data. However,
given the institutional differences (especially related to immigration) in the
three countries and other factors that vary across them, separate regressions
for each country nevertheless yield useful insights. For the United States and
Canada, we estimate specifications for log net business income, and for
Canada and the United Kingdom, we estimate specifications for employment.

In particular, the regressions include an indicator variable for college
degree or higher as a measure of education. We control for group differences
with dummy variables for all major immigrant groups and native-born
ethnic/racial groups. Native-born whites, the single largest ethnic/racial
group, serve as the excluded group.[19] Other covariates include female
indicator, ages 25–29, 30–44 (excluded), 45–59, 60–64; indicator for married;
and indicators for agriculture and construction industries, two industries in
which Indians systematically differ from natives in order to capture inter-
industry wage differentials that may contribute to the Indian-native wage
gap. We also use other specifications with richer industry controls, and the
main results of the article remain unchanged.

U.S. Results

Results for business income regressions for the United States can be found
in the first and second columns in Table 8. Indian entrepreneurs are found
to have 62.3 percent higher earnings than native-born whites before
controlling for other factors.[20] These estimates indicate that the Indian
entrepreneurial earnings advantage holds when the reference group is
native-born whites and when taking logs (which lessens the influence of
high-earnings outliers). In the second specification, we include controls for
education, age, marital status, region, and broad industrial sector.[21] The
earnings differential for Indian entrepreneurs drops substantially (to 14
percent) after including these controls, suggesting that differences in
individual characteristics are largely responsible for why Indian entrepreneurs are so successful in the United States. We return to this finding below
in the decompositions.

The returns to education on business performance are substantial.
Having a college degree increases net business income by over 86 percent.

Table 8. Log Net Business Income Regressions.

Explanatory Variables	U.S. Census 2000		Canada Census 2001	
	(1)	(2)	(3)	(4)
Indian immigrant	0.4843***	0.1314***	0.0583	−0.1855***
	(0.0262)	(0.0246)	(0.0526)	(0.0518)
College graduate		0.6223***		0.5081***
		(0.0041)		(0.0139)
Female		−0.7520***		−0.5185***
		(0.0041)		(0.0130)
Ages 25–29		−0.2540***		−0.2057***
		(0.0079)		(0.0265)
Ages 45–59		0.0023		0.0056
		(0.0040)		(0.0123)
Ages 60–64		−0.1867***		−0.1574***
		(0.0074)		(0.0271)
Married		0.1633***		0.1234***
		(0.0043)		(0.0135)
Agriculture		−0.6274***		−0.4192***
		(0.0083)		(0.0206)
Construction		−0.0545***		−0.0062
		(0.0052)		(0.0165)
Region controls	No	Yes	No	Yes
Mean of dependent variables	10.14	10.14	9.9990	9.9990
Sample size	534,044	534,044	33,676	33,676

Note: (1) The sample consists of self-employed business owners ages 25–64 who work 15 or more hours per week. (2) Additional controls include other Asian immigrant, Asian native, white immigrant, black native, black immigrant, Latino native, Latino immigrant, Native American, other race, and multiple race dummies in the U.S. specifications. Additional controls in the specifications with Canadian data include indicators for being a Chinese immigrant, an immigrant from the Philippines, a Vietnamese immigrant, a Korean immigrant, a white immigrant, a black native, a black immigrant, and Asian native, an immigrant from another Asian country. (3) The left-out categories are white natives and ages 30–44. ***denotes statistical significance at 0.01 level.

The positive connection between the two variables is in itself not a new finding. Indeed, education is found to be a strong determinant of business earnings around the world consistent with this finding (see Parker, 2004, van der Sluis, van Praag, & Vijverberg, 2004, and van Praag, 2005). However, our aim here and in the decompositions is to assess the quantitative impact of education and other observable traits in explaining differences in business income.

The coefficients on the other individual and job characteristics indicate that business income is higher among male owners, married owners, middle-aged owners, and non-agricultural businesses. Differences between Indian entrepreneurs and native-born white entrepreneurs in education and these other characteristics clearly contribute to the relative success of Indian entrepreneurs in the United States. In order to categorize the relative importance of education and the other characteristics we employ decomposition techniques.

Additional Estimates

Before turning to the decompositions, we estimate several additional specifications to check the sensitivity of the estimates (results omitted for brevity). One concern is that education might proxy for wealth instead of skill or aptitude. Limited access to financial resources may result in undercapitalized businesses and restrict the growth of businesses (Fairlie & Robb, 2007, 2008). Measures of total wealth are unavailable in the U.S. Census; however, home ownership is available and the inclusion of this variable in the models does not alter either the estimated effect of Indian immigrants or education on business performance.

We also estimate specifications that include more detailed education levels for the United States. We find that business ownership and income are increasing functions for each higher level of education. The coefficient on the Indian immigrant dummy, however, is not sensitive to the switch from the inclusion of the college dummy variable to more detailed dummy variables. The U.S. Census also allows us to control for English language ability and number of children. The Indian dummy and college coefficients do not noticeably change with the inclusion of these variables.

Finally, we estimate a regression specification that includes dummy variables for the more detailed industries listed in Table 3. The coefficient on the Indian dummy is now 0.176 which is not substantially different than Specification 2 in Table 8, where we include controls only for agriculture and construction. As discussed earlier, the largest under-representation of Indian entrepreneurs relative to the national average are in the low-income industries of agriculture and construction. We continue to include only agricultural and construction sector dummies in the main specifications because of concerns that controlling for more detailed industries might partly proxy for business success.

Decompositions

Estimates from the log business income regressions identify several determinants of business performance. If Indian entrepreneurs differ substantially from the national average in any of these characteristics, then it could explain why Indian entrepreneurs are so successful. To explore these issues further, we employ the Blinder–Oaxaca technique of decomposing inter-group differences in a dependent variable into those due to different observable characteristics across groups (often referred to as the "endowment effect") and those due to different determinants of outcomes (often referred to as the "coefficient or unexplained effect") (Blinder, 1973; Oaxaca, 1973). The standard decomposition of the white-minority gap in the average value of the dependent variable, Y, can be expressed as

$$\bar{Y}^W - \bar{Y}^M = [(\bar{X}^W - \bar{X}^M)\hat{\beta}^W] + [\bar{X}^M(\hat{\beta}^W - \hat{\beta}^M)] \qquad (1)$$

We use log net business income as the dependent variable and define Indian entrepreneurs as the minority group.

Similar to most recent studies applying the decomposition technique, we focus on estimating the first component of the decomposition, which captures contributions from differences in observable characteristics or "endowments." We do not report estimates for the second or "unexplained" component of the decomposition because it partly captures contributions from group differences in unmeasured characteristics and is sensitive to the choice of omitted categories making the results difficult to interpret. Another issue that arises in calculating the decomposition is the choice of coefficients or weights for the first component of the decomposition. The first component can be calculated using either the white or minority coefficients often providing different estimates, which is the familiar index problem with the Blinder–Oaxaca decomposition technique. An alternative method is to weight the first term of the decomposition expression using coefficient estimates from a pooled sample of the two groups (see Oaxaca & Ransom, 1994 for example). We follow this approach to calculate the decompositions by using coefficient estimates from regressions that includes a sample of all racial groups. Finally, Eq. (1) provides an estimate of the contribution of Indian-white differences in the *entire* set of independent variables to the income gap. We further decompose this component into the contributions from each set of independent variables included in the regression.

Table 9 reports estimates from this procedure for decomposing the Indian/white gaps in business outcomes. The most important factor

Table 9. Decompositions of Indian/Native-Born White Gaps in Business Performance.

Dependent Variable	U.S. Log Business	Canada Log Business	Canada	United Kingdom
	Income	Income	Employer	Employer
Indian mean	10.65	10.07	0.4910	0.5360
Native-born white mean	10.17	10.01	0.4410	0.3710
Indian/native-born white gap	0.4781	0.0600	0.0500	0.1650
Contributions from group differences in:				
Education	0.2098	0.1250	0.0177	0.0026
	43.9%		35.4%	1.6%
Female	0.0405	0.0270	0.0056	−0.0006
	8.5%		11.2%	−0.4%
Age	0.0072	−0.0008	−0.0002	0.0022
	1.5%		−0.4%	1.3%
Marital status	0.0258	0.0239	0.0235	0.0194
	5.4%		46.9%	11.8%
Industrial sector	0.0446	0.0438	0.0121	0.0204
	9.3%		24.3%	12.4%
Region	0.0265	0.0296	0.0095	
	5.5%		19.1%	
All included variables	0.3544	0.2484	0.0683	0.0440
	74.1%		136.5%	26.7%

Note: (1) The samples and regression specifications are the same as those used in Tables 8 and 10. (2) See text for more details on decomposition equations.
Sources: U.S. Census 2000, Canada Census 2001, and U.K. Census 2001.

explaining why Indian entrepreneurs perform better on average than white entrepreneurs in the United States is that they have higher levels of education. The education difference explains 43.9 percent of the gap in log business income.[22] The favorable sectoral distribution of Indian entrepreneurs explains 9.3 percent of the log business income differential.[23] In sum, all of the observed variables explain roughly three-quarters of the gap in business income between Indians and native whites. While there is a large enough gap that remains to be explained (cultural or institutional factors may well play a role in explaining this gap), our findings indicate that observable characteristics play a crucial role in explaining the income difference of Indian entrepreneurs.[24]

Canadian Results

We now turn to the results for Canada. Estimates for log net business income regressions are reported in the third and fourth columns in Table 8. Indian entrepreneurs do not have notably higher incomes than native-born white entrepreneurs in Canada. The point estimate in the log business income regression is positive, but small (amounting to a 6 percent difference) and insignificant. This is largely consistent with the estimates for average business income for Indian entrepreneurs and the national average reported in Table 4, but different from what was observed for relative earnings of Indian entrepreneurs in the United States.

Another difference between the results for Canada and the United States is that the return to education is relatively lower in Canada. The coefficients imply that business income for Canadians is over 66 percent higher among college-educated owners, which is lower than the return of over 86 percent found in the United States. The other variables have similar estimated effects as for the United States – business income is higher for male, older, and married entrepreneurs, and lower in agriculture.[25]

One similarity between the Canadian and American results, though, is that controlling for education and other individual characteristics reduces the Indian coefficient substantially. The coefficient is now negative and statistically significant. The point estimate implies that Indian entrepreneurs earn 17 percent less than white entrepreneurs given their education levels and other characteristics. The decomposition estimates discussed below shed light on why this is the case.

We also examine the determinants of whether an entrepreneur hires employees (reported in the first and second columns in Table 10).[26] Having a college education is associated with business success measured by employment. Entrepreneurs with a college education are 7.2 percentage points more likely to hire employees than entrepreneurs with no college education, which is a large effect relative to the mean employment rate of 45 percent. Married, male, and middle-aged entrepreneurs are also more likely to hire employees.[27] Finally, agricultural firms are less likely to hire employees, and construction firms are slightly more likely to hire employees. These results are consistent with those for business income. One difference between the results, however, is that the coefficient on the Indian dummy variable drops from 0.05 to essentially zero. This implies that, in Canadian data, we can entirely explain why Indian entrepreneurs are more likely to hire employees than white entrepreneurs.

Table 10.   Employer Firm Regressions.

Explanatory Variables	Canada Census 2001		U.K. Census 2001	
	(1)	(2)	(3)	(4)
Indian immigrant	0.0510**	−0.0020	0.170***	0.125***
	(0.0250)	(0.0250)	(0.011)	(0.011)
College graduate		0.0720***		0.018***
		(0.0060)		(0.004)
Female		−0.1080***		−0.021***
		(0.0060)		(0.004)
Ages 25–29		−0.0620***		−0.037***
		(0.0120)		(0.007)
Ages 45–59		0.0010		−0.011***
		(0.0060)		(0.004)
Ages 60–64		−0.0430***		−0.052***
		(0.0110)		(0.007)
Married		0.1210***		0.080***
		(0.0060)		(0.004)
Agriculture		−0.1340***		−0.073***
		(0.0090)		(0.007)
Construction		0.0180**		−0.111***
		(0.0090)		(0.004)
Region controls	No	Yes		
Mean of dependent variables	0.45	0.45	0.371	0.371
Sample size	33,676	33,676	84,439	84,439

Note: (1) The sample consists of self-employed business owners ages 25–64 who work 15 or more hours per week. (2) Additional controls in the U.K. specifications include Chinese immigrant, Indian immigrant, Pakistani immigrant, Bangladeshi immigrant, Other Asian immigrant, Asian native, white immigrant, black native, black immigrant, other race, and multiple race dummies. Additional controls in the specifications with Canadian data include indicators for being a Chinese immigrant, an immigrant from the Philippines, a Vietnamese immigrant, a Korean immigrant, a white immigrant, a black native, a black immigrant, and Asian native, an immigrant from another Asian country. (3) The left-out categories are white natives and ages 30–44. ** and *** denote statistical significance at the 0.05 and 0.01 levels, respectively.

Decompositions

To further investigate the importance of various characteristics on income and being an employer firm, we report decompositions for Canada in Table 9. Focusing on the results for log business income first, as in the United States, we find that education contributes substantially to the difference in business income. We do not report percentage contributions in this case because they can be misleading in decompositions when the gaps are relatively small. We instead focus directly on the contribution estimates. Indian entrepreneurs are more educated than white entrepreneurs. Fifty percent have a college degree compared with 25.4 percent of white entrepreneurs. This educational advantage and the large positive returns to education for business income imply that Indian entrepreneurs should earn 12.5 log points more than white entrepreneurs in Canada, all else equal. Of course, not all else is equal, and other factors, which are largely unobservable, work to suppress the incomes of Indian entrepreneurs.

Higher marriage rates, lower female shares, and overrepresentation in British Columbia and Ontario among Indian entrepreneurs contribute slightly to higher business incomes. [28] Differences in industry structure are advantageous for Indian entrepreneurs. Indian entrepreneurs are less likely to locate in agriculture, explaining 4.4 log points of the gap in business income. The decomposition estimates indicate that differences in education and other observable characteristics should result in Indian entrepreneurs earning roughly 25 percent more than white entrepreneurs. Unobservable factors, which may include discrimination, non-transferable credentials, and differences in preferences, reduce this advantage to 6 percent.[29]

The employer decompositions indicate that higher rates of employment among Indian entrepreneurs are partly due to higher education levels.[30] Higher education levels among Indian entrepreneurs contribute 1.8 percentage points to the difference in employment rates (amounting to over 35 percent of the contribution). Higher marriage rates, male shares, and advantaged regional distributions also contribute slightly to why Indian entrepreneurs are more likely to hire employees. Taken together, these factors explain more than the entire gap in employment rates between Indian and white businesses.[31] Similar to the U.S. decompositions of business income, appealing to cultural factors is evidently not needed to explain differences in employment rates of Indian entrepreneurs.

U.K. Results

Estimates for employer regressions for the United Kingdom are reported in the third and fourth columns in Table 10. Unfortunately, we do not have a measure of business income in the United Kingdom, and thus only report results for employment. Indian entrepreneurs are 17 percentage points more likely to hire employees than white entrepreneurs. But the inclusion of education and other covariates decreases the coefficient estimates on the Indian dummy variable to 12.5 percentage points.

Employer firms are more likely among male, married, and middle-aged owners, and non-agricultural, non-construction businesses, which is generally consistent with the results for log business income for the United States and Canada. Most importantly, we find a positive and statistically significant effect of education on employment.[32] The coefficient estimate indicates that college-graduate owners have a 1.8 percentage point higher likelihood of hiring employees than do owners with lower levels of education. The positive effect of education on employment is consistent with the estimated effects of education on log business income in the United States and Canada, but the relative magnitude of the effect is much smaller. The estimated effect on British employment represents roughly 5 percent of the mean employment rate compared to roughly 15 percent on Canadian employment. And, as discussed above, the returns to a college education are also quite high in the United States and Canada, at 86 percent and 66 percent of business income, respectively.

Decompositions
The decomposition estimates reported in Table 9 indicate that high levels of education among Indian entrepreneurs contribute very little to why they are more likely to hire employees. The estimated effect of education on employment is weak even though the educational difference is sizeable. Thirty-six percent of Indian entrepreneurs have the equivalent of a college education compared with 21.4 percent of white entrepreneurs. Instead, higher marriage rates and lower concentrations in agriculture and construction contribute to the higher likelihood of Indian entrepreneurs hiring employees relative to native British entrepreneurs.

Discussion: Immigration Policies and Cross-Country Differences

The finding that Indian entrepreneurs in the United States are more likely to be college educated than Indian entrepreneurs in Canada and the United Kingdom compared to the national average may be due to differences in immigration policies and who decides to move to each country. Although differences in labor markets, credit markets, tax systems, historical ties, geographical proximity, and other institutional and structural differences are all important, immigration policy is clearly one of the most important factors affecting who emigrates. The goal of this article is to fill a gap in the literature by providing a systematic, cross-country description of Indian entrepreneurial success and understanding the explained and unexplained differences in their relative success. As such, a detailed discussion of differences in immigration policies in the United States, Canada, and the United Kingdom, and a structural modeling of the above-mentioned selection issue is beyond the scope of this article. However, a brief discussion of the key differences in how immigrants are admitted into each country might shed light on our findings, especially on why the return to education is higher in the United States and Canada, and why education explains much more of the success of Indian immigrants in these two countries.[33]

Fig. 1 reports immigration admissions by type for the United States, Canada, and the United Kingdom. The breakdown by type is for all immigrants, not just Indians, but the differences are nevertheless interesting. In both the United States and the United Kingdom, immigrants are most likely to enter the country under the "family sponsored" category. Since the 1960s, U.S. immigration policy has strongly favored family reunification (Woroby, 2005) and has been criticized for lowering the skills and education

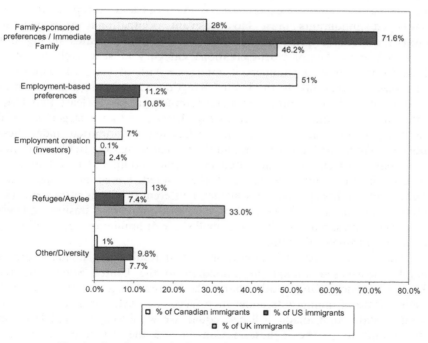

Fig. 1. Immigration by Type of Admission for 1998–2000.

levels of successive waves of immigrants (Borjas, 1995, 1999). The United Kingdom's immigration policies were at one time restricted to citizens of the states in the Commonwealth. However, over the past four decades the policies in the United Kingdom have shifted toward emphasizing family reunification and employment (Bauer, Lofstrom, & Zimmermann, 2000). On the other hand, Canada's point-based system, which awards immigration admission points based on education, language ability (English or French), years of experience in a managerial, professional, or technical occupation, age, arranged employment in Canada, and other factors, leads to more immigrants being skilled when compared to the United States (Borjas, 1993; Woroby, 2005).[34] Because of the point-based system, roughly half of all immigrants are admitted through employment-based preferences (Fig. 1). In contrast, only around 10 percent of immigrants in the United States are admitted under this broad classification.

The related category of employment creation or investors differs across countries.[35] In Canada, these immigrants are categorized as "investors," "entrepreneurs," or "self-employed." There are minimum requirements on net worth and business experience for investors and entrepreneurs; self-employed immigrants must have relevant occupational experience in culture, athletics or farm management.[36] In the United States, immigrants admitted in the "employment creation" category must actively invest at least $1 million in a commercial enterprise with at least 10 employees. "Business" immigrants to the United Kingdom must invest a minimum of £$200,000, and "innovator" immigrants must employ at least two U.K. residents. The estimates reported in Fig. 1 indicate that a larger, but still relatively small, share of immigrants in Canada are admitted under these policies than in the United States and the United Kingdom. In Canada, they represent 7 percent of all admitted immigrants compared to 0.1 and 2.4 percent in the United States and the United Kingdom, respectively. Differences in these policies may attract a different profile of entrepreneurial immigrants and alter the percent of successful immigrant business owners across countries, but overall only a small share of immigrants enter all three countries through this path.

Canada's point based immigration system results in a higher share of employment-based immigrants compared to the United States and the United Kingdom. On the other hand, the United Kingdom admits a much higher share of immigrants under its refugee and asylee programs than the United States or Canada. All else equal, we would expect skill levels of immigrants to be the highest in Canada and the lowest in the United Kingdom. And we expect this to be true for Indian immigrants if they fit the overall pattern. As indicated above, we find some evidence that the educational advantage of Indian immigrants compared to the national average is lower in the United Kingdom than in the United States, which is consistent with these differences in immigration policies. But, we also find that the educational advantage in the United States is higher than it is in Canada, which runs counter to the greater emphasis of Canada's immigration policy on rewarding points for the general skill level of immigrants.

In summary, differences in immigration policies appear to be important in determining the types of entrepreneur who decide to move to a particular country and how successful they become after they move, but they are not the entire story. A model of country selection by entrepreneurs would need to take into account a more complete set of factors. For instance, the positive effect of a greater emphasis on the skill level of immigrants placed by Canada might be undone by a more generous redistribution system, more egalitarian earnings, and other institutional and structural factors, making it less attractive to higher skilled immigrants such as Indian immigrants (Antecol, Cobb-Clark, & Trejo, 2003).

CONCLUSIONS

Over 1 million Indians have migrated to the United States making it the largest receiving country in the world. Nearly another million Indians have migrated to Canada and the United Kingdom, which have received the next largest waves of Indian immigrants besides Bangladesh (World Bank, 2007). Indians also represent either the largest or one of the largest single immigrant groups in each of these countries. In the United States, for example, only immigrants from Mexico, the Philippines, and Germany represent larger shares of the total population. Given the importance of this migration, we use Census microdata from the United States, Canada, and United Kingdom to provide the first comparative examination of the performance of Indian entrepreneurs.

We find that Indian entrepreneurs are much more successful than the national average in the United States. Indian businesses also perform well in Canada and the United Kingdom, but the evidence is not as strong. In the United States, Indian entrepreneurs earn roughly 60 percent more than white entrepreneurs and have the highest average business income of any immigrant group. Estimates from business-level data sources also indicate that Indian firms have higher profits, hire more employees, and have lower failure rates than the average for all U.S. firms (Fairlie & Robb, 2008; U.S. Census Bureau, 2006).

To explain the relative success of Indian entrepreneurs we focus on the role of human capital. Indian immigrants in all three countries have education levels that are higher than the national average, and in the United States the education levels of Indian immigrants are particularly high relative to the entire population; 68 percent of Indian entrepreneurs have a college education which is twice the rate for whites or the national average.

Estimates from regression models for log business income and employment reveal interesting differences across the three countries. When we examine business income, we find large, positive effects of education in the United States and Canada. We also find large positive effects of education on employment in Canada, but smaller positive effects in the United Kingdom. Decomposition estimates provide exact estimates of the contribution of higher levels of education among Indian entrepreneurs to their higher business incomes and employment levels. In the United States, higher levels of education among Indian entrepreneurs result in a business income advantage of 21 log points, which represents 43.9 percent of the gap. High levels of education also contribute substantially to why Indian entrepreneurs earn more in Canada (12.5 log points), but the difference is not as large. The combination of the larger education advantage held by Indian entrepreneurs and the larger return to education is responsible for the increased importance of education as an explanatory factor in the United States compared to Canada. In contrast to these results, the smaller educational advantage and lower returns to education in the United Kingdom result in less explanatory power in the United Kingdom. Lower concentrations of Indian entrepreneurs in agriculture and construction, lower female share, higher marriage rates, and favorable regional distributions also generally contribute to why Indian businesses perform better than white businesses or the national average.

Some of the variation in the education of Indian immigrants across the United States, Canada, and the United Kingdom is likely due to immigration policy that affects the immigrant pool. Another possibility is that the higher returns to education in the United States result in a more selective immigrant pool in the United States compared to Canada and the United Kingdom. Constructing a structured framework that simultaneously examines the determinants of entrepreneurial performance and migration decisions (e.g., immigration policies, credit and labor markets, tax policies, and institutions) using cross-country data would be a useful, but very difficult avenue for future research. Census data, while rich along many dimensions, limit our efforts to answer these types of questions. It is also not clear that the data necessary for research on this topic currently exist and new data, perhaps from linked administrative sources, is needed (e.g. Department of Homeland Security, Census, and IRS data).

Another issue is that it is likely that the returns to education are much larger for entrepreneurs in the countries we study than in India, which causes them to emigrate. Van der Sluis, van Praag, and Vijverberg (2005) conduct a meta-analytical empirical review and note that the return to schooling in terms of enterprise income in developing economies is actually comparable to that of industrial countries. But they also note that educated people prefer wage employment to nonfarm entrepreneurship, an effect that is stronger in economies where agriculture is dominant and literacy rates are lower. Nearly two-thirds of the Indian labor force is in agriculture and only around 60 percent of its population is literate.[37] Therefore, it is likely that educated Indians who want to become entrepreneurs are more likely to start their enterprises in wealthier countries rather than at home.

Indian entrepreneurs contribute substantially to their host economies. Indian firms hire 610,000 employees and have total sales of $88 billion in the United States alone (U.S. Census Bureau, 2006). In Canada, and especially in the United Kingdom, Indian entrepreneurs are more likely to hire employees. From India's perspective, these findings have implications for "brain drain." Although concerns over "brain drain" usually focus on the loss of highly educated workers in professional occupations, the loss of entrepreneurial talent is also important. The loss of Indian entrepreneurial talent to developed countries such as the United States, Canada, and the United Kingdom may have severe consequences for aggregate income, the creation of wealth, and employment. However, as Saxenian (2006) notes, successful entrepreneurs might return home to seed entrepreneurship in their home countries. In other words, "brain circulation," a positive effect, might be operative in addition to "brain drain." What the net effect is to a country with a rich history of emigration would be another research topic to pursue.

NOTES

1. Fairlie, Zissimopoulos, and Krashinsky (2010) examine business ownership and performance patterns in the United States, Canada, and the United Kingdom for Asian immigrants, and Schuetze and Antecol (2006) provide a detailed comparison of immigrant business formation in Australia, Canada, and the United States. Neither study, however, focuses specifically on Indian entrepreneurs examining the causes of high earnings and employment for this group.

2. Sample weights are used for the U.S. Census and Canadian Census to make them representative of their respective populations.

3. The Canadian public use data restrict the detail on exact country of birth, so ethnicity and immigration status are primarily used to categorize Asian immigrants. In the United Kingdom, India, Pakistan, and Bangladesh together are identified as birth countries and "Rest of Asia." Thus, ethnicity is also used here to categorize specific Asian immigrant groups. We did not include N. Ireland and Scotland because the ethnicity variable in the U.K. Census (DETHEW) applies only to England and Wales.

4. The job reported was the one held in the survey week. Persons with two or more jobs in the reference week were asked to provide information for the job at which they worked the most hours.

5. Zissimopoulos, Maestas, and Karoly (2007) show self-employed workers in the United States and England retire at lower rates than wage and salary workers due to differential incentives from pension and health insurance systems.

6. For the U.K. and Canada Censuses, hours per week refer to the survey week, whereas the U.S. Census only provides information on hours worked in the usual week worked over the previous year. Employment status, however, is determined for the survey week.

7. In any case, the exclusion of agricultural industries has little effect on estimates of Indian immigrant entrepreneurship.

8. Level 1 (low education) is held by 18.8 percent of the working age population, levels 2 and 3 held by 18.2 and 6.3 percent of the working age population, respectively, and levels 4 and 5 (high, generally college and above) held by 22.7 percent of the working age population. In addition, 26.3 percent report no qualifications and 7.6 percent report other qualifications.

9. Docquier and Marfouk (2005) report that India is third among the list of skilled emigration countries (behind the United Kingdom and the Philippines), as measured by emigration stocks. But, more pointedly, Agrawal, Kapur, and McHale (2008) note that while the overall tertiary emigration rate from India is about 4 percent, rates from the elite Indian Institutes of Technology are much higher.

10. Median business income among Indian entrepreneurs is 40 percent higher than the median level for all entrepreneurs in the United States.

11. The figure of $54,208 in Table 1 includes Indian immigrants. Income analysis in this article is performed on total annual earnings, instead of hourly earnings, in order to follow the approach taken by most of the existing literature. However, this choice does not impact our overall findings, Indian immigrants and native workers in self-employment do not work significantly different hours per week. As such, the findings on total earnings will be reflected in hourly earnings as well.

12. All source countries with at least 300 observations (representing roughly 6,000 actual businesses in the United States) are reported. Even if the list is expanded further to include very small groups, Indian entrepreneurs remain either the first or second highest income group.

13. Only aggregate data are publicly available from these sources. Confidential and restricted-access microdata from these sources are available after going through an approval and disclosure process with the Center for Economic Studies at the U.S. Census and the IRS.

14. See Georgarakos and Tatsiramos (2009) for evidence on survival rates among immigrant entrepreneurs of major racial groups.

15. At the beginning of 2000, the exchange rate was 1.45 Canadian dollars per U.S. dollar (International Monetary Fund, 2007).

16. The educational advantage of Indians also holds for wage/salary workers in all three countries (see Table A1).

17. Until the mid- to late 1980s, India spent more on higher education than primary and basic education. The large resulting stock of college graduates did not have complementary institutions and other capital to work with in India, and thus emigrated in large numbers to wealthy countries (Goldman, Kumar, & Liu, 2008).

18. Due to data limitations we cannot examine the importance of social capital, which has been found to be important for Indian-owned businesses (see Kalnins & Chung, 2006, for example).

19. We also include dummies for the largest Asian immigrant groups in each specification.

20. Some of the coefficients in the log regressions are too high to warrant their direct interpretation as percentages. Therefore, we report (exp(coefficient)−1) × 100 in the text.

21. We cannot control for year in the country in the U.K. data, and thus do not control for cohort effects (Borjas, 1986; Schuetze & Antecol, 2006), and do not examine assimilation patterns for Indian immigrants (Lofstrom, 2002).

22. We also estimate a decomposition for wage/salary earnings and find that education explains why Indians have higher wage/salary earnings than white natives. The level contributions are very similar and the percentages are larger because the gap size is smaller for wage/salary earnings.

23. Decomposition estimates from including more detailed industries provide a smaller contribution. Industry differences explain 5.8 percent of the gap in log business income.

24. For potential cultural factors, see Helweg and Helweg (1990) for example.

25. We estimate several additional specifications for Canada as robustness checks. First, we checked the sensitivity of the education and Indian immigrant dummies to the inclusion of home ownership. The coefficients are not sensitive to the inclusion of this asset measure. Second, we included more detailed education codes available in the Canadian Census. This also does not have a large effect on the Indian group coefficient. Finally, we included the number of children as an additional control and did not find changes in the Indian group coefficient. Similar to the U.S. results, the Canadian results are robust to alternative specifications.

26. A linear probability model is used for all employer regressions.

27. The correlation between being married and having employees may be partly due to married entrepreneurs hiring their spouses, but the strong association between marriage and net business income suggests it is a factor of independent importance.

28. These are Canada's two most populous provinces, and the largest recipients of immigrants overall.

29. We also estimate a decomposition for wage and salary earnings of Indian immigrants in Canada in comparison with native workers, and find very similar results. In particular, the regression-adjusted earnings for Indian immigrants in the wage and salary sector are significantly lower than earnings of native workers in the wage and salary sector – approximately 36% lower (compared to the estimate of 17% lower business income). And as was the case in the self-employment sector, it is

314					ROBERT W. FAIRLIE ET AL.

also true that Indian immigrants in the wage and salary sector are more educated than their native counterparts – about 42% of all Indian immigrants in this sector have a college degree, whereas only 23.5% of native workers have a similar level of education (see Table A1). As it would be expected, education has a highly significant and positive effect on earnings in the wage and salary sector.

30. A nonlinear decomposition using a logit regression for having employees indicates similar results. See Fairlie (2005) for a discussion of the technique and http:// people.ucsc.edu/ ~ rfairlie/decomposition for examples of SAS and Stata programs.

31. The total contribution from all variables can exceed 100% if there are unobservable factors providing a negative and offsetting contribution to the gap (Blinder, 1973; Oaxaca, 1973).

32. For the United Kingdom, we assessed the sensitivity of the Indian and education dummies to the inclusion of a home ownership indicator in the employer firm regressions and found the estimates were insensitive to this inclusion. Second, we included an indicator for each level of qualifications including no qualifications (with levels 4 and 5 as the excluded group). We find that there is no difference in the effect of level 2 qualifications or level 3 qualifications, relative to level 4 or 5, on business ownership and employer firm. Having no qualifications reduces business ownership and being an employer firm by 1.3 percentage points and 2.6 percentage points, respectively, and having level 1 qualifications reduces business ownership and being an employer firm by 2.6 percentage points and 2.7 percentage points, respectively. These estimates are statistically different from zero, but small. The inclusion of more detailed education indicators has no effect on the Indian dummy. Finally, we included the number of usual household residents in the regressions and found that it had no effect on the estimated Indian immigrant indicators. The U.K. results are thus not overly sensitive to alternative specifications.

33. See Bauer et al. (2000), Antecol et al. (2003), Woroby (2005), and Schuetze and Antecol (2006) for more information on immigration policies.

34. Antecol et al.(2003) find that Canadian immigrants have higher skills than U.S. immigrants, but the disparity disappears after removing Latin American immigrants, which is roughly similar to the finding in Borjas (1993). They argue, however, that policy differences are less important than geographical and historical differences.

35. See Citizenship and Immigration Canada (2007) for more information on the Canadian selection criteria, U.S. Citizenship and Immigration Services (2007) for requirements for employment creation immigrants, and U.K. Border and Immigration Agency (2007) for U.K. investment immigration information.

36. For investors and entrepreneurs, the minimum net worth requirements are $800,000 and $300,000, respectively, and at least 2 years of business experience.

37. See, for instance, World Bank's *India at a Glance*, http://devdata.worldbank. org/AAG/ind_aag.pdf.

ACKNOWLEDGMENTS

We would like to thank Garth Frazer, William Kerr, Josh Lerner, Anna Paulson, Solomon Polacheck, Antoinette Shoar, Leah Nelson, and seminar participants at the AEA Meetings, the University of Wisconsin, the Western

Economic Association Meetings, the Indian School of Business, and the World Bank-Kauffman Conference on Entrepreneurship and Growth for comments and suggestions. We would also like to thank Miranda Smith and Joanna Carroll for research assistance. We thank the Kauffman-RAND Institute for Entrepreneurship Public Policy and the Kauffman Foundation for partial funding.

REFERENCES

Agrawal, A., Kapur, D., & McHale, J. (2008). *Brain drain or brain bank? The impact of skilled emigration on poor-country innovation.* NBER Working Paper 14592.

Antecol, H., Cobb-Clark, D. A., & Trejo, S. J. (2003). Immigration policy and the skills of immigrants. *Journal of Human Resources, 38*(1), 192–218.

Bauer, T. K., Lofstrom, M., & Zimmermann, K. F. (2000). *Immigration policy, assimilation of immigrants and natives' sentiments towards immigrants: Evidence from 12 OECD-Countries.* Discussion Paper. Institute for the Study of Labor, Bonn, Germany.

Blinder, A. S. (1973). Wage discrimination: Reduced form and structural variables. *Journal of Human Resources, 8*, 436–455.

Borjas, G. (1986). The self-employment experience of immigrants. *Journal of Human Resources, 21*(Fall), 487–506.

Borjas, G. (1993). Immigration policy, national origin, and immigrant skills: A comparison of Canada and the United States. In D. Card & R. B. Freeman (Eds.), *Small differences that matter: Labor markets and income maintenance in Canada and the United States* (pp. 21–43). Chicago, IL: University of Chicago Press.

Borjas, G. (1995). Assimilation and changes in cohort quality revisited: What happened to immigrant earnings in the 1980s?. *Journal of Labor Economics, 13*(2), 201–245.

Borjas, G. (1999). *Heaven's door: Immigration policy and the American economy.* Princeton, NJ: Princeton University Press.

Citizenship and Immigration Canada. (2007). *Investors, entrepreneurs and self-employed persons.* Retrieved from http://www.cic.gc.ca/english/immigrate/business/index.asp and http://www.cic.gc.ca/english/immigrate/business/self-employed/index.asp

Clark, K., & Drinkwater, S. (2000). Pushed out or pulled in? Self-employment among ethnic minorities in England and Wales. *Labour Economics, 7*, 603–628.

Clark, K., & Drinkwater, S. (2006). *Changing patterns of ethnic minority self-employment in Britain: Evidence from census microdata.* IZA Discussion Papers 2495, Institute for the Study of Labor (IZA), Bonn, Germany.

Docquier, F., & Marfouk, A. (2005). International migration by educational attainment. In C. Ozden & M. Schiff (Eds.), *International migration, remittances, and the brain drain.* Washington, DC: The World Bank.

Fairlie, R. W. (2005). An extension of the Blinder–Oaxaca decomposition technique to logit and probit models. *Journal of Economic and Social Measurement, 30*(4), 305–316.

Fairlie, R. W., & Robb, A. (2008). *Race and entrepreneurial success: Black-, Asian-, and White-owned Businesses in the United States.* Cambridge, MA: MIT Press.

Fairlie, R. W., & Robb, A. M. (2007). Why are black-owned businesses less successful than white-owned businesses: The role of families, inheritances, and business human capital. *Journal of Labor Economics, 25*(2), 289–323.

Fairlie, R. W., Zissimopoulos, J., & Krashinsky, H. A. (2010). The international Asian business success story: A comparison of Chinese, Indian and other Asian businesses in the United States, Canada and United Kingdom. In J. Lerner & A. Shoar (Eds.), *International differences in entrepreneurship* (pp. 179–208). Chicago, IL: National Bureau of Economic Research Press.

Georgarakos, D., & Tatsiramos, K. (2009). Entrepreneurship and survival dynamics of immigrants to the U.S. and their descendants. *Labour Economics, 16*(2), 161–170.

Goldman, C. A., Kumar, K.B., & Liu, Y. (2008). *Education and the Asian surge: A comparison of the education systems in India and China.* RAND Occasional Paper 218.

Haltiwanger, J. C., Jarmin, R. S., & Miranda, J. (2010). *Who creates jobs? Small vs. Large vs. Young.* NBER Working Paper No. 16300.

Helweg, A. W., & Helweg, U. M. (1990). *An immigrant success story: East Indians in America.* Philadelphia, PA: University of Pennsylvania Press.

International Monetary Fund. (2007). *Representative exchange rates for selected currencies for January 2000.* Retrieved from http://www.imf.org/external/np/fin/data/rms_mth.aspx?SelectDate = 2000-01-31&reportType = REP

Johnson, P. J. (2000). Ethnic differences in self-employment among Southeast Asian refugees in Canada. *Journal of Small Business Management, 38*(4), 78.

Kalnins, A., & Chung, W. (2006). Social capital, geography, and survival: Gujarati immigrant entrepreneurs in the U.S. lodging industry. *Management Science, 52*(2), 233–247.

Ley, D. (2006). Explaining variations in business performance among immigrant entrepreneurs in Canada. *Journal of Ethnic and Migration Studies, 32*(5), 743–764.

Li, P. (2001). Immigrants' propensity to self-employment: Evidence from Canada. *International Migration Review, 35*(4), 1106–1128.

Lofstrom, M. (2002). Labor market assimilation and the self-employment decision of immigrant entrepreneurs. *Journal of Population Economics, 15*(1), 83–114.

Mar, D. (2005). Individual characteristics vs. city structural characteristics: Explaining self-employment differences among Chinese, Japanese, and Filipinos in the United States. *Journal of Socio-Economics, 34.*

Oaxaca, R. (1973). Male-female wage differentials in Urban labor markets. *International Economic Review, 14*(October), 693–709.

Oaxaca, R., & Ransom, M. (1994). On discrimination and the decomposition of wage differentials. *Journal of Econometrics, 61,* 5–21.

OECD. (2005). *SME and Entrepreneurship Outlook – 2005 Edition.* Paris, France: Organisation for Economic Co-operation and Development Press.

Parker, S. C. (2004). *The economics of self-employment and entrepreneurship.* Cambridge, MA: Cambridge University Press.

Saxenian, A. (1999). *Silicon Valley's new immigrant entrepreneurs.* San Francisco, CA: Public Policy Institute of California.

Saxenian, A. (2000). Networks of immigrant entrepreneurs. In C.-M. Lee, W. F. Miller & H. S. Rowen (Eds.), *The Silicon Valley edge: A habitat for innovation and entrepreneurship.* Stanford, CA: Stanford University Press.

Saxenian, A. (2006). *The new Argonauts: Regional advantage in a global economy.* Cambridge, MA: Harvard University Press.

Schuetze, H. J., & Antecol, H. (2006). Immigration, entrepreneurship and the venture start-up process. In S. Parker (Ed.), *The life cycle of entrepreneurial ventures, international handbook series on entrepreneurship* (Vol. 3). New York, NY: Springer.

Singh, S. (2004). Immigration into Canada: Some issues. *Indian Journal of Labour Economics, 47*(2), 349–367.

U.K. Border and Immigration Agency. (2007). *Law and policy: Part 6: Persons seeking to remain in the United Kingdom.* Retrieved from http://www.ind.homeoffice.gov.uk/lawandpolicy/immigrationrules/part6

U.S. Census Bureau. (1997). *1992 economic census: Characteristics of Business Owners.* Washington, DC: U.S. Government Printing Office.

U.S. Census Bureau. (2006). *2002 Economic Census, Survey of Business Owners Asian-owned firms.* Washington, DC: USGPO.

U.S. Citizenship and Immigration Services. (2007). *Employment creation entrepreneur cases.* Retrieved from http://www.uscis.gov/propub/ProPubVAP.jsp?dockey = 987fe2c6b1c 3f9e6725655e39a26a247

U.S. SBA (2010). *Summary of performance and financial information.* Retrieved from http://www.sba.gov/idc/groups/public/documents/sba_homepage/serv_aboutsba_perf_summ.pdf

van der Sluis, J., van Praag, M., & Vijverberg, W. (2004). *Education and entrepreneurship in industrialized countries: A meta-analysis.* Tinbergen Institute Working Paper no. TI 03–046/3, Tinbergen Institute, Amsterdam.

van der Sluis, J., van Praag, M., & Vijverberg, W. (2005). Entrepreneurship selection and performance: A meta-analysis of the impact of education in developing economies. *The World Bank Economic Review, 19*(2), 225–261.

van Praag, M. (2005). *Successful entrepreneurship: Confronting economic theory with empirical practice.* Cheltenham, UK: E. Elgar.

van Stel, A., Carree, M., & Thurik, R. (2005). The effect of entrepreneurial activity on national economic growth. *Small Business Economics, 24*, 311–321.

Wadhwa, V., Saxenian, A.L., Rissing, B., & Gereffi, G. (2007). *America's new immigrant entrepreneurs.* Duke University Report.

World Bank. (2007). *World development report 2007: Development and the next generation.* Washington, DC: World Bank.

Woroby, T. (2005). Should Canadian immigration policy be synchronized with U.S. immigration policy? Lessons learned at the start of two centuries. *American Review of Canadian Studies, 35*(2), 247–265.

Zissimopoulos, J., Maestas, N., & Karoly, L. (2007). *Retirement transitions of the self-employed in the United States and England.* MRRC WP2007-155.

APPENDIX

Table A1. Mean Education and Characteristics Among Indian and
White Wage/Salary Workers.

	United States		Canada		United Kingdom	
	Indians	Whites	Indians	Whites	Indians	Whites
College graduate	77.2%	33.0%	41.3%	23.3%	41.4%	26.8%
Female	35.4%	47.0%	42.3%	47.4%	43.8%	46.6%
Ages 25–29	21.2%	13.0%	15.7%	12.9%	14.2%	14.8%
Ages 45–59	26.7%	36.2%	31.0%	35.8%	33.6%	34.5%
Ages 60–64	3.0%	4.3%	3.9%	3.2%	3.6%	3.9%
Married	82.1%	67.4%	89.7%	61.8%	84.0%	60.4%
Agriculture	0.2%	0.6%	3.1%	3.4%	0.1%	0.7%
Construction	1.3%	5.9%	2.1%	5.1%	5.0%	2.4%
Sample size	21,184	3,316,461	3,764	230,110	4,429	498,433

Note: (1) The sample consists of wage/salary workers ages 25–64. (2) The United Kingdom
includes England and Wales only. For the United Kingdom, "Asian immigrants" group is
defined by country of birth and self-reported ethnicity and does not include all persons born in
Asia and residing in the United Kingdom. For example, it does not include ethnic British born
in India.
Sources: U.S. Census 2000, Canada Census 2001, and U.K. Census 2001.

DATE DUE